Centralizing Fieldwork

Studies of the Biosocial Society

General Editor: **Catherine Panter-Brick**, Professor of Anthropology, University of Durham

The Biosocial Society is an international academic society engaged in fostering understanding of human biological and social diversity. It draws its membership from a wide range of academic disciplines, particularly those engaged in 'boundary disciplines' at the intersection between the natural and social sciences, such as biocultural anthropology, medical sociology, demography, social medicine, the history of science and bioethics. The aim of this series is to promote interdisciplinary research on how biology and society interact to shape human experience and to serve as advanced texts for undergraduate and postgraduate students.

Centralizing Fieldwork

Critical Perspectives from Primatology, Biological and Social Anthropology

Edited by
Jeremy MacClancy and Agustín Fuentes

Berghahn Books
New York • Oxford

Published in 2011 by

Berghahn Books
www.berghahnbooks.com

©2011 Jeremy MacClancy and Agustín Fuentes
All rights reserved. Except for the quotation of short passages
for the purposes of criticism and review, no part of this book
may be reproduced in any form or by any means, electronic or
mechanical, including photocopying, recording, or any information
storage and retrieval system now known or to be invented,
without written permission of the publisher.

Library of Congress Cataloging-in-Publication Data

Centralizing fieldwork : critical perspectives from primatology, biological, and social
anthropology / edited by Jeremy MacClancy and Agustín Fuentes.
    p. cm. -- (Studies of the biosocial society)
  Includes bibliographical references and index.
  ISBN 978-1-84545-690-0 (hardback : alk. paper) -- ISBN 978-1-84545-743-3
(pbk. : alk. paper) 1. Physical anthropology--Fieldwork. 2. Primatology--Field-
work. 3.
Ethnology--Fieldwork. I. MacClancy, Jeremy. II. Fuentes, Agustin.
  GN50.8.C46 2010
  599.9--dc22
                                                                2010018162

British Library Cataloguing in Publication Data

A catalogue record for this book is available from the British Library

Printed in the United States on acid-free paper.

ISBN: 978-1-84545-690-0 (hardback)
ISBN: 978-1-84545-743-3 (paperback)

Contents

List of Figures and Tables

Figures

Tables

Acknowledgements

This book arose from a conference held by the Anthropology Centre for Conservation, the Environment and Development (ACCEND) at Oxford Brookes University, 5th to 6th, May 2007. This was the first of a planned series of interdisciplinary, international gatherings, organized by ACCEND, in its efforts to develop a transdisciplinary anthropology project. The gathering was particularly successful, and enjoyed by all. We were unable to include all the papers presented, and we thank the participant in our event whose contribution is not part of this book. We are deeply grateful to our generous supporters: the School of Social Sciences and Law, Oxford Brookes University; the Sasakawa Foundation; the Japan Foundation; the Biosocial Society; the Royal Anthropological Institute; the Institut Français; University of Notre Dame Institute for Scholarship in the Liberal Arts. We also thank the team at Berghahn Publishers, especially our ever-patient editor, Mark Stanton.

Jeremy MacClancy
Agustín Fuentes

1
Centralizing Fieldwork

Jeremy MacClancy and Agustín Fuentes

Fieldwork is a central method of research throughout anthropology, a much-valued, much-vaunted mode of generating information. It is all the more surprising then, that its nature and process have been seriously understudied in several branches of anthropology. One goal of this book is to ameliorate that imbalance.

Social anthropologists are the exception to this history of neglect. Since the mid-1980s they have made critical scrutiny of their practice a legitimate and revealing topic of study. They have inquired, among other themes, into fieldwork relations and rapport; conflicts, hazards and perils in the field; the continuously negotiated identity of the fieldworker; the blurring of private life and research boundaries; the ethics and the erotics of fieldwork; the status and types of reflexive ethnography; the popularization of the discipline via accounts of fieldwork; and so on (see e.g. MacClancy and McDonaugh 1996; Goulet and Miller 2007; McLean and Leibing 2007; Robben and Sluka 2007). We could make the list longer, but the point is already made. Fledgling research students in social anthropology now go into the field better prepared, because much more knowledgeable about the promise, limits and broad consequences of a panoply of research methods.

In marked contrast, biological anthropologists and primatologists have appeared more reluctant to investigate the wider dimensions of their own approaches in the field. They have long been ready to teach their research students the upsides and downsides of highly particular methods, especially quantitative ones, but have seemed very disinclined to discuss, publicly, much beyond. For instance, in the influential research manual for biological anthropologists, 'Practical human biology' (Weiner and Lourie 1981), we have been able to find only one page (p. 392) which even begins to consider the effect of local cultural dimensions on field research. It is as though primatologists and biological anthropologists thought strength, or perhaps just rigour, came from narrow focus of vision. A key aim of this book is to stretch that view and, in the process, help establish a broad debate about fieldwork as central to the development of their disciplines. Part of the brief we gave our biological anthropology and primatology contributors was to take a step back and to endeavour to look critically at their own research practice. We wanted them to investigate how much of the broader context of fieldwork is relevant to our understanding and assessment of the resulting academic products, and how much (if anything) should be regarded as mere 'corridor gossip'.

The other, key aim of this book is to further the comparative project within a broadly conceived anthropology. Interdisciplinary work in anthropology is usually justified by reference to evolutionary kinship: what we learn from primatology, biological anthropology, and social anthropology could and should illuminate our rounded understanding of the development, since prehistory, of humans and non-human primates. The trouble here is that while some important cross-disciplinary linkages have been made, the attempt can appear all too often as strained and unconvincing. Experienced anthropologists are only too well aware of just how tricky it is to combine the biological and the social in a revealing and academically persuasive manner. Moreover, in a recent review of the status and future of a broad-based anthropology, the social anthropologists Daniel Segal and Sylvia Yanagisako worry that contemporary 'calls for four-field holism and biocultural integration are often … thinly disguised attacks on those strands of cultural-social anthropology—specifically interpretive and constructivist approaches—most visibly in tension with positivism' (Segal and Yanagisako 2005: 11). They fear that four-field holists wish to reduce all forms of anthropology into a singular, dominant, scientific paradigm (ibid.: 13). However, this argument poorly represents the kinds of questions we seek to explore here. We seek a real and open dialogue across arenas of anthropological inquiry, here focusing on biological and primatological areas. In North America, where the term 'holistic' rears its head most often, a modern four-field (holistic) approach does not imply an acceptance of any singular dominant paradigm or theoretical approach. Rather, this 'big tent' anthropology is concerned with mutual interaction and discourse across sub-disciplinary and theoretical boundaries in effort to maximize the transdisciplinary potential of anthropological inquiry. Let us be clear: we have no truck with any reductionist programme, however veiled. Instead, the contributors to this book suggest a different, potentially more fertile way to engage these disciplines, one centred around methodology, not theory. Thus the questions we ask are, what in the pursuit of fieldwork is common to all three disciplines? What is unique to each? How much is contingent, how much necessary? In other words, can we generate well-grounded interdisciplinary generalizations about this mutual research method, and are there are any telling differences?

To this extent, our book may be regarded as a novel, exploratory way to strengthen the promise of the four-fields approach, which has been historically so promoted within sections of American anthropology. As Lederman puts it in her recent defence of this approach, 'Cultivating cross-subfield accents-identifying affinities and openings that make strategic cooperation possible among the subfields-has been, and may continue to be, anthropology's distinctive disciplinary resource' (Lederman 2005: 50). For this reason, and those above, it is an old exercise still very well worth performing. And in this book, by switching the focus from common theory to common method, we hope to breathe new life into this long-established but much contested cross-disciplinary project.

We have chosen to order the contributions in the following sequence, though our apparent logic may seem arbitrary to some. Either way, this précis can serve as a signposting of sorts, for readers who would like a little forewarning, or merely an indication whether it is worth them continuing. We start with a trio of personal but intellectually very revealing essays. In Chapter 2 Geoffrey Harrison, a distinguished biological anthropologist, reviews his fieldwork career, demonstrating just how much research methods and attitudes have evolved, and giving historical depth to our perspectives. Next comes the primatologist Volker Sommer. In a strikingly candid chapter, he reviews the course of his own field researches in order to compare and contrast central dimensions of our three disciplines. In Chapter 4, Robert Sussman takes an autobiographical approach to discuss key but neglected aspects of fieldwork and methods within the contexts of American primatology. Since both Sommer and Sussman underline how fieldwork can easily lead one into the practice of primate conservation, their chapters dovetail neatly with Lee's contribution. For she discusses whether fieldwork can inform approaches to conservation. She wishes to ask whether the outcomes of conservation practice can justify the continued exercise of fieldwork. Of course, there are no easy answers here.

Our three disciplines are all international, taught throughout the world and practised globally. Chapters 6 and 7, both by Japanese primatologists, bear this out. First Yamagiwa portrays the distinctive, interlinked development of primatology and ecological anthropology in his own country. A senior scholar, he has himself experienced much of the history he outlines. Next Kutsukake, who has been educated in both Japanese and Western universities, takes a more distanced stance. He wants to question just how different 'Japanese' and 'Western' primatologies really are. And where they do appear to be mutually distinctive, just what does a 'Japanese primatology' have to offer foreign colleagues?

In Chapter 8 Fuentes notes that biological anthropologists and primatologists go to the field to collect data to improve our overall understanding of being human or being primate. He highlights the often overlooked element that field data are rarely the representative measures we see them as. That is, the data seldom carry the totality of information necessary to fully interpret outcomes. However, even the most skilled field practitioners can inadvertently create substantial problems during field data collection, such as the conflating of measurement with interpretation. This can become a major element in assessing our own fieldwork and its impact.

The following quartet of chapters are by biological anthropologists. Panter-Brick and Eggerman critically analyse their cross-disciplinary fieldwork in the Gambia and Afghanistan. What they come to advocate is an openended attitude to research. Researchers, they argue, need to engage closely with local communities if they are to collect sufficient data and evaluate them meaningfully. In her chapter Rosetta, who has worked in Senegal, France and Bangladesh, illuminates the various pitfalls to avoid when studying biological variables in human populations. Experience leads her to stress the necessity for discretion, tact, confidentiality, respect and a culturally sensitive choice of the most appropriate method of collecting data. Hladik, in Chapter 11, compares the quantitative measurement of food consumption in both primates and humans. Since this kind of research, with humans, could be highly intrusive, Hladik has to emphasize the need for the academics to empathize with the locals and to establish a meaningful consensus with them about the research and its value. For the researchers knew that to do work of any value, locals had to be deeply involved in the project and sufficiently relaxed at measurement times. Froment extends this discussion further by posing the tricky questions which arise when researchers wish to take blood samples, and to conserve them.

After a chapter in which MacKinnon discusses the various productive roles played by primatology field schools, we close with a trio of contributions investigating the ways fieldwork is portrayed in print. Jolly evaluates the pros and cons of a broad, narrative approach to her lifelong fieldsite, compared to the focussed, scientific style she usually employs as a primatologist. Asquith follows. She uses a survey of narrative primatology to argue that her discipline can productively encompass both ethnological and evolutionary perspectives. MacClancy, a social anthropologist, ends the book with an analysis of key themes within popular accounts of fieldwork by primatologists and biological anthropologists.

So much for the individual contributions. In this introductory discussion, we wish to pull out and scrutinize key themes which emerge across the chapters. For expository convenience, we have divided the following into a series of discrete but interlocking sections: an initial historical perspective; international differences in fieldwork; fieldwork as a process and in teams; autobiographical approaches; ethics; studying one group or several; popularizing fieldwork.

A tour around the history of fieldwork

Social anthropologists speak of Bronislaw Malinowski as the key, interwar figure who made fieldwork essential for initiates into their discipline. A Polish expatriate based in London, he was not the first fieldworker, but he was its greatest propagandist, propounding to both academic and popular audiences the value of intensive, long-term research. It was his immediate predecessors who had given up relying on reports sent in from those living in the colonies and made the break into the field. But, unlike them, Malinowski did not stay 'on the verandah', interviewing locals who were brought up to him. Instead he argued social anthropologists should pitch their tents right inside villages, learn the locals' language and endeavour to live as much like them as possible. This is the famous, but impossible concept of 'participant-observation'. It is a magnificent but unachievable ideal, for how can one both participate and observe simultaneously?

In recent years many social anthropologists have felt their subject increasingly under threat, as it has been absorbed into a diversity of other disciplines (most notoriously, cultural studies). For some, social anthropology appears to be losing a sense of its theoretical specificity (e.g. Kapferer in Hirsch et al. 2007: 117). By default, fieldwork has become the most distinctive aspect of a contemporary social anthropology. In this sense, fieldwork is now even more important, more central to the discipline than it was in Malinowski's time. His conception of intensive fieldwork in one area for an extended period of time, usually at least one year, dovetailed well with an idea of sedentary populations with clearly identifiable cultural boundaries. But in recent years, with the increased movements of peoples around the world, some anthropologists have come to laud the value of multi-sited fieldwork, i.e. following the group studied wherever they go. It is felt that this, potentially much more demanding style of fieldwork is more appropriate if studying forced displacement, labour migration, transnational corporations or other forms of mobile populations.

At the same time it is no longer possible to think of a 'culture' in unproblematic terms. Too many people contest the way they are represented by others, or even by members of their own group. Here fieldworkers can choose to make this contest of representation the very focus of their study. Others may choose to research the social life of a thing (say, a carpet, a foodstuff or a piece of art), serially investigating the ways it is used and understood in each of the arenas or cultures it is made to pass through. The sum result of these contemporary changes is that fieldwork remains crucial within social anthropology and has richly diversified in his forms.

The history of field methods within biological anthropology has yet to be written. We can only sketch a segment of it here, greatly assisted by an interview generously granted by Geoffrey Harrison to MacClancy (conducted 6 xi 2007), backed up by his own contribution about different team research trips he was himself involved over the course of his career. The Emeritus Professor of Biological Anthropology at Oxford University sees its postwar development in both Britain and the USA in three overlapping phases. First, the 'descriptive phase', which continued up to the 1950s, where biological anthropologists, usually acting alone, measured stature and blood groups in order to document the variety between and within human populations. As more diagnostic characters were discovered, biological anthropologists formed teams to measure these different dimensions. To begin with, only a small minority fieldworked for more than a few weeks; most of the work was later done in the lab; any subsequent comparison was made within a broad evolutionary framework.

Harrison characterises the second phase as the rise, from the 1950s on, of 'cause and effect approaches'. Here biological anthropologists looked at either the cause or effect of one dimension of variety on human populations. This kind of work necessitated much more fieldwork than descriptive work. For instance one of his students, Melissa Parker, spent two years in the Sudan, investigating the effect of schistosomiasis on the economic productivity of women who worked in the cotton-fields. By day she measured their activity; by night she examined their stool samples. A much longer study was that by Paul Baker and his team, at Pennsylvania State University, who over a ten-year period investigated the effects of altitude on human health, in the Peruvian Highlands (Lasker 1999).

The third phase identified by Harrison is research into 'how populations work'; what is their structure? What effects do they have on the environment, and vice versa? This kind of fieldwork can be so lengthy that it may outlast the research-life of a single academic. The work of Harrison's own team into the population surrounding Otmoor, just outside Oxford, took fifteen years. A further, excellent example here is the work of Neville White in Arnhem Land, northern Australia, which he started as a young man and on which he is still engaged, though now in his sixties. Over that time White has documented the health and wellbeing, in physical terms, of the locals; he has also studied their social organization and the natural environment in which they live as well. In other words, he has been investigating, along multiple dimensions, almost the whole ecology of the area for the last thirty to forty years.

How field methods in French and German biological anthropology developed has yet to be investigated. But the main direction of development within Anglo-American biological anthropology at least is clear: since the Second World War, the main shift has been from primarily laboratory-centred work to field studies, usually of ever longer duration (see e.g. Lasker 1993: 2). Within biological anthropology, 'the field' is now more important than ever.

Primatological fieldwork, often considered a subset of biological anthropology fieldwork in North America, but frequently considered more allied with the biological sciences in Europe, shares a bit more with some of the trends in social anthropology than those in biological anthropology. The primatologist traditionally goes to live with his or her subjects, pitching camp where the monkeys, apes or lemurs are, watching them day in and day out in an attempt to understand the inner workings and general patterns of the particular primate 'society' of interest. While not being able to question their informants as Malinowski and his social anthropology descendants preferred, primatologists seek descriptive answers in the behaviour and inter-individual relationships observable in their primate subjects. Primatological fieldwork lies, in a sense, in an interstitial zone between the ethnography and the bio-assay.

The American physical anthropologist Sherwood Washburn's petition for a new physical anthropology (1951) sounded the initial clarion call for fieldwork in primatology. Washburn's call for a truly biological anthropology advocated multidisciplinary and interdisciplinary approaches to the understanding of human behaviour, biology, and history. One of the cornerstones of this approach was comparative studies of free ranging nonhuman primates. He urged researchers to travel to the locales where these primates lived, to live among them, to record their behaviour, and to initiate understandings of their societies. Washburn's early students became some of the very first primatology fieldworkers and pioneers in the field of North American primatology (e.g. Phyllis (Jay) Dolhinow and Irving DeVore). More than 60 per cent of the North American primatology Ph.D.s produced since the 1950s were by students of Washburn or of Washburn's early students (Kelly and Sussman 2007).

The paleoanthropologist Louis Leakey exploited this call and established the most popular and influential cadre of field primatologists, the trio of Jane Goodall, Biruté Galdikas and Dian Fossey. Interestingly, unlike Washburn's students, two of the three of these most famous of the early primatologists (and probably those most responsible for the primatology explosion in the 1970–80s) were not trained anthropologists. However, Washburn's students and Leakey's 'angels' all practised the anthropological tradition of long-term (one year or more) coexistence with the population of study, often under trying circumstances and with great challenges and difficulties. Beginning in the the 1960s and extending to the modern day, the extended fieldwork trip remains the hallmark of a majority of primatology dissertations (see Fuentes, Jolly, Sommer and Sussman chapters).

Washburn eventually expanded his call to that for a broader biosocial anthropology '… human biology has no meaning without society. For a particular problem in the short run, either biological or social facts may be stressed, but the evolution of man can only be understood as a biosocial problem' (Washburn 1968). This coincided with a linking of biological anthropological field practice with aspects of field practice from primatological and ethnographic approaches, resulting in the relatively recent emergent fieldwork in biocultural anthropology (Dafour 2006; see also Fuentes, Froment and Rosetta chapters).

National styles of fieldwork

A first glance at social anthropology suggests that Malinowski has won. It seems that his promotion of intensive fieldwork has become the dominant model throughout the discipline, worldwide. A slightly finer look, however, suggests that there are at least some international differences. Malinowski's disciples have not triumphed everywhere. According to the Japanese anthropologist Takami Kuwayama, his style of fieldwork should be regarded as only a model, not a norm (Kuwayama 2006: 50). This variety of styles is as uncharted as it is important. As the American social anthropologists Akhil Gupta and James Ferguson point out, 'there might be much to learn from comparing the different kinds of knowledge that such different practices and conventions open up… It seems clear that, in spite of homogenizing tendencies rooted in colonial and neo-colonial histories, practices of 'the field'.are indeed significantly different away from the hegemonic centers of intellectual production' (Gupta and Ferguson 1997: 27–8). All that we attempt here is to broach the topic, to move beyond self-limiting Anglo-American perspectives.

The strongest example comes from Brazil. In a much-quoted article, Alcida Ramos states that fieldwork Malinowski-style tends to produce much fine detail and profound analysis, but with little historical depth. Synchrony is emphasized over diachrony. In contrast Brazilian ethnographers, for a variety of practical reasons, rarely practise longstay fieldwork, but make short trips to Indian areas, usually in the summer months (Ramos 1990). One consequence is that few of them learn to speak the local language well. However, since most of them study some aspect of interethnic relations, that lack is not as big a handicap as it might first appear. Moreover Brazilian ethnographers, unlike their Malinowskian counterparts, make many repeated trips to the same group, over the course of decades. They can thus maintain long-term relations with those they study, gradually building up a profile of them, and tracking their chronological evolution. Ramos likens this difference in fieldwork styles to that between a richly textured still photograph and a film, which focuses on movement over permanence (Ramos 1990: 459).

Anthropologists who practise Malinowski's style are often criticized by inhabitants of the country where they study as 'parachutists': they drop into an area, get their information, and then get out. Some do not go back, and certainly not for repeated visits. But Brazilian ethnographers, who keep on returning to their fieldsites, never really cut off their ties with the locals they work with. These enduring relationships mean that Brazilian anthropologists are almost all actively involved in the struggles of the indigenes with whom they collaborate. This commitment is part and parcel of what they do. As Ramos puts it, 'There is no purely academic research; what there is is the rhetorical possibility and personal inclination to exclude from one's written works the interactive political, moral, or ethical aspects of fieldwork' (Ramos 1990: 454).

Japanese folklorists work in a similar manner. For them, each stay does not exceed a few months, but they visit repeatedly, often for a few decades or even more. In the process they become committed to the welfare of those they study, for example engaged in political activity to improve locals' living standards or informing them about the government's cultural policies and their consequences (Kuwayama 2006). The work of Basque folklorists could be pencilled in here, as the long term studies of these committed amateurs is usually framed within a broad nationalist project. By getting into print the diversities of Basque customary ways they help give substance to a sense of Basque distinctiveness (see, e.g. Azcona 1984).

Midcentury Paris provides our next example. From the 1930s onwards Marcel Griaule propounded the importance of repeated visits, of a few months at a time. But for him the value of going back to his Dogon fieldsite time after time did not lie in a deepening of political commitment or the gaining of a chronological perspective. Instead he saw these return trips as the key way to get an ever more profound insight to indigenous modes of thought; they were the means by which one could serially expose cultural secrets of increasing importance. As the locals came to acknowledge the seriousness of his endeavour, they began, over the years, to reveal more and more of the principles underlying their style of thought (Clifford 1983). Even though a recent re-study of the Dogon has queried the status of material he obtained (van Beek 1991, but see also Calame-Griaule 1991; de Heusch 1991), no one has doubted the ethnographic worth he placed on repeated visits.

Since social anthropology has come 'home' in recent decades, with an increasing number fieldworking within their own country, going back again and again to one's fieldsite, even if only for months at a time, appears to be coming less unusual. Indeed, for many, it is now more and more considered model practice.

In primatological fieldwork practice some similar differences emerge in national schools: most notably between the Japanese and North American schools, and to a lesser extent between the North American and European schools (see Fuentes, Katsukake, Sommer and Yamagiwa chapters). These differences are in part attributable to the home disciplines from which primatologists emerge. In Japan, Kinji Imanishi's hybrid of ethnographic, ethological and ecological approaches contextualized in a particularly complex and holistic view of nature (Imanishi 1941), which influenced methods and orientations. His perspective and training of students laid the groundwork for a long tradition of intensive field observations, a comfort with provisioning as a form of manipulation, and a focus on group social relations as core to understanding primate societies. Members of the North American school, heavily influenced by

Washburn, focussed much of their gaze on the testing of adaptive scenarios and the construction of evolutionary models based on observations and assumptions about the causes of individual primate's behaviour. Finally, the European primatologists were simultaneously influenced initially by the ethologists Lorenz and Tinbergen, and subsequently by ecological approaches and precedence of standardized models for assessing behaviour. Additionally, most North American primatologists were trained in departments of anthropology in United States universities whereas most European primatologists initially emerged from the few major biology or ethology departments in the United Kingdom, Germany, Holland and France.

While major reflection and introspection on practice and impact has not been overly characteristic of primatology in general, since the late 1980s much attention has been focussed on the role of gender in both theory and practice in primatology (Strum and Fedigan 1999). Additionally, the past decade has seen a significantly increased role for reflection amongst primatologists in regard to issues of conservation, engagement with local human populations and the patterns of interaction between humans and nonhuman primates as serious areas for research focus and critical analyses (Fuentes and Sommer chapters).

The social anthropologist Rena Lederman has suggested there may be regional styles in fieldwork. That no matter where an anthropologist comes from, he or she joins a regionally defined community of ethnographers. And each community may have distinct background expectations about scholarly practice, and the conduct of fieldwork, 'e.g. expectations about language competence, conditions for obtaining research permissions..., the duration of fieldwork, and kinds of incorporation into field settings (Lederman 2007: 317). Anecdotal evidence from primatologists suggests that something similar may well be occurring in their own discipline. But, as yet, there has been no systematic study of the phenomenon.

Fieldwork as process, as ethical practice, as training

Fieldwork takes time, lots of it. It is not a state but an open ended process, which evolves and develops on site in a manner often independent of any research agenda however painstakingly formulated back in the fieldworker's university. This is an integral part of the messy, somewhat uncontrolled business that is fieldwork, and one reason why it demands resourcefulness from fieldworkers, who must learn to be adaptable or else choose another profession. As Professor Rodney Needham, MacClancy's supervisor at Oxford, said to him as he left for his first research trip, 'Don't worry. The locals will set the pace.' Too true, but they set the agenda as well. Intending to study indigenous cosmology and ritual, MacClancy arrived in a Pacific archipelago (Vanuatu) undergoing the classical throes of an anti-colonialist struggle for independence. Instead of residing there for one year, he stayed for more than three, and finally returned to Oxford with the material for a doctorate on the cultural dimensions of Melanesian nationalism. Fuentes' supervisor at the University of California, Berkeley, Professor Phyllis Dolhinow, warned him of a similar pitfall in fieldwork practice: falling into the trap of 'I would not have seen it had I not believed it' and reaffirming the consequent. The fieldworker goes into the field well versed in the theory and explicandum related to the topic of focus. But fieldworkers are generally not at all prepared for the fact that their subjects are not indoctrinated into specific academic paradigms or explanatory processes, and thus frequently behave and think in ways that are not best explained via the toolkit the researcher brought to the field. Fuentes went to the field to test a series of hypotheses on the social organization of a monogamous primate. He returned to produce a dissertation and a series of publications demonstrating that few if any primates are monogamous and that most hypotheses proposed for monogamy fail to explain the few primate cases.

The messy, uncontrollable nature of fieldwork forces anthropologists to be resourceful, adaptable. In this way fieldwork is an essentially creative activity, one much more of practice than of prescription. During MacClancy's extended fieldwork on the urban culture of Basque nationalism, a continual task was identifying pertinent phenomena. There had been no earlier work by others in the area, so he had to follow up potential leads and see where they took him. This was a question of recognizing the relevant while repeatedly evaluating processes which unfolded in front of his eyes. Thus at the beginning of his fieldwork he could not have foreseen the contents of his eventual ethnography (MacClancy 2007). Because of this irreducibly creative dimension to our research practice, Judith Okely chooses to call anthropology 'an artistic engagement, not scientific mimicry' (Okely 2007: 359).

Harrison in his chapter, and Panter-Brick and Eggerman in theirs, emphasize this processual aspect of fieldwork in their contributions, even though they come to differing conclusions. Harrison, based on his own experiences, warns against changing the research agenda while in the field. Panter-Brick and Eggerman recommend constant reconsideration of it while fieldworking. They emphasize how they and their team had to learn how to navigate conflicting and contradictory information, how to contextualize the information collected and, perhaps above all, how to assign value to the unexpected. For serendipity is a crucial strength of any fieldwork: the ability to remain open to witnessing an unforeseen event, to work out ways of understanding it and then, if necessary, to adjust accordingly one's comprehension of just what precisely is going on in the fieldsite.

Undergirding the research process there has to be a strong sense of ethics and of good practice. As with all moral debate in a cross-cultural context, there are no easy answers here, no matter how facile the questions may be to pose. The ethics committees of professional anthropology associations may draw up well minded codes of practice for practitioners to implement, but seasoned fieldworkers know all too well that moral judgement in the field is less a simple minded application of ethical verities than a constant, evolving negotiation of responsibility with all those involved in the research enterprise. Researchers do not adjudicate *a priori* precepts; rather they learn to negotiate truths (Meskell and Pels 2005). Froment, Lee, Rosetta and Sommer, in a diversity of different ways, bring up these ethical concerns in their contributions, and demonstrate how easily they can arise in a variety of contexts. Froment discusses some of the key quandaries biological anthropologists can face today: how to negotiate the local perceptions of and the likely reality of benefits for the peoples studied? Under what circumstances, for how long, and for what end may researchers handle human remains and fluids? How can one attempt to balance individual, community and broader rights? One contemporary response is the 'partnership' approach advocated, among others, by the American biological anthropologist Lawrence Schell, who openly admits his intellectual debt to the postmodern debate within social anthropology about reflexivity. He contends that the populations to be studied need to be involved in the research, design and process, at all stages from the beginning. Even though this partnership style of research is more time consuming, the results can be much richer and more valuable for all concerned (Schell et al. 2005, 2007).

Lee's key question in her contribution is central to us all: why do fieldwork? Given the disruption, however mild, it may cause, she asks how we can justify its practice. She examines fieldwork in terms of outcomes, specifically those associated with conservation practices, and so wishes to enquire who, exactly, benefits from fieldwork: the locals, the local habitat, or a local species of concern to conservationists? The crucial point here is how can we ever assess who benefits, and to what extent? Since it is not always obvious that those who identify problems ought to be the people who produce the solutions, Lee argues that the role of anthropological fieldworkers should be to seek solutions which are emergent rather than imposed. Sommer extends the debate in a related direction by contending that conservation has aesthetic as much as ecological consequences. If we make all other primates extinct, the world will become 'poorer, less beautiful, and thus less good'. But why bother to save them, given the crushing weight of forces ranged against their survival? Taking his cue from Camus, Sommer propounds a transcendental heroism: to not give in, to revolt, and not care about defeat or victory.

Fieldwork is processual, but so is the development of any anthropologist's own academic career. Several contributors take an autobiographical approach in their respective chapters (Jolly, MacKinnon, Sussman, and especially Sommer in a disarming and engagingly frank contribution), and so underline the constant interaction between their teaching and their research practice. Besides its other benefits, the personal focus of these contributions emphasizes the longitudinal, dynamic nature of any long term field research.

MacKinnon, in her chapter, focuses on one way to begin this process: primatology field schools. These schools, which are increasingly recognized as fundamental to the initial training of primatologists, fulfil a host of functions. They are opportunities for students to experience another culture, and so reflect back on their own, and their place within it. They can demonstrate just how intertwined issues in social and biological anthropologies are. Also, they may serve to show budding conservationists the agonizing gap between the way things should be and the way they are. In all, as MacKinnon puts it, these schools prepare their graduates well for 'the challenges and epiphanies' which only fieldwork can produce.

Perhaps the most famed of social anthropology field schools is that established in mid-century Mexico by the Spanish exile Angel Palerm. He saw anthropology both as a critical mode of inquiry and as a means to realize the aspirations of the

Mexican Revolution. For him, fieldwork was a way to test anthropological ideas against people's lived reality, and to disturb one's prejudices and bogus certainties. Since he wanted students to integrate theory and practice as early as possible in their anthropological careers, he set up a fieldwork school, in Tepetlaoztoc, near Texcoco. There, mentored by he and his staff and assisted by illustrious north American colleagues, undergraduate anthropologists, even those in only their first year of study, could work on real problems during the day and discuss them with their professors in the evening. In the process Palerm hoped to develop a style of anthropology more attuned to Mexican realities (Wolf 1981; Garcia 2001; Icazuriaga 2005). The school exists to this day.

The fieldworker alone?

Malinowski liked to promote the romantic idea of the ethnographer as an intellectual alone in the bush. Susan Sontag later turned that into the flattering image of 'the anthropologist as hero', a pretentious trope waiting to be punctured (Sontag 1970; MacClancy 1996: 28). Though the practice of fieldwork as a solitary activity is still presented as the dominant style within social anthropology, there has long been competing alternatives. As Gottlieb put it:

> There are strong signs of a macho ethos that pervades the intellectual orientations of many anthropologists, both male and female.... The Marlboro Man-like impulse to celebrate individual achievement rather than collective collaboration may be one component in this tendency ...

> And yet, we are all aware that anthropologists often work in pairs-with a spouse or other domestic partner-and often, as well, in teams of researchers (Gottlieb 1995: 22. See also Foster et al. 1979).

The famous Torres Strait Expedition of 1898 was a very early example of team research, composed in this case of a linguist (Ray), an anthropologist (Haddon), an experimental psychologist (Rivers) and two of his students, plus a medical pathologist (Seligman). Ironically, even though the work of this expedition turned Rivers and Seligman into renowned anthropologists, it seems to have been the sole significant piece of team fieldwork in early British anthropology. And in 1912 Rivers himself came out against teamwork as too disruptive of local life. The only noteworthy exception in subsequent decades was the teamwork method developed during the Second World War by Max Gluckman. Based in Northern Rhodesia, he created groups of white social scientists and African assistants as an effective (and probably the only) way to study the multi-ethnic composition of the Copperbelt (Schumaker 2001; Kuklick 2008: 65, 77–8).

In interwar Paris Marcel Mauss, the leading French anthropologist of his day, told his students that teamwork was the desideratum. In his *Manual of Ethnography*, he argued that the ideal expedition would be composed of a geologist and a botanist, as well as several ethnographers (Mauss 2007). Griaule, especially in the first decades of his Dogon work, also trumpeted the advantages of teamwork. Social reality, he argued, was too complex for any one anthropologist to capture. What was needed was a group of specialists who divided the ethnographic tasks to hand between them. Also, a team, using pen, paper, still and movie cameras, could simultaneously record different aspects of a large, fast moving ritual, though it is hard not to believe the presence of six observers did not change the nature of the ceremony for its participants. Furthermore, members of a team could ask different locals similar questions, in order to check data, account for individual bias, and fill in gaps (Clifford 1983). In this way, his team's short stays could be as intense as, if not more intense than, the prolonged residence of a Malinowskian fieldworker. Though his ideal of teamwork did not become extensively popular, at least one of his followers, Germaine Dieterlin (1903–99), maintained this fieldwork style even into her nineties (Parkin 2005: 204–5). And while Mauss's younger colleague Paul Rivet saw the potential of teamwork to hold a broad based anthropology together, very few in fact practised this collaborative style (Rivet, Lester, Rivière 1935: 516; Blanckaert 1999: 37).

In Japan Kuwayama has similarly praised the benefits of teamwork, among local folklorists. Though different team members play different roles, they usually work together throughout the whole fieldwork period and frequently share information, so they can correct each other's apparent misunderstandings and oversights. By listening to members' opinions, a team may transcend individual subjectivity, by forging a collective inter-subjectivity. In this way, Kuwayama contends, postmodern concerns about fieldworkers' generation of 'partial truths' (Clifford 1986) are, at least, partially overcome (Kuwayama 2006).

Teamwork comes, of course, with its own set of problems. Members of a team, subject to the typical stresses of fieldwork, may turn out to not cooperate in the ways usually expected; expectations may be different; tolerance can fracture as unforeseen difficulties arise. Selecting members of a team becomes a delicate but central task. The American biological anthropologist J.V. Neel said he chose 'people who had been Boy Scouts, or looked as though they had been' (G. Harrison pers. comm.) Evon Vogt, Director of the Harvard Chiapas Project, confessed his team had suffered 'a few celebrated intra-project conflicts' (Vogt 1979: 294). The veteran anthropologist of Papua New Guinea, Mervyn Meggitt, gently understated the challenges of long term teamwork:

> A real problem exists in devising efficient and ethically acceptable procedures for fitting additional investigators into an established or even a nascent program. Such an arrangement must demand delicate handling to ensure that the effectiveness and productivity of the inquiry are not impaired, while at the same time the individual egos (and some anthropologists appear to cherish remarkably tender psyches) remain unbruised and the actors' perceptions of their own integrity are not rudely contradicted... Equity and humility must prevail if the undertaking is not to dissolve into dissension and back biting (Meggitt 1979: 115. See also Lee 1979: 308–9; Scudder and Colson 1979: 234).

Problems can multiply if the team is interdisciplinary. Each member may individually carry out exemplary fieldwork, but putting the results together to generate further insights can prove tricky. Thus the biological anthropologist N.G. Norgan, in an overview of a large landmark study into human adaptability in Papua New Guinea, noted that while the project fulfilled its basic objectives, it was less successful at integrating information from different disciplines (Norgan 1997: 106). The distinguished French practitioner Igor de Garine is candid that collaboration between nutritional and cultural anthropologists 'is not easy to manage':

> Biologists... are not usually trained to establish human contacts. Social anthropologists tend to investigate... factors which are difficult to quantify. 'Hard' scientists are dubious about the scientific validity of the work of 'soft' social scientists, who in turn do not consider their colleagues to be very subtle and object to the intrusiveness of their techniques upon the populations under study (de Garine 2004: 18).

He feels forced to exclaim when mentioning that a team, of which he was a member, 'managed to collaborate for over fifteen years, often working together in difficult environments on fourteen different Cameroonian tribes – and these researchers still talk to one another!' (de Garine 2004: 18. See also Schumaker 2004: 119). Problems may continue once home as, he notes, social scientists tend to take longer than biologists on publishing their data. 'The latter, in order to comply with the publishing style of their specialities, are eager to publish their results very rapidly before others publish similar results' (de Garine 2004: 23). Fledgling team-researcher beware!

Problems are not just internal to the team. Rosetta argues that the quality of the data collected in any project in biological anthropology directly depends on the rapport created by team members with the peoples studied. It is therefore crucial to train participating research students and local assistants well and with sensitivity. Panther-Brick and Eggerman echo this point: the cooperation and engagement of the people being studied is fundamental to research. That does not mean it is usually easily achieved, or maintained.

Starting with biological anthropology in the 1960s and becoming commonplace in primatology by the 1990s, team-based research projects are now in the majority in each of these disciplines. In part due to the radical increase in toolkits (genetic collection and assessment, physiological measurements and assessment, GPS, computer based behavioural analyses, etc.) and the expertise required to utilize and oversee them, one simply cannot do biological anthropological and primatological field work as the lone fieldworker any longer. Both of these areas have also undergone radical expansion in connectivity with affiliated fields such that teams often consist of biological anthropologists and/or primatologists, ecologists, geneticists, student assistants, social anthropologists, and even economists, psychologists, geographers, or botanists.

Anthropologists without anthropology, but just as rigorous

It is all too easy to think of anthropology as practised exclusively, or to any significant extent, by professional anthropologists who were trained in the subject at university and have gained research degrees in it. But even a quick glance at our history reveals that there was a well grounded anthropology before its establishment in centres of higher education, and that educated non-professionals based in the field continued to contribute very productively to the subject even once departments had been set up in universities. The unlikeable truth appears to be that professional anthropologists downplayed the role of their field-based predecessors and contemporaries, in order to boost their already elevated status, to make their own work seem that much more distinctive, and of course to justify their salaries.

Rosalie Wax, in a historical sketch of 'proto-anthropology', has argued that the first Europeans 'to collect and record genuinely useful ethnographic data about alien people were missionaries of the Catholic church and certain ambitious and imaginative merchants', whose exemplar is Marco Polo (Wax 1971: 23). In other words, field ethnography is primarily a product of the thirteenth century. This practice never quite died out, and revived spectacularly in the late nineteenth century, when colonialist expansion stimulated a dramatic renaissance of amateur ethnographic work, some of which remain 'unsurpassable as field descriptions' (Ellen and Harris 2000; Wax 1971). Throughout the British colonies, educated expatriates acted as informants to home-based scholars and published ethnographies, e.g., the long-serving missionary in Fiji Lorimer Fison; the geologist A.W. Howitt who worked with Australian aboriginals; the South Pacific planter, Ewan Corlette, who did ethnographic work among his labourers; the colonial officer E.H. Man, based in the Andaman Islands, whose ethnography was notoriously exploited by the renowned theoretician of structural-functionalism, Arthur Radcliffe-Brown. Brown's own ethnography of the area is generally regarded as inferior to Man's (Corlette 1935; Needham 1974; Tomas 1991: 98; Kuklick 2008: 57). In some British colonies, such as the Sudan, administrators were trained in ethnography and encouraged to submit ethnographically rich reports, some of which, as Evans-Pritchard acknowledged, contained 'interesting, often shrewd observations' (Evans-Pritchard 1940: 1; Johnson 2007).

In the second half of the nineteenth century and subsequent decades, French military administrators were charged to produce tribal *coutumiers,* learned, often highly dense accounts of customary law grounded on native exegesis and sustained fieldwork (Salemink 1991; Parkes 2008). By the early twentieth century, in France there was such a substantial body of colonial administrators who wrote ethnography that 'they created a small army of researchers, and a force that led to epistemological change in the social sciences'. Indeed because so many of Mauss's students were killed in the First World War, these administrator-cum-ethnographers 'were virtually the only persons available to do research at the very time that field research' was defined as central to anthropology. The first methodological essay on field research, published 1925, paid homage to a colonial officer-turned-Africanist, Maurice Delafosse, as much as to Mauss (Sibeud 2008: 101, 106–7. On Delafosse, see Amselle and Sibeud

1998). In Holland, the first prominent anthropologists of Indonesia (ex Dutch East Indies) were both colonial medical officers, A.W. Nieuwenhuis and J.H.G. Kohlbrugge (de Wolf 1999: 3123). Of course, a notable number of missionaries from throughout Western Europe were also important ethnographers, as were the odd planter and adventurer-explorer (Cinnamon 2007; Harries 2007; Hunt 2007). And, as some were well aware, long-term colonial residents often came to know the locals better than bookish visitors who only did fieldwork for a year or so (L'Estoile 2007: 106–107).

These proto-anthropologists did not work alone. Some French and German administrators collaborated with African colleagues, e.g., in French West Africa local schoolmaster-ethnographers, and from German colonies African teaching assistants based in Berlin and Hamburg (Jezequel 2007; Pugach 2007). The same applied further afield. As an expansionist Japan began to colonize its neighbours from the late-nineteenth century on, its government made use of a striking diversity of its expatriates and colonized intellectuals for the production of ethnography: army officers, explorers, formerly imprisoned Marxists, policemen, colonial administrators, linguists, merchants, naval commanders, writers, railroad employees, native scholars untrained in anthropology (Bremen and Shimizu 1998: 6; Nakao 1998; Shimizu 1998: 123, 138; Walraven 1998: 221–3). Perhaps the most surprising example of this anthropology before anthropologists is the 'ethnographic populists' of late nineteenth century Russia. Exiled to Siberia for their activities, politically committed students exploited the opportunity to do fieldwork in local communities there. Their aim was twofold: to contribute to debates on peasant socialism by generating ethnographic material, and to raise local consciousness by taking it down a revolutionary path (Grant 1999; Ssorin-Chaikov 2008).

The first generally acknowledged field primatologist was Clarence Ray Carpenter, who in the 1930s passed several months observing howler monkeys on a Panamanian island. Yet he remained the central pioneer in this work until the 1950s. But non-professionals had already done primate fieldwork before that time. Sussman notes that in the 1890s R.L. Garner, an amateur zoologist, while on an ape-collecting trip, spent '112 days in a cage waiting for gorillas and chimpanzees to wander by' (Sussman 2000: 88). In the 1940–50s the distinguished entomologist A.J. Haddow carried out epidemiological work in East Africa into the interrelations of yellow fever and local primates, especially bushbabies, which led him to carry out sustained field research on them (e.g., Haddow, Dick, Lumsden and Smithburn 1951; Haddow and Ellice 1964). Perhaps the best example, however, of excellent field research in primatology before the subject was established is Eugene Marais, a South African lawyer who carried out sustained observation of baboons in the Outback (Marais 1939). But the intellectual consequence of his innovative work was limited as his major work was not published until decades after his death (Marais 1969).

The chronological process of research development has been similar in biological anthropology. For example, Huss-Ashmore and Ulijaszek, in a review of field research in the Gambia, note that 'It is one of the ironies of human adaptability research in Africa that some of the most interesting work has been carried out by investigators whose primary concern was not in human adaptability' (Huss-Ashmore and Ulijaszek 1997: 82). In other words, excellent field research on an eminently biological anthropological theme was conducted in the Gambia by nutritionists, ecologists, economists, as well as medical and agricultural researchers. There was not an anthropologist among them.

The historical record, as sketched above, suggests that in almost every country where universities created departments of anthropology non-professionals, or the self-trained, produced valuable, at times excellent work in both social anthropology and in primatology, while some of the best work in biological anthropology was carried out by academics from other disciplines. What does this say about us?

If we are to recognize the intellectual contribution made by expatriates, we should at the same time acknowledge that made by locals. Thus, social anthropologists no longer talk of gaining data from 'informants' while in the field, but of collaborating with local 'co-workers'. They now accept that some classic tomes of ethnography were as much produced by their co-worker(s) as by the distinguished anthropologist. It is argued, for instance, that several of Boas's works on the people of the Northwest American Pacific Coast should be authored as 'By Franz Boas and George Hunt', his long-serving local research assistant. A further example: Richard and Sally Price in 2003 re-examined the field diaries Melville and Francis Herskovits kept during their famous 1920s expedition to the Saramkas of Suriname. The Prices note that throughout their time in the field, the Herskovits were accompanied by non-Saramakas, paid for both menial labour and information about the locals, yet their contribution and that of the Herskovits' main Saramaka co-worker are, 'to a startling extent, simply "disappeared" in the publications' (Price and Price 2003: 42). Sanjek provides a depressingly long list of other examples, from around the world, of local fieldworkers who collaborated with famous professional anthropologists, and whose important contribution has still to be properly recognized (Sanjek 1993).

In a similar vein, contemporary primatologists are today much more openly aware of the contribution made by locals who maintain their research sites during their absence. For example, since the 1960s and 70s primary investigators (American, European or Japanese) at many of the best known long term primate research projects in Africa and Asia have had to leave the sites for political, economic and other reasons for varying periods of time. At such prominent sites as Jane Goodall's chimpanzee study at the Gombe Stream Reserve in Tanzania and Biruté Galdikas' orang-utan study at Tanjung Putting in Kalimantan, Indonesia, the projects relied almost exclusively on local trackers and field assistants for their upkeep and continued data collection for significant amounts of time when the foreign researchers were absent from the sites (see also Jolly chapter). The presence and actions of these local participants in the projects enriched the research via their particular insights and perspectives. This core local involvement provided opportunities for researchers to view their primate subjects and the research questions through the eyes of those who lacked the professional training but lived through long term exposure and cultural contexts in which primates were central or at least permanent fixtures of the local ecologies and sometimes mythologies (e.g., Fuentes and Wolf 2002). Hans Kummer makes a comparable point in the closing pages to his popular 'In quest of the sacred baboon'. There he argues that 'the crucial aspect of the scientific approach' is 'to strive for a differentiated view, free from contradictions, one that does justice to the object observed and corrects our prejudices' (Kummer 1995: 308). His best example of this comes from his encounter with Mahdi, a twelve year old Bedouin. The lad amazes the academic with the precision, range and incisiveness of his baboon observations. Here 'was a nomad boy who had never been to school and, purely for his own interests, had observed a wild animal and understood it just as I try and do … Mahdi was a born scientist, more than I am'(Kummer 1995: 312).

Either way, whether discussing self-trained non-professionals or indigenous savants, the general point is still clear: it is not only university educated outsiders who produce anthropological knowledge, and we ignore that at our peril. Today not all locals fill this role of the non-professional. In countries where primates reside naturally the 1990s saw an increase in indigenous primatologists receiving degrees in North America, Japan or Europe and, increasingly, (in the last decade) in their own countries. In many primate-rich countries, such as Indonesia and Brazil, the majority of researchers engaged in primate studies will soon be nationals as opposed to foreigners. This has led to some friction as the passing of the post-colonial baton has been slow and not without controversy.

Fieldworking anthropology, broadly speaking

The fieldworking specificities of each sub-field may be particular, but some commonalities are already clear:

Length of fieldwork

Social anthropologists like to pride themselves on the duration of their fieldwork: one year at least; two years better. An increasing number make repeat trips, but there may well be long gaps between those visits. But even that level of commitment pales in the face of primatological practice. For some primatologists maintain field research sites where a Director may supervise, over the course of decades, the continuous observation of the primate population by an overlapping series of graduate students and local workers. Sommer, in his contribution, describes the establishment of one such site.

The benefits of repeated, or better protracted fieldwork are obvious. What might have seemed lasting, on an anthropologist's first trip, may turn to be historically contingent on a subsequent one. In primatology, Sussman (in this volume) argues similarly: he underlines the worth of very protracted fieldwork, conducted by several researchers, because local history can be just as influential as ultimate, selective explanations.

A further benefit of long term fieldwork is the potential of an illuminating serendipity: the unexpected event which can make us revise our understanding of local life. Its value has long been noted and lauded in social anthropology, where unforeseen occurrences have radically altered many fieldworkers' comprehension of life around them (see, e.g., MacClancy 2002). Kutsukake, in this volume, discusses the central significance of the previously unseen, and how it can change primatological fieldworkers' approach to the locals they are studying.

But there are of course downsides to very long term team fieldwork. A key worry here is who is habituating to whom, and to what effect? One very striking example: by 1975, the Harvard-Chiapas project, which had involved over 140 anthropologists, into the town of Zinacantan had lasted so long that half of its 11,000 or so inhabitants could not have known what it was like to live without the scrutiny of an anthropologist. In the words of one commentator:

> It is difficult to believe a community of this size ... exposed to twenty years of outsiders prying and probing has not been profoundly affected by it. A body of trained and paid informants has grown up, two of whom can 'type in both Tzotzil and Spanish, and have learnt to footnote when they come to a difficult passage to translate'. On occasion an informant has also been shipped to Cambridge, Massachusetts, 'to be available for interviews to students'.
>
> It seems safe to assume, however, that it is in the interests of some Zinacantecos to keep the information flowing and the project rolling (Anon 1977).

At times like these, the obsessions of anthropologists can take on surrealist tones, and the status of the information generated appears to float off into uncharted realms. In a similar fashion some primatologists have voiced concerns that the chimpanzees at Goodall's original field site, Gombe, have been habituated for so long and so intensively that we can legitimately query the origins and contexts of the behaviour studied.

Fieldwork reality and representation

Many social anthropologists and some primatologists might still try to maintain the fiction of the lone intellectual in the bush or other challenging environment. But this literary pose has been well exposed for the rhetoric that it is. Even if not working within a team of colleagues, no field anthropologist is ever truly alone. Malinowski might have lived with the Trobriand Islanders for years, but he also spent valuable time with nearby planters and missionaries (Young 2004). The same applies to primatologists. As Jolly and MacClancy point out in their contributions to this volume, one is rarely studying only one group of local primates, whether human or non-human. No matter our original focus, other groups can easily impress themselves onto us, and enter our field of research vision, whether we desire them there or not. But such is in the very nature of field research. In their comparative work on field research, the historian of anthropology Henrika Kuklick and the sociologist of science Robert Kohler underline this point. Field sites, unlike laboratories, are natural locations. They are public spaces, never exclusively scientific domains, and fieldworkers share those spaces with all their residents, whether indigenous or not. Scientists may be able to exclude all others from their labs; fieldworkers cannot do that. In the field, the distinction between the purportedly 'professional' and the often dismissed 'amateur' becomes much, much more blurred, and usually to the benefit of the discipline (Kuklick and Kohler 1996: 4).

Schumaker makes the related point that early anthropologists had to find ways to make their fieldwork-centred approach acceptable to gatekeepers in the field (Schumaker 2004). Fieldworkers were not to indulge in behaviour which might endanger their continued stay in the field. This caveat applies just as strongly today, and just as strongly to field primatologists and biological anthropologists as well. It is a further reminder that we are not alone in the field, but must take account of those within it, especially those in positions of power over us.

Moreover, the research practice of many social anthropologists is often much more varied than they would give us to know. Instead of relying almost exclusively from living with locals in the field, many have in fact also gained from a somewhat wider diversity of sources. Judith Okely, who investigated social anthropological practice, found that fieldwork, in reality, 'included searches in archives, scrutiny of national legislation and participant observation among local officials' (Okely 2007: 360). Lederman argues that it is for this reason of diversity that a renowned paper by a leading commentator of contemporary anthropology, George Marcus, praising the power of multi-sited fieldwork (Marcus 1995) has been so multi-cited: Marcus's paper was, unintentionally, less a prospective programme than a summary of much present activity (Lederman 2008: 315). Primatology also participates in this trend to an extent. No longer is most primatology practiced simply via observations and recoding of behaviour. Today practice in primatology ranges from basic observations, to field experiments involving the manipulation of food and individuals, to genetic analyses via faecal collection, to follows of animals via global positioning satellite (GPS) enabling the researchers to view the animals though a computer screen rather than a pair of binoculars. Additionally, although not 'multi-sited' ethnography, primatologists are realizing the substantial importance of studying the same species at different locations and in different ecologies in order to better understand the patterns and ranges of variability. However, despite some parallels with multi-sited fieldwork, a major difference between modern primatology and modern social anthropology (vis-à-vis Lederman 2008) remains that only a small minority of primatologists actively promote a concept of diversity both in location and in theoretical perspectives in theory and practice (i.e., Fuentes 2007 and Fuentes chapter here).

The morality of it all

These days it is made patent to all fledgling fieldworkers, no matter their discipline, that ethics is not a latter-day 'add-on' to research. On the contrary, continuous ethical negotiation is central and primary to all styles of fieldwork, no matter the discipline. The respective learned bodies may draw up 'Ethics guidelines' for field practitioners, but it is generally accepted that these prescriptions, despite their authors' best intentions, must remain by definition generalized guides. While striving to maintain key principles from the beginning to what is seen as the end of research, neophyte fieldworkers have to be forewarned that they will probably encounter moments when principles may diverge or even clash, and that they may well be forced to choose which ethical road to go down. In these moments, inaction is not a withdrawal of responsibility, but a chosen form of action in itself, which can be subject to ethical assessment. Once in the field, there is no easy escape from ethical involvement.

The qualitative and the quantitative

Most social anthropologists shy from any suggestion of quantitation in their studies, as though the very act of measuring numerically was itself suspect. And in many cases their fears are well-grounded, for their aim is to discover in an open-ended mode other people's visions, and not to triangulate them via questionnaires constituted in anthropologists' categories (MacClancy 2002). Statistical data, if needed, are only generated in the latest stages of fieldwork, and even then in a very diffident manner. In sharp contrast quantitative material is integral to most primatology. Qualitative observations, as Kutsukake notes in his contribution, are usually regarded as secondary. His question is whether that is appropriate.

Contemporary biological anthropologists, as Panter-Brick and Eggerman underline, work to integrate the two. Quantitative research gives them the numerical data they require, while qualitative work guides what data they wish to produce, and helps them interpret the significance of the data they do generate. And, as Hladik demonstrates in his chapter, there can be common quantitative approaches between biological anthropology and primatology: the statistical work of one can illuminate that of the other.

Kutsukake exemplifies a different style of crossing boundaries: the use of primatological field techniques to study both human child development and other animals, such as meerkats. In this way the interconnections between the research styles and aims of our three disciplines can be shown to be as unexpected as they are multiple.

Who knows tomorrow? Quantitation may yet become fashionable again within social anthropology.

The academic, the popular

All too often academics distance their writing from allied, but popular work. It is as though they regarded non-academic books as unworthy of academics' attention, even if they covered the same terrain. Yet it is very easy to argue that this academics' division of labour is short-sighted, self-serving and dangerously misleading (MacClancy 1996). While there are very few popular works in biological anthropology so far, both social anthropology and primatology are well-known to a broad non-academic public thanks to the bestsellers produced by a series of practitioners who each had a story to tell and knew how to tell it. They have portrayed fieldwork, whether among gorillas or witches, chimpanzees or crack dealers, as an exciting adventure of self-realization and academic advance. In the process they have swelled the ranks of our disciplines and, perhaps, facilitated their sustained funding. Both Asquith and MacClancy, in their contributions, focus on popular publications in primatology, exposing the key moments in this literary style and the underlying agendas. Taken together, this pair of chapters demonstrates that, from the beginning, primatologists have looked beyond the boundaries of the academy for their audience. Just as was the case for social anthropology (MacClancy and McDonaugh 1996), if we wish to understand the development of primatology in a rounded manner then we need to examine how literary-minded primatologists have expressed themselves to others.

* * *

Perhaps what has surprised us both is the number of dimensions of fieldwork common to all three disciplines: the need to habituate oneself as well as the group studied; having to deal with multiple groups; the permeable boundaries of the field; accommodating for the unexpected; bonding with the studied; fieldwork and its ethics as process; and so on. Even that great, supposed divider – language – is revealed as only a relative difference, with primatologists gawping at their occasional ability to engage in inter-species communication. Also, we can identify national styles of fieldwork within both social anthropology and primatology, while at the same time recognizing that these styles are dynamic, may well subsume a diversity of practices, and may influence one another. They are not fixed categories.

It is simplistic to characterize any one discipline in unitary terms. There are always competing theories, different schools of thought vying for pre-eminence. Our space, however, was limited. We could not give room to all. For example, we have not included a comparative discussion of field notes – what is taken as conventional and sufficient for fieldworkers in each of our disciplines (see, e.g., Sanjek 1990). Nor did we wish to mask difference within a discipline. Thus some of our contributions point in different directions; a few are even opposed to one another. We regard this diversity of viewpoints positively. We wished to stimulate discussion, not foreclose it. We wished to open up our comparative topic, not impose an authoritarian, bogus unity. Similarly, we have not covered all topics related to fieldwork which cut across our disciplines. Our aim, after all, was to instigate debate, to inspire primatologists and biological anthropologists to step back and critically assess their fieldwork practice. In the process they just might get us all to reconfigure the comparative project within anthropology, broadly speaking. For this is a project which could benefit us all.

Acknowledgements

We are grateful to Simon Bearder, Peter Parkes and Stan Ulijaszek, and two anonymous reviewers for comments and suggestions.

References

Amselle, J.L. and E. Sibeud (eds). 1998. *Maurice Delafosse. Entre orientalisme et ethnographie: l'itinéraire d'un africaniste (1870–1926)*. Paris: Maisonneuve et Larose.

Anon. 1977. 'Ethnographic cuckoos', *Times Literary Supplement*, 4 February, p. 128.

Azcona, J. 1984. *Etnía y nacionalismo vasco. Una aproximación desde la antropología*. Barcelona: Anthropos.

Blanckaert, C. 1999. 'Introduction. Histoires du terrain. Entre savoirs et savoir-faire', in C. Blanckaert (ed.) *Le terrain des sciences humaines. Instructions et enquétes (XVIIIe—XXe siècle)*. Paris: L'Harmattan, pp. 9–56.

Calame-Griaule, G. 1991. 'On the Dogon restudied', *Current Anthropology* 32(5): 575–7.

Cinnamon, J.M. 2007. 'Colonial Anthropologies and the Primordial Imagination in Equatorial Africa', in H. Tilley (ed.) *Ordering Africa: Anthropology, European Imperialism, and the Politics of Knowledge*. Manchester: Manchester University Press, pp. 225–51.

Clifford, J. 1983. 'Power and dialogue in ethnography. Marcel Griaule's initiation', in G.W. Stocking (ed.) *Observers Observed: Essays on Ethnographic Fieldwork. History of Anthropology*, vol. 1. Madison: University of Wisconsin Press, pp. 121–56.

——— 1986. 'Introduction: partial truths', in J. Clifford and G.E. Marcus (eds) *Writing Culture: The Poetics and Politics of Ethnography*. Berkeley: University of California Press, pp. 1–27.

Corlette, E.A.C. 1935. 'Notes on the Natives of the New Hebrides', *Oceania* 5(4): 474–87.

De Garine, I. 2004. 'Anthropology of Food and Pluridisciplinarity', in H. Macbeth and J. MacClancy (eds) *Researching Food Habits: Methods and Problems*. Oxford: Berghahn, pp. 15–28.

de Heusch, L. 1991. 'On Griaule on trial', *Current Anthropology* 32(4): 434–7.

de L'Estoile, B. de. 2007. 'Internationalization and "scientific nationalism": the International Institute of African Languages and Cultures between the wars', in J. MacClancy and C. McDonaugh (eds) *Popularizing Anthropology*. London: Routledge, pp. 95–118.

de Wolf, J. 1999. 'Colonial Ideologies and Ethnological Discourse: A Comparison of the United Faculties at Leiden and Utrecht', in J. van Bremen and A. Shimizu (eds) *Anthropology and Colonialism in Asia and Oceania*. Richmond: Curzon, pp. 307–25.

Ellen, R. and H. Harris. 2000. 'Introduction', in R. Ellen, P. Parkes and A. Bicker (eds) *Indigenous Environmental Knowledge and its Transformations*. London: Gordon and Breach, pp. 1–34.

Evans-Pritchard, E.E. 1940. *The Nuer: A Description of the Modes of Livelihood and Political Institutions of a Nilotic people*. Oxford: Oxford University Press.

Foster, G.M., T. Scudder, E. Colson and R.V. Kemper (eds). 1979. *Long-Term Field Research in Social Anthropology*. London: Academic Press.

Fuentes, A. 2007. 'Social Organization: Social Systems and the Complexities in Understanding the Evolution of Primate Behavior', in C. Campbell, A. Fuentes, K. MacKinnon, M. Panger and S. Bearder (eds) *Primates in Perspective*. Oxford: Oxford University Press, pp. 609–21.

Garcia, V. 2001. *Bringing Anthropology Home: Latino/a Students, Ethnographic Research, and US Rural Communities*, Occasional Paper no. 57, Latino Studies Series, Julian Samora Research Institute, Michigan State University.

Gottlieb, A. 1995. 'Beyond the lonely anthropologist: collaboration in research and writing', *American Anthropologist* 97(1): 21–6.

Goulet, J-G. A., and B. G. Miller (eds). 2007. *Extraordinary Fieldwork: Transformations in the Field*. Lincoln: University of Nebraska Press.

Grant, B. 1999. 'Foreword', in L. Shternberg *The Social Organisation of the Gilyak*. Anthropological Papers of the American Museum of Natural History, no. 82. Seattle: University of Washington Press.

Gupta, A. and J. Ferguson. 1997. 'Discipline and Practice: "the Field" as Site, Method, and Location in Anthropology', in A. Gupta and J. Ferguson (eds) *Anthropological Locations: Boundaries and Grounds of a Field Science.* Berkeley: University of California Press, pp. 1–46.

Haddow, A.J., G.W.A. Dick, W.H.R. Lumsden and K.C. Smithburn. 1951. 'Monkeys in relation to the epidemiology of yellow fever', *Transactions of the Royal Society of Tropical Medicine and Hygenie,* 45: 189–224.

Haddow, A.J. and J.M. Ellice. 1964. 'Studies in bush-babies (Galago spp.) with special reference to the epidemiology of yellow fever', *Transactions of the Royal Society of Tropical Medicine and Hygiene,* 45: 521–38.

Harries, P. 2007. 'From the Alps to Africa: Swiss Missionaries and Anthropology', in H. Tilley (ed.) *Ordering Africa: Anthropology, European imperialism, and the Politics of Knowledge.* pp. 201–24.

Hirsch, E., B. Kapferer, E. Martin and A. Tsing. 2007. '"Anthropologists are talking" about anthropology alter globalization', *Ethnos* 72(1): 102–26.

Hunt, N.R. 2007. 'Colonial Medical Anthropology and the Making of the Central African Infertility Belt', in H. Tilley (ed.) *Ordering Africa: Anthropology, European imperialism, and the Politics of Knowledge.* pp. 252–84.

Huss-Ashmore, R. and S. Ulijaszek. 1997. 'The contributions of field research in the Gambia to the study of human adaptability', in S. Ulijaszek and R. Huss-Ashmore (eds), *Human Adaptability: Past, Present, and Future.* Oxford: Oxford University Press, pp. 82–101.

Iczuriaga Montes, C. 2005. 'La influencia de Angel Palerm en el CIESAS (Alocución en la inauguración de la cátedra)', http://www.ciesas.edu.mx/Catedra/archivos/Icazuriaga_CAPalerm.pdf. Accessed 18 January 2008.

Jezequel, J-H. 2007. 'Voices of their own? African participation in the production of colonial knowledge in French West Africa', in H. Tilley (ed.) *Ordering Africa: Anthropology, European imperialism, and the Politics of Knowledge.* Manchester: Manchester University Press, pp. 145–72.

Johnson, D. 2007. 'Analytical anthropology in the Sudan', in H. Tilley (ed.) *Ordering Africa: Anthropology, European imperialism, and the Politics of Knowledge.* Manchester: Manchester University Press, pp. 309–35.

Kuklick, H, and R.E. Kohler. 1996. 'Science in the field: introduction' in H. Kuklick and R.E. Kohler (eds) 'Science in the field', special issue of *Osiris* 11: 1–16.

Kuklick, H. 2008. 'The British tradition', in H. Kuklick (ed.) *A New History of Anthropology.* Oxford: Blackwell, pp. 52–78.

Kuwayama, T. 2006. 'Anthropological fieldwork reconsidered: with Japanese folkloristics as a mirror', in J. Hendry and H. Wah Wong (eds) *Dismantling the East-West Dichotomy.* London: Routledge, pp. 49–55.

Lasker, G. 1993. 'Planning a research project', in G.W. Lasker and C.G.N. Mascie-Taylor (eds) *Research Strategies in Human Biology: Field and Survey Studies.* Cambridge: Cambridge University Press, pp. 1–19.

——— 1999. *Happenings and Hearsay: Experiences of a Biological Anthropologist.* Detroit: Savoyard.

Lederman, R. 2005. 'Unchosen grounds: cultivating cross-subfield accents for a public voice', in Segal and Yangasiko (eds) *Unwrapping the Sacred Bundle.* Durham, NC: Duke University Press, pp. 49–77.

——— 2008. 'Anthropological regionalism', in H. Kuklick (ed.) *A New History of Anthropology.* Oxford: Blackwell, pp. 310–25.

Lee, R.B. 1979. 'Hunter-gatherers in process: the Kalahari Research Project, 1963–1976', in G.M. Foster, T. Scudder, E. Colson and R.V. Kemper (eds) *Long-term Field Research in Social Anthropology*. London: Academic Press, pp. 302–22.

MacClancy, J. 1996. 'Popularizing anthropology', in J. MacClancy and C. McDonaugh (eds) *Popularizing Anthropology*. London: Routledge, pp. 1–57.

—— 2002. 'Taking people seriously', in J. MacClancy (ed.) *Exotic No More: Anthropology on the Front Lines*. Chicago: University of Chicago Press, pp. 1–14.

—— 2007. *Expressing Identities in the Basque Arena*. Oxford: James Currey.

MacClancy, J. and C. McDonaugh (eds). 1996. *Popularizing Anthropology*. London: Routledge.

Marais, E. 1939. *My Friends the Baboons*. New York: Robert M. McBride.

—— 1969. *The Soul of the Ape*. London: Antony Blond.

Marcus, G. 1995. 'Ethnography in/of the world system: the emergence of multi-sited ethnography', *Annual Review of Anthropology* 24: 95–117.

McLean, A. and A. Leibing (eds). 2007. *The Shadow Side of Fieldwork*. Oxford: Blackwell.

Meggitt, M. 1979. 'Reflections occasioned by continuing anthropological field research among the Enga of Papua New Guinea', in Foster et al. (eds) *Long-Term Field Research in Social Anthropology*. London: Academic Press, pp. 107–26.

Meskell, L. and P. Pels (eds). 2005. *Embedding Ethics*. Oxford: Berg.

Needham, R. 1974. *Remarks and Inventions*. London: Tavistock.

Nakao, K. 1998. 'Japanese colonial policy and anthropology in Manchuria', in J. van Bremen and A. Shimizu (eds) *Anthropology and Colonialism in Asia and Oceania*. Richmond: Curzon, pp. 245–65.

Norgan, N.G. 1997. 'Human adaptability studies in Papua New Guinea', in S. Ulijaszek and R. Huss-Ashmore (eds) *Human Adaptability: Past, Present, and Future*. Oxford: Oxford University Press, pp. 102–25.

Okely, J. 2007. 'Response to George E. Marcus', *Social Anthropology* 15(3): 357–61.

Parkes, P. 2008. 'Canonic ethnography: Hanoteau and Letournex on Kabyle communal law', in R. Parkin and A. de Sales (eds) *Out of the Study and into the Field: Ethnographic Theory and Practice in French Anthropology*. Oxford: Berghahn Books (in process of publication).

Price, R. and S. Price. 2003. *The Root of Roots, or How Afro-American Anthropology Got Its Start*. Chicago: Prickly Paradigm Press.

Pugach, S. 2007. 'Of conjunctions, comportment, and clothing: the place of African teaching assistants in Berlin and Hamburg, 1889–1919', in H. Tilley (ed.) *Ordering Africa: Anthropology, European imperialism, and the Politics of Knowledge*. Manchester: Manchester University Press, pp. 119–44.

Ramos, A. R. 1990. 'Ethnology Brazilian style', *Cultural Anthropology* 5(4): 452–72.

Rivet, P., P. Lester and G-H. Rivière. 1935. 'Le laboratoire d'Antropologie du Muséum', *Archives du Muséum National d'Histoire Naturelle* 6e serie XII: 507–31.

Robben, A.C.G.M. and J.A. Sluka (eds). 2006. *Ethnographic Fieldwork: An Anthropological Reader*. Oxford: Blackwell.

Salemink, O. 1991. '*Mois* and *Maquis*. The invention and appropriation of Vietnam's Montagnards from Sabatier to the CIA', in George W. Stocking (ed.) *Colonial Situation: Essays on the Contextualization of Ethnographic Knowledge*. Madison: University of Wisconsin Press, pp. 243–84.

Sanjek, R. 1993. 'Anthropology's hidden colonialism. Assistants and their ethnographers', *Anthropology Today* 9(2): 13–18.

—— (ed.). 1999. *Fieldnotes: The Making of Anthropology*. Ithaca: Cornell University Press.

Schell, L.M., J. Ravenscroft, M. Cole, A. Jacobs, J. Newman and Akwesasne Task Force on the Environment. 2005. 'Health disparities and toxic exposure of Akwesasne Mohawk Young Adults: a partnership approach to research', *Environmental Health Perspectives* 113(12): 1826–32.

Schell, L., J. Ravenscroft, M. Gallo and M. Denham. 2007. 'Advancing biocultural models by working with communities: a partnership approach', *American Journal of Human Biology* 19: 511–24.

Schumaker, L. 1996. 'A tent with a view: colonial officers, anthropologists, and the making of the field in Northern Rhodesia, 1937–1960', in H. Kuklick and R.E. Kohler (eds.) 'Science in the field', special issue of *Osiris* 11: 1–16.

——— 2001. *Africanizing Anthropology: Fieldwork, Networks and the Making of Cultural Knowledge in Central Africa*. Durham: Duke University Press.

——— 2004. 'The director as significant other: Max Gluckman and team fieldwork in the Rhodes-Livingstone Institute', in R. Handler (ed.) *Significant Others: Interpersonal and Professional Commitments in Anthropology*. Madison: University of Wisconsin Press, pp. 91–130.

Scudder, T. and E. Colson. 1979. 'Long-term research in Gwembe valley, Zambia', in G.M. Foster, T. Scudder, E. Colson and R.V. Kemper (eds) *Long-term Field Research in Social Anthropology*. London: Academic Press, pp. 227–54.

Segal, D, and S. Yanagisako. 2005. 'Introduction', in Segal and Yangasiko (eds) *Unwrapping the Sacred Bundle*. Durham, NC: Duke University Press, pp. 1–23.

Shimizu, A. 1998. 'Colonialism and the development of modern anthropology in Japan', in J. van Bremen and A. Shimizu (eds) *Anthropology and Colonialism in Asia and Oceania*. Richmond: Curzon, pp. 115–171.

Sibeud, E. 2008. 'Ethnology in France, 1839–1930', in H. Kuklick (ed.) *A New History of Anthropology*. Oxford: Blackwell Publishing, pp. 96–110.

Sontag, S. 1970. 'The anthropologist as hero', in E.N. and T. Hayes (eds.) *Claude Lévi-Strauss: the Anthropologist as Hero*. Cambridge, MA: MIT Press, pp. 184–97.

Ssorin-Chaikov, N. 2008. 'Political fieldwork, ethnographic exile, and state theory: peasant socialism and anthropology in late-nineteenth century Russia', in H. Kuklick (ed.) *A New History of Anthropology*. Oxford: Blackwell, pp. 191–206.

Sussman, R.W. 2000. 'Piltdown Man: the father of American field primatology', in S.C. Strum and L.M. Fedigan (eds.) *Primate Encounters: Models of Science, Gender and Society*. Chicago: University of Chicago Press, pp. 85–103.

Tilley, H. (ed.). 2007. *Ordering Africa: Anthropology, European Imperialism, and the Politics of Knowledge*. Manchester: Manchester University Press.

Tomas, D. 1991. 'Tools of the trade: The production of ethnographic observations on the Andaman Islands, 1858–1922', in G. Stocking (ed.) *Colonial Situations: Essays on the Contextualizing of Ethnographic Knowledge*. Madison: University of Wisconsin Press, pp. 75–108.

van Beek, W.E.A. 1991. 'Dogon restudied: a field evaluation of the work of Marcel Griaule', *Current Anthropology* 32(2): 139–67.

Vogt, E.Z. 1979. 'The Harvard Chiapas Project: 1957–1975', in G.M. Foster, T. Scudder, E. Colson, & R.V. Kemper (eds.) *Long-Term Field Research in Social Anthropology*. London: Academic Press, pp. 279–302.

Walraven, B. 1998. 'The natives next-door: Ethnology in colonial Korea', in J. van Bremen and A. Shimizu (eds) *Anthropology and Colonialism in Asia and Oceania*. Richmond: Curzon, pp. 219–44.

Wax, R. 1991. *Doing Fieldwork: Warnings and Advice*. Chicago: University of Chicago Press.

Weiner, J.S. and J.A. Lourie. 1981. *Practical Human Biology*. London: Academic Press.

Wolf, E. R. 1981. 'Ángel Palerm Vich (Obituary)', *American Anthropologist* 83(3): 612–15

Young, M. 1972. *Fighting with Food: Leadership, Values and Social Control in a Massim Society*. Cambridge: Cambridge University Press.

——— 2004. *Malinowski: Odyssey of an Anthropologist, 1884–1920*. New Haven CT: Yale University Press.

2

The Dos and Don'ts
of Fieldwork

Geoffrey A. Harrison

Research in the biological anthropology of recent human populations has largely focused on documenting the great variation that occurs within and between such populations and in attempting to explain the causes for it. Where the variation is mainly of genetic origin, as for example in blood groups, the principal cause of similarity between groups is recent common ancestry: so analyses of such characters will therefore tend to reveal evolutionary relationships between populations. Where, however, the variation has a large component of environmental determination and arises directly from the particular conditions under which individuals develop, similarity and differences may have little to do with ancestry. For many years such variation was perceived as a nuisance, but increasingly it has been recognized that it provides insight into the quality of environments and into characteristics which facilitate survival in those environments, i.e., it is adaptive.

Examination of these issues clearly requires fieldwork and biological anthropologists have examined and measured people all over the world. Initially, such work was undertaken by individuals but as the number of characteristics which needed to be taken into account increased, studies were conducted by teams composed of various specialists. Periods spent in the field, however, tended to be short, rarely more than a few weeks, and most of the time was spent analyzing data back in laboratories. This chapter is concerned with contrasting the experience of two expeditions in the 1950s and early 1960s: one to Namibia and the other to Ethiopia.

The original aim of the Namibian study was to document the genetic variety among the various indigenous populations of that country, Bantu, Hottentot, San Bushmen and some hybrid groups, and to determine affinities between them and with people in surrounding countries. Quite a lot was known of physical appearance characters, but only a little of genetic markers. At the time many new blood markers were being discovered: more blood groups, various serum proteins and red blood cell enzymes. Special interest was to be given to the so-called Black Bushmen of the

Caprivi Strip and surrounding areas about which almost nothing was known. The focus of the field study was therefore to collect blood samples from the various groups and get them back to Johannesburg for testing.

The scientific team consisted of five males from South Africa, the UK and Germany but none had any experience of the Kalahari. Arrangements were somewhat complicated by a logistic collaboration with a different team of physiologists who were concerned with examining the cold tolerance of San Bushmen but none of them had Kalahari experience either. Although some support staff knew Afrikaans, no one had any knowledge of local languages and much of the contact with the local people was arranged through Finnish missionaries. The main transport was a large lorry specially designed for going through the Kalahari sands and loaned to the expedition for testing. It turned out to be especially designed for getting stuck in the sand! And almost all the food for the expedition was donated by South African food companies who were varyingly generous.

Clearly, all the components for a disaster were there but the crucial one was a decision in the field for a complete change of aims. Various papers had just been published indicating that some blood groups and particularly the ABO system were subject to natural selection and one in particular claimed experimental evidence for an antigenic overlap between ABH substances and the bubonic plague bacterium. On arrival in the area the team learned that there had just been an epidemic of bubonic plague in the populations along the Okavango River. It seemed to be too good an opportunity to miss and all the resources of the expedition were turned to determining the impact of the epidemic on the genetic markers. What was not known and was never established was which of the populations had been most affected, what the mortality rates were and what were the age distributions of those affected. Nor was any realistic estimate made of the sample sizes required for the detection of effects under different levels of selection. All that was recognized was that the sample number would have to be very large. The expedition was short of many things but not of venules. So a massive blood collection of all and sundry was started and there was no shortage of subjects since local chiefs gave their full support in thanks for the help of the Finnish missionaries and the gift of a few trade goods. It was, however, not only the ethics which were at fault: the set up was incapable of adequately coping with the preservation and transport of the large numbers of blood samples; much larger than were expected for the original aims. The refrigerator carried was too small to supply sufficient ice and the vacuum flasks too few for transportation. What is more, the communication links were insufficiently robust for the job. Most of the samples went rotten on their way back to Johannesburg.

Thus the whole venture was a catastrophe yet a few simple calculations showed that even if the practical side had worked satisfactorily the sample sizes required to detect likely selection levels were far greater than those that could be collected. Only two small scientific papers were ever published, one on skin colour and one on the distribution of the ABO blood groups along the Okavango, it being possible to determine ABO status from rotten blood samples! All that was really achieved was a collection of horrifying after dinner stories.

At least lessons were learned for the Ethiopian researches. The basis for these rested on a number of years of experimental work on the effects of climatic factors on the growth and development of mice. With them it was possible to use highly inbred strains, in which all individuals of a strain were essentially identical, and F1 hybrids between them. It was thus possible to examine direct environmental effects on development separately from genetic factors. The main environmental factor studied was temperature variation but large differences in temperature on earth involve great distances and peoples living far apart are likely to be genetically very different. The only great climatic differences that are to be found in small geographical distances are those associated with altitude especially the partial pressure of oxygen. In the Simien of Ethiopia the land rises gradually to an altitude of 10–15,000 feet then falls away in a spectacular precipice in almost zero geographical distance to an altitude of 4–5,000 feet. Both habitats are quite heavily populated and it was for these reasons that Ethiopia was chosen for an examination of the direct environmental effects on human growth and development: the nearest one could get to the experimental mouse situation.

The study involved extensive measurement in adults of various morphological features, respiratory function, haematology and health status. Blood was also collected for genetic analysis to confirm that the populations in the two environments were essentially the same and advantage was taken of some migration between the two altitude zones. It was conducted by six investigators: four British, including one who was long resident in Ethiopia and two of which were female, and two Ethiopians. So there were no communication difficulties. Although the study focused on adults, a clinic was held each morning for children and this was much appreciated by the population. As each subject came to be measured a Polaroid photograph was taken which confirmed identification when all the people examined during a week were asked to return on a Saturday for blood collection. At this time they were given their photograph which was greatly valued. Collected samples were first taken by mules to the nearest roadway, then transported overnight by motor vehicle to Gondar, where the expedition had available a small aircraft to fly the samples to the international airport in Addis Ababa for onward carriage to Europe. Samples reached the laboratory in London within thirty-six hours of collection and all were in perfect condition. The expedition was provisioned with the British Army rations purchased from Aden and these were excellent.

The contrast with the Namibian venture could not have been greater and the scientific results met all the planned aims and made a major contribution to the understanding of high altitude adaptation in humans. The study also led to follow-up investigations into other aspects: for example, into child development, and the secondary consequences of the climatic difference which affected infectious disease prevalence, and forms of economy, which affected nutritional status.

So, what of general relevance is to be learned from these two experiences? Clearly, the worst that happened on the Namibian expedition was the total change of aims once in the field. This must be an exceptional circumstance but it highlights the general point of the difficulty of making important judgements under conditions of some stress. What, back home, can be seen as absolutely absurd may be considered to be exciting and important when people are tired, frustrated, hungry and disoriented, and it is to be noted that the decision to change was not just made by one person but by the whole team. Clearly all field projects need to be monitored continuously and faults corrected but it should constantly be in a fieldworker's mind that judgements made in the field are particularly fallible.

Perhaps a more general point concerns the composition of a team and the personal qualities and experience of individual workers. Clearly the Ethiopian study benefited enormously from having local people not only in the team but as senior members of it. And this was not only because it overcame language barriers but also because of knowledge and understanding of the customs and expectations of the people being studied. So far as individual personal qualities are concerned it is not easy to predict the kind of person who can withstand the deprivations that fieldwork inevitably involves. In my experience both in Namibia and Ethiopia and in many other expeditions, nationality and gender are unimportant but it does seem that the 'nice guys' of our society are not the ones who stand up best to field work situations. J.V. Neel is reportedly to have said that he wanted people in his teams who had been boy scouts or the like in their youth. I think there is much sense in this view. What is definitely true is that every expedition needs a single leader, who should take ultimate decisions or be responsible for them. Full discussion is vital but committee decisions don't work in the field.

Then there is the issue of the rights of the subjects especially when body fluids, such as blood, urine, saliva are being sought. The critical requirement today is informed consent, but this is open to various interpretations. Even in one's own society with detailed explanations of procedures and purposes, it is questionable whether all subjects fully understand what is involved. The procedures used in Namibia would not obtain ethical consent today, and rightly so. Most of the subjects just did what their chief told them to do. In Ethiopia much more attention was paid to the decisions of individuals. The provision of an early morning child clinic run by an Ethiopian doctor brought many families to the expedition's camp and those adults who volunteered to join the study were given a detailed explanation of what was involved. The question remains whether or not this was enough. Today one needs ethical approval from various institutions such as one's university, local government and the community in which the work is being done. More importantly one has to make as sure as one can that each individual is truly a volunteer. Some workers pay for their samples but this changes totally the relationship between researchers and subject. Then there is the question of who benefits from the work other than the researchers. Clearly it is best if one can truly conclude that at least in the long run the community will benefit, and among some Australian peoples it is required that the individual donor benefits. Ownership of samples can also be a difficult question. In Australia where these issues are foremost, there is a general view that while the results of analyses belong to the investigator, the original samples as long as they exist belong to the donors.

To more practical matters, the Namibian experience demonstrates just how important communication is, especially in connection with transport of specimens. This issue was made priority one in the Ethiopian work. Today keeping in touch is much easier than it was fifty years ago but it is still necessary to try and cover every eventuality and to have backup for failure at critical points such as the handover of specimens from one carrier to another. What had not been anticipated in Ethiopia was the local law closing roads at night as a protection against bandits. The problem was solved by demonstrating the value of a Polaroid camera to the authorities, who then provided a military escort!

Finally there is the issue of provisions, especially food provisioning. It is quite unforgivable to take food from local sources when food is short, even if it is paid for. In Ethiopia the British Army rations, occasionally supplemented by an invitation to dine with local people, provided an excellent diet but everything that was available in Namibia came from cans, and particularly canned fish. It is sometimes considered that all worthwhile fieldwork must be tough but there is no doubt that the best work is done when workers can enjoy some comfort. And a crucial member of a field team is an experienced daily logistics manager and supplier.

Population biology field work today tends to be focused much more on human ecology questions and this is best undertaken by single workers spending long periods of time in the field and learning local languages and social customs. It is thus much more similar operationally to what social anthropologists do. However, not all the lessons from the past have become redundant.

Acknowledgements

I am grateful to Professor E.J. Clegg for his helpful comments on this chapter.

3

The Anthropologist as a Primatologist:

Mental Journeys of a Fieldworker

Volker Sommer

A well-travelled discipline

Experiencing destinations far from home is a dream that feeds the tourism industry. Those who explore foreign scenery, customs, food, nature, wildlife as professionals are called anthropologists. According to Greek etymology, the diversity of humans (anthropos) is the subject of their words and wisdom (logos).

But anthropologists do not travel. They conduct 'fieldwork', a term that rings of wilderness. A German equivalent of the term has a truly poetic tinge to it: 'Freilandforschung', meaning 'research in free land'. For long and intensive periods, far from home and family, these researchers are thoroughly immersed in 'the other', taking shelter with natives, learning their tongue, sharing food and rituals, partaking in strange ways of life and death while filling stacks of notebooks. Solid fieldwork is a core research method of anthropology. Once returned, these voyagers become objects of fascination themselves, exuding their strange experiences in lectures and monographs. Fieldwork marks anthropologists of good standing and mythical proportions can be attained if the quest was difficult. For example, 'Argonauts of the Western Pacific' (1922): who could have dreamed up a better title for that first major field study, which turned Bronislaw Malinowski (1884–1942) into an icon?

Fieldwork can be gripping because of inherent surprises and unpredictability. The popularity of fictional anthropologists such as 'Indiana Jones' reflects this. Many would want to go on treasure hunts and tell heroic stories of survival. Admittedly, my portrayal of the anthropologist as a fieldworker is outdated. Often, anthropologists do not work in the field and those who do might be a far cry from the cliché of the lone explorer roughing it amongst natives. Contemporary research is less likely conducted amongst tribes of the Trobriand Islands than in a Sari store in India, a hospital in Thailand or a beauty salon in Nigeria. In any case, few places remain 'remote' given electronic mail and satellite phones, and given that even casual tourists can visit locations which until recently were far off the beaten track.

Nevertheless, fieldwork in far-flung places has produced staple knowledge in anthropology and set paradigmatic standards of the discipline. However, the conduct of 'traditional' fieldwork has rarely been scrutinized within primatology and biological anthropology. I at least, a seasoned fieldworker with a quarter of a century's experience, operate without an explicit intellectual framework and know hardly any colleagues who have one. This essay will thus touch upon explicit and, more importantly, implicit factors which shape fieldwork and its narratives. I do this from my perspective as a primatologist, i.e., as somebody who studies monkeys and apes in nature. Such research is anthropology too, given the multi-field approach, which includes biological (or physical) anthropology; archaeology or prehistory, linguistic anthropology, and social or cultural anthropology (Miller 2005).

The four-field approach is foremost a North American affair whereas British anthropology is largely equated with 'social anthropology'. Here, biological anthropology comes across as an addendum, often only grudgingly tolerated by their more socially minded colleagues. Quite the reverse is true for German-speaking countries where virtually all anthropology departments are exclusively dedicated to biological dimensions, while separate disciplines deal with 'Völkerkunde' (human cultures), 'Archäologie' (prehistory) and 'Sprachwissenschaften' (linguistics).

Social anthropologists have thought more about fieldwork than biological anthropologists, perhaps because measurements from blood, bones, and body dimensions appear less fuzzy than descriptions of wedding ceremonies or genital mutilation. Applying cultural anthropological discourses to research on wild primates, which I attempt here, might reveal parallels and peculiarities, and enlighten both disciplines about merits and shortcomings. For reviews of social anthropological theory, I rely on own amateur attempts (Sommer 1992) as well as on Barbara Miller's superb textbook 'Cultural Anthropology' (2005).

My 'primates' are non-human primates. This is purely for brevity. Of course, humans are primates as well, but the dynamics of my essay are largely generated because different ethical dimensions still apply to research on humans and 'non-humans', while for me, as a dedicated primatologist, such distinctions have become less and less tenable.

In the woods of Brothers Grimm

My home department of anthropology still interviews all undergraduate applicants. Most assert a fascination with foreign cultures but are perfectly foggy about underlying academic contents. If it comes to biological anthropology, exotic peoples are replaced by furry monkeys. Scientific reasoning is again hard to come by. Even if applicants have read introductory literature, pictures of blonde and pretty Jane Goodall gently touching hands with an infant chimpanzee had very likely a far greater impact on the choice of career. I tell these hopefuls that a passion for Goodall's chimpanzee adventures, or Dian Fossey's gorilla tragedy, or Biruté Galdikas' orang-utan exploits

(Goodall 1971; Fossey 1983; Galdikas 1995) qualifies them perfectly well to pursue primatology. This is because academic skills can be learned, but a love for wild animals cannot. And without that, you better not go anywhere near our wild kin.

This untidy conviction – fascination equals qualification – has to do with my own childhood. I grew up in a village in the German heartlands, frolicking in the farms of my parents' families. I wasn't interested in domesticated animals; they were too tame, too unchallenging, devoid of mysteries. I loved 'wild' creatures: deer, boar and tiny game such as beetles, ants and butterflies. I pursued them at forest edges and in mighty oak woods nearby.

In this very area, one and a half centuries earlier, the Brothers Grimm had recorded their fairy tales. That animals spoke, that they had secrets and guarded treasures made perfect sense to my innocent mind. I invented a religion grounded in the conviction that wildlife was conscious and able to communicate with me upon performance of prayers and rituals. Soon, insects, frogs and owls would plead with me to save them, as tracks became tarred roads and small fields and hedges gave way for monocultures which, in the 1960s, replaced much of the mosaic agricultural landscape. Many beautiful critters literally disappeared from one summer to the next, as the bears of Goldilocks' and Little Red Riding Hood's wolf had already. In my pantheism, I was a lone eco-warrior. As an adolescent, I indulged in the fictional travel stories of Karl May, transferred to the wild Sahara, North American plains, and India. There was always a lion to escape from, a grizzly to fight with, or an elephant to ride on.

To observe animals professionally was thus rooted in a mystical connection with nature: sincerely childish, pure and uncompromising, coupled with an adolescent thirst for adventure. This mixture slightly matured through hardcore, non-fictional input at high school and studies of biology, chemistry and theology at the nearby University of Göttingen. I stumbled upon monkeys as research subjects for my doctoral thesis because the professor who lectured best and was most approachable happened to study monkeys. Christian Vogel was a comparative morphologist who realized that bones would tell him only so much about evolution. To truly understand forces that brought about particular designs would require studies 'in the flesh'. Thus my fieldwork career took off, with three pivotal periods:

- langur monkeys in the Great Indian Desert (since 1981), with about three years of fieldwork (Sommer 1987, 1996, 2000);
- gibbons in Thailand's primary rainforest at Khao Yai National Park (since 1989), with close to two years at the site (Reichard and Sommer 1997; Sommer and Reichard 2000);
- chimpanzees in Nigeria's mountainous Gashaka-Gumti National Park (since 1999), with so far two years in the field (Sommer et al. 2004; Fowler and Sommer 2007; Sommer and Ross 2011).

In India, I resided in a Hindu temple outside the city of Jodhpur, and became even competent at conducting Shivaistic rituals. This tied in well with my monkeys who were holy and used to people feeding them, so one could sit right next to them. The landscape was open and arid. Sexual and reproductive strategies was my main research, with infanticide by males a rather nasty ingredient. I used a motorbike to reach study groups. In Thailand, I rode another motorbike, while residing at the rainforest edge in a townhouse resort equipped with swimming pools. The social structure of gibbons (monogamous or not?) and relationships between several groups tolerant of human observers was a major research interest. Gibbon songs swept through the canopy, with leeches, ticks, bears and tigers as creatures of concern. In Nigeria, I founded what is now one of the largest research and conservation projects in West Africa. We first set up tents in the wilderness and now have a sizeable research station with a round-the-clock power supply from a state-of-the-art combination of hydroelectric and photovoltaic energy. During the dry season, four wheel drive vehicles can make it to the camp; during rains, we cope with precarious river crossings, plus hours of walking towards the highlands. The chimpanzees are still hard to find, and much research is indirect, based on calls, faecal samples and discarded tools.

My fieldwork experience is therefore of the old-fashioned type, with extended periods as a solitary researcher in places far away from my native lands. Against this experiential tapestry I will contemplate explicit and implicit dimensions of cultural and biological anthropology.

Armchairs, verandas and wildernesses

Cultural anthropology was not born in the wild, but in the study rooms of wealthy gentlemen when, since the mid-nineteenth century, 'armchair anthropologists' summarized exploits of missionaries and explorers. 'The Golden Bough' (1890), the monumental compilation of myths, rituals and symbols by James Frazer, provides an eminent example. Research became 'open' during the heydays of British imperialism as anthropologists interviewed native informants on the porches of colonial settlements. This 'verandah anthropology' lost its appeal, once Polish-born Malinowski went out to study the Trobrianders, setting new standards for fieldwork. Research on our animal relatives also comes in tame variants of 'verandah primatology'. Jane Goodall lured baboons and chimpanzees with the proverbial bananas into her Tanzanian camp. Similarly, holy monkeys would hang out at my Indian temple, while I noted identities and travel pattern. Most primatological fieldwork, however, takes place in open space (typical for the 'field') where physical challenges can be considerable. Hilly terrain and dense forest soaked up some of my blood (imagine leeches and scrapes from thorns and falls), a lot of my sweat (imagine scorching sun, mean slopes, and deliriums of flu and malaria), and more than a few of my tears (imagine lost love …). Primatological fieldwork is not of the vintage version unless initiated with such fluids.

Malinowskian 'participant observation' comprises extended and intense periods, in a place removed from Western life, living with locals, learning their language, learning to feel in local terms and trying to participate as much as ethically possible. Some of these qualities have equivalents in primate fieldwork; others, by definition, cannot.

The main cause for the 'long-term perspective' is scientific. Social anthropologists try to cover at least one annual cycle of subsistence activity. Seasonal fluctuations in, for example, food availability and parasite load also strongly influence primate physiology and behaviour. Given that three initial months at a new site are often necessary to set up logistics, one looks at a solid fifteen month stretch for a typical doctoral research project: about 2 per cent of the average Western life span.

Another long term aim can be the need to establish 'rapport', the process during which cultural anthropologists build trusting relationships with their study population. In this respect, field primatologists must master a double burden of rapport: with local people *and* animals. Locals might assist primatologists to run a camp, track animals, collect data. Contact with indigenous outsiders can be trickier. At my Indian site, monkeys raid crops and sneak unnoticed into gardens to munch pomegranates, rose buds or vegetables. I, following suit, was invariably spotted. Politely, farmers refrained from chasing the monkeys away so as to not disturb my apparently important work. This not only made me feel bad, but also distorted records about the monkeys' raiding success. In Nigeria, the situation is reverse: locals complain to students who follow crop-raiding baboons that 'their' monkeys inflicted damage.

Establishing rapport with study animals is called 'habituation', a process during which animals get used to human observers. The provisioned Indian monkeys tolerate people at close proximity, but elsewhere, one needs to invest extended periods and a succession of fieldworkers, ideally generations of masters or Ph.D. students. In Nigeria, we designed a rota for several field assistants to try to daily contact the shy chimpanzees. After two years, we see initial success, but are aware that years of hard work lie ahead to earn the apes' trust.

Well-habituated primates obviously make better study animals. However, much of the social dynamics happen between groups, including emigrations, immigrations, extra-group sexual relationships and violent encounters. But neighbours are rarely habituated, which may considerably distort the characterisations of certain primates. For example, gibbons were thought to be firmly monogamous and territorial. This was largely an artefact of following a single group. Neighbours would flee (creating the impression of strict territoriality) and not physically interact: sexual unfaithfulness was therefore not observed. Once we habituated neighbouring groups in Thailand, we were able to document overlapping home ranges as well as extra pair copulations. Only a handful of sites run real long term data collection regimes, taking into account that monkeys and apes may live for decades, and that important events may be very rare. For example, after six, seven or even eight observation years, one might be convinced that gibbon pairs mate 'for life'. This, however, would be another artefact of a too brief study period since our data demonstrate that couples often split after ten years!

Primate societies, like those of humans, also experience spaced-out 'historic' events with high mortality that shape populations for decades to come. Examples are droughts, violent storms, epidemics or 'wars' between chimpanzee communities. Innovations may likewise influence a group's future. For example, our Nigerian chimpanzees swallow certain leaves which expel parasitic worms. Such self-medication is observed in various ape populations, but records are not yet long enough to document the initial invention of such traditions.

While primatologists invest additional energy in habituation, they don't have to master languages, as we can't. This has drawbacks, but also minimises the danger to misinterpret utterances. Margaret Mead's allegedly misconstrued reports about the laissez-faire lifestyle of Samoan adolescents are a prominent example (see e.g., Freeman 1983). Cultural anthropologists may also be duped by the Hawthorne effect, i.e., that informants try to please researchers and consequently alter behaviour or say what one wants to hear. Wild primates are not apparently motivated by impulses of politeness or the lure of gifts and wages. There is thus less danger of misinterpreting what is going on.

However, primate research can certainly change the animals' behaviour:
- worshippers feed my Indian langurs, and the monkeys therefore habitually investigate any bag a researcher carries around.
- 'My' gibbons at times despise my presence and purposefully urinate down on me. At other times, they seem to like the midget who trails them somewhere down below. Perhaps they connect human presence with the absence of predatory cats.
- 'Our' Nigerian chimpanzees do not tolerate us at close quarters. If we unexpectedly bump into them, scaring them off, they may fall quiet for days.

Cultural anthropologists strive to live 'like a local'. Participation in primate lives is more partial. Indian langurs use my arched back as a springboard for graceful jumping displays. Occasionally, I elbow a monkey to make room under some narrow sandstone cliff to also secure a small strip of shade for me. Lowly built chimpanzee nests offer the opportunity to feel a bit like an ape. These sleeping platforms are quite comfortable, swaying gently under one's weight.

The quintessential Malinowskian fieldworker is supposed to be a lone foreigner, intense *solitariness* only mitigated by visits from relatives or friends and acquaintance with locals. Solitariness during the actual act of data collection is certainly advisable for research into primate behaviour, as another person's presence compromises one's attention and sensitivity to notice subtle events. Here, fewer eyes will see more.

For better or worse, roads, mobile phones and e-mail increasingly alleviate the isolation that comes with remoteness, although I pity the deprived students who suffer bewildering episodes of isolation, when time creeps slowly, letters take weeks to arrive, with monkeys as the most frequent social contacts. Our site in Nigeria retains much of this aura, not least because one has to cross rivers to get to this place where all roads end.

But overall, fewer and fewer fieldworkers experience that healthy trauma known as *culture-shock*. I had the privilege to receive a full dose, during my first fifteen months in India. Imagine a Byzantine telephone system which I overcame only once, on Christmas day, for that singular phone-call to Europe; think Hindu Gods and rat worshippers, nights under an oozing Milky Way, and all sounds, smells and tastes Indian. Such clichés add up to a grand and life-changing experience I would never want to miss.

Less enriching was the *reverse culture shock* upon return, when all things German seemed odd. People eating cows, dressing drably, and cleaning up after elimination with toilet paper instead of water: something was deeply wrong with this culture.

Persons versus primates

Primatologists can do a lot that cultural anthropologists cannot or should not do, and much of this difference stems from the widely accepted notion that only people are persons.

For example, 'undercover' research on humans is not condoned. *Informed consent* is required; human data have to be anonymised. Such rules can be cumbersome and hard to implement. How can illiterates sign a form of consent? How can indigenous people understand what a mouth-swab means in the hands of molecular anthropologists?

Field primatologists can ignore such considerations. We even lift our study subjects from anonymity and *give* them names! Many primatologists take this a step further and consider primates to not only have personalities, but be *persons*. The 'Great Ape Project', initiated by Australian philosopher Peter Singer (Cavalieri and Singer 1993), demands basic liberties for orang-utans, gorillas, chimpanzees and bonobos: such as a right to live (to kill and eat apes should be illegal), a ban on torture (medical experiments should be outlawed), and a right to freedom (habitat destruction should stop). I support these goals, and, in 2003, sent a letter to my university's data protection office. I stated that I consider apes to be persons, and asked about implications for my studies. I didn't receive an answer. Perhaps I should not push this further, as a recognition that apes are persons would render me a criminal before ethics committees, given the kind of data I collect. Because not only might I stare at my study subjects from a hideout, but I also employ extreme voyeuristic attitudes about defecation, urination and sexual behaviour. Completely unashamed, I collect records on menstrual flow, colour of labiae, penis morphology, erections, pelvic thrusts, sex with juveniles, clitoral stimulation, incest, homosexual behaviour, and so on. Interestingly, much basic data for the topics just listed are missing for humans, although our physiology is extensively studied in medical research. Certainly, unexplored frontiers still exist for cultural anthropologists.

But if 'sex and the jungle' is not an issue with respect to primates, it is an issue with respect to primatologists. Colleagues regularly pair up with natives from primate habitat countries whom they meet in transit to and from the site. Such acquired roots will often enhance long term prospects of research. Onsite sex can be more problematic. Some projects ban relationships between researchers and field assistants: perhaps because this may confer an air of exploitation or manipulation or because it may produce jealousy. Such a ban is probably a human rights violation but is also rarely effective, as illustrated by at least occasional transcontinental breeding success.

Relationships between Western fieldworkers are viewed as less problematic and are certainly more common. Remoteness and isolation have turned many a student of average beauty and qualification into the prettiest girl or boy on the island. Onsite matches, given surrounding wilderness, have romantic qualities but may incur the added pain of breaking up with somebody left at home. The limited mate-choice opportunities in the wild may seem to render the process suboptimal. But then, one has to factor in the benefits of assortative mating, as those who meet at remote field sites have already much in common, making them actually rather suitable partners.

Touchier is the potential transcendence of animal-human boundaries. Folk-stories abound about human/ape hybrids, which (even if not true) must root in ultimate fantasies. Primatologists have not been implicated in such unions. But given what people do with domesticated animals, a disclaimer is needed. Personally, I hold only academic interest in bottoms and breasts of female monkeys and apes. But I do know woman researchers who admit to being turned on by the magnificently muscled appearance of male apes. We can be fairly certain, though, that things have never been taken further, given hard to negotiate logistics of severe sexual dimorphism in physical strength and proportions.

Low and high, wild and civilized

Primate fieldwork analyses how behaviour and morphology is shaped by environmental factors (predators, food resources, pathogenes, climate, social structure). Virtually everybody agrees that biological anthropology has evolutionary theory at its heart – while fieldwork in cultural anthropology is embedded in less blatant reasoning. If and how evolutionary theory should be integrated at all is a major bone of contention and fuels many of its paradigmatic battles.

Anthropological thought came into its own in the wake of the Enlightenment. Literal Biblical explanations for origins of life and distribution of organisms across the globe were slowly amended and ultimately replaced by theories of change. The founding fathers of anthropology were influenced by Charles Darwin's understanding of natural selection as well as by ideas from Karl Marx about forces that create power-differentials in human societies. The buzzword was 'progress', nourished by expansions of the British Empire as well as fallouts of the industrial revolution. Thus, change in evolutionary and societal terms was equated with a dynamic movement from less developed to advanced stages. Consequently, early cultural anthropologists such as Lewis Henry Morgan in the US, and Edward Tylor and James Frazer in England were evolutionists. They explained differences between human populations as a gradual move from a 'primitive' state (as exemplified by Non-Western people) to that of 'civilization' (achieved by Western, and in particular, Anglo-American societies).

Primate taxonomy was built on similar principles, in that 'lower' forms were distinguished from 'higher', with the latter of course more closely related to humans. Similar discrimination is embodied by the distinction between 'prosimians' such as lemurs, galagos and lorises (who fail to be true simians?) and 'anthropoids' such as monkeys and apes (who fail to be true humans?) This value-laden taxonomy contrasts with an explicitly neutral interpretation of evolutionary change, which most evolutionary biologists nowadays adopt. In this view, evolution has no direction or progressive trajectory, and does not even proceed from 'simple' to 'complex' forms. Change simply reflects adaptive radiation: some creatures will cope better than others with certain environmental conditions, thus creating an ever varied portfolio of biodiversity. As Darwin said: 'It is not the strongest of the species that survive, nor the most intelligent, but the most responsive to change.'

Such a 'neutral' view mirrors the rejection of evolutionist ideas in cultural anthropology by German-born Franz Boas. He developed the concept of 'cultural relativism': cultures are not to be judged by standards of others, rather, values and ideas are to be understood in their own terms and historical context. However, despite the concept of neutral evolutionary change, primatology is much less explicit in its rejection of distinctions between 'high' and 'low' forms. One reason is surely that labels conferred upon monkeys and apes do not offend these primates.

Nevertheless, some researchers take offence. Those who study gibbons are an example. The singing and swinging apes of Southeast Asia are often referred to as 'Lesser apes', in contrast to 'Great apes' such as orang-utans, gorillas and chimpanzees. The word 'lesser' can simply mean 'smaller in size', but may be read as 'less significant'. Gibbon researchers therefore push the term 'Small apes'. But those who study 'Great apes' are in no hurry. Nobody proposes a change to 'Big apes', away from more prominent thesaurus explanations of 'great' as 'very significant or important', 'powerful and influential'.

In addition, more primatologists who switch study animals follow the subliminal trajectory from 'low' to 'high' (i.e., from monkeys to apes) than vice versa. I am an example in kind, with my move from langur monkeys via small apes to big apes. I believe this reflects my increasing interest in primate cognition which had me look for models as closely related to humans as possible. But I cannot exclude that I gravitated towards great apes because they confer more 'status'. They certainly generate more interest amongst the public, media, and funding agencies.

Few isolated human cultures remain unstudied, whereas field primatology still offers opportunity to consort with true wilderness. In some ways, monkeys and apes have even replaced the tribes explored by early cultural anthropologists, in that romanticising and sensationalist labels once reserved for strange peoples are now bestowed upon primates. One of my books may serve an example, as it is entitled 'Our Wild Kin' ('Unsere wilde Verwandtschaft'). Other primatologists have described baboons as 'almost human' or gorillas as 'gentle giants'. Jane Goodall portrayed her chimpanzees initially as 'better humans'.

The latter term is subject to one's moral agenda. For example, wild primates might be commended, because they do not kill or betray conspecifics, because they are monogamous, or not gay and thus not 'perverted'. Of course, none of these generalizations is correct. There are numerous taxa, which kill conspecifics, are not monogamous or which, even if pair-living, indulge in extra-pair copulations; some populations also prefer same-sex sex to heterosexual sex, and could thus equally well qualify as a cause celebré for gay activism.

While these attributes are prolongations of the myth of the 'noble savage', extensions of the 'dangerous savage' are also found – most prominently for chimpanzees as 'unmasked humans'. Late in her research, Jane Goodall began to record 'lethal raids' against neighbouring communities and cannibalization of conspecifics (Goodall 1986). This changed the stereotype of the 'better humans' to those of 'innocent killers' and 'demonic males' (Wrangham and Peterson 1996). My own thoughts underwent a similar transition. I had started out with the belief that animal behaviour serves the 'good of the species', and that slaughter of conspecifics is pathological. Eight months into my studies, I began to witness systematic killings of babies by langur males. I since emphasize the selfish side of behaviour, and entitled a book about India's revered monkeys as 'Heilige Egoisten' ('Holy Egotists').

Another important point is the (largely Western) fascination with the 'natural' and 'exotic'. In Berlin, London or Los Angeles, I am the centre of attention if I espouse tales about wild animals. In Bangkok, Lagos or New Delhi, my stories will be met with perplexity and puzzlement. Why does a well-educated person not seek a well paid job in banking, a law firm or government office? This explains why primatologists from so-called habitat countries are difficult to recruit: if parents can provide good education, they don't want their children to waste this investment on something useless and silly such as roaming around with monkeys. Our Nigerian students will thus not easily confide to their families that they study primates, while happily reporting receipt of a bursary from England, creating the belief that this will secure them a desk in an office.

Economics influence these perceptions. In nineteenth century Europe, naturalist studies were largely the privilege of wealthy gentlemen such as Alexander von Humboldt and Charles Darwin. Similarly, in twenty-first century Europe and North America, young people from middle- and upper-class backgrounds embark on a career as anthropologists, because they can. It's a bit like poetry, painting or playing in a rock-band. The theory of 'costly signalling' (Zahavi and Zahavi 1997) explains this beautifully: one's status comes with and depends on the ability to 'waste' time and energy on enterprises not designed to make money.

Explicit and implicit narratives

The common research philosophy of biological anthropologists is deduction, where data are gathered to test a preconceived hypothesis. This viewpoint, in social anthropological terms, is etic, i.e., imposed from the outside. The research attempts to be 'objective'. Because the great majority of social anthropologists reject this 'top-down' approach, most biological anthropologists regard social anthropological discourse as 'just talk'. Social anthropologists might reply that how the talk is talked is exactly the point. They tend to strive for an emic approach, trying to understand how the locals view the world. As a result, social anthropologists tend to adopt a research philosophy of 'induction', a 'bottom-up' approach in which information is gathered without pre-hoc hypotheses, stressing local cultural contexts.

Though many primatologists might strive to be objective gatherers of data which they can turn into statistical outputs, much field primatology is in fact purely descriptive and conducted outside the umbrella of deduction. Description is revered, because much of what we know about different species is grounded in 'natural history' reports, free from meta-theory. Konrad Lorenz, founder of comparative ethology, was excellent in such descriptions. He relished 'Gestaltwahrnehmung': a holistic perception of animal behaviour, which requires much patience (Lorenz 1959) and often physical immersion into animal habitats. But that does not mean that natural history experiences in field primatology can be equated with the 'emic' perspective of cultural anthropology. The philosopher Thomas Nagel once asked 'What is it like to be a bat?' (Nagel 1974). Answer: We will never know, not for bats, and not for primates either. But equally, I will never know, how it feels like to be you, another human being.

So, what do I assume about the relationship between me and my study animals? That humans become true companions, establishing some sort of 'mystical complicity', is probably more in researchers' heads than in those of the primates. The media may like to portray researchers as those who 'live with the apes' or are 'part of the group', but only Tarzan has ever 'lived' with apes. Researchers are at best like zookeepers: regular features in the apes' lives. No less, but also no more.

Well-habituated Great apes may certainly care about particular researchers. Ian Redmond illustrates lectures with a picture of him posing beside a wild mountain gorilla male. Ian describes him as a friend who is happy when he shows up again. There is no reason to belittle such stories of friendship. After all, we would not discount them for cats and dogs. As for wild gibbons or monkeys, I believe they do not have much positive feeling about those who study them. 'My' animals certainly recognised me, but I can't imagine they missed me when I was gone. Research into primate cognition has a lot to say about a potential divide in the ability to take mental perspectives, with prosimians, monkeys and small apes being rather bad at it, while humans, apes and domesticated animals are rather good at it (Wynne 2001).

Even if animals don't care much about researchers, this doesn't prevent researchers from entering into an emotional affair, no matter how one-sided. Those who work with individually identifiable animals are almost bound to develop a 'bond' with them, particularly as following a study group on a daily basis is like watching a soap opera. One becomes anxious not to miss the next episode, and one is also likely to take sides. Some characters are clearly nasty, others are self-infatuated beaux, responsible grandmothers, up-and-coming beauties, etc. Consequently, primatologists will sometimes name their study animals in a way which reflects their perceived personality: 'David Greybeard' surely sounds more benign than 'Satan'. Our Nigerian chimpanzees are not yet named, and I consider auctioning names as a fundraiser. If you look for immortality by having a wild chimpanzee named after yourself, your chance might soon come. Let's hope, your names are Bill and Melinda.

Stories about monkey personalities and field adventures make good stuff for popular books. Here, primatologists have to navigate fewer problems than cultural anthropologists who report about other humans, with all the dangers of sounding patronising or neo-colonialist. Women seem to be more successful and prolific in this genre (apart from Goodall, Fossey, Galdikas, think, e.g., Strum 1984, Strier 1992, Jolly 2004) compared to men (Schaller 1963, and then a long time nothing until Sapolsky 2001). Women are perhaps more prolific, because they are more likely to be admired by the readership: Men who brave the wilderness and kiss-and-tell come across as boastful machos, whereas women are seen as heroines. The rise of feminism may have also credited women with an ability to perceive the world in a better or at least different way than the good old boys did. Primatology has certainly not been untouched by postmodern deconstruction discussed so intensely in cultural anthropology (Haraway 1989). For example, early fieldwork was heavily biased by a 'gendered subjectivity' that focussed on male primates – simply because they are louder and more boisterous. Women researchers such as Sarah Blaffer Hrdy corrected this view and worked out how female primates drive social dynamics (Hrdy 1981).

The next paradigmatic frontier might be an exploration of animal sexuality that transcends the male/female dichotomy in favour of concepts of multiple sexualities and 'animal queerdom'. I was always interested in the related topic of same-sex sexual behaviour ('no': one doesn't have to be gay for this, while 'yes': one can be). Because my study animals are 'wild', I could deflate statements that animal homosexual behaviour is a pathology brought about by captivity. This research (Sommer and Vasey 2006) inspired parts of the gay and lesbian movement and produced tangible result in how laws were changed. Who would have thought that an Indian female monkey rubbing her clitoris on the back of a troop-mate and seemingly enjoying it would become a matter of politics in Europe?

Ethics on the edges

Social anthropologists have often tried to apply the results of their fieldwork to public policy. Many regard as an almost unquestionable good the need to value and sustain diversity (Miller 2005). The equivalent within field primatology is nature conservation, given that animals disappear with alarming speed, due to habitat destruction, hunting for bush meat and trophies, trade in wildlife and pets, and infectious diseases. In this respect, comparisons of wild primate populations reveal that extinction is not only forever with respect to biodiversity. Behavioural diversity is likewise lost. Thus, in primates, human or non-human, extinction is genocide *and* culturecide.

The situation at my Indian site is paradoxical. Jodhpur's human population has tripled since the mid-1960s. So did the monkeys; they were 700 in 1965 and currently there are more than 3000. This is easily explained: more Hindus hand out more food to holy monkeys who can thus make more monkeys. Isn't this a good thing for a primatologist? Perhaps 'yes', but certainly also 'no'. The Jodhpur habitat once consisted of isolated groves, gardens and cliffs around ponds and lakes, but has become increasingly urbanized. Monkeys therefore find less natural vegetation and instead of sleeping in trees, roost on rooftops. In sum, diversity is lost, and yet another habitat is homogenized.

It may seem straightforward and 'good' to work towards the continuation of cultural and biological diversity. But that's easier said than done, as this requires decisions between what is 'right' and what is 'wrong'. For example, should we blow the whistle when unwanted newborn girls are killed in rural India? Should we defend the traditional opium trade in Northern Thailand? Should we oppose the coming-of-age rite of female genital cutting in Nigeria? Tricky questions. They become even trickier, if conservation agendas of cultural anthropologists and primatologists clash over issues such as local spiritual beliefs, handicraft skills or traditional medicine:

- shouldn't locals have a right to practise their religion? At my Indian site, priests selected a picturesque wood to erect a new temple. The surrounding feeding trees of langurs were quickly cut down for fuel.

- Shouldn't locals have a right to extract non-timber forest products? Spirit houses and temples in Thailand are imbued with incense smoke. The raw material was for centuries collected in forests. Most have disappeared, but incense trees are still found in the Khao Yai jungle, where their exploitation contributes to the destruction of remaining gibbon habitat.
- Shouldn't locals have a right to follow indigenous beliefs? Local healers in Nigeria advise the killing of chimpanzees, as the meat from this human-like animal gives strength.

In any case, primatological careers are increasingly likely to move from academic to conservationist. The 'trimates' of chimpanzee, gorilla and orang-utan fame, Jane Goodall, Dian Fossey, Biruté Galdikas, are renowned examples. Like them, I became also more and more entangled in the extinction crisis. Much of my time and energy goes into efforts to delay what seems like the inevitable. If perhaps the most famous living scientist, Jane Goodall, cannot prevent the fatal decline of chimpanzees at 'her site' at Gombe in Tanzania, what hope is there for the rest of us?

Similarly, cultural anthropological research is more and more conducted in zones of violent conflict, becoming 'frontline anthropology' (Miller 2005), and thus increasingly overlapping with frontlines which primatologists are battling. The former United Nations Secretary-General Kofi Annan, in a foreword to the 'World Atlas of Great Apes and their Conservation', points out that people often treat primates better 'when they treat each other better, as a result of education, good governance, and reduced poverty' (Caldecott and Miles 2005). This echoes the mantra of well-meaning conservationists about 'sustainable development'. Unfortunately, we seem to have run out of time for this vision to become reality. Because even if we succeeded to educate 5,000 children and pull them out of poverty in the buffer zone of Gashaka-Gumti National Park, another 10,000 children would have been born into the area or migrated there with their parents, thus annihilating our efforts. The park's apes would have gone in the meantime. Therefore, in my eyes, fortress conservation has to take precedence. Otherwise nothing worth protecting will be left (Oates 1999).

On top of what people in habitat countries may inflict upon their primates, it is our Western lifestyle which creates much of the dynamics of destruction. Vast stretches of the Niger delta, ancient home of chimpanzees, have been remodelled beyond recognition to satisfy our thirst for oil. Hunters provide bushmeat for miners, who provide coltan ore to companies such as Sony and Motorola, who use it in mobile phones. Those hunters have killed thousands of lowland gorillas in DR Congo. Every text message fuelled by ape blood. Better not to think about it.

Primate extinction will have severe economic and ecological consequences: even if it is only that forests cannot regenerate when vital seed-dispersers are cut out. Another, perhaps even sadder, consequence is the erosion of aesthetic dimensions. For the Greek, the 'good' was the 'beautiful'. Without primates, this planet will be poorer, less beautiful, and thus, less good. So, if all is lost, why care? Because of pride and dignity. Albert Camus writes about a doctor, in his novel 'The Plague'. The medic treats the sick, although he is aware that they will die anyway. For Camus, such heroism transcends us: to not give in, to revolt, and not care about defeat or victory.

Resumé of a naturalist's mind

Little did I know that my childhood mission as a pantheistic eco-warrior would lead to a late career as a serious conservationist. And little did I know that my childhood infatuation with butterflies, ants and exotic travels would one day embroil me in philosophical and political controversies: just because I love to roam about with wild monkeys and apes. I woke up to such entanglement, when I was first accused of being a fascist. I had lectured about killings of infants by monkey males, and how infanticide seems to be driven by a reproductive selective advantage, as immigrant males will shorten the period of temporary sterility associated with nursing. In a classic case of 'naturalistic fallacy', somebody attending my talk concluded that my explanations were intended as a justification to kill others.

Soon, I became streetwise when reporting on behaviours of wild primates behaviours which are deemed 'controversial' if exhibited by humans, such as cannibalism, rape, sex with immatures or killings of conspecifics. I dutifully emphasize that what 'is' in nature should not be confused with what 'ought' to be. I point out that my reports are predictive, not normative, and that I am therefore not responsible for the actions of monkeys. In the same way a seismologist is not at fault for the lamentable suffering and loss of life during earthquakes (Sommer 2000). Interestingly, one can always count on a lay audience's sympathy if one describes how primates self-medicate with herbs, how they bring up young, and how humans endanger them. These stories come across as harmless and likeable and elicit everybody's parenting instinct. However, such conversations sharpen my mind less than controversial debates which help and force me to be conscious and explicit about my positions.

For a resumé, not of my credentials, but my credos, I would resort to a portfolio of heuristic principles, my intellectual working tools. These are helpful for arriving at a solution but do not claim to constitute 'proof'. All principles developed during my times 'in the wild', and I feel passionate about them:

- **Materialism.** I assume the natural world (including what humans produce and can think of) is governed by laws of physics. I do not believe in supra-natural beings. There is no intelligent designer. Intergalactic or evolutionary processes constitute change, not progress. There is no purpose to life. Humans and other primates are similar, because their ancestors shared periods of evolutionary change.
- **Determinism.** I assume every effect (such as behaviour) has a cause. This is not identical with the simplistic assumption that genes or hormones 'cause' behaviour. The environment can be a cause as well. However, my determinism makes me sceptical about the 'agency' approach of cultural anthropology according to which humans are free to consciously change the direction of developments. Free will, for me, would depend on the ability to act without cause, and this would require circumventing the laws of nature. I don't assume that monkeys or apes act without cause. Human behaviour might be more complicated, but I assume that it is also channelled by incremental accumulations of past events.

- **Reductionism.** I adhere to parsimony and apply the simplest explanation I can think of. This anti-holistic stance prevents me from hiding behind humble, but rather unproductive statements such as 'reality is immensely complex'.
- **Individualism.** Malinowski and others subscribed to a holistic view of functionalism: as various organs support a biological organism, so do belief systems or traditions contribute to the functioning of a whole culture which is the unit perpetuated through time. Consequently attempts to dissect or particularize social networks would be ill-founded. However, as long as I can get away with it, I will assume that the whole is not more than its parts. Furthermore, I assume that selection operates upon individuals, not societies. Individuals will cooperate when it is advantageous (and it often is, as primate groups illustrate convincingly). But individuals (or better, the genetic information they encode) are inherently 'selfish', metaphorically speaking (Dawkins 1976).

My heuristic approach is closely linked to my conviction that all scientists conduct their own 'hermeneutics', and that data are meaningless unless we ascribe a meaning, an interpretation, to them. The term, derived from Hermes, messenger of the Gods in Greek mythology, reminds us that 'objective data' (the 'Gods' of science which embody 'plain truth') make no sense by themselves. It is up to us to play Hermes, and translate encoded information into something meaningful.

Nevertheless, my colleagues from cultural anthropology generally have a hard time with these positions of a 'radical naturalist': I study animals in nature, and I happily use my insights to extrapolate about human behaviour. But the nature/culture dichotomy, like the nature/nurture dichotomy, has become blurred for those who recognize flexibility and intra-specific behavioural diversity also amongst our closest living relatives.

To make a perhaps slightly irrelevant point that I live what I preach: My son Kalind is the first human named after an ape – and thus personal testimony to my belief in the beauty of the gradualist, naturalistic paradigm. Latest by now, my field primatology joins the navel-gazing exercises of cultural anthropologists published as 'reflexive anthropology': 'Everyone is changed through the anthropological enterprise because it is a social process itself' (Miller 2005: 36). Indeed.

References

Caldecott, J. and L. Miles (eds). 2005. *World Atlas of Great Apes and Their Conservation*. Los Angeles: University of California Press.

Cavalieri, P. and P. Singer (eds). 1993. *The Great Ape Project: Equality Beyond Humanity*. New York: St. Martin's Press.

Daly, M. and M. Wilson. 1983. *Sex, Evolution, and Behavior*. Belmont, CA: Wadsworth.

Dawkins, R. 1976. *The Selfish Gene*. New York: Oxford University Press.

Dunbar, R.I.M. 1988. *Primate Social Systems*. London: Croom Helm.

Fossey, D. 1983. *Gorillas in the Mist*. London: Hodder & Stoughton.

Fowler, A. and V. Sommer. 2007. 'Subsistence technology in Nigerian chimpanzees: A contribution to cultural primatology', *International Journal of Primatology* 28(4).

Fowler, A., Y. Koutsioni and V. Sommer. 2007. 'Leaf-swallowing in Nigerian chimpanzees: Assumed evidence for self-medication', *Primates* 48: 73–6.

Freeman, D. 1983. *Margaret Mead and Samoa: The Making and Unmaking of an Anthropological Myth*. Canberra: Australian National University Press.

Galdikas, B.M.F. 1995. *Reflections of Eden: My Years with the Orangutans of Borneo*. Boston: Little, Brown.

Goodall, J. 1971. *In the Shadow of Man*. London: Collins.

——— 1986. *The Chimpanzees of Gombe: Patterns of Behavior*. Cambridge, MA: Belknap of Harvard University Press.

Haraway, D.J. 1989. *Primate Visions: Gender, Race, and Nature in the World of Modern Science*. New York: Routledge.

Hrdy, S.B. 1981. *The Woman That Never Evolved*. Cambridge, MA: Harvard University Press.

Jolly, A. 2004. *Lords and Lemurs: Mad Scientists, Kings With Spears, and the Survival of Diversity in Madagascar*. New York: Houghton Mifflin.

Kay, C.E. 1994. 'Aboriginal overkill. The role of native Americans in structuring western ecosystems', *Human Nature* 5: 359–98.

Lorenz, K. 1959. 'Die Gestaltwahrnehmung als Quelle wissenschaftlicher Erkenntnis. Z. angew. Experiment', *Psychologie*. 6: 118–65 Reprinted in K. Lorenz 1965. *Über tierisches und menschliches Verhalten II*. München: Piper, pp. 255–300.

McGrew, W.C. 2004. *The Cultured Chimpanzee: Reflections on Cultural Primatology*. Cambridge: Cambridge University Press.

Miller, B.D. 2005. *Cultural Anthropology*. Boston: Pearson.

Nagel, T. 1974. 'What is it like to be a bat?', *Philosophical Review* 83: 435–50.

Oates, J. 1999. *Myth and Reality in the Rainforest: How Conservation Strategies are Failing in West Africa*. Berkeley: University of California Press.

Reichard, U. and V. Sommer. 1997. 'Group encounters in white-handed gibbons (Hylobates lar): Agonism, affiliation, and the concept of infanticide', *Behaviour* 134: 1135–74.

Sapolsky, R.M. 2001. *A Primate's Memoir: A Neuroscientist's Unconventional Life Among the Baboons*. New York: Touchstone.

Schaller, G.B. 1963. *The Mountain Gorilla: Ecology and Behavior*. Chicago: University of Chicago Press.

Sommer, V. 1987. 'Infanticide among free-ranging langurs (Presbytis entellus) at Jodhpur (Rajasthan / India). Recent observations with a reconsideration of hypotheses', *Primates* 28: 163–97.

——— 1992. *Feste - Mythen - Rituale. Warum die Völker feiern*. Hamburg: GEO / Gruner und Jahr.

——— 1996. *Heilige Egoisten. Die Soziobiologie indischer Tempelaffen*. Munich: C.H. Beck.

——— 2000. 'The holy wars about infanticide. Which side are you on? And why?' In C. van Schaik and C. Janson (eds) *Infanticide by Males and its Implications*. Cambridge: Cambridge University Press, pp. 9–26.

Sommer, V., J. Adanu, I. Faucher and A. Fowler. 2004. 'The Nigerian chimpanzee (*Pan troglodytes vellerosus*) at Gashaka: Two years of habituation efforts', *Folia Primatologica* 75: 295–316.

Sommer, V. and U. Reichard. 2000. 'Rethinking monogamy: the gibbon case' in P. Kappeler (ed.) *Primate Socioecology: Causes and Consequences of Variation in the Number of Males*. Cambridge: Cambridge University Press, pp. 159–68.

Sommer, V. and P. Vasey (eds). 2006. *Homosexual Behaviour in Animals: Evolutionary Perspectives*. Cambridge: Cambridge University Press.

Sommer, V. and G. Ross (eds). 2011. *Primates of Gashaka*. New York: Springer.

Strier, K.B. 1992. *Faces in the Forest: The Endangered Muriqui Monkeys of Brazil*. New York: Oxford University Press.

Strum, S. 1984. *Almost Human: A Journey into the World of Baboons*. New York: Random House.

Whiten, A., J. Goodall, W.C. McGrew, T. Nishida, V. Reynolds, Y. Sugiyama, C.E.G. Tutin, R.W. Wrangham and C. Boesch. 2001. 'Charting cultural variation in chimpanzees', *Behaviour* 138: 1481–516.

Whiten, A., V. Horner and S. Marshall-Pescini. 2003. 'Cultural panthropology', *Evolutionary Anthropology* 12: 92–105.

Wrangham, R. and D. Peterson. 1996. *Demonic Males: Apes and the Origins of Human Violence*. London: Bloomsbury.

Wynne, C.D.L. 2001. *Animal Cognition: The Mental Lives of Animals*. New York: Palgrave.

Zahavi, A. and A. Zahavi. 1997. *The Handicap Principle*. New York: Oxford University Press.

4
Primate Fieldwork and its Human Contexts in Southern Madagascar

Robert W. Sussman

Introduction

The re-evaluation of fieldwork in social anthropology has been a worthy subject of study and has enriched anthropological understanding, both in the way ethnographic knowledge has been assessed and in the way we train our students. In this book, the authors have been asked to explore whether comparable re-evaluation of experiences in fieldwork in biological anthropology and primatology might not further enrich our understanding of anthropological research generally. In this chapter, I have chosen to reminisce over my past thirty-five years plus of fieldwork experience and, in doing so, I attempt to answer many of the questions posed by the editors of this volume. Some of my answers might seem to be more from my personal experiences than answers for the field in general. This is because many of these questions have not been openly discussed in the primatology literature and because many of the questions actually are personal in nature. However, by discussing them in this volume, perhaps these aspects of field research and methodology in primatology will become more openly discussed in the future. Further, the editors have asked me to attempt to put this reminiscence into the context of the history and developments of USA primatological approaches to fieldwork, and how these approaches have changed, or not, over the years. This I have attempted to do.

In the beginning

I began fieldwork as a graduate student collecting data for my Ph.D. thesis at Duke University in 1969. Today, most Ph.D. students have taken a field course or have done preliminary field research with their faculty, at an established field site, or at their future thesis research site. In the 1960s there were very few established field sites and no primate-oriented field courses. In fact, this was quite early in the history of field primatology. I had never done field work before and, in fact, never been outside of the United States, except to visit Mexico by car with high school pals as part of summer and spring breaks, a fairly common jaunt for teenagers from Los Angeles.

Although Darwin had put man in his place with the rest of the animal kingdom and especially as a close cousin with non-human primates (for practical purposes, primates from now on), in the late nineteenth and early twentieth century, although social anthropology was quite active, there were few scientists interested in venturing into the forests to see what our closest primate relatives were actually doing. In fact, before 1950, there was essentially no discipline of field primatology, either in biology or anthropology (Sussman 2007). There were a few fits and starts, however. In the 1890s, a zoologist and animal collector, Richard L. Garner (1848–1920) visited Gabon to study the speech of great apes. He spent 112 consecutive days and nights sitting in a large cage with his rifle waiting for gorillas and chimpanzees to wander by and, in fact, a few did (Garner 1896).

In 1929, Robert Yerkes (1876–1956), a psychologist, and his wife Ada Yerkes (1874–1963) published 'The Great Apes' and in it compiled a summary of the current knowledge of primates in the field. There was no systematic field research to report, only anecdotal information. In the same year, Yerkes was establishing a great ape breeding facility as part of the Yale Laboratories of Primate Biology (later the Yerkes National Primate Research Centre). In this context, he sponsored two expeditions to Africa to study the behaviour of apes in their native habitat, to aid his captive breeding program, and to collect animals for the facility (Yerkes 1943). In 1929, Harold Bingham was sent to the Congo to study gorillas and, in 1930, Henry Nissen traveled to French Guinea to study chimpanzees (Nissen 1931; Bingham 1932).

Yerkes also was instrumental in getting another psychologist interested in studying primates. C. Raymond Carpenter (1905–1975) had just completed his Ph.D. on the sexual behaviour of birds when Yerkes and Frank M. Chapman, an ornithologist, convinced Carpenter to study monkeys at Chapman's field site Barro Colorado, a manmade island in the Panama Canal. Between 1931 and 1935, Carpenter spent a number of months studying the social organization, social interactions and demographics of howler and spider monkeys in Panama. In fact, Carpenter was the only primatologist before 1950 to dedicate much of his life to field primatology and worked in the field until his death in 1975. However, it was not until after World War II that the discipline of field primatology could be considered a sub-discipline in itself. Before this, studying primates was not considered anything different from studying birds or other non-human mammals. Although a few anthropologists wrote about the importance of primates to anthropology (Kroeber 1928; Hooton

1942, 1954; Sahlins 1959), an interest in the natural behaviour of primates was not incorporated into our discipline until the 1950s (see Sussman 2000, 2007).

From the mid 1950s to early 1960s many essays were written (e.g., Washburn 1951; Bartholomew and Birdsell 1953) and books edited (Gavan 1955; Tax 1960; Washburn 1961; Howells 1962; Washburn 1963; Howell and Bourliere 1963) on the importance of the study of non-human primates to understanding human nature and evolution. Sherwood Washburn (1911–2000) was the prime mover in incorporating field primatology into anthropology. Papers by him, stressing the need for primate field research, appeared in each of the above edited volumes, including the classic papers by Washburn and DeVore (1961; DeVore and Washburn 1963) on baboon and early human ecology and behaviour. On the jacket cover of his 1961 volume, 'Social Life of Early Man', Washburn wrote:

> The social relationships that characterize man cannot have appeared for the first time in the modern human species ... Since Man is a primate who developed from among the Old World simian stock, his social behaviour must also have evolved from that of this mammalian group. Thus the investigation of man's behaviour is dependent upon what we know of the behaviour of monkeys and apes.

Thus began the field study of non-human primates in anthropology. Although there were a few studies of primates in the 1950s, most were not within the paradigm of the 'New Physical Anthropology' (Washburn 1951). However, the Japanese school was an exception and their work could easily be seen as having an anthropological perspective, following the view of the world expressed by Imanishi (1941; see Fedigan and Strum 1999). This is discussed in detail by Yamagiwa (this volume).

It was not until the next decade that field primatology finally emerged as an identifiable discipline. The idea that the study of primates could help us understand the evolution of human behaviour and human nature stimulated many biological anthropologists to travel to the tropics and study these animals. In the 1960s, a number of conferences on free-ranging primates were held and related edited volumes began to appear (Southwick 1963; DeVore 1965; Altmann 1967; Jay 1968). The international journal Folia primatologica was founded in 1963; the Japanese journal Primates was first published in English in 1959. Southwick (1963: iii) stated in the introduction to his book: 'Quite apart from the obvious values of primates in medical and psychological research, primate studies are yielding new perspectives into basic problems of group dynamics, human sociality, behavioural ecology, and the evolutionary history of man.'

Back to the beginning

As mentioned above, I arrived to conduct my dissertation research in Madagascar in 1969, relatively early in the history of the discipline. In fact, only two other scientists had conducted systematic fieldwork on the living primates of Madagascar by that time. The French zoologist Jean-Jacques Petter (1962, 1965) had done an extensive survey with notes on the behaviour of many species of lemur and Alison Jolly (1966) had conducted an exceptional study of the ringtailed lemur and the Verreauxi's sifaka in a private reserve in southern Madagascar (Jolly, this volume). I was a third generation Washburn student (my dissertation advisor was Jack Prost, though he moved from Duke to University of Illinois, Chicago while I was in the field and John Buettner-Janusch became the chair of my thesis committee). In the spirit of Washburn's paradigm, my research focused on a question being debated in the early human evolution literature. Since two species of australopithecines had been discovered living in proximity, the question had arisen as to whether two closely related species of humans or primates could co-exist in the same area. My research focused on whether two closely related, morphologically very similar lemurs, ringtailed and brown lemurs, could co-exist in the same forest and, if so, how.

Methodologies

One of my major concerns in conducting my field research was how could I compare two different species or the same species living in two different forests? When preparing for my field work, I was frustrated and quite surprised that there were no tried and true methods available in field primatology to collect the comparative quantitative behavioural ecology data needed to answer my questions. To answer my questions, I needed to have statistical comparisons. I was very concerned with measuring and measuring accurately.

I scoured the literature and finally discovered one paper in which the time that animals spent in various activities, on what substrates, and in eating various items was actually measured! Crook and Aldrich-Blake (1968) had introduced a method of scan sampling – sampling the number of individuals doing a particular activity at a particular time, much like an instantaneous photograph – that enabled them to quantify and compare three sympatric ground-dwelling primate species in Ethiopia. I decided to use this method and, in fact, on my way to Madagascar, Alison Jolly showed me a paper in press at the time in which Alison Richard (1970) had adopted Crook's and Aldrich-Blake's method to compare howler and spider monkey behaviour in Barro Colorado. Richard (1973) was soon to follow me to Madagascar to conduct her thesis research comparing two populations of sifaka living in very different types of habitats and using the same quantitative instantaneous sampling methods. In 1974, Jeanne Altmann published a paper summarizing the various quantitative methods used in field primatology and in this paper she described the instantaneous scan sampling method. This paper remains one of the most cited papers in primatology today and variations on the instantaneous scan sample technique is a method of choice in the field.

The relationship between 'understanding' our subjects of research and 'measuring' or quantifying their behaviour is another and complicated question, and is dependent upon our questions (see also Fuentes, this volume). Primatologists must measure the behaviour of their subjects and, from the numbers, they must attempt to understand the meaning of the behaviour. To do this they attempt to follow the animals, usually the whole group, from dawn to dusk. Social anthropologists normally cannot follow the people they study from dawn to dusk, nor can they observe the whole study group or population (though, see Tanaka 1976, 1980). However, social anthropologists can ask people questions about their current, past, and even projected future behaviour. In this way they can fill in for missing times and get historical perspectives. This can be both an advantage and a problem. Primatologists must try to understand their animals by interpreting what they see – and they are often limited by what they don't see and by having to guess what the animals are thinking and why they are doing what they do. They also can be limited by their preconceptions. Social anthropologists have to compare what they see with what they are told and the two stories don't always match. People don't always tell the truth and they don't always remember accurately. Also, human subjects don't always interpret what they are doing in a 'functional' or 'practical' way, or they interpret their behaviour in a ritualized way, or different people describe the same behaviours or their functions in different ways; the question of emic vs. etic interpretations. However, even in social anthropology, the best results often involve a combination of qualitative and quantitative techniques (Nichter 1978; Sussman 1981, 1983; Sussman et al. 1987; Bernard 2002; Kempf-Leonard 2005). Measuring is not just the job of biological anthropologists, and a degree of qualitative understanding is necessary for all scientific study.

Thus, language makes social anthropology more interesting, develops more ways to interpret what one sees, and complicates understanding by creating multiple levels of reality. Although different populations of the same primate species do show differences in behaviour in the different localities and habitats in which they are found, these differences are exceedingly trivial compared to differences that social anthropologists encounter even between peoples living side by side. This is true even among our closest relatives, the chimpanzees. Social anthropologists must deal with the problems created by the capacity, or one might say the necessity, of humans to create their own worlds. Primates, of course, do vary their behaviour given different environments and different circumstances. However, if one travels from one chimpanzee site to another, for example, the differences between populations are relatively minor. The animals generally have the same dietary patterns, they have the same general social organization effected mainly by demographic differences, they communicate similarly, they defend themselves the same way, their mating behaviour and patterns are very similar. This is not true of human populations.

I would argue that primates relate to the world mainly as it relates to their physiology and biological senses, they are what one might say is 'at one with nature.' I say this in contrast to the way in which humans react to the world. Humans see and react to the world through a lens of culture; to a great extent they create their world through this lens. Thus, what is edible, who is a possible mating partner, who are your relatives, who is dominant or even a leader is often purely symbolic and has little to do with biologically restricted mental or physical aptitude or behaviour. Of course human behaviour is ultimately based on biology. Humans are biologically different from chimpanzees and gorillas. However, part of human biology is the necessity of culture which leads to incredible behavioural flexibility and the necessity for an extended learning period.

To my mind, culture makes many social anthropologists' methods very different from those of field primatologists. Primatologists can attempt to study the evolution of protoculture but primates do not have culture. Thus, primatologists measurements attempt to see how the animals deal directly with their environments and among themselves and how this relates to their evolution and current adaptations. Social anthropologists must also deal with another dimension – they must deal with the filter that culture 'imposes' between how people deal with the environment and themselves. I believe that this leads to measuring and understanding at another and different level. Instantaneous scan sampling can only do so much.

Timing

When I began my study, most fieldworkers were planning their studies for at least one year in order to see the effects of seasonality on their study species and with the belief that the longer one studied the animals, the more one could understand their behaviour and ecology. However, at this point, there are three typical timelines for primatological field studies, depending upon the types of questions being asked, as well as on practical concerns.

I think that most primatologists would agree that a twelve to twenty-four month study of a previously unknown species or a studied species at a new site is the minimal time needed to obtain a good idea of the basic natural history of the study population. This is the typical length of a preliminary but intensive study of a primate population and is necessitated by the need to observe the animals throughout all seasons and through their reproductive cycle. After a year to eighteen months one usually has a relatively good idea of the general patterns of behaviour of the population as well as of its social structure and organization, general ecology, etc. However, shorter-term studies are often done to answer specific questions, conduct preliminary surveys of specific areas, or to survey and collect preliminary data on future study populations.

Finally, shortly after primatology became an established discipline, in the 1960s to 1970s, a number of long-term research sites were established. These included the well known sites in Tanzania at Gombe Stream Reserve established by Jane Goodall and at Mahale Mountain Reserve established by the Japanese primatologists Itani and Nishida. However, there were many other long term sites, including, Karidoke, Uganda (gorillas), Tanjung Putting, Borneo (orang utans), Amboseli, Gilgil/Chololo, Gombe, and Mikumi, Africa (savannah baboons), Erer-Grota and Awash, Ethiopia (Hamadryas baboons), Jodhpur, India (Hanaman langur), Arashiyama and Takasakiyama, Japan (Japanese macaques), Barro Colorado Island, Panama (howler monkeys), Caratinga, Brazil (muriquis), Berenty and Beza Mahafaly, Madagascar (ringtailed lemurs and sifakas). This list is not exhaustive but emphasizes the importance placed on studies of the same population for many generations and over the lifetime of these long-lived animals.

These studies demonstrate the value of life history, demographic and ecological data on identified individuals and genealogical lines, and provide evidence that behaviour and ecology varies over time as well as across groups and species. They also illustrate that local history often can provide as much an explanation for current, proximate events as can ultimate selective explanations (Fedigan and Strum 1999; Strier 2003). The importance of these long-term studies, over many generations, is now understood and, where possible, primatologists are attempting to establish these sites in all countries in which primates naturally occur. Once these sites are established many shorter-term, problem-oriented studies are often conducted on the study populations and many students and specialists are drawn to these established sites to conduct research. However, this should not deter young primatologists to study species and populations in remote sites where they have not yet been observed. Many species that seem to be very well studied have only been observed in very few research sites.

Although timelines in primate studies normally are determined by the questions being posed by the researchers, they also are constrained by practical issues and political contingencies. Most biological anthropologists and primatologists teach in universities or colleges. Many important studies of primates in the field are conducted for Ph.D. dissertations. Thus, though I haven't researched this topic, I would say that many primate field studies are twelve to eighteen months because this is the time span allowed for leave from teaching, the duration of many government and foundation grants, and about as much time a graduate student can afford in the field for a dissertation project. Short-term, problem-oriented field studies are most likely usually of two to three month duration because they are conducted during summer breaks in the university schedule. Long term studies, over many primate generations, normally are a combination of the above plus include the collaboration of many scientists. Very few primatologists have the luxury of remaining in the field over many consecutive years and funds for long-term studies are difficult to maintain.

Being an anthropologist and a primatologist

I presume that primatologists with an anthropological perspective might differ in their perspectives from those who consider themselves biologists and not necessarily, or even desirably, anthropologists. There also can be a division between those who like working in the forest with the primates but avoid or even deplore working with the local, in-country people. I presume that some of these scientists wish that naturally occurring primates still existed in the US or Europe. I have always considered myself an anthropologist first, with a subdisciplinary focus on primatology. When I left North Carolina to conduct my research, there was some trepidation that I would be unable to find an adequate site where ringtailed and brown lemurs coexisted sympatrically. Because of master degree and dissertation qualifying examinations given both at UCLA and at Duke University, where social anthropology was the dominant focus, I had had to prepare for more hours of examination on social anthropology and archaeology than physical anthropology. Two of my social anthropology professors had suggested that I conduct ethnographic work on the local people if I was unable to find an adequate primate site and had advised me accordingly. I brought a classic ethnography with me as a sample just in case.

Thus, being alone in the field for me was an experience both as an anthropologist, interested in the people, and as a primatologist. My fiancée (now my wife), Linda Kaye Sussman, accompanied me to the field. At the time, she was a senior at Duke majoring in psychology and math but becoming more and more interested in anthropology.

As with many social anthropologists, I always felt relatively alienated from my own culture as did Linda. This alienation, I believe (and as has often been discussed in the anthropological literature) enables many social anthropologists to understand that the world view of their own culture is not the only, or necessarily correct one. This enables one to enter into other cultures with not a value-free but a less value-laden attitude. Although, during my thesis research, much of our time was spent in a tent in the forest, for the majority of the time we lived in a very remote village in southwestern Madagascar, Vondrove. Depending on road conditions, it took a minimum of five days by four-wheel drive vehicle to reach the only large village in the area, Manja. From Manja it took another two hours (50 kilometres) to reach our village, when the road was passable. To get to one of my study forests, Antserananomby, it took another hour (15 kilometres). Besides our Landrover, there were no other automobiles in Vondrove, a village of around 40 families. Travel was done by ox cart and by foot. Few, if any, of the children under the age of ten had ever seen a *Veza*, or white foreigner, in their lives (Figure 4.1).

Being alone in the field to me and Linda was magical, exciting, educational and extremely enlightening, both in the village and in the forest. Although we only

Figure 4.1. Linda Sussman and our research assistant Folo Emmanuel upon our arrival at Vondrove. Few, if any, of the children under the age of ten had ever seen a Veza, or white foreigner, in their lives.

spoke rudimentary Malagasy and only a few of the villagers spoke French, we were completely at home and accepted. We felt privileged and I felt I had the best of both worlds of an anthropologist. I could enjoy living in this exotic and different world, taking part in village life, and learning what I pleased. Yet I was not obliged to collect ethnographic data. However, over the year and a half, Linda and I collected a limited amount of ethnographic data and later published papers on the local practice of divination (Sussman and Sussman 1977), games (R.W. Sussman 1989), and Malagasy cuisine and ritual (L.K. Sussman 1989a, 1989b). We learned that people from very different cultures are indeed very different while being much the same. Although difficult to express, our lives were permanently changed for the better from this experience. In fact, Linda decided to become a social anthropologist.

In the forest, one also gets the feeling of privilege and acceptance. Before a primatologist can study his primate group(s), it is necessary to habituate the animals. This takes a different amount of time depending upon the species and the conditions. The two species of lemur that I studied at Antserananomby were protected from hunting by local taboos and were accustomed to seeing people. They were quite easy to habituate and, within a few weeks, I was 'accepted' into the groups. It may seem strange, but I felt honoured. One feels as if you are being accepted into some primeval nature, into the natural world. While studying a species, one comes to understand that different species are very different indeed. The ringtailed lemurs were like business people, they got up early, gathered energy by a particular sunning behaviour, and then were off to find their food throughout the day in the hottest areas, outside of the canopy forest, with only a short rest period at midday, and retired for the evening just at dusk. They did all of this in fairly large groups and had quite strict dominance hierarchies.

Brown lemurs were more laid back – I referred to them as the hippies of the forest. They woke up early and fed, then spent most of the day resting in tight clumps. They then became active again late in the day and were active into the night. They lived in smaller groups, always remained in the canopy forest, and had no noticeable hierarchies. While studying the two species, I had to have quite different activity cycles and a very different attitude.

Later, while doing an eighteen month study of long tailed macaques in Mauritius, I found another, entirely different personality or 'gestalt'. Although I hate to admit it, the macaques were more intelligent. They live in much larger groups, have more complex social interactions, and manipulate the environment in more complex ways. The macaques had been hunted and, although we did habituate them, they were never as trusting of us as were any of the lemurs that I studied. Besides the lemurs and macaques, over the years I have now studied a number of neotropical monkey species and have found each to have their own gestalt. I also have found that in each country I have worked (Madagascar, Mauritius, Panama, Costa Rica and Guyana) the people and their cultures differ. I believe these experiences enable most sensitive anthropologists, ethnographers as well as primatologists, to realize that no one culture has all the correct answers, that there are many ways to see the world, and that answers are always dependent upon the questions asked. Furthermore, there are often many potentially correct answers to the same question. Whether studying humans or primates, obtaining the best answer to a question often depends upon how the question is posed and using the best method to answer the specific question, while always being aware of your preconceptions.

In any case, as Alison Jolly and I have stated elsewhere:

> These studies of the early 1970s were the end of an age of innocence – or perhaps of ignorance. Westerners could imagine themselves as pure scientists following untrammelled intellectual curiosity. They took for granted their privilege as the heirs of Rousseaux – and Commerson – in love with the romance of far-off wilderness, and boosted like multistage rockets by the funds of the Paris Museum or the NSF. (Jolly and Sussman 2007: 30–1).

Transition period

By the mid 1970s, the world economy and political unrest in many tropical countries was making field work a bit more problematic. Between 1973 and 1985, I made eight field trips to Madagascar, three to Mauritius, one to Panama, and spent a summer doing museum research in Europe. My field work during this period was dictated as much by academic schedules, world politics, and chance as by any strict research agenda.

Upon completing my Ph.D., I obtained academic positions and, thus, was only able to conduct research during summer breaks until my first sabbatical in 1979. Two of my field research projects (accounting for five trips) resulted from unplanned events. In 1973, Ian Tattersall and I went to northern Madagascar to study sympatric groups of brown and mongoose lemurs. However, we discovered that the mongoose lemur, a species thought to be diurnal, turned out to be completely nocturnal during our visit. Thus, I decided to spend two summers studying this species. In the summer of 1977, my wife was to do preliminary research in Madagascar for her Ph.D. thesis in social anthropology. However, because of political unrest, we were forced to go to Mauritius. Because of our tight time schedule, we decided to do our research there. Beginning in 1979, I spent my sabbatical year studying the Mauritian long-tailed macaques while Linda did her dissertation research on the poly-ethnic medical practices in Mauritius.

In 1972, the First Malagasy Republic fell. There was objection to French domination of the school systems and of government jobs. By 1975, with Didier Ratsiraka as President, relations between the US and Western Europe and Madagascar were strained and close relations were open with Russia, North Korea, and China. The US Ambassador departed. One of the early acts of the Malagasy Government was to cancel research visas for western scientists. In Madagascar, as well as in many other tropical countries, research strategies and approaches by foreign scientists needed to change. The faux-Colonial period was over and local needs and aspirations needed to be considered.

In fact, luckily, Alison Richard and I had come to similar conclusions even before the Ratsiraka government. In the early 1970s, we had begun to work with one of our close Malagasy colleagues Guy Ramanantsoa, the then Chair of the Department of Water and Forests, School of Agronomy, University of Madagascar, in an attempt to establish a reserve for conservation, research and education. In establishing this reserve, we knew it was necessary to have the blessings of the local inhabitants and to compensate them for use of their land with development projects requested, designed and managed by them. This necessitated a long-term commitment and the need for an interdisciplinary team of collaborators, as well as close collaboration with Malagasy scientists as well as the local people.

Primatology in a socio-political context

In the early days of primatology, most primate-inhabiting countries were still in a neo-colonial haze and local governments and people were often treated as one of the many nuisances that one had to endure while doing field work. However, as in Madagascar, by the mid 1970s, many primatologists were forced to begin thinking about how their work impacted or was impacted by national and local politics and economics because of the dissatisfaction of in-country scientists, and local inhabitants and governments, and the resultant rules they began to set for foreign scientists.

Although many primatologists still see the local people and policies as either just a nuisance or as a major enemy of their animals and the cause of forest destruction, most researchers recognize the problems faced by extremely poor governments and people. It is difficult to take land and protect primate species, and to host rich westerners driving massive shining vehicles and having equipment that obviously could feed a village for months, while the people surrounding your protected site are poor and starving. Primatologists are beginning, and must continue, to understand that long term conservation of their study sites and animals will depend upon mutual understanding and real cooperation with local governments and people. Local people can help us manage and improve our research into the future but this will take the understanding and education of the primatologists, as much as the local people, to achieve. The question is how do we protect our animals in the long run and still help preserve local populations and traditions? This ethical question is still being debated in primatology, especially in relation to habitat conservation and to hunting. Complicating this question is the involvement of large corporations, such as oil, timber or mining companies that negatively affect local habitats and animals, as well as the local people. What can biological anthropologists and primatologists do to help abate the massive destruction often caused by these absentee corporations with massive resources. In many cases, these could be the ultimate cause of extinction of many of our animals and many of the cultures that we study as anthropologists. These types of questions have driven much of my most recent research.

Since the mid 1970s, probably first stimulated by the dissatisfaction of local scientists, primatologists began to include local scientists in their projects and to develop programs to train them. As an example, Alison Richard and I had worked with Malagasy scientists from the beginning of our thesis research. A local botanist had identified our plants, and work with Guy Ramananstoa had begun early in our research. These collaborative and equal relationships enabled us to establish the Beza

Mahafaly Nature Reserve and the interdisciplinary research and education project that are still very active today.

During the 1970s, when research visas were not being granted to western scientists, Alison Richard and I were able to continue to enter Madagascar with the aid of our Malagasy scientific collaborators and continue to work with Ramanantsoa to find and establish our reserve. I made five visits to Madagascar in this regard between 1977 and 1981. In the early 1980s, the economy in Madagascar had begun to fall apart and the Malagasy realized that nationalization was not working. In 1983, at the request of the Malagasy Government, a workshop was held at the Jersey Wildlife Trust. Shortly thereafter, a commission was established to vet foreign research requests and western science was once again allowed in Madagascar, but with stipulations to have Malagasy collaborators, train Malagasy students, and make results of research available locally. Our ongoing, under the radar, program already had these components and, in 1985, Beza Mahafaly was officially inaugurated as a Special Government Reserve with much pomp and circumstance (Figure 4.2). In 1986–1987, Alison and I were able to begin long term multi-disciplinary, collaborative studies (including social anthropology), and education and economic development projects at Beza Mahafaly. The reserve is now being managed by the School of Agronomy, University of Antananarivo and is a centre for Malagasy and western scientific research (Sussman and Ratsirarson 2006). In fact, a large number of Malagasy primatologists have received degrees from this program (Ratsirarson et al. 2001). This is just one example of a massive effort now underway to train and work with local primatologists worldwide.

Figure 4.2. Alison Richard and Robert Sussman, with a number of Malagasy dignitaries, at the official inauguration of the Beza Mahafaly Special Reserve in 1985.

Teamwork

I began working with teams in earnest on the Beza Mahafaly project. Working with fairly large teams on multidisciplinary projects often removes one from the joy of that one-on-one relationship with the animals. However, it allows the fieldworker to expand research in many directions simultaneously and to discover a great deal about the animals and their environment not possible in any other way. During the Beza Mahafaly project, I have had the opportunity to work directly with western and Malagasy botanists, ecologists, zoologists, agronomists, social anthropologists, medical pharmacologists, medical doctors, geologists, earth and planetary scientists, as well as other primatologists. Team work also allowed us to develop our education and development projects while continuing to conduct scientific research on the animals. This collaborative effort was not without unexpected conflicts and harmonies. For example, one cannot always predict that a scientist will understand or be sensitive to local traditions because of his/her scientific training. We have had instances where social anthropologists were completely insensitive to the local tradition, and others in which geologists or botanists were completely integrated into the local community. We also have had instances where non-local Malagasy were less compatible with local inhabitants than were foreign scientists. In my experience, it is often personality, and a level of sensitivity and humility, rather than scientific training that makes a person able to work harmoniously in multidisciplinary, collaborative projects and in difficult and foreign circumstances. Care should always be taken in choosing collaborators. When a team is working well it is exciting and ideas and innovations abound. However, conflict can be very destructive and must be resolved quickly.

Recent historical phases of primate fieldwork

Fedigan and Strum (1999, 2000) have divided primate research since World War II into four stages: The Natural History Phase (1950–1965); the Discovery and Dilemma of Variability Phase (1965–1975; my Problem-Oriented Phase); The Era of Sociobiology (1975–1985); and The Advent of Behavioural Ecology (1985–present). I would agree with their assessment but consider that each of the earlier phases is still current and important. There are still primate taxa for which we have little or no natural history data and some known only from one or a few sites. For example, although ringtailed lemurs have been the subject of intensive research for over forty years, almost all of this is from two sites and these sites do not represent the habitat in which most of ringtails live (Goodman et al. 2006; Sussman et al. 2006).

Most current primate field research is still of the quantitative, comparative, problem-oriented variety. Many modern primatologists would be considered sociobiologists and would consider this to be the dominant paradigm and conventional wisdom in primatology today, though an increasing number of young primatologists are recognizing the anomalous observations that do not fit the adaptationist, individual maximization, selfish gene, and biological reductionist models of sociobiology. However, as stated by Fedigan and Strum (1999: 267), the most recent stage of primate studies is difficult to characterize because it is currently ongoing and unfinished, but also a result of 'the growing fragmentation and specialization within the discipline and increasingly complex interactions among theories, methods, and other intrinsic aspects of science, as well as between science and its larger context.' In this modern phase, primatologists are attempting to answer old questions with new theories and methods, and with modern technology (e.g., using genetic, hormonal, and biomedical analyses, GIS, satellite imagery, biotelemetry, digital video data). Finally, the results from many long term research sites are changing the way we see primate biology (see Strier 2003, for example).

My research has changed over the years. Although I am still involved in some natural history and problem-oriented studies, the main thrust of my research in Madagascar in recent years has been more global and heavily vested in modern technology. I have left most of the research on ringtailed lemurs at Beza Mahafaly to two of my former students, Michelle Sauther and Lisa Gould, and to my Malagasy colleagues and their students. Using satellite imagery, GIS, and ecological and ethnographic techniques, with a US and Malagasy interdisciplinary team, I have been conducting research on deforestation and its effects on the ecology and behaviour of the lemurs in general and of ringtails specifically, and on the rural Malagasy people (Green and Sussman 1990; Sussman et al. 1996, 2003, 2006).

Species specialists and serendipity?

I have done research on ringtailed lemurs for a long time and I don't think that I have gone ringailed, though my research on them has probably slanted my views to some degree. However, it is probably harder to 'go ringtail' than it is to 'go chimp.' In another sense, it is interesting that the term 'go chimp' is used commonly because of a taxonomic bias that has prevailed in primatology. For a very long time, it was thought that most, if not all, primates lived in groups in which the males migrated and the females were philopatric. This was based mainly on research on baboons and their relatives, and mainly on Old World monkeys. However, in her classic paper, *Myth of the Typical Primate,* Karen Strier (1994a), who studies New World monkeys, illustrated that this, among other popular beliefs, was a myth based on taxonomic bias. In a similar manner, there is a tendency for a decreasing knowledge of the general primate literature as one looks at those studying species 'up the taxonomic latter'. Students of prosimians feel the need to be aware of the work done on all primate taxa, those studying New World species usually know the Old World monkey and ape literature, Old World monkey researchers are aware of the ape literature, and ape people often only know what is going on with the apes. It is rare that a chimpanzee specialist will be current on the research being done on lorises.

Besides being careful about our taxonomic biases, basing grand evolutionary theory on relatively few observations or relatively short studies, especially in relation to evolutionary time, is usually unwise. We rarely observe revelatory moments happening unexpectedly before our own eyes. As stated by Ehrlich (2000): 'The secret of biological evolution ... is vast amounts of time (p. 15)... The average levels of selection implied by the fossil record are almost impossible to detect in what is called 'ecological time' (p. 34). It would be very impressive to see evolution occur before one's eyes but, in reality, I suspect that this rarely happens.

Gendered primatology?

Most would agree that women primatologists have lent a gendered approach to fieldwork and theory in biological anthropology (e.g., Fedigan 1982, 1994, 1997; Haraway 1989; Strum and Fedigan 2000). I will only provide a few examples. Adrienne Zihlman (Tanner and Zihlman 1976; Zihlman 1978, 1987, 1997) has used the primate literature to challenge the male biased Man the Hunter theory, pointing out that it is normally female primates that make and use tools, spread innovations, socialize the young, are the repositories of group knowledge, are the centre of society, and the core of group stability (see Hart and Sussman 2005). Shirley Strum (1978, 1882) was among the first to challenge the complete male domination and aggression view of baboon society, and to document the importance of 'friendships' between males and females. She stated (1987: 81–82):

> It was a remarkable set of findings. No male dominance. The reduced effectiveness of aggression to obtain what one wanted. Complementary roles within the troop for both males and females ... Females certainly had an elevated place in Pumphouse when compared with the early descriptions of baboons that had had such an impact on anthropological thinking... the baboons pointed in another direction: complementary equality... I suspected that no one would be happy with my findings ... There was no guarantee that I would even be believed.

The importance of friendships and the role of females in primate societies was soon after recognized by a number of other female primatologists (e.g., Altmann 1980; Smuts 1982, 1985; Rasmussen 1983; see also Rowell 1974). As mentioned above, Strier (1994a, 1994b) was among the first to question the myth of the male-biased view of the patrilocal, male dominated, 'typical' primate society. She had studied the muriquis of Brazil and found that they lived in non-hierarchical, egalitarian societies, in which the males lived in peaceful 'brotherhoods'. 'The peaceful societal relationships at the core of muriqui society were an unexpected discovery that set muriquis apart not only from baboons, but also from nearly all other primates that were known at the time' (Strier 2007). From the beginning primatology has attracted female scientists and this may be even more so today. I am teaching two primatology classes this semester and over 70 per cent of fifty-one students are women. I believe this is a positive sign for primatology.

A personal note

Personal 'ethnographies' or 'primate ethnographies' have been a feature of modern primate field work from the beginning and many of these have been important in making the field well known and well received among the educated public, and in stimulating literary and scientific exchange among scientists. Schaller's 'The Year of the Gorilla' (1964), Goodall's 'My Friends, the Wild Chimpanzees' (1967), Jolly's 'A World Like Our Own' (1980) and Kummer's 'In Quest of the Sacred Baboon' (1995) are excellent examples of this genre. I believe that it is important to continue this trend and have recently, with Natalie Vasey, initiated a series in primate field monographs with Pearson-Prentice Hall in which we encourage an ethnographic approach (see Swedell 2006; Gursky 2007; Porter 2007; Atsalis 2008; Pruetz 2009; Bartlett 2009). I have also recently completed my first tome for a popular audience with fellow primatologist, Donna Hart (Hart and Sussman 2005, 2009). I believe that if we can't romanticize about our experiences as field primatologists, it would be hard to romanticize about any scientific endeavour. However, romanticizing should not be equated with intellectual dishonesty or exaggeration. When writing for a popular audience, we have an obligation to be both honest and scientifically rigorous. Bad science and dishonesty led to the acceptance of Social Darwinism and eugenics in the past and this could easily happen again.

One of my fondest experiences was doing a T.V. episode with Marlin Perkins for Wild Kingdom. Another will be when I write my romanticized version of more than thirty years of conducting fieldwork on primates in remote places. Romanticizing anthropology can be a good thing. After all, our field of study should be among the most interesting, important and enlightening fields in the world today. Who else is better able to understand and solve the problems humans face and create in the modern world of globalization?

References

Altmann, J. 1974. 'Observational study of behaviour: sampling methods', *Behaviour* 49: 227–67.

_____ 1980. *Baboon Mothers and Infants.* Cambridge, MA: Harvard University Press.

Altmann, S.A. (ed.). 1967. *Social Communication among Primates.* Chicago: University of Chicago.

Atsalis, S. 2008. *A Natural History of the Brown Mouse Lemur.* Upper Saddle River, NJ: Pearson-Prentice Hall.

Bartholomew, G.A. Jr., and J.B. Birdsell. 1953. 'Ecology and the protohominids', *American Anthropologist* 55: 481–98.

Bartlett, T.Q. 2009. *The Gibbons of Khao Yai: Seasonal Variations in Behaviour and Ecology.* Upper Saddle River, NJ: Pearson-Prentice Hall.

Bernard, H.R. 2002. *Social Research Methods: Qualitative and Quantitative Approaches.* Thousand Oaks, CA: Sage Publications.

Bingham, H.C. 1932. 'Gorillas in a native habitat', *Carnegie Inst. Pub.* 426: 1–66.

Crook, J.H. and P. Aldrich-Blake. 1968. 'Ecological and behavioural contrasts between sympatric ground dwelling primates in Ethiopia', *Folia primatologica* 8: 192–227.

DeVore, I. (ed.). 1965. *Primate Behaviour: Field Studies of Monkeys and Apes.* New York: Holt, Rinehart and Winston.

DeVore, I. and S.L. Washburn. 1963. 'Baboon ecology and human evolution', in F.C. Howell and F. Bourliere (eds) *African Ecology and Human Evolution.* Chicago: Aldine, pp. 335–67.

Ehrlich, P.R. 2000. *Human Natures: Genes, Cultures, and the Human Prospect.* Washington, DC: Island Press.

Fedigan, L.M. 1982. *Primate Paradigms: Sex Roles and Social Bonds.* Montreal, Eden Press.

—— 1994. 'Science and the successful female. Why there are so many women Primatologists', *American Anthropologist* 96: 10–20.

Fedigan, L.M. 1997. 'Is primatology a feminist science?' in L. Hager (ed.). *Women in Human Evolution.* New York: Routledge. pp. 56–75.

Fedigan, L.M. and S.C. Strum. 1999. 'A brief history of primate studies: national traditions, disciplinary origins, and stages in North American field research', in P. Dolhinow and A. Fuentes (eds) *The Nonhuman Primates.* London: Mayfield, pp. 258–69.

—— 2000. 'Changing views of primate society: a situated North American perspective', in S.C. Strum and L.M. Fedigan (eds) *Primate Encounters: Models of Science, Gender, and Society.* Chicago: University of Chicago, pp. 3–49.

Garner, R.L. 1896. *Gorillas and Chimpanzees.* London: Osgood, McIlvaine.

Gavan, J.A. (ed.). 1955. *The Nonhuman primates and Human Evolution.* Detroit: Wayne State University.

Goodall, J. 1967. *My Friends, The Wild Chimpanzees.* Washington, DC: National Geographic Society.

Goodman, S., S.V. Rakotoarisoa and L. Wilmé. 2006. 'The distribution and biogeography of the ringtailed lemur (*Lemur catta*) in Madagascar', in A. Jolly, R.W. Sussman, N. Koyama, H.R. and S.V. Rasamimanana. (eds) *Ring-tailed Lemur Biology: Lemur catta in Madagascar.* New York: Springer, pp. 1–13.

Green, G.M. and R.W. Sussman. 1990. 'Deforestation history of the eastern rainforests of Madagascar using satellite images', *Science* 248: 212–15.

Gursky, S.L. 2007. *The Spectral Tarsier.* Upper Saddle River, NJ: Pearson-Prentice Hall.

Haraway, D. 1989. *Primate Visions: Gender, Race, and Nature in the World of Modern Science.* New York: Routledge.

Hart, D. and R.W. Sussman 2005. *Man the Hunted: Primates, Predators, and Human Evolution.* New York: Westview.

—— 2009. *Man the Hunted: Primates, Predators, and Human Evolution: Expanded Edition.* New York: Westview.

Hooton, H. 1942. *Man's Poor Relations.* New York: Doubleday.

—— 1954. 'The importance of primate studies to anthropology', *Human Biology* 26: 179–88.

Howell, F.C. and F. Bourliere (eds). 1963. *African Ecology and Human Evolution.* Chicago: Aldine.

Howells, W.W. (ed.). 1962. *Ideas on Human Evolution: Selected Essays 1949–1961.* Cambridge, MA: Harvard University Press.

Iminishi, K. 1941. *The World of Living Things.* Tokyo: Rikusuisha. [Translated by P.J. Asquith 2002. *A Japanese View of Nature: The World of Living Things.* London: Routledge Curzon.]

Jay, P.C. (ed.). 1968. *Primates: Studies in Adaptation and Variability.* New York: Holt, Rinehart, Winston.

Jolly, A. 1966. *Lemur Behaviour.* Chicago: University of Chicago Press.

—— 1980. *A World Like Our Own: Man and Nature in Madagascar.* New Haven: Yale University Press.

Jolly, A. and R.W. Sussman. 2007. 'Notes on the history of ecological studies of Malagasy lemurs', in L. Gould and M. Sauther (eds): *Lemurs: Ecology and Adaptation.* New York: Springer, pp. 19–39.

Kempf-Leonard, K. (ed.). 2005. *Encyclopedia of Social Measurements.* Amsterdam: Elsevier.

Kroeber, A.L. 1928. 'Sub-human culture beginnings', *Quarterly Reveiw of Biology* 3: 325–42.

Kummer, H. 1995. *In Quest of the Sacred Baboon: A Scientist's Journey.* Princeton, NJ: Princeton University Press.

Nichter, M. 1978. 'Patterns of resort in the use of therapy systems and their significance for health planning in South Asia', *Medical Antropology* 2: 29–56.

Nissen, H.W. 1931. 'A field study of the chimpanzee' *Comp. Psychology Monograph* 8: 1–122.

Petter, J-J. 1962. 'Ecological and behavioural studies of Madagascar lemurs in the field', *Annals of the New York Academy of Sciences* 102: 267–81.

——— 1965. 'The lemurs of Madagascar', in I. DeVore, (ed.). *Primate Behaviour: Field Studies of Monkeys and Apes.* New York: Holt, Rinehart and Winston, pp. 292–319.

Porter, L.M. 2007. *The Behavioural Ecology of Callimicos and Tamarins in Northwestern Bolivia.* Upper Saddle River, NJ: Pearson-Prentice Hall.

Pruetz, J.D.E. 2009. *The Socioecology of Adult Female Patas Monkeys and Vervets in Kenya.* Upper Saddle River, NJ: Pearson-Prentice Hall.

Rasmussen, K.L.R. 1983. 'Influences of affiliative preferences upon the behaviour of male and female baboons during consortships', in R.A. Hinde (ed.) *Primate Social Relationships: An Integrative Approach.* Sunderland, MA: Sinauer Associates, pp. 116–20.

Ratsirarson, J., J. Randrianarisoa, E. Ellis, R.J. Emady, J. Efitroarany, J. Ranaivonasy, E.H. Razanajoanarivalonaand, A.F. Richard. 2001. *Bezà Mahafaly: Ecologie et Réalité Socio-économiques.* Série Sciences Biologiques, No. 18. Antananarivo: Université d'Antananarivo.

Richard, A.L. 1970. 'A comparative study of the activity patterns and behaviour of *Alouata villosa* and *Ateles geoffroyi*', *Folia Primatologica* 12: 241–63.

——— 1973. *Social Organization and Ecology of* Propithecus verreauxi *Grandidier 1867.* Ph.D. Thesis, University of London.

Rowell, T.E. 1974. 'The concept of social dominance', *Behavioral Biology* 11: 151–54.

Sahlins, M. D. 1959. 'The social life of monkeys, apes and primitive man', *Human Biology* 31: 54–73.

Schaller, G.B. 1964. *The Year of the Gorilla.* Chicago: University of Chicago Press.

Smuts, B. 1982. *Special Relationships between Adult Male and Female Olive Baboons* (Papio anubis). Ph.D. Thesis, Stanford University.

——— 1985. *Sex and Friendships in Baboons.* New York: Aldine.

Southwick, C.H. (ed.). 1963. *Primate Social Behaviour.* New York: Van Nostrand Reinhold.

Strier, K.B. 1994a. 'Myth of the typical primate', *Yearbook of Physical Anthropology* 37: 233–71.

——— 1994b. 'Brotherhoods among atelins', *Behaviour* 130: 151–67.

——— 2003. 'Primatology comes of age', *Yearbook of Physical Anthropology* 122: 2–13.

——— 2007. *Primate Behavioural Ecology, Third Edition.* Boston: Allyn and Bacon.

Strum, S.C. 1978. 'Dominance hierarchy and social organization: strong or weak inference?' Paper for Wenner-Gren Conference, *Baboon Field Research: Myths and Models.*

——— 1982. 'Agonistic dominance in male baboons: an alternative view', *International Journal of Primatology* 3: 175–202.

——— 1987. *Almost Human: A Journey into the World of Baboons.* New York: Random House.

Strum, S.C. and L.M. Fedigan (eds). 2000. *Primate Encounters: Models of Science, Gender, and Society.* Chicago: University of Chicago.

Sussman, L.K. 1981. 'Unity in diversity in a polyethnic society: the maintenance of medical pluralism on Mauritius', *Social Science and Medicine* 15B: 247–60.

——— 1983. *Medical Pluralism on Mauritius: A Study of Medical Beliefs and Practices in a Polyethnic Society.* Ph.D Thesis, Washington University, St. Louis.

——— 1989a. 'Ramazava: Madagascar's national dish', *Faces V*: 7.

——— 1989b. 'Following the ways of the ancestors', *Faces V*: 27–31.

Sussman, L.K., L.N. Robins and F. Earls. 1987. 'Treatment-seeking for depression by black and white Americans', *Social Science and Medicine* 24: 187–96.

Sussman, R.W. 1989. 'Katra: a Malagasy Game of Strategy', *Faces V*: 24–26.

——— 1997. 'Primate field studies', in F. Spencer (ed) *History of Physical Anthropology: An Encyclopedia.* New York: Garland, pp. 842–48.

——— 2000. 'Piltdown Man: the father of American field primatology', in S. Strum, and L. Fedigan (eds) *Primate Encounters: Models of Science, Gender, and Society.* Chicago: University of Chicago, pp. 85–103.

——— 2007. 'A history of primate field studies' in C.J. Campbell, A. Fuentes, K.C. MacKinnon, M. Panger and S. Bearder (eds) *Primates in Perspective.* New York: Oxford University Press, pp. 6–10.

Sussman, R.W., G.M. Green, I. Porter, O.L. Andianasolondraibe and J. Ratsirarson. 2003. 'A survey of the habitat of *Lemur catta* in southwestern and southern Madagascar', *Primate Conservation* 19: 32–57.

Sussman, R.W., G.M. Green and L.K. Sussman. 1996. 'The use of satellite imagery and anthropology to assess the causes of deforestation in Madagascar', in L.E. Sponsel, T.N. Headland, and R.C. Bailey (eds) *Tropical Deforestation: The Human Dimension.* New York: Columbia University Press, pp. 296–315.

Sussman, R.W. and J. Ratsirarson. 2006. 'Beza Mahafaly Special Reserve: a research site in southwestern Madagascar', in A. Jolly, N. Koyama, H.R. Rasamimanana and R.W. Sussman (eds.) *Ring-tailed Lemur Biology: Lemur catta in Madagascar.* New York: Springer, pp. 41–9.

Sussman, R.W. and L.K. Sussman. 1977. 'Divination among the Sakalava of Madagascar', in J. Long (ed.) *Parapsychology and Anthropology.* New York: Scarecrow Press, pp. 271–91.

Sussman, R.W., S. Sweeney, G.M. Green, I. Porton, O.L. Andrianasolondraibe, and J. Ratsirarson. 2006. 'A preliminary estimate of *Lemur catta* population density using satellite imagery', in A. Jolly, R.W. Sussman, N. Koyama, and H.R. Rasamimanana (eds) *Ringtailed Lemur Biology.* New York: Springer, pp. 14–29.

Swedell, L. 2006. *Strategies of Sex and Survival in Hamadryas Baboons: Through a Female Lens.* Upper Saddle River, NJ: Pearson-Prentice Hall.

Tanaka, J. 1976. 'Subsistence ecology of Central Kalahari San', in R.B. Lee and I. DeVore (eds) *Kalahari Hunter-Gatherers: Studies of the Kung San and Their Neighbors.* Cambridge, MA: Harvard University Press, pp. 98–119.

——— 1980. *The San Hunters-Gatherers of the Kalahari: A Study in Ecological Anthropology.* Tokyo: Tokyo University Press.

Tanner, N., and A. Zihlman. 1976. 'Women in evolution: innovation and selection in human origins', *Signs* 1: 585–608

Tax, S. (ed.). 1960. *The Evolution of Man.* Chicago: University of Chicago.

Washburn, S.L. 1951. 'The new physical anthropology', *Transactions of the New York Academy of Sciences Series II: Vol. 13* No. 7: 298–304.

——— (ed.). 1961. *Social Life of Early Man.* Chicago: Aldine.

——— (ed.). 1963. *Classification and Human Evolution.* Chicago: Aldine.

Washburn, S.L. and DeVore, I. 1961. 'Social behaviour of baboon and early man', in S.L. Washburn (ed.) *Social Life of Early Man*. Chicago: Aldine, pp. 91–105.

Yerkes, R.M. 1943. *Chimpanzees: A Laboratory Colony.* New Haven: Yale University Press.

Yerkes, R.M. and Yerkes, A.W. 1929. *The Great Apes.* New Haven: Yale University Press.

Zihlman, A. 1978. 'Women in human evolution. Part II, subsistence and social organization among early hominids', *Signs* 4: 4–20.

Zihlman, A. 1987. 'Sex, sexes, and sexism in human evolution' *Yearbook of Physical Anthropology* 30: 11–19.

Zihlman, A. 1997. 'The Paleolithic glass ceiling: women in human evolution', in Hager L. (ed.) *Women in Human Evolution*. London: Routledge, pp. 91–113.

5
Problem Animals or Problem People?
Ethics, Politics and Practice or Conflict between Community Perspectives and Fieldwork on Conservation

Phyllis C. Lee

Introduction

This chapter sets out to consider one explicit aim of this volume: to critically examine fieldwork practice in the context of outcomes. The specific outcomes explored here are those associated with conservation practices, and I ask whether our fieldwork can inform conservation practices, and whether we can find justifications for fieldwork in terms of conservation outcomes. I also consider ethical issues as applied to conservation related fieldwork: who benefits from fieldwork? Is it the local people, the local habitat, or a species of conservation concern, and how most importantly can we ever assess who benefits and to what extent?

Biological anthropology holds no claim to an exclusive or even unique perspective on either fieldwork or conservation. It is but one among a number of relevant disciplines, although biological anthropology can at times argue that it is capable of integration across a wider variety of sub-disciplines, possibly because its own *raison d'être* is so poorly defined. It can be all things to all researchers, and in this lies some of the discipline's strengths, as well as the potential for a lack of focus. In addition, biological anthropologists work with species (primates, including lemurs and apes) that are often highly threatened and live in forest habitats that are subject to extreme human exploitation. Primates and their habitats thus typify the problems of high human density and land or resource use in areas of significant conservation value (Cincotta et al. 2000; Myers et al. 2000; Balmford et al. 2001). Other than the highly charismatic nature of our subjects, the basic problems associated with human exploitation and environmental degradation are probably the same whether we are working on wetlands, marine habitats or deserts. I use examples from primates and another charismatic but vulnerable mega-fauna, the elephant, to illustrate concerns and actions affecting the welfare and conservation of these species as well as impacting on the human populations that live nearby.

I explore the nature of the questions we address during fieldwork, of how we apply answers to our original study questions, and how our justifications for fieldwork have changed over time given the dramatically altering dynamics of human interactions with the natural world. I aim to examine the pressures and political dilemmas of doing fieldwork on species that are either 'problem' animals (pests, crop-raiding, or dangerous) or in areas where local needs (poverty, health, land tenure, resource extraction) are unmet. I illustrate some of these dilemmas with outcomes in the form of perceptual or attitudinal data from communities, and discuss attempts to mitigate conflict and negative perceptions. Finally I ask how do we, as fieldworkers, use data to justify prioritizing land-use practices between competing conservation and human development interests?

Human-wildlife interaction

It seems apparent that humans hold views of self, or shared groups of selves, versus 'other', where 'wildlife' can easily be constructed as 'other'. The very term wildlife evokes the nature of such species; unmanaged and unconstrained by humans, these are life forms that are independent of humanity (although not unaffected by human actions) (see also Adams 1996).These so-called others are thus conceptually removed from being treated as intrinsically worthwhile or having justifiable needs, especially when their needs are in conflict or direct competition with those of people. Wildlife, taken here to represent large and small wild mammals and birds, can represent a threat to human livelihoods and lives, as well as competing for grazing, water and space. A phenomenon that has probably existed since modern humans emerged as a distinct species, codified in some religions and texts such as the Judeo-Christian Book of Genesis, this perceptual clash of interests between coexisting communities of people and the surrounding wildlife is now dignified with the name of 'human–animal conflict'. We establish the context, the control and even the potential outcomes by our use of such language. We define species as 'pests' because their interests compete with our own. In the course of making a living, non-humans become a construct of enmity. Such a construct has obvious implications for conservation.

There is no question but that conflict does exist in the interactions between humans and wildlife. There can be conflict between human communities and wildlife over destruction of human resources, restriction of human access to resources, loss of income, and at the most extreme, loss of human life (Madden 2004; Patterson and Wallis 2005; Lee and Graham 2006). It is also clear that in the course of this conflict, humans will 'win'. Since we establish the playing field, the nature of the game, and set the goalposts, wildlife can never 'win'. We define the problem, and by doing so make a problem (Riley 2006). Wildlife can, at times, hold its own when tolerance rather than conflict is the mode of interaction. Such contexts are however, unfortunately for wildlife, relatively rare. They depend on low densities of both humans and wildlife, large areas of land over which both can move independently and a cultural tradition of non-consumption or non-utilization, as for example was historically found among the pastoralist Maa speakers of East Africa (Kangwana 1993; Kuriyan 2002). Controlled resource use, as might be argued occurs among the Kayapo of Amazonia, is also relatively rare, and represents a form of shared, agreed policing in the context of egalitarian societies where no surplus can be monopolised and where the extent of resource exploitation is by agreement among all (Zimmerman et al. 2001). In addition there are a number of religious or cultural traditions that provide some protection to wild animals such as primates (Fuentes et al. 2005; Lee and Priston 2005). By contrast, modern western values could be best exemplified by the Tragedy of the Commons (Hardin 1968) directly applied to conservation paradigms (e.g., Ostrom 1990; Rosenberg et al. 1993). In this context, the individualistic scramble for the greatest amount of a resource leads to depletion when there is no consensus or inadequate policing of the 'common good'. That a global tragedy of the commons is currently being played out, the net effect of which will be to the detriment of humans as well as other species, can hardly be debated.

What, then, establishes the context for conservation, and how does fieldwork relate to this context? It can be argued that the primary determinant of conservation contexts is one of power, and especially economic power. When participation in conservation-related activities provides benefits, these benefits can be unequally distributed along the lines of power, wealth or gender, leading to exclusion and disillusionment (Colchester 1997). We can also define situations where benefits derived from conservation activities create dependencies, possibly as applicable to EU Common Agricultural Policies as they are to schemes that share revenues from hunting or tourism such as Zimbabwe's CAMPFIRE programme (Murombedzi 2001). For most field anthropologists, their role and indeed dilemma is one of assessing where the imbalance of power lies – with animals or communities – and attempting to either research or mitigate the imbalance. They thus risk being central to perceptions of responsibility for the actions of their research subjects. Nonetheless, developing an understanding of the potential alternative values that may be culturally placed on animals such as primates (e.g., Cormier 2006) or elephants as mentioned above, is a role that can and should be fulfilled by both biological and social scientists.

Conservation with development

Since the late 1980s, a shift has taken place in the ways in which conservation is approached by donors and practitioners, with a move from fortress perspectives (protected area conservation) to those of community-based conservation paradigms or integrated conservation with development programmes (ICDP) (Barbier 1992; Brown and Wychoff-Baird 1992; IIED 1994; Adams 2001). It has been suggested that Millennium Development Goals can only be met in the context of sustainable land or resource use practices (Brown 2004), and hence the emphasis on the interaction between conservation and development. ICDP conceptually offer four key features guaranteed to appeal to fieldworkers: equity, participation, rural development and conservation (MacKinnon 2001). Biological anthropologists are no exception in shifting to this newer perspective of working with and in the interests of those communities that experience wildlife conflicts, although some field researchers have remained emphatically rooted in the concept of protected areas and protected species (see Oates 1999; Struhsaker et al. 2005).

Conservation with development projects tend to reflect several distinctive approaches (Pimbert and Pretty 1997; Adams and Hulme 2001; Woodman 2005). The first is participatory, where stakeholders directly engage with and participate in the planning of development and resource management structures (see Zeba 2000). A second approach is that of projects which seek to link conservation with livelihoods and use economic incentives to foster both development and conservation (IIED 1994; Salafsky and Wollenberg 2000). ICDP is seen as a route to conservation, while community-based conservation is seen as a means of development. Both the participatory and the incentive based approaches emphasise the sustainable exploitation or harvesting of resources on a community basis but can differ in whether the management of the resource is extractive and driven from the top downwards or traditional and emergent from the end-users (Brandon and Wells 1992; Metcalfe 1994; McNeeley et al. 1997; du Toit 2002). While elephants can be (and are) harvested to provide benefits, the majority of those from primates are associated with non-consumptive viewing or eco-tourism, designed to contribute to conservation as well as facilitate local community participation. Eco-tourism is hardly a panacea (see Treves and Brandon 2005), of necessity and by design being limited to a niche tourist market, highly vulnerable to local political instability, and with a significant carbon cost.

Community-based perspectives raise a number of questions for fieldworkers (Agrawal and Gibson 1999). The first is how best to define a community and how to assess the commonalities amongst individuals. Typically, households are taken as the basic unit of shared economic production and resource utilisation in many developing economies, and thus characterization of this economic unit is key to many quantitative and qualitative explorations. There are however, significant problems with ethnicity or origins. In many communities, different ethnic groups co-reside in the 'community', including groups indigenous to the area and in-migrants. Defining social cohesion in a community conservation project can be problematic in the face of kinship networks that extend over large areas and where migration determines inter- and intra-community linkages. Finding commonalities in attitudes to resource ownership and resource sharing become unlikely (Gillingham 2001). Each group within a community may have different traditions of relating to wildlife, different levels of tolerance or avoidance, hierarchical power structures and gendered exclusions (Nabane and Matzke 1997; Fuentes and Wolfe 2002; Flintan 2003; Lee and Priston 2005). Social exclusion within even small communities can be a significant problem in that educational level, gender, wealth, status, and power determine who 'wins' in the acquisition of wildlife-related benefits when these are not equitably distributed (Gillingham 1998; Table 5.1). Social exclusion can lead to low participation in conservation programmes due to the potential costs of expending time and effort, and the perception of availability of incentives that are constrained by status or gender.

Table 5.1. Summary of factors influencing rural villagers' attitude to protected areas in southern Tanzania (Gillingham and Lee 1999).

Factor level	Context	Responses to questions about protected areas and protected resources
Historical / Political *Situation in the political ecology*	Arusha declaration ('That all citizens together possess all the natural resources of the country in trust for their descendants') sets legislative and perceptual context	Majority positive about the existence of protected areas and recognise the importance of mega-fauna to the state
Educational / Economic *Mapping of the interfaces between project and beneficiaries*	Awareness of national benefits derived from wildlife and habitat conservation	Majority positive about the protection of wildlife from threats and poachers
Local *Dynamics of actors and interactions – implementation and change*	Land use – farming	Majority negative about the local presence of wildlife
	Land use – pastoralists	Neutral or mildly positive
	Pest perception; experience of crop losses	Majority negative when in contact with wildlife
	Personal benefits from quota meat	Recipients positive – economic incentives rewarding
	No quota meat	Non-recipients hostile to managers and concept of incentives
	Income / status	Low – negative as incentives not available
		High – positive when incentives are distributed

Finally, given the neo-colonial context of many conservation with development projects, restricted ownership of land, resources or wildlife are significant negative characteristics associated with such projects. Land titles are rarely clear, and ownership of natural resources is thus problematic or the domain of the state. Typically, few people perceive that wildlife benefits local people or themselves personally, rather than benefiting the nation (Gillingham and Lee 1999). In addition, the government, the governmental resource management authorities and/or foreign tourists are seen as the principal beneficiaries of wildlife in such schemes (Gillingham and Lee 1999). All of these problems pose a significant challenge to conservation projects that have development goals or work in a poverty alleviation context. In addition, as a mechanistic point, the training of ICDP practitioners may be inadequate in a domain that combines the social sciences with zoology or botany, lacking the capacity to integrate across discipline boundaries. Interdisciplinary biological anthropologists can certainly contribute here.

Perceptions and conservation success

Numerous studies have demonstrated consistent effects in attitudes to conservation programmes and protected areas (Bell 1984; Conover and Decker 1991; Newmark et al. 1993, 1994; Fiallo and Jacobson 1995; Naughton-Treves 1997; De Boer and Baquette 1998; Gillingham 1998; Hill 1998; Gillingham and Lee 1999, 2003; Hill et al. 2002; Priston 2005; Webber 2006). People responding to questionnaires tend to be split roughly 50:50 between positive and negative attitudes to protected areas and the livelihood restrictions that these impose. Positive perceptions are most likely when employment and revenue generation are associated with the protected area, when there is adequate and effective protection of people and their property given conflicts between humans and wildlife, and finally when the local people have a tradition of aesthetic or religious valuing of an area or animals. Negative perceptions are associated with heavy-handed enforced compliance with protection, exclusion from historical resources and conflicts of interest over access to benefits which exacerbate inequalities. In particular a lack of participation (or a perception of exclusion) in decision-making over resource management is a significant factor shaping conservation attitudes. This is followed by a lack of support for the external institutions responsible for the implementation of conservation strategies. When wildlife or resource management continues to be perceived, to villagers' disadvantage, as the domain of the state, and the institutional context is imposed and centralised, local dissatisfaction and lack of compliance can result. Neither are productive of good conservation outcomes or positive and sustainable local initiatives and support (see Balmford et al. 2001; Infield and Namara 2001).

Conflict paradigms and possible outcomes

Biological anthropologists and particularly those working with non-human primates, often realise that their study species is actually a significant problem for local communities. 'Pest' primates are ubiquitous; wherever humans, their crops or activities and primates coexist, the primates are seen as trouble. Even arboreal leaf eaters, such as the threatened Zanzibar red colobus (Siex and Struhsaker 1999), are not immune to this negative perspective, and some primate populations pose such problems to humans and their livelihoods (e.g., the Barbary macaque on Gibraltar; Fa and Lindt 1996) that culling may be discussed as the only viable 'solution'. The activities of a small number of individuals, such as a garbage-raiding troop of baboons (Strum 1994), temple-raiding monkeys (Eudey 1994), or vervets and other species that terrorise tourists (Brennan et al. 1985; Chapman et al. 1998), contribute to the perception that all these animals are pest primates, and thus are thought to require management or interventions.

Among crop pests, primates tend to rank higher as a perceived pest than might be expected from the quantity of damage that they inflict (Hill 1997, 2000; Naughton-Treves 1997; De Boer and Baquette 1998; Gillingham and Lee 2003; Priston 2004; Lee and Priston 2005; Reynolds 2005; Webber 2006). Farmers focus on extreme events and damage to crops is seen as significant because the pest is highly visible, mobile, elusive and intelligent. Non-lethal deterrence is difficult to devise and implement since primates can leap most barriers and learn to manipulate or avoid traps, alarm systems, aversive stimuli and human guards. It is hardly surprising that even when the majority of economic loss is due initially to soil type, rainfall regimes and plant diseases, and then to rodents, insects, and birds, among the mammals, primates come top of the hit list of culprits. Interestingly, where wild pigs are a significant problem, they tend to be rated relatively accurately as a pest (Priston 2004). Large-bodied behaviourally aggressive primates which raid in large groups, such as baboons or macaques, and mega-herbivores such as elephants tend to be singled out for perceptual negative attention (Gillingham and Lee 2003; Webber 2006). As Webber (2006) has noted, the risks to humans and their activities due to crop-raiding by primates such as baboons are not proportional to other risks. Internalized risks, those due to soil, plant fertility, fire, seasonality etc., are distinct from external risks, which enter the domain of field from outwith the human habitat. Thus crop loss from a baboon raid may be perceived more negatively than equal crop losses due to poor soil fertility.

The perceptual mismatch is significant, since the resulting actions tend to involve the removal or destruction of all the pest populations whether pest or not (Horrocks and Baulu 1988; Strum 2005). There are however some contexts where pests, such as macaques, are tolerated. Priston (2005) reports that her villagers responded with comments such as, 'If you don't want [animal] damage, don't plant a garden'. The type of crop, size of farm and income from farm were significant predictors of how much damage was experienced, although the subjective perception of level of damage tended to be highly skewed; farmers over-estimated damage when their experience with damage was limited and the macaques raided only infrequently. Monkey factors were important, in that a high frequency of raids tended to promote more negative perceptions. Other features of the specifically human environment determined attitudes to the pest monkeys and an increased distance of a farm from the village enhanced a perception of vulnerability unrelated to the frequencies or intensity of raids.

The ranking of 'pests' can at times represent a form of local protest over the impacts of conservation strategies constraining traditional activities (Gillingham 1998; Lee and Graham 2006) or due to linkage with unsuccessful development projects (Webber 2006). The overstatement of losses or negative perspectives may result from resentment over limitations on resource-use imposed by land-use controls, conservation legislation or wildlife/central administrative representatives (Madden 2004). That respondents exaggerate depredation by wildlife illustrates the importance of the social dimension to human-wildlife conflict.

Crop-raiding species such as macaques, baboons, pigs and elephants cause measurable losses, suggesting that a strategy needs to be found to reduce losses if their conservation is a goal. Again, here we see the conflict between the fieldwork practitioner and the consequences of his or her study. What are the solutions available? The first of these is the mitigation of conflict, damage, or loss; a strategy which may be difficult to devise and implement when there are costs to the animals. Is the role of the research to identify a problem or to solve it? And where do our loyalties as fieldworkers lie: with study animals or with our human hosts? When dealing with proposed removal or death of highly social, long-lived and intelligent animals which may be of considerable conservation concern, do fieldworkers have a special obligation to consider the ethical issues around animal welfare? In other words, how do we square the circle of competing interests and emotions?

The so-called African 'elephant problem' is graphic illustration of the fieldworkers' conservation dilemmas. At the end of the twentieth century, as at the end of the nineteenth, African elephant populations faced a continent-wide crisis of decline. Remaining populations were compressed into smaller areas, while simultaneously human populations expanded and transformed land previously occupied at low densities into sites of conflict with wildlife, especially the mega-fauna such as elephants. Human-elephant conflict or HEC is now an established sub-discipline in conservation biology (Kangwana 1995; Hoare and du Toit 1999; Lee and Graham 2006). Relatively few studies have focused on the fact that elephants, a species that requires huge ranges, can act as a surrogate for political and legislative land tenure struggles. Politics more than livelihoods imperil the future of elephants in many areas of east and southern Africa. I would suggest that HEC cannot be solved without changing the expectations of the people involved. To achieve this, fieldworkers need to create a perceptual context where elephants have value as elephants; to minimize conflict zones by creating expectation of shared resource use; and to establish alternative sources of income that cannot be trampled or eaten by elephants. These are not easy tasks. The alternatives are the consumptive use of elephants (du Toit et al. 2004) for trophy hunting, meat or elephant-back safaris, which again pose severe ethical dilemmas in their treatment of the animals.

Economics, conservation and cultures

We are however faced with other problems when establishing the paradigms for field research in conservation. A clear distinction between sustainable ecosystems versus sustainable economic systems is seldom made. Modern practitioners are involved in valuing wild species, in valuing ecosystem services, and in creating market systems for wildlife (Leader-Williams and Albon 1988; Alper 1993; Balmford et al. 2002). The alternatives to commoditization of wildlife are seldom examined in the rush to create market economies which allegedly benefit local 'stakeholders' (but see Fullerton and Stavins 1998). As modern field practitioners, we seem not to questions the relevance of these emerging market economies, again potentially leading to the collapse of unsustainable systems and the conservation practices that depend upon them. Should we be asking to whom is the market answerable? For shareholders in a company (aka stakeholders in an ecosystem), the priority is to maximise returns; legal entities are required to ignore social consequences when in these are in conflict with profits or returns. The negative consequences of such ignorance can be global, as seen in the 2008 'credit crunch'.

A second question is: who responds to markets? Are these markets an expression of public interests and aims? Conservation markets may be limited to those who have the power to buy, not those who are forced to consume what is made available. Finally, we need to consider the social effects of markets and of commodities; we ignore externalities and marginal considerations in our development of such schemes. We field practitioners are either poor economists, or poor at considering the consequences of our commoditization, or both. In sum, valuing wildlife and ecosystem services can be extremely problematic for sustainable conservation (Balmford and Whitten 2003).

An additional issue is that responses to conflict can engender a 'compensation culture'. Crop damage, loss of resources to wildlife, injury or death are effectively rewarded financially and one outcome thus can be to perceive conflict as having a potential reward. If such a system develops, then communities can develop dependencies on compensation handouts (a situation not unknown in relation to the Common Agricultural Policy of the EU). A further issue is that the local population becomes risk averse with regard to wildlife. What are the alternatives that can be explored? At this stage relatively few exist or have been tried by fieldworkers. Some system of valuation or reward equivalent to the current UK Environmental Stewardship scheme run by Defra, which values the farmer's input specifically for encouraging and sustaining wildlife in combination with crops and other land uses, could generate a reliable income from the coexistence of wildlife with crop-lands. Other proposals can be imagined: giving wildlife or forests value in the form of financial gains to local residents from simple proximity to animals, which might create a context for or expectation of tolerance. In line with the current obsession with costing the natural environment, ecosystem or animal 'services' could be given proximity values. None of these solutions are ideal; we have no structure for generating income, subsidies or fees in the long-term in the absence of utilisation. As Balmford et al. (2002) note, we need a strategy for ensuring that the conservation 'opportunity costs' are met outside the local community in order to produce effective conservation support within communities.

Additional considerations apply. For example, the benefits proposed must be those desired by residents in the community. Access to wildlife-related benefits or non-timber forest products do not, of themselves, lead to the establishment of mutually beneficial partnerships for wildlife management between rural communities and the state. Schools and dispensaries do not equate to or trade-off with forests or reserves; to local residents they simply represent education and health (see also Oates 1999). Conservation initiatives need to be bottom-up rather than top-down: emerging from local communities and filtered through the conservation stakeholders. Can any such programmes realized? In addition, benefits must be seen to be (and indeed must be) equally distributed. No programme will work unless it tackles social exclusion and gender (Flintan 2003). Obtaining and distributing benefits must be self-sustaining, reducing dependence on NGOs and Government agencies. Funding conservation and development solutions sustainably is a key aim and in order to meet this aim, we need to ensure that the funding lifespan of the projects we initiate is greater than the lifespan of NGO participation. This could be attained via the participation of multiple institutions with nested hierarchies of structures and infrastructures.

The challenges to fieldworkers

Should anthropological fieldworkers take responsibility for finding solutions to the kinds of conservation problems that I have outlined above? It is not always clear whether those who identify problems should or can be those who produce solutions. But fieldworkers are often in a specific and unique social, demographic and economic context. The profile of an anthropological field researcher, who represents a context for decision making, policy planning and finding solutions to conservation dilemmas, is typically that of an educated, wealthy (or at least funded) person who is not reliant on the forests, animals or land for his or her survival. Furthermore, they are often outside language and cultural expectations, and possibly most importantly not gendered (and therefore empowered) in the context of the local community. They are also committed and highly motivated. As an additional positive attribute, they tend not to be Governmental representatives and thus can be viewed by the community as independent or unbiased.

Their role, then, can be to seek solutions that are emergent rather than imposed. They can address conflicts of interests and confront asymmetric power relations such as those between the state and the individual. It is, however, crucial to distinguish between the community's priorities, which may be local development and poverty alleviation, and those of the state, which may be prioritizing conservation. Fieldworkers in the absence of an institutional or political context are unable to operate effectively. In order to achieve outcomes, equality amongst participants needs to be ensured. This equality might be attained via institutional mechanisms to ensure equitable distribution of project benefits, which take account of gender, education, corruption and or social and political power. In addition a key mechanism could be via community or 'group-ranch' land titles to sustain active community participation in resource management.

Fieldworkers are faced with a series of questions in the context that I have framed above. Can we operate in this context? Should we? And how do we take responsibility over such decisions? Solving political problems of land ownership and land titles could help, as could empowering the disenfranchized. But these are political acts, which benefit people. Developing the understanding of the dynamics of exchange among processes related to resource use, its protection and the agents and actors involved could be part of the role of fieldworkers. These are ethical dilemmas faced by fieldworkers in the changing global conservation climate. We, and our students, need at the very least to examine our roles in such activities before they become themselves unsustainable.

Acknowledgements

I thank Jeremy MacClancy for inviting me to participate in the workshop, Sarah Gillingham, Nancy Priston, Jo Woodman, Amanda Webber and Max Graham for sharing their results and passions with me, Bill Adams for broadening my perspectives, and Keith Lindsay for sharpening the arguments. Thanks also to Kim Hockings, Jeremy MacClancy and Agustin Fuentes for helpful comments on the draft manuscript.

References

Adams, W. 1996. *Future Nature*. London: Earthscan.
_____ 2001. *Green Development: Environment and Sustainability in the Third World*, Second edition. London: Routledge.
_____ 2004. *Against Extinction: The Story of Conservation*. London: Earthscan.
Adams, W. and D. Hulme. 2001. 'Conservation and Community: Changing Narratives, Policies and Practices in African Conservation', in D. Hulme and M. Murphree (eds) *African Wildlife and Livelihoods: The Promise and Performance of Community Conservation*. Oxford: Heinemann and James Currey.
Agrawal, A. and C. Gibson. 1999. 'Enchantment and Disenchantment: The Role of Community in Natural Resource Conservation', *World Development* 27: 629–49.
Alper, J. 1993. 'Protecting the Environment with the Power of the Market', *Science* 260: 1884–5.
Balmford, A. and T. Whitten. 2003. 'Who Should Pay For Tropical Conservation, and How Could the Costs Be Met?', *Oryx* 37: 238–50.
Balmford, A., J.L. Moore, T. Brooks, N. Burgess, L. Hansen, P. Williams and C. Rahbek. 2001. 'Conservation Conflicts Across Africa', *Science* 291: 2616–19.
Balmford, A., A. Bruner, P. Cooper, R. Constanza, S. Farbert, R.E. Green, M. Jenkins, P. Jefferiss, V. Jessamy, J. Madden, K. Munro, N. Myers, S. Naeem, J. Paavola, M. Rayment, S. Rosendo, J. Roughgarden, K. Trumper and R.K Turner. 2002. 'Economic Reasons for Conserving Wild Nature', *Science* 297: 950–3.
Barbier, E. 1992. 'Community Based Development In Africa', in T.M. Swanson and E.B. Barbier (eds) *Economics for the Wilds: Wildlife, Wildlands, Diversity and Development*. London: Earthscan, pp. 103–35.
Bell, R.H.V. 1984. 'The Man-Animal Interface: An Assessment of Crop-Damage and Wildlife Control', in E. McShane-Caluzi (ed.) *Conservation and Wildlife Management in Africa:*

The Proceeding of a Workshop Organised by the US Peace Corps at Kasungu National Park, Malawi. Washington, DC: US Peace Corps, pp 387–416.

Brandon, K. and M. Wells. 1992. 'Planning for People and Parks: Design Dilemmas', *World Development* 20: 557–70.

Brennan, J., J.G. Else and J. Altmann. 1985. 'Ecology and Behavior of a Pest Primate: Vervet Monkeys in a Tourist Lodge Habitat', *African Journal of Ecology* 23: 35–44.

Brown, M. 2004. 'Conserving Biodiversity for Development'. SciDev.Net: *www.scidev.net/dossiers/index.cfm.*

Brown, M. and B. Wychoff-Baird. 1992. *Designing Integrated Conservation and Development Projects: Revised Edition.* Washington DC: Biodiversity Support Programme, WWF.

Chapman, K.L., M.J. Lawes and M.M. Macleod. 1998. 'Evaluation of Non-Lethal Control Methods on Problematic Samango Monkeys in the Cape Vidal Recreation Reserve, Greater St. Lucia Wetland Park', *South African Journal of Wildlife Research* 28(3): 89–99.

Child, B. 1996. 'The Practice and Principles of Community-Based Wildlife Management in Zimbabwe: The CAMPFIRE Programme', *Biodiversity and Conservation* 5: 369–98.

Cincotta, R.P., J. Winewski and R. Engelman. 2000. 'Human Population in the Biodiversity Hotspots', *Nature* 404: 990–2.

Colchester, M. 1997. 'Salvaging Nature: Indigenous Peoples and Protected Areas', in K. Ghimire and M. Pimbert (eds) *Social Change and Conservation: Environmental Politics and Impacts of National Parks and Protected Areas.* London: Earthscan.

Conover, M.R. 2002. *Resolving Human-Wildlife Conflicts: The Science of Wildlife Damage Management.* London: Lewis Publishers.

Cormier, L. 2006. 'A Preliminary Review of Neotropical Primates in the Subsistence and Symbolism of Indigenous Lowland South American Peoples', *Ecological and Environmental Anthropology* 2: 14–32.

De Boer, W.F. and D.S. Baquette. 1998. 'Natural Resource Use, Crop Damage, and Attitudes of Rural People in the Vicinity of the Maputo Elephant Reserve, Mozambique', *Environmental Conservation* 25(3): 208–18.

du Toit, J.T. 2002. 'Sustainable Wildlife Utilization in Africa: A Contest Between Scientific Understanding and Human Nature', in P. Schmuck and W.P. Schultz (eds) *Psychology Of Sustainable Development.* London: Kluwer Academic Publishers, pp. 197–207.

du Toit, J.T., B.H. Walker, and B.M. Campbell. 2004. 'Conserving Tropical Nature: Current Challenges for Ecologists', *TREE* 19: 12–17.

Eudey, A. 1994. 'Temples and Pet Primates in Thailand', *Terre et Vie* 49: 273–80.

Fa, J. and R. Lind. 1996. 'Population Management and Viability of the Gibraltar Barbary Macaques', in J.E. Fa and D.G. Lindburg (eds) *Evolution and Ecology of Macaque Societies.* Cambridge: Cambridge University Press, pp. 235–62.

Fiallo, E.A. and S.K. Jacobson. 1995. 'Local Communities and Protected Areas: Attitudes of Rural Residents towards Conservation and Machalilla National Park', *Environmental Conservation* 22: 241–9.

Flintan, F. 2003. *Engendering Eden Volume I: Women, Gender and ICDPs: Lessons Learnt and Ways Forward – Summary Document.* London: IIED Wildlife and Development Series No. 16.

Fuentes, A. and L.D. Wolfe. 2002. *Primates Face To Face: The Conservation Implications of Human-Nonhuman Primate Interconnections.* Cambridge: Cambridge University Press.

Fuentes, A., M. Southern and K. Ged Suaryana. 2005. 'Monkey Forests and Human Landscapes: Is Extensive Sympatry Sustainable for *Homo sapiens* and *Macaca fascicularis* on

Bali', in J.D. Patterson and J. Wallace (eds) *Primate–Human Interaction and Conservation*. Toronto: American Society of Primatologists Publications, pp. 168–95.

Fullerton D., and R. Stavins. 1998. 'How Economists See the Environment', *Nature* 395: 433–4.

Getz, W.M., L. Fortmann, D. Cumming, J. du Toit, J. Hilty, R. Martin, M. Murphee, N. Owen-Smith, A.M. Starfield and M.J Westphal. 1999. 'Sustaining Natural and Human Capital: Villagers and Scientists', *Science* 283: 1855–1956.

Gibson, C.C. and S.A. Marks. 1995. 'Transforming Rural Hunters into Conservationists: An Assessment of Community-Based Wildlife Management Programs in Africa', *World Development* 23: 941–57.

Gillingham, S.G. 1998. *Giving Wildlife Value: A Case Study of Community Wildlife Management around the Selous Game Reserve, Tanzania*. Ph.D. Thesis, Cambridge University.

_____ 2001. 'Social Organization and Participatory Resource Management in Brazilian *Ribeirinho* Communities: A Case Study of the Mamirauá Sustainable Development Reserve, Amazonia', *Society and Natural Resources* 14: 803–14.

Gillingham, S.G. and P.C. Lee. 1999. 'The Impact of Wildlife-Related Benefits on the Conservation Attitudes of Local People around the Selous Game Reserve, Tanzania', *Environmental Conservation* 26: 218–28.

_____ 2003. 'A Preliminary Assessment of Perceived and Actual Patterns of Wildlife Crop-Damage in an Area Bordering the Selous Game Reserve, Tanzania', *Oryx* 37: 316–25.

Happold, D.C.D. 1995. 'The Interactions between Humans and Mammals in Africa in Relation to Conservation: A Review', *Biodiversity Conservation* 4: 395–414.

Hardin, G. 1968. 'The Tragedy of the Commons', *Science* 162: 1243–8.

Hill, C.M. 1997. 'Crop-Raiding by Wild Vertebrates: The Farmer's Perspective in an Agricultural Community in Western Uganda', *International Journal of Pest Management* 43: 77–84.

_____ 1998. 'Conflicting Attitudes towards Elephants around the Budungo Forest Reserve, Uganda', *Environmental Conservation* 25: 244–50.

_____ 2000. 'Conflict of Interest between People and Baboons: Crop Raiding in Uganda', *International Journal of Primatology* 21: 299–315.

Hoare, R.E., and J.T. du Toit. 1999. 'Coexistence between People and Elephants in African Savannas', *Conservation Biology* 13: 633–9.

IIED. 1994. *Whose Eden? An Overview of Community Approaches to Wildlife Management.* Report to ODA. Nottingham: Russell Press.

Infield, M. and M. Namara. 2001. 'Community Attitudes and Behaviour towards Conservation: An Assessment of a Community Conservation Programme around Lake Mburo National Park, Uganda', *Oryx* 35: 48–60.

Kangwana, K.F. 1993. *Conservation and Conflict: Elephant-Maasai Interaction in Amboseli Kenya*. Ph.D. Thesis, Cambridge University.

_____ 1995. 'Human–Elephant Conflict: The Challenge Ahead', *Pachyderm* 19: 11–14.

Kuriyan, R. 2002. 'Linking Local Perceptions of Elephants and Conservation: Samburu Pastoralists in Northern Kenya', *Society and Natural Resources* 15: 949–57.

Leader-Williams, N. and S.D. Albon. 1988. 'Allocation of Resources for Conservation', *Nature* 336: 533–5.

Lee, P.C. and M.D. Graham. 2006. 'African Elephants (*Loxodonta africana*) and Human–Elephant Interactions: Implications for Conservation', *International Zoo Yearbook* 40: 9–19.

Lee, P.C. and N.J. Priston. 2005. 'Human Attitudes to Primates: Perceptions of Pests, Conflict and Consequences for Primate Conservation', in J.D. Patterson and J. Wallace (eds) *Primate–Human Interaction and Conservation*. Toronto: American Society of Primatologists Publications, pp. 1–23.

MacKinnon, K. 2001. 'Editorial: Integrated Conservation and Development Projects – Can They Work?' *Parks* 11: 1–7.

Madden, F. 2004. 'Creating Coexistence between Humans and Wildlife: Global Perspectives on Local Efforts to Address Human–Wildlife Conflict', *Human Dimensions of Wildlife* 9: 247–59.

McNeely, J. 1993. 'People and Protected Areas: Partners in Prosperity', in E. Kemf (ed.) *The Law of the Mother: Protecting Indigenous Peoples in Protected Areas*. San Francisco: Sierra Club Books.

McNeely, J., M. Rojas and F. Vorhies. 1997. 'Incentives and Disincentives to Conservation'. In G. Borrini-Feyerabend (ed.) *Beyond Fences: Seeking Social Sustainability in Conservation, Vol. 2: A Resource Book*. Gland: IUCN.

Metcalfe, S. 1994. 'The Zimbabwe Communal Areas Management Programme for Indigenous Resources', in D. Western, P.M. Wright and S.C. Strum (eds) *Natural Connections: Perspectives on Community-Based Conservation*. Washington, DC: Island Press, pp. 161–93.

Murombedzi, J. 2001. 'Why Wildlife Conservation Has Not Economically Benefited Communities in Africa', in D. Hulme and M. Murphee (eds) *African Wildlife and African Livelihoods: The Promise and Performance of Community-Based Conservation*. Oxford: James Currey, pp. 208–26.

Myers, N., R.A. Mittermeier, C.G. Mittermeier, G.A.B. da Fonseca and J. Kent. 2000. 'Biodiversity Hotspots for Conservation Prorities', *Nature* 403: 853–5.

Nabane, N. and G. Matzke, 1997. 'A Gender-Sensitive Analysis of a Community-Based Wildlife Utilisation Initiative in Zimbabwe's Zambezi Valley', *Society and Natural Resources* 10: 519–35.

Naughton-Treves, L. 1997. 'Farming the Forest Edge: Vulnerable Places and People around Kibale National Park, Uganda', *The Geographical Review* 87: 27–46.

_____ 1998. 'Predicting Patterns of Crop Damage by Wildlife around Kibale National Park', *Conservation Biology* 12: 156–68.

Naughton-Treves, L., A. Treves, C. Chapman and R.W. Wrangham. 1998. 'Temporal Patterns of Crop-Raiding by Primates: Linking Food Availability in Croplands and Adjacent Forest', *Journal of Applied Ecology* 35: 596–606.

Newmark, W.D., N.L. Leonard, H.I. Sariko and D-G.M. Gamassa. 1993. 'Conservation Attitudes of Local People Living Adjacent to Five Protected Areas in Tanzania', *Biological Conservation* 63: 177–83.

Newmark, W.D., D.N. Manyanza, D-G.M. Gamassa and H. I. Sariko. 1994. 'The Conflict between Wildlife and Local People Living Adjacent to Protected Areas in Tanzania: Human Density as a Predictor', *Conservation Biology* 8: 249–55.

Oates, J. 1999. *Myth and Reality in the Rainforest: How Conservation Strategies are Failing in West Africa*. Berkeley: University of California Press.

Ostrom, E. 1990. 'Reflections on the Commons', in E. Ostrom (ed.) *Governing the Commons: The Evolution of Institutions for Collective Action*. Cambridge: Cambridge University Press.

Patterson, J.D., and J. Wallace. 2005. *Primate–Human Interaction and Conservation*. Toronto: American Society of Primatologists Publications.

Pimbert, M. and J. Pretty. 1997. 'Parks, People and Professionals: Putting 'Participation' into Protected Area Management', in K. Ghimire and M. Pimbert (eds) *Social Change and Conservation: Environmental Politics and Impacts of National Parks and Protected Areas.* London: Earthscan.

Priston, N.E.C. 2005. *Crop Raiding by Macaca ochreata brunnescens in Sulawesi: Reality, Perceptions and Outcomes for Conservation.* Ph.D. Thesis: Cambridge University.

Reynolds, V. 2005. *The Chimpanzees of the Budongo Forest.* Oxford: Oxford University Press.

Riley, E.P. 2006. 'Ethnoprimatology: Toward Reconciliation of Biological and Cultural Anthropology', *Ecological and Environmental Anthropology* 2: 75–86.

Rosenberg, A.A., M.J. Fogarty, M.P. Sissenwine, J.R. Beddington and J.G. Shepherd. 1993. 'Achieving Sustainable Use of Renewable Resources', *Science* 262: 828–9.

Salafsky, N. and E. Wollenberg. 2000. 'Linking Livelihoods and Conservation: A Conceptual Framework and Scale for Assessing the Integration of Human Needs and Biodiversity', *World Development* 28: 1421–38.

Siex, K.S. and T.T. Struhsaker. 1999. 'Colobus Monkeys and Coconuts: A Study of Perceived Human Wildlife Conflicts', *Journal of Applied Ecology* 36: 1009–20.

Songorwa, A.N. 1999. 'Community-Based Wildlife Management (CWM) in Tanzania: Are the Communities Interested?' *World Development* 27: 2061–79.

Struhsaker, T.T., P.J. Struhsaker and K.S. Siex. 2005. 'Conserving Africa's Rain Forests: Problems in Protected Areas and Possible Solutions', *Biological Conservation* 123: 45–54.

Strum, S.C. 1994. 'Prospects for the Management of Primate Pests', *Terre et Vie* 49: 295–306.

_____ 2005. 'Measuring Success in Primate Translocation: A Baboon Case Study', *American Journal of Primatology* 65: 117–40.

Treves, A. and K. Brandon. 2005. 'Tourist Impacts on the Behaviour of Black Howling Monkeys (*Alouatta pigra*) at Lamanai, Belize', in J.D. Patterson and J. Wallace (eds) *Primate–Human Interaction and Conservation.* Toronto: American Society of Primatologists Publications, pp. 146–67.

Wells, M. and K. Brandon. 1992. *People and Parks: Linking Protected Area Management with Local Communities.* Washington DC: World Bank.

Webber, A. 2006. *Primate Crop Raiding in Uganda. Actual and Perceived Risks around Budongo Forest Reserve.* Ph.D. Thesis: Oxford Brookes University.

Woodman, J. 2004. *Between Bureaucrats and Beneficiaries: The Implementation of Ecodevelopment in Pench Tiger Reserves, India.* Ph.D. Thesis: Cambridge University.

Zeba, S. 1998. *Community Wildlife Management in West Africa: A Regional Review.* London: IIED, Evaluating Eden Series Working Papers.

Zimmerman, B., C. Peres, J. Malcolm and K. Turner. 2001. 'Conservation and Development Alliances with the Kayapo of South-Eastern Amazonia, a Tropical Forest Indigenous Peoples', *Environmental Conservation* 28: 10–22.

6
Ecological Anthropology and Primatology:
Fieldwork Practices and Mutual Benefits

Juichi Yamagiwa

The roots of Japanese primatology

Fieldwork efforts in anthropology and primatology at Kyoto University have been based on the traditions of AACK (Academic Alpine Club of Kyoto), established by Kinji Imanishi and his colleagues in 1931. Their activities were characterized by the motto 'ascent of virgin peaks'. They attempted to climb uncharted mountains and made several expeditions to unknown parts of Asia. Their expeditions were always motivated by academic interests and composed of an interdisciplinary research team typically consisting of anthropologists, zoologists, botanists, geologists, etc. After World War II, the club splintered into several academic fields, but the resulting groups still have frequent exchanges (Figure 6.1). Imanishi was based in the Department of Zoology, Kyoto University, and started his field studies on feral horses at Cape Toi in Miyazaki Prefecture. The aim of his study was to understand species society and to thus trace the evolution of human society (Asquith 1991, 2000; Takasaki 2000). The concept of species society had developed from his study on mayflies skittering around a river in Kyoto. He observed four species of mayflies favouring different habitats from each other and called this phenomenon 'habitat segregation'. He proposed a new definition of society as a combination of an organism and its habitat and applied it to all living things (Imanishi 1941). Based on the idea of Espinas (1877) that the principles of family and troop are different and incompatible in animal societies, Imanishi postulated that human society had evolved to solve the conflicts between these principles (Imanishi 1951). He proposed four conditions (exogamy, incest taboo, division of labour, and neighbourhood relationships) for the formation of a human family (Imanishi 1961).

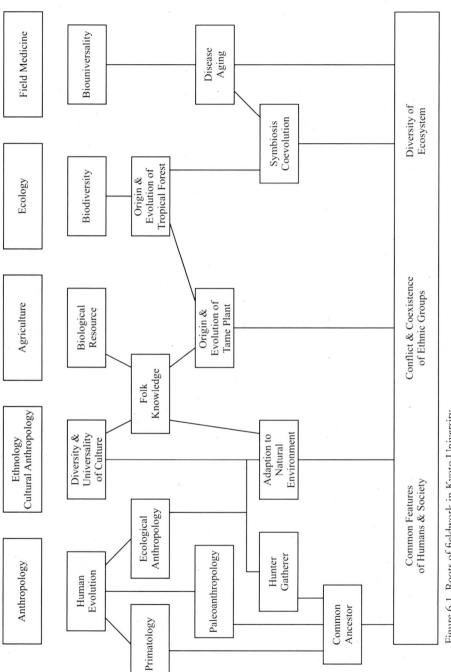

Figure 6.1. Roots of fieldwork in Kyoto University.

By the late 1940s, Imanishi and his students started work in animal sociology to study Japanese deer, horses and captive rabbits. They liked to read the books of Seaton and called themselves Seatonians. Unlike most Western zoologists who strictly avoided anthropomorphism, they identified each individual they observed and named it, as did Seaton in his books. Imanishi thought this method to be essential for illustrating social interactions among individual animals. During their fieldwork on horses at Cape Toi in 1948, Imanishi and his students Junichiro Itani and Shunzo Kawamura encountered a troop of Japanese macaques. Although it was very brief, they were impressed by this encounter and expected a more complex social structure in macaques than horses. They formed the Primate Research Group in 1951 and visited many habitats of Japanese macaques to find the best study site. They tried to habituate macaques with provisioning (feeding them with sweet potatoes, wheat or soy beans) and finally succeeded in provisioning at several sites, such as Koshima (Miyazaki Prefecture) and Takasakiyama (Oita Prefecture).

This method enabled the human observers to shorten their distance from the macaques and to record their interactions at close proximity. They continued to name each individual for recording social interactions. Individual identification by marking had previously been used by Carpenter for rhesus macaques at Cayo Santiago Island, but Japanese primatologists identified each individual by the features of face and body (shape, colour and scars). Imanishi devised a guide to field studies by first adopting methods of comparative sociology, secondly basing work on individual identification, and thirdly recording social interactions from prolonged continuous observations. The fieldwork accomplished by this method produced many findings on the social structure of Japanese macaques, such as linear dominance rank, basic and dependent rank, leadership system and kin relationships (Itani 1954; Kawamura 1958a).

The first generation of Japanese primatologists thought that social structure was not a mere reflection of individual survival or reproductive strategies but reflected a norm of species-specific sociality (Itani 1972, 1985). Another important scheme was 'culture'. Imanishi (1952) defined this as non-hereditary, acquired behaviour that was acknowledged socially. He used the term 'kaluchua' in Japanese in a much broader sense than culture defined in human-centred terminology (Nakamura and Nishida 2006). Social structure and behaviour, such as leadership system, paternal care, or flexibility in individual aggregation, communication, and dominant/ subordinate relationships were regarded as culture, sometimes using the term 'sub-culture' or 'pre-culture' (Itani 1954, 1959; Kawamura 1959; Kawai 1965). However, after the findings on newly acquired techniques of Japanese macaques to eat artificial foods (washing human-provided potatoes in sea water) at Koshima and on various tool-using behaviours of chimpanzees at Gombe and Mahale in Tanzania, this term has been restricted to complex feeding skills or techniques. Recently, the concept of culture and its learning process have been reconsidered and used to explain subtle social customs or behavioural variations in group-living primates (de Waal 1999, 2001; Nakamura et al. 2000; McGrew 2004; Nakamura and Nishida 2006).

Ape expeditions and establishment of the anthropological course

The Japan Monkey Center (JMC), a non-governmental (supported by the Nagoya Railway Company) institute, museum and zoo for primates and primatology, was established at Inuyama (Aichi Prefecture) in 1956. It was a successful collaboration between the Primate Research Group and the Experimental Animal Research Group (based at Tokyo University), and Itani and Kawai obtained early research posts there. The JMC started to publish *Primates*, the first international journal of primatology, in 1956, and the Japanese primatologists disseminated their discoveries to the world in English two years later. *Primates* remains among the top primatology journals today.

The first two overseas expeditions were dispatched in 1958. Kawamura conducted a preliminary survey on gibbons in Thailand (Kawamura 1958b). Imanishi and Itani visited several countries in Equatorial Africa in order to find a long-term study site for gorillas. The JMC supported three expeditions in Africa, and they met several researchers dispatched from different academic fields at the Virunga volcanoes on the border of Uganda, Rwanda and Democratic Republic of Congo (DRC). Osborn and Donisthorp were funded by Louis Leakey and Reymond Dart, paleoanthropologists who discovered fossil hominids in East and South Africa, and they tried to habituate gorillas with provisioning (Baumgartel 1977). Emlen and Schaller were sponsored by the New York Zoological Society, and tried to habituate gorillas without provisioning (Schaller 1963). The fieldwork projects having three different interests (animal sociology, anthropology and zoology) met at the Virungas to study mountain gorillas in the late 1950s. Unfortunately, the outbreak of civil war in the Belgian Congo interrupted their work in 1960, and Itani decided to change the study subject from gorillas to chimpanzees after travelling in Uganda and Tanzania (Itani 1961). Dian Fossey, who was dispatched by Leakey, resumed fieldwork on mountain gorillas at the Virungas in 1967 and succeeded in habituating them without provisioning (Fossey 1983).

Imanishi became the head of the Division of Social Anthropology at the Research Institute for Humanistic Studies, Kyoto University in 1959. He organized a group of primatologists, social anthropologists, ecologists and botanists, and started anthropological expeditions in Tanzania in 1961. They constructed a research base at the Gape Kabogo, on the eastern shore of Lake Tanganyika, and started fieldworks on chimpanzees and people heavily dependent on nature, such as hunter-gatherers and slash-and-burn agriculturalists (Imanishi 1966; Itani 1977). In 1962, the Course of Anthropology (CA) was opened in the Department of Zoology, Kyoto University, and Imanishi became the first professor of this course. Itani obtained the post of associate professor and Yukimaru Sugiyama, who conducted fieldwork on hanuman langurs in India and reported the first observation of infanticide among non-human primates (Sugiyama et al. 1965), joined as an assistant professor. Jiro Ikeda also joined as an associate professor of physical anthropology. After the retirement of Imanishi in 1965, Itani led the studies in primatology and ecological anthropology. From the beginning, CA promoted three different studies for understanding human evolution.

The Primate Research Institute of Kyoto University (PRI) was established at Inuyama in 1967. Researchers of brain science, psychology, morphology, phylogeny, biochemistry, genetics, veterinary science, sociology and ecology began working together with primate subjects. Kawai and Kawamura assumed the post of associate professor there. Both CA and PRI had graduate schools where many students learned primatology and produced brilliant works. These institutions and their traditional ways of teaching and learning are called the 'Kyoto School' (Takasaki 2000). I discuss here only about CA where I learned my field and am now working as a professor.

Lessons from the Course of Anthropology at Kyoto University

When I entered the Graduate School in CA in 1975, graduate students were actively pursuing research projects on human evolution from three different dimensions. First, the paleo-anthropological approach involved, studies of human bones from ancient times excavated in Japan and the Middle East (later in Africa). Second, the primatological approach focused on social and behavioural features of the Japanese macaques and the African great apes. Third, studies in ecological anthropology, concentrated on the lives of people having a high dependence on nature in Japan and Africa. The main subject of fieldwork then was chimpanzees living in the Mahale Mountains of Tanzania. After several researchers searched for the best site to study chimpanzees on the western shore of Lake Tanganyika, Toshisada Nishida succeeded in provisioning them at Mahale in 1965. Although studies on wild chimpanzees had been pursued by Jane Goodall since 1960 at Gombe, about 100 km north of Mahale, Nishida and Kawanaka were the first to illustrate their social structure consisting of multiple males and females with female transfers between unit-groups (Nishida and Kawanaka 1972; Kawanaka and Nishida 1975). Nishida, one of Itani's students, was an associate professor in the Department of Anthropology, Tokyo University, at that time. Graduate students in both Tokyo and Kyoto Universities joined the research project on chimpanzees at Mahale. Fission-fusion social features based on complex social relationships, tool using, hunting and food sharing were discovered and reported by them (Itani 1970, 1977; Nishida 1970, 1981). Takayoshi Kano, another student of Itani and an associate professor of Ryukyu University at that time, had created a research site for bonobos at Wamba, DRC, in 1973. Suehisa Kuroda, a graduate student of Kyoto University, joined him to habituate them and succeeded in provisioning efforts in 1975. Other graduate students also joined them to conduct fieldwork at Wamba, making various new findings such as the cohesive social structure with female transfer, genito-genital rubbing, food sharing and strong mother-son bonds (Kano 1980, 1992; Kuroda 1980, 1984).

The research projects on hunter-gatherers and slash-and-burn farmers were also conducted at that time. Under the supervision of Itani, Reizo Harako, an assistant professor, created a field site in the Ituri Forest, DRC, and conducted participatory fieldwork on pygmy people with a few graduate students. Makoto Kakeya lived in a village of Togwe people in Tanzania, and after obtaining qualification as a witch doctor he conducted an ethnobotanical survey. Jiro Tanaka, one of Itani's students, conducted participatory fieldwork on the Bushmen in Botswana in the 1960s. He was accompanied by his family, including two young children, and they followed nomadic people extensively in the Kalahari Desert. He obtained a post at PRI and started new fieldwork on pastoral people with graduate students of Kyoto University in northern Kenya in the 1970s. Most graduate students learning ecological anthropology went to the Okinawa Islands in Japan to do their first fieldwork on fishermen using traditional fishing methods in the master course and later joined the ongoing projects in Africa.

The graduate students were encouraged to broaden and deepen their interests based on their curiosity about certain phenomena that they encountered in the field, rather than to narrowly define a research object and methodology and gather data in accordance with a pre-determined framework (Ichikawa 2004a). They were directed to collect data by following their intuition and curiosity, and especially first-hand data concerning forms of phenomena that had gone unnoticed. Underlying the emphasis on this approach was a tacit understanding that we should refrain by all means from squeezing the young hopefuls of learning, full of growth potential, into a small number of moulds. The phrase 'Let the data speak' was the catchphrase of our research at the time.

Lessons in the study site of Japanese macaques

I was interested in the evolution of human societies, and I selected the primatological approach. During the lessons of graduate school at Kyoto University, I learned how to collect first-hand data and to contemplate how to pose new questions based on such data. During the master course, I visited nine habitats of Japanese macaques from the northern limit to the southern limit of their distribution. I collected data on their external non-metrical features and analyzed intra-specific variation in their morphological features. The degree of sexual dimorphism in some features was distinctly different between habitats. In the second year of the master course, I selected Yakushima Island where I found the highest degree of sexual dimorphism and started fieldworks on social features of Japanese macaques without provisioning in their natural habitat.

In the 1970s, provisioning appeared to have a great influence on troop size and social interactions. The number of provisioning sites increased to thirty-seven, mainly for the purpose of tourism (Nihonzaru Editorial Committee 1977). Provisioning improved nutritional conditions of Japanese macaques and increased the survival rate and birth rate, especially for dominant-class females (Sugiyama and Ohsawa 1982). Furthermore, provisioning created factors that encouraged the macaques to engage in crop damage. This was probably caused by the loss of habitats after large-scale logging throughout Japan in the 1960s and early 1970s. Macaques dispersed from logged areas and began raiding crops in the low foothills, where fewer people were engaged in agriculture due to mechanization. Provisioning may have accelerated the process of their invasion. These observations led us, the young generation of Japanese primatology, to conduct field studies in natural habitats without provisioning.

The fieldwork projects at Yakushima were characterized by the absence of strong leadership. The graduate students formed a research group with schoolteachers and local people to plan and conduct fieldwork (Yamagiwa 2008). Although we returned to Kyoto University once or twice a year to analyze and present the results of our fieldwork, we usually stayed in Yakushima to continue our work. Instead of using the telephone due to its high cost, we frequently wrote letters to Itani, our supervisor, who always replied to us with a long letter when he was in Japan. Itani had experienced a visit to Yakushima with Kawamura in 1952 and expected certain social features of the macaques unique to Yakushima, such as strong inter-troop antagonism, small troop size and small home range (Itani 1952). He thought that several troops living in partly overlapping ranges might represent the population structure of Japanese macaques in natural habitats. However, because of the success in provisioning at Koshima just after their visit, fieldworks were concentrated on single and isolated troops and did not resume at Yakushima until the 1970s. Although his main interest was in chimpanzees and ecological anthropology at that time, Itani sent us useful suggestions, recalling his past experience at Yakushima.

We conducted fieldwork without professional guides or assistants. Tamaki Maruhashi, a graduate student of PRI at that time, initiated habituation of Japanese macaques without provisioning in the subtropical/warm-temperate forest at Yakushima in 1975, and Kuroda and I joined him one year later. First we confirmed Itani's predictions (Maruhashi 1982; Iwano 1983). These features were attributed to rich food production in the warm-temperate forest at Yakushima. However, unlike the Western primatologists who usually seek ecological factors shaping social structure and relationships (Wrangham 1980; van Schaik 1983), we focused on the social features that maintained the small troop size with high SSR (socionomic sex ratio: the number of reproductive males/the number of reproductive females within a troop).

We frequently observed several troop fissions and troop takeovers by non-troop males in our study troops. Based on these observations, we found many differences in social organizations of Japanese macaques between Yakushima and other habitats, especially in comparison with provisioned troops (Maruhashi 1982; Yamagiwa 1985; Furuichi 1985; Oi 1988, Sprague 1991; Hill and Okayasu 1996). Troop fission occurred at smaller troop size in Yakushima than in other habitats. This was caused by non-troop males and estrous females with kin groups during the mating season. A large number of non-troop males appeared around the study troops soliciting mating with estrous females (Yamagiwa 1985). The majority of these males visited the study troops for a short period and some of them immigrated into the study troops as the highest or the lowest ranking males (Sprague 1992). When troop takeover occurred by non-troop males, females extended estrous period and showed strong proceptivity (Okayasu 2001). Hill and Okayasu (1996) found the absence of 'youngest ascendancy' in the dominance relations among sisters in the study troops at Yakushima, while it is common in provisioned troops of Japanese macaques (Kawamura, 1958a).

In order to analyze the socio-ecological factors shaping these social features of Japanese macaques at Yakushima, we compared such features and environmental conditions with those at Kinkazan, where long term field studies had been conducted in the cool-temperate forest without provisioning since 1982. We formed several working groups to compare various aspects of ecological and social features between the two habitats. In summary, female Japanese macaques living at Yakushima have higher-quality and more abundant foods, while they more severely compete for resources within and between troops (Agetsuma and Nakagawa 1998; Maruhashi et al. 1998). Such competition leads to strong antagonism between troops, which poses the risk of troop extinction or decreased birth rate of the subordinate troops after a bad fruiting season (Saito et al. 1998; Suzuki et al. 1998; Takahata et al. 1994, 1998; Sugiura et al. 2000, 2002). Female macaques at Yakushima more positively solicit non-troop males to associate with them during the mating season (Yamagiwa and Hill 1998; Okayasu 2001). Such a tendency may promote frequent male movement between troops and diverse entries, frequent troop fissions by estrous females and non-troop males, and frequent non-agonistic interactions among males within a troop (Takahashi and Furuichi 1998; Sprague et al. 1998). These social features may contribute to the small group size with high SSR.

Lessons in the study sites of gorillas

In the second year (1978) of my doctorate course, I was dispatched to Kahuzi-Biega National Park, DRC, to study eastern lowland gorillas. The Park was known as a site of gorilla tourism where visitors observed wild gorillas in their natural habitats. I made a population census and tried to observe the social interactions of two habituated gorilla groups (Yamagiwa 1983). However, due to incomplete habituation, I could not observe their behaviour at close proximity. As suggested by Itani, I visited Karisoke Research Center at the Virunga Volcanoes, Rwanda, and decided to study mountain gorillas under the supervision of Dian Fossey in 1980. Her methods of habituating gorillas were different from those I had learned for habituating Japanese macaques: I had to immerse myself in the gorillas' behaviours, communicating with them in their manner. She named each individual as do Japanese primatologists. By the 1970s this methodology had become popular among Western primatologists, especially among ape field workers (Goodall 1971; Fossey 1983). To observe the behaviour of apes in the wild, we naturalized ourselves into their behavioural characteristics. While spending the daytime within a group of apes, we shared a special experience with them. We usually use these experiences to find important features of their behaviour and social organizations and to consider new insights on the social and behavioural continuities between primates, including humans.

For example, I had a strange experience with a male gorilla. He made a prolonged gaze on my face within a short distance. The same episode was observed frequently among gorillas in various contexts. A prolonged gaze constitutes a mild form of threat in most group-living primates; it is usually avoided by subordinate animals. However, prolonged gazing or eye contact between gorillas may fail to elicit submissiveness by the recipients (Yamagiwa 1992). This behaviour may promote various kinds of social interactions to reduce social tension in the great apes and humans. Observations of homosexual behaviour among male gorillas also brought me new perspectives for male life history in the non-matrilineal society of gorillas (Yamagiwa 1987, 2006). New findings on ape behaviour in their natural habitats, such as genito-genital rubbing, grooming hand-clasp, social scratch, tool using, food sharing, display and greeting, have enabled fieldworkers to present new arguments on social features and social evolution of the great apes (Kuroda 1980, 1984; Mori 1983; Nishida 1987; Kano 1986; Kitamura 1989; Nakamura et al. 2000; Yamakoshi 2004).

Based on these experiences and observations, we can imagine behavioural and social similarities between apes and us. However, description of animal behaviour in human language is limited, and sometimes this leads us to misunderstand it as anthropomorphism. A prudent classification of animal behaviour could reduce such negative effects (Itani 1987). Long-term observation with individual identification may enable us to recognize the visible interactions of primates and their actual relationships. For example, intervention by a third party in agonistic interactions is based on different motivations of mediators: to support the winner, to support the loser, to dominate both participants, or just to stop the fight. These variations have been empirically identified from the precise records of individual life histories. Although human language does not directly contribute to an understanding of an animal's social cognition, it may enable us to find a behaviour's function at different social levels.

Principle of fieldwork in ecological anthropology

Ecological anthropology was initially aimed at finding clues to the evolution of human society by studying the life of people who depend heavily on nature (hunter-gatherers, slash-and-burn agriculturalists and pastoralists). Researchers followed the guidelines of Imanishi for primatology and spent all of their time with subject people (participatory observation) instead of staying in a nearby village and inviting them to give information. Based on the perspectives of Itani, the early research projects focused on subsistence activities, dietary life, food sharing and social organization of hunter-gatherers in Africa. Their ritual performance and face-to-face interactions were recorded partially by adopting the methods of primatology. Itani (1988) answered the question 'How are your primatology and ecological anthropology interrelated?' with 'For the investigation of evolution of human society, these two fields (non-human primates in the wild and the nature-dependent people) are prerequisite.'

Itani (1977) thought that social structure of chimpanzees and hunter-gatherers were homologous. Both societies are based on a fission-fusion nature, patrilineal features and strong alliance between males. The presence of family is the only difference between them. He hypothesized that our ancestral society started as a patrilineal troop with a fission-fusion nature and later developed the family structure in it.

Unlike Imanishi who proposed an anti-Darwinian theory for evolution (Asquith 1991), Itani challenged the concept of 'natural man' by Rousseau (1755). In order to clarify man's state of nature, Itani promoted ecological anthropology. Rousseau illustrated the process from human equality at the primitive state to inequality at the civil state. His 'natural man' lacks sociality. Itani pointed out that most non-human primates have already graduated from such a stage. The primitive state assumed by Rousseau may correspond to the elemental society of nocturnal prosimians. Itani (1985, 1988) proposed the possible evolutionary pathway from the equipotent state of elemental society, equality of monogamous society, and inequality of group-living non-human primates to the conditional equality of human society (Figure 6.2). The inequality principle is seen typically in the society of Japanese macaques. Dominant/subordinate relationships appear in situations of conflict, and the subordinate always retreats from the source of conflict. Such a norm and cognition plays an important role in the coexistence of macaques within a troop.

By contrast, the equality principle of human society does not have as firm a foundation as the inequality principle. It is founded only on the negation of the inequality principle, and it functions in a society ruled by the inequality principle as if that principle were non-existent. It is supported by an implicit agreement for achieving peaceful coexistence among the troop members. Itani suggested some forms of conditional equality in non-human primates, especially in the great apes. He took up play interactions (Hayaki 1985), food sharing (Kuroda 1984), and socio-sexual interactions (Kitamura, 1989), for example. Social staring of gorillas or peering of bonobos may also be classified as interactions based on conditional equality (Yamagiwa 1992; Idani 1995).

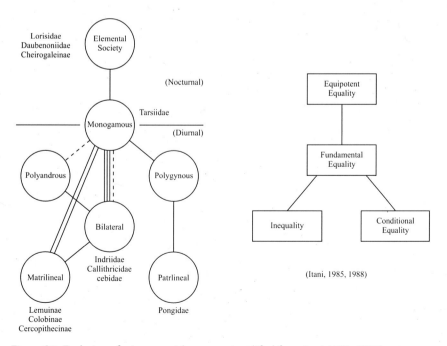

Figure 6.2. Evolution of primate social structure (modified from Itani 1985, 1988).

In the graduate school, students participating in primatology, ecological anthropology and physical anthropology attended the same seminars to discuss their works in relation to human evolution. These experiences enabled them to expand their perspectives: to illustrate the natural life of hunter-gatherers in the past and the cultural life of early hominids just after differentiation from the common ancestor with chimpanzees. Food sharing behaviour was analyzed in both hunter-gathers and chimpanzees in order to elucidate the evolution of human sociality (Tanno 1976; Ichikawa 1982; Kitanishi 1996, 1998). Based on Itani's perspectives, social features of hunter-gatherers, pastralists, and slash-and-burn farmers were discussed in relation to their subsistence ecology (Kakeya 1976; Harako 1976; Tanaka 1980; Ichikawa 1983, 1996; Ohta 1986; Terashima 1985).

The CA was divided into the Laboratory of Physical Anthropology and the Laboratory of Human Evolution Studies in 1981 (Figure 6.3). Itani obtained a post of professor in the latter and led both primatology and ecological anthropology. The Graduate School of African Area Studies was created in 1986, and Itani became a director concurrently. Some ecological anthropologists (Tanaka, Kakeya, Ichikawa and Ohta) educated by Itani obtained posts there. Itani left the post in the Graduate School of Science in 1988 and retired from Kyoto University in 1990. His students took over his posts in the Laboratory of Human Evolution Studies and the Department of African Area Studies.

Contribution of primatology and ecological anthropology to conservation

The Japanese primatologists contributed to conservation of primates and their habitats from the beginning of their fieldwork. Based on the appeals of the Primate Research Group, the Japanese Government legislated that Japanese macaques at several sites were national treasures, and included their habitats in the National Reserves and Parks. JMC, CA, and PRI have frequently been at the centre of these appeals. After the establishment of the Primate Society of Japan (PSJ), the president of PSJ had routinely sent letters to the central and local governments to demand that stronger conservation measures be taken for the Japanese macaques.

At Yakushima, our study site was included in the National Park in 1964. But the level of protection was low and logging was not restricted. We formed a group of primatologists and demanded repeatedly that the protection level of our study site be raised. We also organized several NGO's with local citizens to consider the appropriate way of achieving conservation with local development. Our study site was included in the first level of protection and hunting was prohibited in 1982. The high-level protected area (21 per cent of forest), including our study site, was designated as a World Heritage Site by UNESCO in 1993.

However, despite our conservation efforts and habituation methods without provisioning, crop damage by macaques increased at Yakushima (Yamagiwa 2008). The farmers tried a variety of methods to keep the macaques away from cultivated fields. But they were not successful and the local governments decided to shoot the macaques. We discussed with farmers the best methods to keep them away without killing them. Kagoshima University and Kyoto University made a joint project to examine a new system of protection using an animal sensor. We organized international and national symposia to discuss the problems of crop damage by macaques with the local government and local farmers. Primatologists and university students made a population census and estimated the number of macaques surviving in the coastal area including all cultivated fields at Yakushima (Yoshihiro et al. 1998).

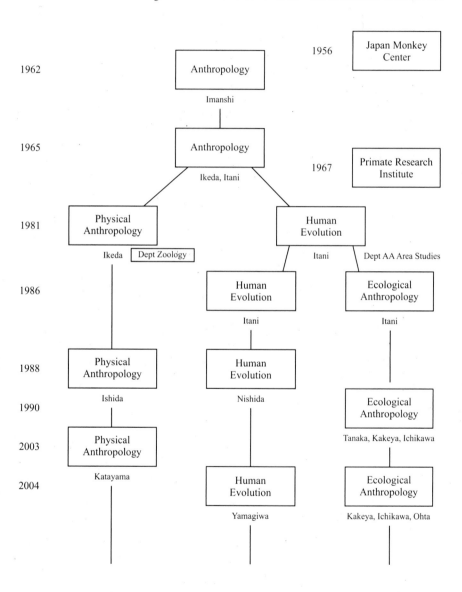

Figure 6.3. Transition of Anthropological Course in Kyoto University.

Furthermore, we protested the decision of Kagoshima Prefecture to expand a road in our study site in 1993. This plan would have damaged the forest and prevented the vertical distribution of plants and the movements of animals. Many local people joined our protest and supported us, and finally Kagoshima Prefecture decided to suspend the project in 1998.

Human pressure also increased in the habitats of the great apes. Deforestation, cattle encroachment and hunting for bush-meat have posed a large threat to wildlife everywhere. Itani and Nishida requested that the Tanzanian government create a national park at Mahale to protect chimpanzees in their natural habitats and demanded the support of the Japan International Cooperation Agency (JICA 1980; Itani 1993). The Mahale Mountain area was designated as the eleventh Tanzanian national park in 1985. Moreover, the Japanese primatologists played important roles in the establishment of the Luo Scientific Reserve at Wamba in DRC for the protection of bonobos, the Ndoki National Park in Congo for the protection of gorillas and chimpanzees and the Kalinzu Reserve in Uganda for the protection of chimpanzees.

I had learned from Fossey that continuous conservation efforts and long term field studies were vital to supporting a healthy population of gorillas at Karisoke Research Center. But her murder in 1985 also taught me the importance of harmonious relationships with the local human community; although it was the most effective way to save gorillas at that time, her 'active conservation' provoked the hostility of local people.

When I resumed my fieldwork on wild gorillas in eastern DRC in 1986, I tried to extend my lessons and experience at Karisoke to the new study sites. I implemented two policies in my research project: first, to conduct long-term studies with Congolese scientists, and secondly to raise the awareness of local people on the need to conserve gorillas and their natural habitats. Fortunately, I became associated with two gifted colleagues, and joined the establishment of an NGO called POPOF (Pole Pole Foundation), consisting of people living near the park, as an external adviser in 1992. I thought that the most important requirement for research on gorillas and thus their conservation was to work with local people, since the major obstacle to achieving conservation was conflict: conflict between gorillas and humans and conflict between groups of people in struggles for life (Basabose 2001; Yamagiwa 2003).

POPOF tried to mitigate the increased conflicts between the local people and the park authorities. A tree nursery, a handicraft centre and a school for women and children were established for community-based conservation education. POPOF played an important role in the spread of conservation knowledge and in the reduction of poaching during the civil war in 1996 and 1998. I established POPOF-Japan (a branch office in Japan) in 1994 to support the activities of POPOF in Kahuzi. We invited the members of POPOF to Japan to participate in several conferences and symposia on conservation of natural environments and eco-tourism in 2001. They visited Yakushima and discussed community-based conservation in the World Heritage Sites with guides and local NGOs.

Ecological anthropology has also changed its focus. Although it has so far developed as a human ecology in a broad sense, it has come to include the scope of conservation. Ichikawa (2004b) regards it as a combination of the three types of ecology, namely cultural ecology, historical ecology and political ecology. The first ecology seeks to understand how and to what extent the hunter-gatherers depend on the central African forest. It is important to describe their unique forest culture in detail and to shed light on the relationship between their culture and the forest environment. The second ecology aims to interpret the ecological system of an area as the interdependence between humans and nature with a long history of interactions. We should evaluate positive effects of human activities on forest conservation. The third ecology attempts to elucidate the relations between the microscopic aspects of the lives of forest people and the community of the broader world, in particular their relations with macro-level political and economic systems. The forest people are not just a group of vulnerable people buffeted by the raging waves of globalization, by forces such as the market economy, destruction of the environment, and nature conservation movements. It is necessary to understand how the forest people are coping with these forces and to identify the ways in which they can maintain their autonomy.

It is important to increase the participation of rural populations in forest conservation and management. This may activate local economies and act as a brake on the migration of people and their heavy reliance on bushmeat. Although eco-tourism is a promising method for sustainable use of natural resources in the protected area, habituation of great apes may increase the risk of disease transmission from human to apes and may weaken the viability of their population (Woodford et al. 2002). Due to the genetic proximity of non-human primates to humans, transmission of animal-borne diseases to humans is also becoming a great risk when a number of primates are put on sale. Interdisciplinary studies between natural and social sciences are urgently needed to establish peaceful and safe relationships between human and non-human primates.

Recent scope of primatology and ecological anthropology

Primatologists have recently concentrated their attention on conservation of primates and their natural habitats. In particular, fieldworkers studying the great apes have become seriously concerned with conservation activities. The Great Ape Survival Plan (GRASP) was established by the United Nations Environment Programme (UNEP) in 2001. It aims to coordinate efforts to halt the decline in great ape populations and to ensure their long-term survival in their natural habitat.

Adding to these top-down approaches, we have established GRASP-Japan mainly based on a bottom-up approach with local NGOs, including us, in 2003. We selected seven long-term study sites and have promoted unified conservation measures while exchanging information with each other. We employed postdoctoral students who had experience in ecological anthropology in our project to facilitate our understanding of conflicts between wildlife and people. We are applying our accumulated discussion and knowledge among primatologists and ecological anthropologists in the Kyoto School. We have also organized SAGA (Support Asian and African Great Apes), an annual consortium of researchers, zoo keepers, curators, NGO volunteers, and journalists to discuss first conservation of the great apes in their natural habitats, secondly, enrichment of the great apes in captivity, and thirdly promotion of experimental studies with non-invasive methods since 1998. Many graduate and undergraduate students who are engaged or interested in studies of the great apes have attended the conference.

Nothing has changed in our way of teaching at present. However, the lessons of fieldwork require more time and care than before. Prior to fieldwork, students are expected to discuss their plans with us in seminar and to get full agreement from most of us. At the initial stage of fieldwork, one or more professors or teaching assistants take students to the field and teach them how to lead their life safely and appropriately. Due to the increasing insecurity in some habitats of primates, it has become risky to leave inexperienced students alone at study sites. Actually several researchers and students evacuated during the civil wars in DRC and Congo in the 1990s. We need to take precise measures for security in the countries of our study sites and to find reliable assistants and supporters among resident people to protect fieldworkers. Native collaborators (researchers) sometimes work with students and supervise them.

We usually conduct fieldwork with resident researchers or students based on our agreements on cooperative research between Kyoto University and academic institutions of resident countries. We have accepted several graduate students from these countries and they learned primatology toward earning the doctor's degree in Japan. Nowadays, graduate students are requested to take the doctor's degree within a set term (five years including master course). They are also encouraged to publish their doctor's thesis in international journals within one year after taking the degree. Such trends have forced them to narrowly define a research object and methodology and gather data in accordance with a predetermined framework, always sticking fast to the established discipline. We usually advise students to write a paper with solo authorship, because it can reflect their own thoughts and ideas. However, we have a large amount of data accumulated from long term field studies made by many people in the past. In order to raise the quality of papers and to satisfy statistical requirements, students need such long term data. Before starting or during fieldwork, we sometimes recommend that students ask about co-authorship with previous workers or colleagues currently working with them. So far, little conflict has arisen among students and researchers on co-authorship.

Recently graduate students tend to do their fieldwork at long-term study sites, instead of creating new sites. It seems easy for them to collect data on well-habituated and known individuals. They can reduce the time needed to proper conditions for observations and also use the existing records at these sites. Given these trends, we must accept an increased role in mitigating conflict between students with similar themes and subjects. Although it is becoming difficult to promote our traditional way of teaching in the manner of 'the deserted child' in the field conducting participatory observations, I still recommend independent fieldwork and encourage students to broaden their interests through interdisciplinary discussions. I believe that the continuous fusing of primatology, ecological anthropology and physical anthropology will bring us new perspectives on human evolution and the appropriate conservation measures in the near future.

Acknowledgements

This paper was originally prepared for the international symposium 'Fieldwork: Examining its practice among biological anthropologists and primatologists' held 5–6 May, 2006 in Oxford Brookes University, United Kingdom. I would like to express my heartfelt thanks to Professor Jeremy MacClancy for giving me the opportunity to present the history of my laboratory and Japanese primatologists and ecological anthropologists. I am also greatly indebted to Professor Simon Bearder for his help and hospitality throughout the conference. My travel grant was supported by the JSPS-HOPE Project.

References

Agetsuma, N. and N. Nakagawa. 1998. 'Effects of habitat differences on feeding behaviours of Japanese monkeys: Comparison between Yakushima and Kinkazan', *Primates* 39: 275–91.

Asquith, P.J. 1991. 'Primate research groups in Japan: orientations and East-West differences', in L.M. Fedigan and P.J. Asquith (eds.) *The Monkeys of Arashiyama*. Albany: SUNY Press, pp. 81–98.

Asquith, P.J. 2000. 'Negotiating science: internationalization and Japanese Primatology', in S.C. Strum and L.M. Fedigan (eds.) *Primate Encounters*, Chicago and London: University of Chicago Press, pp. 165–83.

Basabose, A.K. 2001. 'Causes of poaching, consequences, proposed solutions and agencies that could implement them', *Gorilla Journal* 22: 6–8.

Baumgartel, W. 1924. *Up Among the Mountain Gorillas*. New York: Hawton Books, INC.

Espinas, A. 1924. *Des Societes animals*, 3rd edn. Paris: Felix Alcan.

Fossey, D. 1983. *Gorillas in the Mist*. Boston, MA: Houghton Mifflin.

Furuichi, T. 1985. 'Inter-male associations in wild Japanese macaque troop on Yakushima Island, Japan', *Primates* 26: 219–37.

Goodall, J. 1971. *In the Shadow of Man*. Boston: Houghton Mifflin.

Harako, R. 1976. 'The Mbuti as hunters: A study of ecological anthropology of the Mbuti pygmies (1)', *Kyoto University African Studies* 10: 37–99.

Hill, D.A. and N. Okayasu 1996. 'Determinants of dominance among female macaques: nepotism, demography and danger', in J.E. Fa and D.G. Lindburg (eds) *Evolution and Ecology of Macaque Societies*. Cambridge: Cambridge University Press, 459–72.

Idani, G. 1995. 'Function of peering behaviour among bonobos (*Pan paniscus*) at Wamba, Zaire', *Primates* 36: 377–83.

Ichikawa, M. 1982. *Hunters in the Tropical Forest*. Kyoto: Jinbun-Shoin, (in Japanese).

―――― 1983. 'An examination of the hunting-dependent life of the Mbuti Pygmies, eastern Zaire', *African Study Monographs* 4: 55–76.

_____ 1996. 'Co-existence of man and nature in the African rain forest', in R. Ellen and K. Fukui (eds) *Redefining Nature: Ecology, Culture and Domestication*. Oxford: Berg, pp. 467–92.

_____ 2004a. 'Benefit of Foresight: From evolutionary interest to global environmental problems', *Before Farming* 1–5.

_____ 2004b. 'The Japanese Tradition of Central African Hunter-gatherer Studies: with Comparative Observation on the French and American Traditions', in A. Barnard (ed) *Hunter-Gatherers in History, Archaeology and Anthropology*. Oxford: Berg, pp. 103–14.

Imanishi, K. 1955. *The World of Living Things*. Tokyo, Kobunsha. (Translated by Asquith, P.J., H. Kawakatsu, Yagi, Shusuke and H. Takasaki, 2002, Routledge Curzon).

_____ 1951. *Pre-human Societies*. Tokyo: Iwanami-shoten (in Japanese).

_____ 1952 'Evolution and humanity', in K. Imanishi (ed) *Man*. Tokyo: Mainichi-shinbunsha, pp. 36–94 (in Japanese).

_____ 1961. 'The origin of human family: a primatological approach', *The Japanese Journal of Ethnology* 35(3): 119–38 (in Japanese with English Summary).

_____ 1966. 'The purpose and method of our research in Africa', *Kyoto University African Studies* 1: 1–10.

Itani, J. 1942. *Natural Society of Yakushima Macaques*. Primary Research Group of Kyoto University, (in Japanese).

_____ 1954. *The Monkeys of Takasakiyama*. Nihon Dobutsuki vol II. Tokyo: Kobunsha. (in Japanese).

_____ 1959. 'Paternal care in the wild Japanese monkey, *Macaca fuscata*', *Primates* 2: 61–93.

_____ 1961. *The Forest of Gorillas and the Pygmies*. Tokyo: Iwanami-shoten (in Japanese).

_____ 1972. *Primate Social Structure*. Tokyo: Kyoritsu-shuppan (in Japanese).

_____ 1977. *In Search of Chimpanzees in the Wilderness*. Tokyo: Heibonsha (in Japanese).

_____ 1985. 'The evolution of primate social structure', *Man* 20: 539–611.

_____ 1988. 'The origin of human equality', in M.R.A. Chance (ed). *Social Fabrics of the Mind*. Hove and London: Lawrence Erlbaum associates, pp. 137–56.

_____ 1983. 'On the shore of Lake Tanganyika', *Primate Research* 9 (1993): 215–24.

Iwano, T. 'Concluding remarks on the socioecological characteristics of the Yakushimazaru', *The Nihonzaru* 5: 86–95 (in Japanese).

JICA. 1980. *Mahale: Study for the proposed Mahale Mountains National Park*, Final Report. Tokyo: The Japan International Cooperation Agency.

Kakeya, M. 1976. 'Subsistence ecology of the Tongwe, Tanzania', *Kyoto University African Studies* 10: 143–212.

Kano, T. 1980. 'Social behaviour of wild pygmy chimpanzees (*Pan paniscus*) of Wamba: A preliminary report', *Journal of Human Evolution* 9: 243–60.

_____ 1986. *The Last Ape: Pygmy Chimpanzee Behaviour and Ecology*. Tokyo Dobutsusha (in Japanese). (English translation, 1992, California: Stanford University Press).

Kawai, M. 1965.' 'Newly-acquired pre-cultural behaviour of the natural troop of Japanese monkeys on Koshima Island', *Primates* 6: 1–30.

Kawamura, S. 1958a. 'The matriarchal social order in Minoo-B troop: A study on the rank system of Japanese monkeys', *Primates* 1: 149–56 (in Japanese).

_____ 1958b. 'The preliminary survey on the white-handed gibbon in Thailand', *Primates* 1: 157–58.

_____ 1959. 'The process of sub-culture propagation among Japanese macaques', *Primates* 2 (1959): 43–60 (in Japanese).

Kawanaka, K. and T. Nishida. 1975. 'Recent advances in the study of inter-unit group relationships and social structure of wild chimpanzees of the Mahali Mountains', in S. Kondo, M. Kawai and A. Ehara (eds). *Proc. Symp. 5th Congr. Int. Primat. Soc.* Tokyo: Japan Science Press, pp. 173–86.

Kitamura, K. 1989. 'Genito-genital contacts in pygmy chimpanzee (*Pan paniscus*)', *African Study Monographs* 10: 49–67.

Kitanishi, K. 1996. 'Variability in the subsistence activities and distribution of food among different aged males of the Aka hunter-gatherers in northeastern Congo', *African Study Monographs* 17: 35–57.

—— 1998. 'Food Sharing among the Aka hunter-gatherers in northeastern Congo', *African Study Monographs Supplementary Issue* 25: 3–32.

Koyama, N. 1970. 'Changes in dominance rank and division of a wild Japanese monkey troop in Arashiyama', *Primates* 11: 335–90.

Kuroda, S. 1980. 'Social behaviour of the pygmy chimpanzees', *Primates* 21: 181–97.

—— 1984. 'Interaction over food among pygmy chimpanzees', in R.L. Susman (ed). *The Pygmy Chimpanzee: Evolutionary Morphology and Behaviour*. New York: Plenum: 301–24.

Maruhashi, T. 1982. 'An ecological study of troop fission of Japanese monkeys (*Macaca fuscata yakui*) on Yakushima Island, Japan', *Primates* 23(3): 317–37.

Maruhashi, T., C. Saito and N. Agetsuma. 1998. 'Home range structure and inter-group competition for land of Japanese macaques in evergreen and deciduous forests', *Primates* 39: 291–302.

Mori, A. 1983. 'Comparison of the communicative vocalizations and behaviours of group ranging in eastern gorillas, chimpanzees and pygmy chimpanzees', *Primates* 24: 486–500.

Nakamura, M. and T. Nishida 2006. 'Subtle behavioural variation in wild chimpanzees, with special reference to Imanishi's concept of Kaluchua', *Primates* 47: 35–42.

Nakamura, M., W.C. McGrew, L.F. Marchant and T. Nishida. 2000. 'Social scratch: another custom in wild chimpanzees', *Primates* 42: 237–48.

Nihonzaru Editorial Committee. 1977. 'Changes in population of Japanese macaques at Monkey Parks in Japan', *Nihonzaru* 3: 113–20 (in Japanese).

Nishida, T. 1970. 'Social behaviour and relationship among wild chimpanzees of the Mahali Mountains', *Primates* 11: 47–87.

—— 1981. *The World of Wild Chimpanzees*. Tokyo: Chuokoronsha (in Japanese).

—— 1987. 'Local traditions and cultural transmission', in B.B. Smuts, D.L. Cheney, R.M. Sayfarth, R.W. Wrangham and T.T. Struhsaker (eds) *Primate Societies*. Chicago: University of Chicago Press, pp. 462–74.

Nishida, T. and K. Kawanaka. 1972. 'Inter-unit-group relationships among wild chimpanzees of the Mahali Mountains', *Kyoto University African Studies* 7: 131–69.

Ohta, I. 1986. 'Reciprocity among the Turkana, northwestern Kenya', in J. Itani and J. Tanaka (eds). *Anthropology of Natural Society*. Tokyo: Academia, pp. 181–215 (in Japanese).

Oi, T. 1988. 'Sociological study on the troop fission of wild Japanese monkeys (*Macaca fuscata yakui*) on Yakushima Island', *Primates* 29: 1–19.

Okayasu, N. 2001. 'Contrast of estrus in accordance with social contexts between two troops of wild Japanese macaques on Yakushima', *Anthropological Science* 109: 121–39.

Rousseau, J.J. 1755. *Discours sur l'origine et les fondement de l'inegalite parmi les hommes*. Harmondsworth: Penguin (English translation in 1984).

Saito, C., S. Sato, S. Suzuki, H. Sugiura, N. Agetsuma, Y. Takahata, C. Sasaki, H. Takahashi, T. Tanaka and J. Yamagiwa. 1998. 'Aggressive intergroup encounters in two populations of Japanese macaques (*Macaca fuscata*)', *Primates* 39: 303–12.

Schaller, G.B. 1963. *The Mountain Gorilla: Ecology and Behaviour.* Chicago: University of Chicago Press.

Sprague, D.S. 1991. 'Mating by non-troop males among the Japanese macaques of Yakushima macaques of Yakushima Island', *Folia Primatologica* 57: 156–8.

Sprague, D.S. 1992. 'Life history and male intertroop mobility among Japanese macaques (*Macaca fuscata*)', *International Journal of Primatology* 13: 437–54.

Sprague, D.S., S. Suzuki, H. Takahashi and S. Sato. 1998. 'Male life history in natural populations of Japanese macaques: migration, dominance rank, and troop participation of males in two habitats', *Primates* 39: 351–64.

Sugiura, H., C. Saito, S. Sato, N. Agetsuma, H. Takahashi, T. Tanaka, T. Furuich and Y. Takahata. 2000. 'Variation in intergroup encounters in two populations of Japanese macaques', *International Journal of Primatology* 21: 519–35.

Sugiura, H., N. Agetsuma and S. Suzuki. 2002. 'Troop extinction and female fusion in wild Japanese macaques in Yakushima', *International Journal of Primatology* 23: 69–84.

Sugiyama, Y. 1976. 'Life history of male Japanese monkeys', *Advances in the Study of Behaviour* 7: 255–84.

Sugiyama, Y., K. Yoshibaa and N.D. Parthasarathy. 1965. 'Home range, mating season, male group and inter-troop relations of hanuman langurs (*Presbytes entellus*)', *Primates* 6: 73–106.

Sugiyama, Y. and H. Ohsawa. 1982 'Population dynamics of Japanese monkeys with special reference to the effect of artificial feeding', *Folia Primatologica* 39: 238–63.

Suzuki, S., N. Noma and K. Izawa. 1998. 'Inter-annual variation of reproductive parameters and fruit availability in two populations of Japanese macaques', *Primates* 39: 313–24.

Takahashi, H. and T. Furuichi. 1998. 'Comparative study of grooming relationships among wild Japanese macaques in Kinkazan A troop and Yakushima M troop', *Primates* 39: 365–74.

Takahata, Y., D.S. Sprague, S. Suzuki and N. Okayasu. 1994. 'Female competition, co-existence, and mating structure of wild Japanese macaques on Yakushima Island, Japan' in P.J. Jarman and A. Rossister, (eds) *Animal Societies: Individuals, Interaction and Organization*, Kyoto: Kyoto University Press, pp. 163–79.

Takahata, Y., S. Suzuki, N. Agetsuma, N. Okayasu, H. Sugiura, H. Takahashi, J. Yamagiwa, K. Izawa, T. Furuichi, D.A. Hill, T. Maruhashi, C. Saito, S. Sato, and D.S. Sprague. 1998. 'Reproduction of wild Japanese macaque females of Yakushia and Kinkazan Islands: A preliminary report', *Primates* 39: 339–50.

Takasaki, H. 2000. 'Traditions of the Kyoto School of field primatology in Japan', in S.C. Strum and L.M. Fedigan (eds) *Primate Encounters*. Chicago and London: University of Chicago Press, pp. 151–64.

Tanaka, J. 1980. *The San: Hunter-Gatherers of the Kalahari – a Study of Ecological Anthropology.* Tokyo: University of Tokyo Press.

Tanno, T. 1976. 'The Mbuti net-hunters in the Ituri forest, eastern Zaire: their hunting activities and band composition', *Kyoto University African Studies* 10: 101–35.

Terashima, H. 1982. 'Variation and composition principles of the residence group (band) of the Mbuti pygmies: beyond a typical/atypical dichotomy', *African Study Monographs Supplementary Issue* 4: 103–20.

van Schaik, C.P. 1983. 'Why are diurnal primates living in groups?', *Behaviour* 87: 120–44.

Wrangham, R.W. 1980. 'An ecological model of female-bonded primate groups', *Behaviour* 75: 262–300.

Woodford, M.H., T.M. Butynski and W.B. Karesh. 2002. 'Habituating the great apes: the disease risks', *Oryx* 36: 153–60.

Yamagiwa, J. 1983. 'Diachronic changes in two eastern lowland gorilla groups (*Gorilla gorilla graueri*) in the Mt. Kahuzi Region, Zaire', *Primates* 24: 174–83.

Yamagiwa, J. 1985. 'Socio-sexual factors of troop fission in wild Japanese monkeys (*Macaca fuscata yakui*) on Yakushima Island, Japan', *Primates* 26: 105–20.

—— 1987. 'Intra- and inter-group interactions of an all-male group of Virunga mountain gorillas (*Gorilla gorilla beringei*)', *Primates* 28: 1–30.

—— 1992. 'Functional analysis of social staring behaviour in an all-male group of mountain gorillas', *Primates* 33: 523–44.

—— 2003. 'Bush-meat poaching and the conservation crisis in Kahuzi-Biega National Park, Democratic Republic of Congo', *Journal of Sustainable Forestry* 16: 115–35.

—— 2006. 'Playful encounters: the development of homosexual behaviour in male mountain gorillas', in V. Sommer and P.L. Vasey (eds) *Homosexual Behaviour in Animals*. Cambridge: Cambridge University Press, pp. 273–93.

—— 2008. 'History and present scope of field studies on *Macaca fuscata yakui* at Yakushima Island, Japan', *International Journal of Primatology* 29: 49–64.

Yamagiwa, J. and D.A. Hill. 1998. 'Intra-specific variation in the social organization of Japanese macaques: past and present scope of field studies in natural habitats', *Primates* 39: 257–74.

Yamakoshi, G. 2004. 'Evolution of complex feeding techniques in primates: is this the origin of great ape intelligence?' in A.E. Russon and D.R. Begun (eds). *The Evolution of Thought*. Cambridge: Cambridge University Press, pp. 140–71.

Yoshihiro, S., T. Furuichi, M. Manda, N. Ohkubo, M. Kinoshita, N. Agetsuma, S. Azuma, H. Matsubara, H. Sugiura, D.A. Hill, E. Kido, R. Kubo, K. Matsushima, K. Nakajima, T. Maruhashi, T. Oi, D.S. Sprague, T. Tanaka, T. Tsukahara and Y. Takahata. 1998. 'The distribution of wild Yakushima macaque (*Macaca fuscata yakui*) troops around the coast of Yakushima Island, Japan', *Primate Research* 14: 179–88.

7
Lost in Translation:
Field Primatology, Culture, and Interdisciplinary Approaches

Nobuyuki Kutsukake

Hatsusikure
Saru mo Komino wo
Hosikenari

Winter downpour - even the monkey needs a raincoat
in Sarumino (1691) by Matsuo Basho (a Japanese *Haiku* poet)

Introduction

This Japanese haiku, written about 300 years ago, describes how the famous poet Matsuo Basho and a Japanese macaque were freezing in winter and 'sharing' the same experience. The poem nicely demonstrates the connection Japanese people felt with macaques, and their feelings of close intimacy and empathy towards animals in general. There is no doubt that this attitude, and a sense of value towards nature or animals, is reflected in not only artistic, but also everyday human activities. Academic research is not an exception. Fieldwork and research in primatology and anthropology reflect the identities, thoughts and culture of researchers, irrespective of whether these reflections are explicit or implicit processes unto themselves. This is because different countries and cultures have their own social, religious, and historical backgrounds. There may be differences in attitudes towards nature, or in the lasting effect left by the founder of an academic discipline, and research traditions may also place constraints on current fieldwork practices.

Japanese primatology is one such example (Asquith 1986, 2000; Takasaki 2000; de Waal 2001, 2003). Japanese primatology began earlier and independently of primate research in Western countries (Europe and North America) and is unique in its perspective and history. Superficially, there seem to be no differences in fieldwork activities and practices between Japan and in Western countries, terms of employing habituation and individual identification of study animals, and quantitative measurements of their behaviour and ecology. However, it is also true that many researchers detected 'Japaneseness' in fieldwork studies by Japanese primatologists. It is important to examine how various perspectives produce a different understanding of the same research subject when discussing whether it is possible and meaningful to converge these divergent research traditions and fieldwork practices into an 'internationally standardized' natural science. In the first part of this chapter, I will discuss characteristics of fieldworks by Japanese primatologists and several related topics. This issue is not new and has been discussed previously by several researchers (Asquith 1986, 2000; Takasaki 2000; de Waal 2001, 2003). Indeed, the aim of this chapter is neither to conduct a comprehensive review of the history of Japanese primatology, nor to exhaustively list the characteristics of Japanese primatology; all of this information can be found in other publications (Asquith 1986, 1989, 2000; Takasaki 2000; de Waal 2001, 2003; Yamagiwa in this volume). Rather, this chapter reflects the views of a young researcher in his early thirties who has not been heavily influenced by traditions in Japanese primatology.

In the latter part of the chapter, I will discuss how research practices in primatology can be applied to the field study of other biological systems. Primate research is distinct from research on nonprimate animals because primates have distinct biological characteristics (e.g., large brain size relative to the body, long life history, and so on), and experiments are difficult to conduct both because of these distinct characteristics and for ethical reasons. Because of this, the field of primatology itself has unique characteristics. For example, there is a greater risk of anthropomorphism in this field than in other research areas. These unique biological characteristics inevitably shape our fieldwork practices and implicit biases when we interpret the study species, and these invisible tendencies are unnoticed as long as the researchers study only (nonhuman) primates. Therefore, it is important to discuss how gaining an interdisciplinary perspective on primatology and other research fields can contribute to both areas.

Brief history of Japanese primatology

In 1948, shortly after the end of World War II, Japanese primatologists (Dr Kinji Imanishi and his students at Kyoto University) began studies of the wild Japanese macaque, *Macaca fuscata,* on Koshima Island in the southern part of Japan (Takasaki 2000; Yamagiwa in this volume). Japanese primatologists have an advantage over European or American primatologists because they are able to study endemic primate species. There are no endemic primate species in Europe or North American, so European and American primatologists must go abroad to study wild primates. Provisioning, individual identification, and long term field studies are characteristics of classic Japanese primatology (although provisioning and individual identification were previously used by Western researchers: Asquith 1989, 2000; Yamagiwa in this volume). Since the 1950s, systematic observations of Japanese macaques have been conducted and have continued to the present day at multiple field sites. As a result, four study sites of provisioned Japanese macaques have been maintained since then. Study sites where researchers habituate and study macaques without provisioning were established in 1976 on Yakushima Island, and in 1982 on Kinkazan Island; these sites also continue to be maintained (Yamagiwa and Hill 1998).

In 1958, Japanese primatologists extended their surveys to various primate species located abroad. Long term field studies on African apes may be the most famous and successful of Japanese primatology projects. Researchers have also studied species in other regions, including Old World monkeys, New World monkeys, and prosimians (Takasaki 2000).

Early Japanese primatology studies strongly influenced not only primatology, but also general animal behaviour research. Individual identification and long-term studies are commonly used in current animal behaviour research. The contribution of Japanese primatology is not only methodological, but also academic. For example, sweet potato washing behaviour by Japanese macaques (Kawai 1965) was the first novel behaviour acquired via social learning to be reported. This study is now the basis for current animal culture research. Other important findings from early Japanese primatology include the first documentation of infanticide in the Hanuman langur, *Semnopithecus entellus* (Sugiyama 1965); the discovery of a stable group ('unit group' or 'community') of wild chimpanzee, *Pan troglodytes* (Nishida 1968); and long term field study of the wild bonobo, *Pan paniscus* (Kano 1992). These findings were published, in part, in the international journal *Primates,* published by the Japan Monkey Centre. *Primates*, which has been published since 1957, is the oldest primatological journal in the world. de Waal (2003) described the contribution of Japanese primatology to animal behaviour research as a 'silent invasion' because the Japanese origins of commonly used animal research techniques and ideas had gone largely unnoticed by Western researchers.

Traditions of Japanese primatology and my perspectives

As discussed, fieldwork studies have been conducted all over the world for decades and can be regarded as a speciality of Japanese primatology. The considerable number of publications by Japanese primatologists that appear in international academic journals and at international conferences demonstrates the important position that Japanese primatology occupies in this field. Despite its international status, Japanese primatology has several unique characteristics. It is led mainly by researchers of the 'Kyoto School' at Kyoto University (Takasaki 2000). Takasaki (2000) summarises their characteristics as follows: the strategic use of anthropomorphism; a belief in the power of good descriptive data; highly valued long term fieldwork; and a structural view of primate societies. In Japan, most primatologists study primates from an anthropological or comparative psychology perspective, but rarely from the perspective of behavioural ecology or evolutionary biology. Non-academic researchers often play important roles in studies of Japanese macaques such as the long term data collection describing sweet potato washing behaviour (de Waal 2001) and the continuous recording of demographic events (e.g., birth, death, immigration and emigration) by staff of the Monkey Parks tourist sites (Huffman 1991).

Western primatologists (i.e., American or European) occasionally argue that Japanese primatology has a different perspective and different fieldwork practices than primatology in Western countries. Most obviously, Japanese primatology is based on narrative descriptions with an overabundance of detailed data, and usually lacks theories or hypotheses to be tested. On the other hand, some Western researchers have recently begun paying attention to Imanishi's holistic perspectives towards understanding primates (Imanishi 1941; de Waal 2003). Why, then, does Japanese primatology differ from primatology in other countries or in other cultures? What are the pros and cons of Japanese primatology, and how do the unique perspectives of Japanese primatology contribute to the future of the disapline?

Before discussing these questions, several potential biases included in this chapter should be noted. Although it is tempting to simply dichotomise Japanese versus Western primatology, we need to be careful of this classification because there is variation among researchers both within Japan and within Western countries, and also because Western countries have different histories, traditions, and approaches (e.g., van Hooff 2000; Hinde 2000). However, Japanese primatology must adapt to current international standards for research practices. Therefore, the differences between Japanese primatology and that of Western countries must be relative, rather than absolute.

Also, it is necessary to note my position in primate research in Japan. For my undergraduate and masters work, I studied wild provisioned Japanese macaques (snow monkeys) at the Jigokudani Monkey Park in Nagano, Japan. At this study site, park staff have provisioned macaques for the benefit of tourists and have made detailed records of demographic events that have occurred since its establishment in 1962. When I studied Japanese macaques, I was not affected by the traditional fieldwork practices of Japanese primatology because I was only an academic researcher at this site and had little opportunity to interchange with the Kyoto School researchers. For my doctoral work, I studied wild chimpanzees at the Mahale Mountains National Park in Tanzania. Since 1965, Toshisada Nishida, Emeritus Professor at Kyoto University, has directed a long-term research project at this site with his colleagues and students. This was the first time I experienced the traditional fieldwork practices of Japanese primatology. My career as a primatologist, beginning with the Japanese macaque and continuing with chimpanzees, represents a 'standard' course for students of Japanese primatology. However, my education in Japanese primatology was relatively atypical for a number of reasons. I was educated in a 'Westernised' style because my promoter, Dr Duncan L. Castles, was a Scottish primatologist. My supervisor, Professor Toshikazu Hasegawa at the University of Tokyo, studied primates from a behavioural ecology perspective and had experience of studying in the UK. Therefore, in this semi-Western environment, I was educated to be a behavioural ecologist or evolutionary biologist, rather than a primatologist or anthropologist. Because I have never studied at Kyoto University, I have never been in a position to be influenced by either Imanishi or the Kyoto School of Primatology.

I have not been an enthusiastic reader of the theories by Imanishi or his students (e.g., Jun-ichiro Itani), and most of my knowledge has come from secondary sources. During my postdoctoral period, I participated in fieldwork organised by a research team from the UK, which helped me to learn how Western fieldwork practices differ from Japanese fieldwork practices (see below).

From my 'hybrid' perspective as a Japanese 'Western primatologist', I have mixed feelings about the different fieldwork practices in Japan and Western countries. I have experienced both styles and have learned that each style has advantages and disadvantages. Through such experience, I will discuss the current status and characteristics of Japanese primatology. Again, these discussions are not intended to be a comprehensive review of this topic; my aim is to reflect the opinions of one Japanese primatologist who has a different background and perspective than the majority of Japanese primatologists.

Characteristics of Japanese primatology

Fieldwork studies are composed of several processes including research planning before going to field, preliminary observation and data collection in the field, data analyses, and interpretation of the results. Here, I discuss four characteristics of Japanese fieldworks which I believe are the most explicit characteristics of Japanese primatology. These include ones that occur during the process of data collection in the field (data collection, observational methods, and researchers' priority) and during other processes (education, style of researches, and research planning).

Understanding and measuring

Researchers need to understand the study species to accurately measure it. By getting to know the study species, observers can identify its behavioural repertoire, predict individual behaviour from known behavioural sequences, promote efficient observation and develop plausible and testable predictions.

I sometimes suspect that Japanese primatologists believe it is more important to study a species than to obtain scientific measurements. There may be several reasons for this. First, Japanese primatologists appear to be obsessed with long-duration observation ('dusk to dawn' observation) and are sometimes called 'field-workaholics' by Western colleagues. Many Japanese primatologists (myself included) rarely take holidays while in the field and try to observe the study animals for as long as possible. The reason for these extensive observations may be the idea that an understanding of the study subject increases linearly or exponentially with observation time, particularly at the start of a study. In contrast, some Western primatologists of my acquaintance cease their observations and return to the field camp when they have finished collecting the data they need.

Second, some Japanese primatologists from the Kyoto School believe that it is better to not have any previous knowledge about the study species; in fact, veteran Japanese Kyoto School primatologists have advised me not to go to the library to read previous publications. Proponents of this style of research (which I call the 'from scratch' style) say that new question about the study species should be developed through intensive observation. I am often disappointed to find that many graduate students do not conduct extensive literature surveys when deciding upon their research plan. Whereas it is important to not have pre-existing prejudices about the study species and to cast healthy doubt on previous findings, it is a waste of time and energy for graduate students to report results that were first reported years earlier. I suspect that this research method prevails in Japanese primatology because it places a high priority on developing a personal understanding of the study subject, rather than on the scientific method.

Data collection and long term fieldwork

In current field studies of primates and also of other animals, long term continuous field research has become common practice. Many students, myself included, partake of the advantages of detailed demographic information contained in long-term field records. For example, I performed field studies at sites for the study of Japanese macaques and chimpanzees thirty-five years after the fieldwork was first begun. At both field sites, all of the individuals were habituated and had been identified, and detailed long term demographic information was already available.

Japanese primatology has a tradition of long term fieldwork, which has provided researchers with the unique opportunity to test hypotheses using a very large sample size (Yamagiwa and Hill 1998). However, although it sounds paradoxical, I believe that the systematic long term studies at most Japanese field sites do not meet current standards for long term field research. This is because whereas each researcher has his or her independent research topic, the data of different researchers are not combined, which means that only basic demographic data and not other long term data are available for these sites. This contrasts with several other long term field sites where multiple types of data (e.g., ecological, behavioural, and molecular) were collected by multiple researchers following the same protocol. The absence of long term field sites in Japan may result from the emphasis of Japanese primatologists on personal understanding over scientific measurement or from the fact Japanese researchers have had no good models for such long term field research. In addition, Japanese primatologists suffer from a lack of volunteers or research assistants who will remain in the field for long periods of time. In Western countries, researchers benefit from field assistants who stay in the field for long periods of time and collect data for the project in a standardized way. As a result, Western graduate students and researchers have larger sample sizes available to them than they could have collected by themselves over the short term. Because few primatology research projects in Japan have such research assistants in the field, Japanese students or researchers must collect all of their data on their own, resulting in small sample sizes and only short-term data, except for basic demographic data. At one field site on Yakushima Island, Japan, volunteers play a major role and have high scientific output (e.g., Yoshihiro et al. 1999; Hanya et al. 2003), but such fieldwork is still rare in Japan. Furthermore, there are no assistants or volunteers who remain in the field for long periods of time.

Anti-reductionism: descriptive approaches, holistic approaches and lack of theory

Some Western researchers have noted that Japanese primatology is characterized by a descriptive approach, without a clear theoretical framework or specific hypotheses to be tested (Asquith 2000; Strum and Fedigan 2000; but see de Waal 2001). This tendency remains strong. For example, at the annual conference of the Primate Society of Japan, both veteran and young primatologists show endless descriptive notes that lack biological explanations or clear hypotheses. Although I understand the effort made by researchers to collect this detailed data, I cannot find any rationale for these studies. The scientific significance of these papers cannot be understood, leaving the reader with feelings of 'so what?'

I admit that description is a fundamental process in natural science including field studies, because it usually precedes explanation or hypothesis testing (Altmann and Altmann 2003). Although it is impossible to judge for researchers which descriptive data will be a basis for theory-oriented studies in future, a descriptive approach has several pitfalls. For example, when using a descriptive approach, it is difficult to make other researchers understand the study's significance. In addition, the collected field data have low statistical power, which makes it difficult to draw useful conclusions. Why, then, do Japanese primatologists persist in using a descriptive style when the 'dominant paradigm' of current primatology is based on reductionism and a deductive framework? This question was analysed nicely by Asquith (2000), who concluded that many Japanese primatologists do not feel comfortable with reductionist research or hypothesis testing because such approaches may overlook the nature of the study species. In other words, Japanese primatologists do not like to 'squeeze the information out of nature' (Asquith 1986). Takasaki (2000) states that the different style of traditional Japanese primatology is an alternative to Western approaches. However, I disagree with this opinion unless such studies have clear ways to quantitatively and systematically explain the significance of the data.

It is easy to conclude that the historical and social environment has shaped the style of Japanese primatology. For example, the founder of Japanese primatology, Dr. Kinji Imanishi, was highly influential for later generations of Japanese primatologists and has been regarded as an icon of the holistic approach. In addition, I propose that the descriptive and holistic style has also been influenced by bicultural effects. Recent cultural psychology studies have shown that there are general differences in how East Asian (Japanese, Chinese and Korean) and Western people grasp the characteristics of an object (Nissbet 2004). Several experiments by Nissbet and his colleagues show that North East Asian people focus on the contextual aspects of objects and emphasize relational aspects between the focus object and other objects (Nissbet 2004). In contrast, Western people have a more focused analytical perspective towards objects. These cultural differences, if they also operate in academic research, may be related to the unique characteristics of Japanese primatology. Thus, I predict that primatologists in other Asian countries (China, Thailand, Indonesia or Vietnam) may use a different research style from the Western style that is based on their own culture and history (see Yamamoto and Alencar 2000 for Brazilian primatology as an example of a non-Western approach). Although the views of researchers from these countries are not included in this discussion of the cultural influences of primate researchers, it would be interesting to compare the styles among various countries.

Education system

The characteristics of Japanese primatology studies may be a result of Japan's educational system. When candidate graduate students in Japan begin their own research, they are not required to submit a formal research proposal or win a competitive scholarship; they are only required to pass the graduate school's entrance examination. As a result, graduate students can begin fieldwork, even if they do not have clear research plans and specific questions to be addressed through their fieldwork. Because of this, it is not uncommon for graduate students to finish the degree without having clearly specified the hypotheses or theory to be tested. Most undergraduate students do not have enough experience in field research or data collection, which may also hinder systematic and efficient research. Prospective students do not need to have experience as a research assistant in the field or to have actively volunteered at a field site before starting their research in graduate school.

Field researchers, in particular young graduate students, receive strong influences on their fieldwork practices from their supervisor, field colleagues and laboratory members. In other words, fieldwork practices are culturally inherited from generation to generation. In this regard, Japanese primatology is relatively closed to different fieldwork practices. Few Japanese primatologists have studied abroad, and most remain at the same university or research institute throughout their educational career. This viscosity of researchers derives an opportunity for Japanese young researchers to experience various fieldwork practices. To my knowledge, no Japanese primatologist has received a tenured position at a Western university. In contrast, Western researchers commonly move to new institutions and countries, where they are exposed to different research atmospheres and groups. These experiences influence their own studies and how they educate the next generation.

Advantages of Japanese primatology

Although I have been rather critical of many characteristics of Japanese primatology, the system also offers several advantages. First, many long term field sites are available to graduate or undergraduate students beginning their own fieldwork. These sites offer the potential for powerful long term data sets from multiple field sites, once data collection systems are introduced. Second, the different perspective and approach of Japanese primatology, relative to the Western style, raises new questions. For example, Japanese primatologists have been interested in personality and individual differences in primate species, and this is now the focus of current primatology research (e.g., Gosling et al. 2003). Japanese primatologists have been interested in social structures and interpersonal relationships, or contextual approaches to social behaviour. Currently, various analytic methods such as the emergence of complexity from simply ruled agents (Hemelrijk 2002; Rands et al. 2003), social network theory (Flack et al. 2006), and pattern detection from sequential data (Anolli et al. 2005) are available for primatologists. The introduction of these advanced methods will allow Japanese researchers to address new questions that have been difficult to investigate in the past.

In addition to these possibilities, I next discuss two areas where Japanese views may play important roles: conservation and case studies.

Primate conservation

Primate conservation has become an increasingly urgent problem in recent years. Several large-scale conservation projects to conserve primates and other animals or plants in developing countries have been conducted by Western researchers or conservationists. The success of primate conservation strategies partly depends on the understanding and cooperation of the local people. Given that the local people in each country or culture have a different history, religion, attitude, and sense of the value of nature, conservation strategies based on the Western mindset may not be viable everywhere. In some situations, a conservation strategy based on Western ideas may not be understood by the local people and may cause conflict. The perspective of Japanese primatology may provide a different primate conservation strategy.

Currently, primate conservation is a growing topic in Japanese primatology. Conservation and management problems for Japanese macaques, such as crop damage, have become one of the biggest issues faced by Japanese primatologists. In recent years, approximately 10,000 Japanese macaques have been removed each year in Japan. The genetic distinctness of the Japanese macaque is threatened by hybrid crosses with the rhesus macaque and Taiwanese macaque, which have been introduced into Japan. There are various opinions about how to deal with these problems. The 'best' strategies should be based not only on scientific efficiency but also on the sense of value that the Japanese people have towards nature. This is because understanding and cooperation by local people is indispensable in conservation activities. Here, Japanese primatologists can understand and sympathize with the sense of value of the local people, by which means the conservational strategies may be able to reflect the local opinion efficiently. Conservational issues that Japanese primatologists face are not restricted to Japanese macaques but can be found in other cases. In countries where Japanese primatologists have been conducting long-term research (i.e., Tanzania, Uganda, Indonesia, and so on), many Japanese primatologists commit the conservation activity on their study species. Conservation policies that are based on Japanese ideas may be better accepted by the local people in some countries where the local people have different ideas or sense of the value of nature from Western countries. Long term studies by Japanese primatologists will be a basis of communicating and understanding the local people's ideas. Therefore, even though various aspects of Japanese primatology may not be efficient in some basic areas of science, they may provide a slightly different conservation strategy from Western ones.

Tension between hypotheses testing and anecdotes or case studies

Another type of study where the traditional Japanese approach may prove advantageous are studies where N = 1. The N = 1 type of observations (i.e., anecdotes and case studies) are difficult to replicate, and general conclusions are difficult to draw. Therefore, such studies have sometimes received less value than studies that test hypotheses. However, N = 1 observations can demonstrate the occurrence of behaviours or social events that are too rare for systematic data collection to detect (e.g., infanticide, tool use, deception, group fission and dramatic changes in social condition). N = 1 studies have played an important role in primatology because of the difficulty in conducting primate experiments. Most primatologists think that such observations are as valuable as quantitative studies when there is enough theoretical rationale, when observational bias and subjective interpretation can be avoided by employing systematic observation methods, and when the generality of the results can be checked through further systematic studies.

One serendipitous example is the turnover in dominance between an alpha and a beta male in the Japanese macaque (Kutsukake and Hasegawa 2005). During more than fifty years of research on Japanese macaques and in primate behavioural research, only a few records have detailed agonistic turnovers between a top-ranked male and a group member(s) because of the unpredictability of such events and the difficulty in observing them. In addition, reports on dominance turnover contain data with substantial bias because systematic observation methods were not used. During my studies, I was fortunate not only to observe the whole process of dominance turnover, but also to use observation methods that exclude biases. That is, I used the focal-animal sampling method and the all-occurrence method to examine social interactions among six males. This allowed me to provide unbiased quantitative data and analyses of male–male aggression and coalition formation in probably the first systematic data on 'monkey politics' (Kutsukake and Hasegawa 2005).

Fieldwork with long-duration observations should theoretically result in more chances to view unusual events. However, it may not be possible for fieldworkers who collect data that are only sufficient to test specific hypotheses to systematically analyse a sudden event in context. In my case, I had collected data without purpose before the dominance turnover. Using that data, I could compare behaviour in the post-turnover period to behaviour in the pre-turnover period. These analyses may not have been possible if I had only collected data necessary for hypothesis testing. Thus, the descriptive data and long-duration observations of Japanese primatology have and will have much potential to provide many quantified case studies.

Application of primatological perspectives to other biological systems

Up to this point, I have contrasted the research practices within Japanese and Western primatology. I will now discuss the uniqueness of primatology relative to other subjects such as anthropology, psychology, and animal behaviour. What can primatological perspectives contribute to these other studies, and how do these different subjects promote our understanding of primates? Given that primates have several unique biological characteristics and that some researchers believe the separation between primatology and other academic areas is a problem (Harcourt 1993; Hauser 1994), it is also important to recognise the uniqueness and biases of primatology.

I have been fascinated with the application of methodologies or questions developed from primate studies to other species because such experiences offer a unique perspective on the understanding of both primates and other species. Here, I briefly introduce two example species to which primatological perspectives have been applied: human children and meerkats. I then discuss how the interchange of perspectives is fruitful for both primatology and other research areas.

Primatological perspectives on child development

The first project examined social development among Japanese children at a nursery school in Tokyo, Japan. The correlation between cognitive development in young children and sociality, and the effects of cultural background on behaviour are both interesting topics in behavioural science. In collaboration with a developmental psychologist, we have applied the observational and analytical methods developed in primate behavioural research to the study of child behaviour, including conflict resolution, prosocial behaviour, reciprocity and social networks (Fujisawa et al. 2005, 2006, 2008a, 2008b, 2009). This collaboration is fruitful because the primatological view cultivates new research areas in developmental psychology. The best example is studies of reconciliation. Reconciliation is defined as an affiliation between former opponents soon after aggression (de Waal and van Roosmalen 1979; Aureli et al. 2002) and is commonly observed in social primates (about forty species: Arnold and Aureli 2006). Primatologists developed an ethological observation method (the PC-MC method: de Waal and Yoshihara 1983) to study post-aggression behaviour. Primatological perspectives and the use of the PC-MC method have promoted a new understanding of reconciliation among children. For example, the primatological perspective provided empirical evidence for a function of reconciliation (the stress reduction in victim children: Fujisawa et al. 2005; see Lindburg et al. 1999), which had not been studied in traditional developmental psychology researches (Sackin and Thelen 1984; Laursen and Hartup 1989). Since studies that employ the primatological perspective use a standard observational method, it is possible to compare the results of studies from different countries. This has resulted in the new discovery of intercultural variation in the tendency and process of reconciliation (Butovskaya 2000, 2001; Fujisawa et al. 2005, 2006).

Experiencing European fieldwork practices through nonprimate fieldwork

I also apply primatological perspectives in field studies of the nonprimate social carnivore, meerkat (*Suricata suricatta*). This species lives in groups with multiple males and females in which the membership is relatively stable. It is a cooperatively breeding species in which nonparents rear the offspring of the dominant individuals

(Clutton-Brock et al. 2001). Since the mid-1990s, wild meerkats have been studied in the Kalahari Desert, South Africa, by a research team headed by Professor Tim Clutton-Brock of the University of Cambridge.

During my postdoctoral studies, I joined the meerkat project hoping to ask a bold question: are primate societies really 'complex' relative to nonprimate animals? Although it is generally thought that sociality in primates is more 'complex' than in other animals, there are no robust data on social behaviour in nonprimate species with which to make comparisons (see Kutsukake 2009). Thus, I sought an opportunity to study nonprimate social mammals using observational methods and research questions that I had used in primate research. I found several examples of strategic social behaviour (Kutsukake and Clutton-Brock 2006a, 2006b, 2008a, 2008b, 2010).

In addition to these findings, I was interested in experiencing a fieldwork system organised by a team of Western researchers. The meerkat project involves researchers, graduate students, and volunteers from Western countries, and I was the first researcher from an East Asian country to join the project. Several characteristics of the meerkat project differed from Japanese fieldwork practices, including the collective data collection systems staffed by volunteers following a specific observation protocol, hypothesis-driven research, and concentrated observation, rather than lengthy observations within a day. Most of the volunteers were students who wanted to experience fieldwork before beginning graduate school, so their motivation was high. This experience offered me the chance to be objective about the research practices of primatology in general and of Japanese primatology in particular.

However, I did feel that something was missing from this style of fieldwork. For example, in the meerkat project, observations were taken at two times during the day, in the morning and in the evening. Researchers and volunteers thought that there was no value in daytime observation because the animals are active mainly during the cooler morning and evening periods and do little or retreat into the burrow during the daytime. Thus, there had been no attempt to conduct an all-day observation. I conducted two weeks of all-day observations in the Kalahari Desert, where the maximum temperatures exceed 40°C and found that the previously held thought was incorrect: the meerkats were active during the daytime. I observed many interesting behaviours such as surreptitious mating of the dominant female with a rover male, group encounters with a bat-eared fox, and others. I felt that I had gained a new understanding of the meerkat; I tried to convey the significance of all-day observations to my Western colleagues, but they did not seem to understand my attitude. This experience taught me that my fieldwork style is quite 'Japanese,' although I preferred a Westernized paradigm when I studied primates.

In studying meerkats and recognizing the difficulties in labelling their behaviour, I realised that primatologists need to be more critical about how they define or label behaviour in primates. Meerkats creep in a ritualized fashion when subordinates approach dominant individuals. Because the morphology and behavioural repertoire of meerkats is quite different from that of humans and other primates, the behaviour was too subtle to be a definite subordinate signal. Therefore, researchers need to be very careful in their decisions about such behaviour. To determine whether this creeping behaviour is a subordinate signal requires confirmation that it is not used in other social contexts and examination of other contexts in which it occurs. Although I do not hesitate to use a word that represents the function of a particular behaviour, e.g., reconciliation or friendship, this experience made me recognise the risk of anthropomorphic labelling by primatologists, which may result in a distance between primatologists and researchers of behaviour in nonprimates.

One example of this issue comes from our primatological study. Ritualized nonagonistic behaviour typically observed during an encounter between individuals is often called 'greeting' behaviour. Greeting behaviour has been reported in various mammal species (e.g., East et al. 1993). Before we began our observations of greeting behaviour in black-and-white colobus monkeys (*Colobus guereza*: Kutsukake et al. 2006), we conducted an extensive literature survey on greeting behaviour. We were surprised to find that few previous studies actually investigated its function empirically. This is problematic because the a priori use of the term 'greeting' reminds us of the prejudice for the functions of behaviours, which may lead us to incorrect conclusions.

In sum, I feel that interdisciplinary approaches and fieldwork experiences in a different culture would facilitate unexpected findings and deep considerations on our study subjects. Such activities must be important for all researchers because, as discussed in this chapter by exemplifying Japanese primatology, the fieldwork practices are shaped by histories, traditions and culture that are specific to their affiliations. I have also considered that fieldwork practices and research paradigms of the traditional Japanese primatology are distinct from the current 'dominant paradigm' of primate studies. Comparative discussion of fieldwork practices will offer an interesting opportunity to rethink how the divergent perspectives will affect our scientific understanding of study subjects.

Conclusions and limitations

In this chapter, I discussed how different perspectives and cultures affect academic activity. Inevitably, this chapter has limitations. First, the discussion stems from my personal activity over the past nine years, both in Japan and abroad. Therefore, other Japanese primatologists must have different opinions and perspectives. The readers must be careful to avoid excessive generalization or the creation of a simple dichotomy between Japanese and Western styles. This will lead to incorrect conclusions because primatology in Western countries also has diverse perspectives and histories and because the differences may be absolute and not relative. I compared the fieldwork practices used in primate and nonprimate studies, which differ in various respects. I did not discuss the language barrier or research funding problems, which may be the greatest issues in current animal research.

In concluding, I have both comfortable and uncomfortable feelings about both traditional Japanese primatology and Western fieldwork practices. Being Japanese, I understand the practices and perspectives of traditional Japanese primatology because it is natural for the Japanese to seek an understanding of animals and of nature. However, I have also noticed that traditional Japanese primatology approaches are not efficient and cogent in the current dominant paradigm in natural sciences. As a researcher, I respect the efficiency of Western fieldwork practices, but the style makes me uncomfortable because I feel something is missing in these approaches and because they are not a natural way of understanding study subjects to the Japanese. I feel that I am a stranger to both circumstances, like the character played by the actor Bill Murray in the movie 'Lost in Translation' (2003). Perhaps mixing the advantages of both circumstances will offer a new perspective for future primatology and a way for a Japanese primatologist to 'negotiate' science (Asquith 2000).

Acknowledgements

Many thanks to Jeremy MacClancy for inviting me to the excellent conference 'Fieldwork: examining its practice by biological anthropologists and primatologists', which provided an opportunity to think about my fieldwork practices. I thank Jeremy MacClancy and Agustin Fuentes for editing the book and constructive comments, Juichi Yamagiwa and Hideshi Ogawa for discussion, participants of the conference for stimulating discussion and for an enjoyable time, and Keiko K Fujisawa for his support. This study was financially supported by Japan Society for Promotion of Science, RIKEN Special Postdoctoral Researchers Program, and The Japan Foundation.

References

Altmann, S.A. and J. Altmann. 2003. 'The transformation of behaviour field studies', *Animal Behaviour* 65: 413–23.

Anolli, L., S. Duncan, and M. Magnusson. 2005. *The Hidden Structure of Social Interaction: from Genomics to Cultural Patterns*. Amsterdam: IOS Press.

Arnold, K. and F. Aureli. 2006. 'Postconflict reconciliation' in C.J. Campbell, A. Fuentes, K.C. MacKinnon, M. Panger and S.K. Bearder (eds) *Primates in Perspective*. New York: Oxford University Press, pp. 592–608.

Asquith, P.J. 1986. 'Anthropomorphism and the Japanese and Western traditions in primatology' in J.G. Else and P.C. Lee (eds) *Primate Ontogeny, Cognition and Social Behavior*. Cambridge: Cambridge University Press, pp. 61–71.

_____ 1989. 'Provisioning and the Study of Free-ranging Primates: History, Effects and Prospects', *Yearbook of Physical Anthropology* 32: 129–58.

_____ 2000. 'Negotiating science: internationalization and Japanese primatology' in S. Strum and L.M. Fedigan (eds) *Primate Encounters: Models of Science, Gender, and Society*. Chicago, Illinois: University of Chicago Press, pp. 165–83.

Aureli, F., M. Cords, and C.P. van Schaik. 2002. 'Conflict resolution following aggression in gregarious animals: a predictive framework', *Animal Behaviour* 64: 325–43.

Butovskaya, M.L. 2001. 'Reconciliation after conflicts: Ethological Analysis of Post-conflict Interactions in Kalmyk Children' in J.M. Remirez and D.S. Richardson (eds) *Cross-

cultural Approaches to Aggression and Reconciliation. Huntington, NY: Nova Science Publishers, pp. 167–90.

Butovskaya, M.L., P. Verbeek, T. Ljungberg, and A. Lunardini. 2000. 'A Multicultural View of Peacemaking among Young Children' in F. Aureli and F.B.M. de Waal (eds) *Natural Conflict Resolution*. London: University of California Press, pp. 243–58.

Clutton-Brock, T.H., A.F. Russell, L.L. Sharpe, P.N.M. Brotherton, G.M. McIlrath, S. White and E.Z.Cameron. 2001. 'Effects of helpers on juvenile development and survival in meerkats', *Science* 293: 2446–9.

East, M.L., H. Hofer and W. Wickler. 1993. 'The Erect Penis is a Flag of Submission in a Female-dominated Society: Greetings in Serengeti Spotted Hyenas', *Behavioral Ecology and Sociobiology* 33: 355–70.

Flack, J.C., M. Girvan, F.B.M. de Waal, and D.C. Krakauer. 2006. 'Policing Stabilizes Construction Social Niches in Primates', *Nature* 439: 426–9.

Fujisawa, K.K., N. Kutsukake and T. Hasegawa. 2005. 'Pattern of Reconciliation after Aggression among Japanese Preschool Children', *Aggressive Behavior* 31: 138–52.

_____ 2006. 'Peacemaking and Consolation in Japanese Preschoolers Witnessing Peer Aggression', *Journal of Comparative Psychology* 120: 48–57.

_____ 2008a. 'Reciprocity of Prosocial Behavior in Japanese Preschool Children', *International Journal of Behavioral Development* 32: 89–97.

_____ 2008b. 'The Stabilizing Role of Aggressive Children in Affiliative Social Networks among Preschoolers', *Behaviour* 145: 1577–600.

_____ 2009. 'Social Network Analyses of Positive and Negative Relationships among Japanese Preschool Classmates', *International Journal of Behavioural Development* 33: 193–201.

Gosling, S.D., S.O. Lilienfeld, and L. Marino. 2003. 'Personality' in D. Maestripieri (ed.) *Primate Psychology*. Cambridge, MA: Harvard University Press, pp. 254–88.

Hanya, G., S. Yoshihiro, K. Zamma, R. Kubo, and Y. Takahata. 2003. 'New Method to Census Primate Groups: Estimating Group Density of Japanese Macaques by Point Census', *American Journal of Primatology* 60: 43–56.

Harcourt, A.H. 1993. 'Does Primate Socioecology Need Nonprimate Socioecology?', *Evolutionary Anthropology* 7: 3–7.

Hauser, M.D. 1994. 'Primatology: Some Lessons from and for Related Disciplines', *Evolutionary Anthropology* 5: 182–6.

Hemelrijk, C.K. 2002. 'Understanding Social Behaviour with the Help of Complexity Science', *Ethology* 108: 655–71.

Hinde, R.A. 2000. 'Some Reflections on Primatology at Cambridge and the Science Studies Debate' in S. Strum and L.M. Fedigan (eds) *Primate Encounters: Models of Science, Gender, and Society*. Chicago, Illinois: University of Chicago Press, pp. 104–15.

van Hooff, J.A.R.A.M. 2000. 'Primate Ethology and Socioecology in the Netherlands' in S. Strum and L.M. Fedigan (eds) *Primate Encounters: Models of Science, Gender, and Society*. Chicago, Illinois: University of Chicago Press, pp. 116–37.

Huffman, M.A. 1991. 'History of the Arashiyama Japanese macaques in Kyoto, Japan' in L.M. Fedigan and P. Asquith (eds) *The Macaques of Arashiyama: Thirty-five Years of Study in Japan and the West*. New York: SUNY Press, pp. 21–53.

Imanishi, K. 1941. *Japanese View of Nature: The World of Living Things*. Translated 2002 by P.J. Asquith. H. Kawakatsu, S. Yagi, H. Takasaki (eds.). New York: Routledge Curzon.

Kano T. 1992. *The Last Ape: Pygmy Chimpanzee Behavior and Ecology*. California: Stanford University Press.

Kawai, M. 1965. 'Newly-acquired pre-cultural behavior of the natural troop of Japanese monkeys on Koshima islet', *Primates* 6: 1–30.

Kutsukake, N. In press. 'Complexity, dynamics and diversity of sociality in group-living mammals', *Ecological Research* 24: 521–31.

Kutsukake, N. and D.L. Castles. 2001. 'Reconciliation and variation in postconflict stress in Japanese macaques (*Macaca fuscata fuscata*): testing the integrated hypothesis', *Animal Cognition* 4: 259–68.

Kutsukake, N. and T.H. Clutton-Brock. 2006a. 'Aggression and submission reflect reproductive conflict between females in cooperatively breeding meerkats', *Behavioral Ecology and Sociobiology* 59: 541–8.

—— 2006b. 'Social function of allogrooming in cooperatively breeding meerkats', *Animal Behaviour* 72: 1059–68.

—— 2008a. 'The number of subordinates moderates intra-sexual competition among males in cooperatively breeding meerkats', *Proceedings of the Royal Society of London, Series B* 275: 209–16.

—— 2008b. 'Do meerkats engage in conflict management following aggression? Reconciliation, submission, and avoidance', *Animal Behaviour* 75: 1441–53.

—— 2010 'Grooming and the value of social relationships in cooperatively breeding meerkats', *Animal Behaviour* 79: 271–79.

Kutsukake, N. and T. Hasegawa. 2005. 'Dominance turnover between an alpha and a beta male and dynamics of social relationships in Japanese macaques', *International Journal of Primatology* 26: 775–800.

Kutsukake, N., N. Suetsugu and T. Hasegawa. 2006. 'Pattern, distribution, and function of greeting behaviour among black-and-white colobus', *International Journal of Primatology* 27: 1271–91.

Laursen, B. and W.W. Hartup. 1989. 'The dynamics of preschool children's conflicts', *Merrill Palmer* Q 35: 281–97.

Nisbett, R. 2004. *The Geography of Thought: How Asians and Westerners Think Differently...and Why.* Free Press.

Nishida, T. 1968. 'The social group of wild chimpanzees in the Mahali Mountains', *Primates* 9: 167–224.

Rands, S.A., G. Cowlishaw, R.A. Pettifor, J.M. Rowcliffe, and R.A. Johnstone. 2003. 'The spontaneous emergence of leaders and followers in foraging pairs', *Nature* 423: 432–44.

Sackin, S. and E. Thelen. 1984. 'An ethological study of peaceful associative outcomes to conflict in preschool children', *Child Development* 55: 1098–102.

Strum, S. and L.M. Fedigan. 2000. *Primate Encounters: Models of Science, Gender, and Society.* Chicago, Illinois: University of Chicago Press.

Sugiyama, Y. 1965. 'On the social change of hanuman langurs (*Presbytis entellus)* in their natural condition', *Primates* 6: 381–418.

Takasaki, H. 2000. 'Traditions of the Kyoto School of field primatology in Japan' in S. Strum and L.M. Fedigan (eds) *Primate Encounters: Models of Science, Gender, and Society.* Chicago, Illinois: University of Chicago Press, pp. 151–64.

de Waal, F.B.M. 2001. *The Ape and the Sushi Master.* New York: Basic Books.

—— 2003. 'Silent invasion: Imanishi's primatology and cultural bias in science', *Animal Cognition* 6: 293–9.

de Waal, F.B.M. and A. van Roosmalen. 1979. 'Reconciliation and consolation among chimpanzees' *Behavioral Ecology and Sociobiology* 5: 55–66.

de Waal, F.B.M. and D. Yoshihara. 1983. 'Reconciliation and redirected affection in rhesus monkeys', *Behaviour* 85: 224–41.

Yamagiwa, J. and D.A. Hill. 1998. 'Intraspecific variation in the social organization of Japanese macaques: past and present scope of field studies in natural habitats', *Primates* 39: 257–73.

Yamamoto, M.E. and A.I. Alencar. 2000. 'Some characteristics of scientific literature in Brazilian primatology' in S. Strum and L. M. Fedigan (eds) *Primate Encounters: Models of Science, Gender, and Society*. Chicago, Illinois: University of Chicago Press, pp. 184–93.

Yoshihiro, S., M. Ohtake, H. Matsubara, K. Zamma, G. Han'ya, Y. Tanimura, H. Kubota, R. Kubo, T. Arakane, M. Hirata, M. Furukawa, A. Sato, and Y. Takahata. 1999. 'Vertical distribution of wild Yakushima macaques (*Macaca fuscata yakui*) in the Western area of Yakushima Island, Japan: preliminary report', *Primates* 40: 409–15.

8

Measuring Meaning and Understanding in Primatological and Biological Anthropology Fieldwork:
Context and Practice

Agustín Fuentes

After the study of fossils and living animals, when theories have taken definite form, then experiments should be planned. Particularly the importance of adaptive complexes and the precise nature of adaptation can be advanced far beyond the level of individual opinion.
–Sherwood Washburn 1951

We are primates, products of the evolutionary process, and the promise of primatology is a better understanding of the peculiar creature we call man.
–Sherwood Washburn 1973

Introduction

In the North American school of biological anthropology and primatology our modern call to action in fieldwork owes a great deal to the inspiration of Sherwood Washburn. His emphasis, amongst other facets, was on the importance fieldwork as a main baseline for the construction of testable hypotheses. In the Japanese tradition, as illustrated by Pam Asquith, Juichi Yamagiwa, and Nobu Katsukake in this volume, Kinji Imanishi for played a similar role. As primatologists and biological anthropologist our goals for fieldwork can be summarized by a few salient questions (Table 8.1). The answers to these questions are then the driving forces behind the creation and modification of our methodologies.

Table 8.1. Goals for fieldwork in primatology and biological anthropology.

What is human and how do we know it? Fieldwork across cultures and populations provides a view of what humans do on a regular basis – the patterns and variations in human behaviour
How do humans function? Fieldwork provides us with substantive data on human physiological structure and function that can be modeled and tested in the laboratory
Can we see Primates as primates and People as primates? By studying nonhuman primates as well as human primates (the comparative approach) we derive an understanding of both primate wide trends and primate particularities that are present only in specific lineages of primates …this fieldwork is extremely important for the understanding of the phylogenetic origins of behaviour and structure

Because we are interested in understanding why human and nonhuman primates do what they do, and what our measurements of behaviour and structure mean, we go to the field to collect data. Because we rely on field data as the most accurate reflection of real-world functioning of human and primate bodies the meaning of our data is extremely important to our overall understanding of being human or being primate. That is, we see field data as those data that provide us with the greatest insight into how organisms actually function in the complex reality of day to day existence as opposed to the carefully controlled assessments of particular facets of behaviour and physiology that we can examine in the lab.

Field data are rarely the true measures we see them as. That is, the data seldom carry the totality of information necessary to fully interpret outcomes. This is well known to researchers and we practice and teach care when collecting field data. However, even the most skilled field practitioners can inadvertently create substantial problems during field data collection. We can fall prey to the conflating of measurement with interpretation, we can make the assumption that assessing data is equal to understanding data, and we can fail to recognize and incorporate important biases during our initial assessments of data. These problematic patterns are largely due to the attraction of seeing wild or free ranging behaviour as it happens, which immediately stimulates our desires to understand what we are seeing.

The goal of collecting field data is the measurement of behaviour and bodies, ostensibly the facts of existence. To avoid inherent bias these data should be analyzed only after they have been collected, not simultaneously with collection. However, many of us fail to remember that we cannot and should not interpret what we are seeing as we are collecting data. This is best illustrated by Phyllis Dolhinow's use of the phrase 'I would not have seen it had I not believed it' (Dolhinow 1999). That is, data are of the highest quality when we do not attempt to interpret what we are seeing as we see, and record, it. For the experienced fieldworker it is very difficult not to see the beginning of a behaviour and immediately think 'aha, I know what is going to happen next.' Even if we are correct in our assumptions (as we frequently are) this frame of mind can alter the records we are collecting. For this very reason we use structured data collection tools and methodologies that attempt to inhibit our ability to interpret while recording.

Simply because we can assess the data and discover patterns within it does not imply that we understand the underlying function and/or origin of the patterns. While understanding emerges from repeated assessment and testing, we have to be careful not to make the leap from one to the other quickly. Also, biases created by the constraints of field situations, such as temporal restrictions on field activities, personal experiences and the paradigms from which we derive our basal understandings of how patterns emerge, also impact the data we collect.

In response to these issues this chapter examines the various confounds at play in the collection and assessment of field data in primatology and biological anthropology. While nothing presented here is new, it remains a very important aspect of any discourse on fieldwork and thus in a book on fieldwork should be one of the focal points.

Basic confounds: context and methods

The first significant component of understanding and meaning in our fieldwork is context. Here by context I propose that the (sub-)discipline of the fieldworker (biological anthropology vs. primatology) and the regional and national history of that arena of inquiry has substantial impact on how one goes about asking questions. The issue of nationality is eloquently examined by Pam Asquith and Nobu Katsukake (this volume) so I will not dwell on it in this chapter. However, I will add my voice as an emphatic reminder that much of what we do is rooted in deep traditions of various field work cultures and that one should be aware of his or her cultural history as he/she embarks on data collection or reads the published work of others.

A relevant component of context is the degree to which an individual is engaged with, or by, the various perspectives that ally with biological anthropology and primatology. A biological anthropology fieldworker strongly allied with a psychological approach may seek out different data than one with an evolutionary biology perspective even if asking a similar question. Thus researchers allied with multiple fields and paradigms can embark on data collection from distinct contexts relative to one another and their datasets may look different even when examining the same subjects.

The second and probably most critical component that shapes our field data is the methods by which we collect it. This is a basic point of information that all researchers are taught, but even the most practiced fieldworker can fall into the trap of tunnel vision in regards to methodologies. Here I suggest that different methodologies provide distinct lenses with which to view behaviour and physiology and thus careful consideration and examination of the choice of lens utilized can inform us about the data produced from such activities. Different practitioners favour different methods based on their interest, training and the questions at hand, however, that does not imply that the choices are always the correct ones or that other methods applied to the same data sets will show the same outcomes.

Methodologies in primatology and biological anthropology

When considering field work in primatology and biological anthropology we can see that there are some general similarities despite working on human and nonhuman organisms. In collecting physiological measures one can overlap in the assessment tools to a large degree due to the phylogenetic relationships between primates. For example, many of the hormone metabolite tests used on nonhuman primates are those that were developed for humans and the same is true for many of the genetic markers (DiFiore and Gagneux, 2007; Lasley and Savage, 2007; Ray, 2007). However, the converse is less practiced in that those markers developed for nonhuman primates are seldom used on humans. This does give us some assuredness that we are measuring similar physiological systems, but it does not immediately tell us the meaning of those systems in the organism of interest. For example, the work of Robert Sapolsky on behaviour and endocrine function in baboons has led to similar work with humans. However, these same stress response systems appear to have some important differences in outcomes (meanings) in human and baboon societies (Sapolsky 2004).

In observational measures there are methodological similarities when collecting data to construct general or daily activity budgets (Table 8.2). The patterns and formats by which observers record ad-libitum, or by chance, notes are also quite similar between primatology and biological anthropology. Over the last forty years there has been cross-fertilization between ethnography and primatology producing a methodological practice of observation that has become incorporated into modern biological anthropological approaches to observing humans. However, these similarities (between methods of observing nonhuman primates and humans) are among fairly superficial measures (activity budgets and gross behavioural profiles) and can potentially create false similarities in interpretation of the data.

Table 8.2. The Methodological differences and similarities between primatology and biological anthropology.

Methodological differences in primatology and biological anthropology	
Primatology	**Biological Anthropology**
Scan samples	Informant focus data collection
Group scans	Third party reports
Focal scans	Interviews
All-occurrence samples	Culturally limited all-occurrence samples
Continuous	Continuous
Select variables	Select variables
Limits of observation	Limits of Cultural context
Biomarkers w/capture	Biomarkers w/o capture
Observer impact	Participant observation/impact

In the arena of differences between primatology and biological anthropology we see the greatest potential for miscommunication across research results. For example, primatologists are limited by access to the group ('solved' via habituation, which may create its own problems) and by the observation conditions (one can lose a monkey in forest cover). Observing Humans on the other hand one can encounter a variety of cultural limitations on observability and access. Thus the gender/age of the fieldworker and his/her linguistic/social engagement with the people being observed can radically impact the observations themselves. This may lead to problems when attempting to generalize or universalize results across these related spheres of interest. For example, comparing results of nonhuman primate studies reporting on male-male competitive behaviour inherently produces a distinct set of data than a similar male-male competition study in humans. In this same example we might measure reproductive investment in two very different ways; using occasional behavioural protection of an infant by a male langur monkey versus social investment in a child's education, food and housing by an adult male human. In this case we must ask ourselves: are these measures equal when attempting to assess meaning and understand a system of male mating investment? Even two studies of similar behaviour in humans by different fieldworkers can produce distinct data sets if appropriate controls are not utilized.

The use of similar biomarkers in nonhuman primates and humans can produce distinct types of data as the nonhuman primates must usually be trapped and sedated prior to drawing samples whereas the humans are not. Even the use of fecal samples produced distinct patterns as human cultural rules and contexts surrounding defecation and urination vary substantially more than nonhuman primate behavioural restrictions on such behaviour. This comes into play when moving back and forth between human and other primates in the recent discussions about field data relative to hormone levels such as testosterone, cortisol and oxytocin for example (Carter 2004; Sapolsky 2004).

Of course, language also complicates the methodological endeavour. We are more reliant on interpretive meaning of data from nonhuman primates, which is not to say that a good deal of human data are also open to broad interpretation. Rather, we are not able to question the primates in the same manner we can humans. We have no access to linguistic clues and symbolic manipulation to contextualize the behaviours we observe and record in the free ranging nonhuman primates. This is can also be a confound in interpreting human data; language and symbol greatly enhance our ability to deceive and manipulate meaning. Language, and its concomitant cognitive context, also allows us to 'think' ourselves into the mind of another human in a way that we cannot with another primate, even when we share a multitude of similar physiological and morphological patterns with those primate cousins (see related discussion in Fuentes 2006).

Finally, it is also worth noting that the human subjects protocols and the animal subjects protocols, and the ethical issues surrounding them, differ. Researchers must acquire these permissions prior to engaging in research projects, and the differences can also shape the methodologies and subsequent data generated by such projects.

Therefore data from field studies in primatology and biological anthropology can be different even when similar methods are used. This is an important consideration in trying to assess data derived from these two intertwined sub-disciplines. Similarities may be superficial such as in the case of activity budget, or they may not be (even in the same case). However, simple one-to-one correlations across primates and humans are fraught with complexity thus field data should not be taken at face value without multiple assessments of the issue at hand.

Care must be taken when comparing data derived from similar methodologies on humans and primates even when constructing primate wide trends. Caution must also be used when making comparisons (such as in mating behaviour, aggression, infant care-taking, etc ...) and using those comparisons to initiate research agendas (as per Washburn's 'New Physical Anthropology'). In other words, our use of field-work to test and construct hypotheses about primates and humans is in and of itself a complex exercise filled with both superficial and substantive similarities. The methods utilized and the contexts in which those methods are employed can have substantial impact on the resulting data and therefore on our attempts to assign meaning to the data and derive understanding from those meanings.

What constitutes natural behaviour?

In addition to the context and the methodologies we practice, the conceptualization of natural in the field, assumptions about what we see in the field, the proclivity to think in terms of species-specific behaviour, and the potential conflicts created by the differences between approaches favoring inductive and deductive approaches are relevant to thinking about the production and assessment of field data.

A major problem revolving around the concept of natural encountered in fieldwork scenarios is the notion that field observations (of humans or other primates) are recording behaviours in an environment that is minimally anthropogenically altered and/or that is disconnected from facets of the global ecosystem. This is seen in primatology with the drive to find new or novel sites at locations distant from human settlement and in human studies by a focus on tribal or forager peoples in settings remote relative to urban centres (seen also as 'remote' from modernity or even post-modernity and representing a possible 'link' to our forager past). Over the past few decades it has become readily apparent that these assumptions about isolation or minimalization of modern impact are potentially serious errors.

A second fallacy of natural is the concept that measuring one population or subpopulation can present a reliable measure of a species norm, or what is typical (read natural) behaviour for a given species. Primatology has only recently emerged from this misconception as multiple site studies on the same species continued to demonstrate remarkable variability in behavioural and physiological responses at the same time that some distinct common patterns emerge/remain (Campbell et al. 2007).

A main assumption in both the issues of natural and of species specificity is the notion that the anthropogenic impact and local histories are minimal enough to ignore when in most cases they are not. An example from primatology exemplifies this. Sapolsky and Share (2004) provide an example from their study of two groups of baboons. This study began with observations of two groups, one who frequented a tourist lodge garbage dump and another that lived in the forest away from the human activity. The two groups had somewhat distinct behavioural and ecological profiles. Over time the higher ranking adult males from the forest group began to forage occasionally in and around the tourist lodge group. These adult males were highly aggressive and frequently would have to fight with the males and other individuals in the tourist lodge group for access to the high quality refuse at the forage site. At one point in time a quantity of tainted meat was dumped by local humans at the site resulting in the tourist lodge group and the aggressive males from the forest group suffering substantial mortality. The remaining males in the forest group happened to be rather pacific in their behavioural profile, especially relative to the highly aggressive males that died from the tainted meat forage. Over time as young males matured in the group they acquired the pacific behavioural patterns of the surviving males and the whole behavioural profile of the group shifted radically from aggressive to affiliative.

This example challenges both what is natural and what is typical simultaneously. The baboon males exhibited the capacity for both aggressive and pacific temperaments and the foraging and demographic patterns were affected by anthropogenic interactions, even in the forest group where most individuals did not interact with humans of human areas. Observers not viewing this entire sequence (local history) and only collecting data at specific 'slices' of time would report very different patterns of behaviour in the forest group and potentially offer quite different explanations of their meaning.

It is common to assume that what we see in the field reflects an adaptive response to specific selective environments. This was often seen as a simple truth: that field behaviour is natural, thus has arisen as an adaptation in response to selection pressures as organisms strive towards optimal solutions. The reality of fieldwork interceded by at least the 1980s and this simple assumption about optimality transitioned into the current paradigmatic parsimony explanation based on functional hypotheses. That is, if the behaviour we see is potentially 'costly' for the organism in terms of energy or reproductive output then it must have arisen (or is maintained) through some selective influences and, thus, may be seen as a response to selective challenges. The problem with this perspective is that it results in assuming we understand the meaning (or function) of a behaviour simply because of its occurrence in a field setting. Seeing a behaviour commonly expressed in a field setting does not necessarily tell us that the behaviour is functional, adaptive or even the best response to a given challenge. These understandings come from much greater analyses of the behaviour in and across contexts. While most fieldworkers are well aware of this confound it remains a common assumption amongst practitioners. If a behaviour is exhibited in the field in a 'relatively' normal environment, or in a particularly challenging environment, then we usually assume it is a functional response. This is a potential error of assigning meaning and assuming understanding prior to careful analyses.

While fieldworkers are less and less likely to assume species-specific behaviour and physiologies today, it does still occur and is relevant to this discussion. Multiple factors (Table 8.3) will impact what our data look like and each plays an important role in the creation of meaning and subsequent understanding. The representative sampling issue is of particular importance in regards to human biology and behaviour studies. Many psychologically allied approaches in biological anthropology particularly in mating strategies theory (Buss and Schmidt 1993, Miller 2000) and game theory/cooperation studies (see Barrett et al. 2002) rely heavily on student samples as proxy for field conditions. While this is a practical response to the difficulty of getting subjects and controlling for subjects in cross-cultural contexts this remain a real problem as college students are a relatively poor representative sample of the human species

Table 8.3. Multiple factors impact what our data look like and each plays an important role in the creation of meaning and subsequent understanding in short vs. long term studies.

| Short vs. long term studies |
| Individuals vs. Group vs. Groups vs. Populations – representative sampling |
| Inter- & Intra-specific comparisons |
| Researcher vs. Research team vs. Multiple teams |

A final additional confound, the conflict between inductive and deductive (a posteriori and a priori) approaches in fieldwork, is worth mentioning. I tend to think of this as a pseudo conflict because I believe it should not be a problem for researchers. However, under certain paradigmatic perspectives deductive approaches based on apriori hypotheses are more highly valued than inductive approaches and basic natural history/baseline data collection (van Schaik and Kappeler 2002). This is a problem as assumptions of sufficient baseline understandings change the meaning of data. If we assume we already know how a system works, then there is a higher likelihood of our data reinforcing this assumption. This is why both inductive and deductive approaches should be equally valorized as complementary approaches, not hierarchically related methodologies. The conflict interpretation is best combated by researchers being open to diverse paradigmatic perspectives, employing multi-disciplinary approaches and realizing that baseline data collection and hypothesis testing are equally valid partners rather than steps on a hierarchy of value. It is also worth noting that recent emerging complexity in both evolutionary and biocultural theory comes with a built in connectivity between apriori and aposteriori approaches (Odling-Smee et al. 2003, Stamps 2003, West-Eberhardt 2003).

A case study

Here I review a case study from primatology to demonstrate the complexities inherent in measuring meaning and understanding in fieldwork discussed above. The case of gibbon social organization and behaviour provides a robust exemplar of how context, methods, and paradigmatic orientation combined with a significant temporal factor can influence and structure the ways in which field data are understood and assessed. Here I give a brief summary of the broader review presented in Malone and Fuentes (in press) and Fuentes (2000).

The gibbons are a group of apes found throughout parts of South and Southeast Asia. They are represented by four genera and twelve species making up the family Hylobatidae. Aside from humans they are the most geographically widespread apes. Even in the earliest stages of primatological investigations the Hylobatids, or lesser apes, played a significant role in method and theory. The fieldwork by Carpenter (1940) is amongst the first examples of modern primatological field studies and set a basal stage for the expansion of primatology as a discipline in North America. Interestingly, Sherwood Washburn was a research assistant on one of Carpenter's main research trips to Asia and the experience he had there, melding primate observation and anatomical/morphometric analyses, may have laid a portion of the impetus and theoretical perspectives eventually resulting his call for a 'New Physical Anthropology'. Although cautious in his assertions about what he saw and recorded, Carpenter did report that the gibbons appeared to occur in groups that resemble nuclear families: an adult male, an adult female and one or more offspring. Carpenter and his team observed a few groups with apparently more than two adults, but gave them little consideration (Fuentes 2000). This assumption of a 'nuclear family' grouping pattern become the normative state for baseline perceptions of gibbons from the 1940s on. It began to be associated with a set of particular characteristics, the most prominent of which is the 'pair bond' and its assumed monogamous social structure.

The 'pair bond' or predictable, stable and long-lasting relationship between two unrelated adults is, for some, the basal unit of social organization in many primate taxa. Several authors proposed the pair bond as the central aspect in models of the evolution of lemur, gibbon, and human societies (Jolly 1998; van Schaik and Kappeler 1997; Lovejoy 1981; Palombit 1999; Wrangham et al. 1999). In these cases the pair bond is associated with monogamous mating and a suite of behavioural characteristics that act to maintain the mating and social bond between the pair. The focus on the pair bond is primarily rooted in the search for its evolutionary or functional origins, the manner in which selection pressures may have produced pair bonds, their associated behavioural profiles, and how pair bonding relates to individuals' genetic fitness (see Fuentes 1999, 2002). As such, the occurrence and maintenance of the pair bond becomes a critical basal element in the theorizing on the evolution of primate, and human, social organization. This status combined with the strong positive socio-moral association of monogamy and pair bonds (frequently shorthanded as 'marriage') in North American and European society and Judeo-Christian traditions make monogamy/pair bonds very interesting to both evolutionary theorists and individuals searching for explanations of our current moral and social systems (Fuentes 2000; Hrdy, 1981; Symons 1979; Wrangham et al. 1999).

In this context study of the gibbons moves beyond being simply a primatological endeavour and plays a prominent role in the construction of broader evolutionary hypotheses for the occurrence of two adult, pair-bonded, or 'monogamous' social organization (Mitani 1984; Palombit 1999; van Schaik and Dunbar 1990; Tilson 1980; Wittenberger and Tilson 1980). From the earliest field studies to more recent fieldwork (Brockelman and Srikosamatara 1984; Chivers 1974; Ellefson 1974; Leighton 1987; Mitani 1984), the hylobatids were seen as the 'paragons of fidelity', the model family unit, and the standard bearers of the monogamous primates. This then acted to provide impetus for their study in regards to the potential insight they could provide to the functional understandings of said theoretical perspectives (monogamy, in this case).

However, as early as 1940 Carpenter warned, 'It was found that the gibbon family pattern with limited variations characterized gibbon societies. ... But this description may be an overgeneralization' (Carpenter 1940). So, while there were tentative warnings and cautionary statements regarding the use of gibbons as 'model' monogamous systems, they still were held as the prototypical primate to study to understand monogamy, with the caveat that 'some extremes to a strictly monogamous patterns have been observed, but typically in extreme circumstances' (Chivers 2005). Thus deviations from the expected grouping pattern were aberrant and not included in data based attempts to understand gibbon social and evolutionary patterns. The 'monogamous' model for the gibbons included a suite of associated characteristics that fieldworkers expected to see during their data collection. These included a species-ubiquitous pattern of pair bonded adults residing in nuclear families, monogamous mating within the pair, long term fidelity between the pair, territoriality and aggression between neighbouring groups/pairs, and expulsion of offspring by the same-sex parent at or near sexual maturity because of their potential as competitors. These assumptions combined with the broader perceptions of monogamy as a social system led to a suite of hypotheses constructed to take to the field in order to test the specific apriori models (Fuentes 2000, 2002; van Schaik and Dunbar 1997; Wittenberger and Tilson 1980).

Because of the accumulation of fieldwork knowledge over the past three decades we now have sufficient data to warrant not only Carpenter's caution, but a full reassessment of both how gibbons live and interact and how we gather and represent field datatsets. The above mentioned apriori models for gibbon social evolution and behaviour have to be modified. Substantial field work demonstrates that, currently, we cannot best describe the gibbons as living exclusively in nuclear family groups, exhibiting only monogamous mating, or necessarily exhibiting other facets in the expected behavioural profiles of monogamous social systems (Bartlett 2007; Brockelman et al. 1998; Fuentes 1999, 2000; Malone and Fuentes 2009; Reichard 2003; Reichard and Sommer 1997). Based on accumulated fieldwork we can assert that monogamy per se is not a social system (it is a mating pattern) and that two-adult groups as a species norm are very rare for primates (as in all mammals). Even when two-adult groups do occur in primate species, they vary dramatically in their behavioural and mating profiles and occurrence in a two-adult group does not necessarily imply monogamous mating or other any specific pair bond behaviour (Fuentes 2002). In other words, the basal assumptions underlying much of the status of gibbons as the iconographic models for monogamy in primates are misunderstandings and overstatements of the meaning of previous field data and incorrect assumptions about what 'monogamy' is on the whole.

Why did perspectives on gibbons change? Why are our understandings and our interpretation of the meaning of gibbon behaviour different today? Fieldwork at both long term and short term field sites resulted in a set of data that challenge previous assumptions/assertions. Eight of twelve gibbon species have been reported to occur in larger than two adult groups (at least 18 per cent of all groups observed) (Fuentes 2000; Malone and Fuentes 2009). Observed dispersal distances from natal (birth) groups are short (averaging less than 1000m) and mating outside of the group does occur, suggesting that genetic relationships between neighbouring groups may be close (Fuentes 2000; Reichard 1995, 2003). Long term observations demonstrate that many groups are not made up of only parents and offspring (they are not nuclear families) and that groups undergo changes in adult composition as adult pairs dissolve and form over time (Brockelman et al. 1998; Reichard 2003). Different species show variation in by sex behavioural patterns, especially in regards to inter-adult intragroup interactions (Fuentes 2000). Local populations of gibbons appear to have a level of supra-group social organization, resulting in communities or neighbourhoods with complex genetic and experiential relationships between groups. This suggests that the traditional focus on the single group as the sole centre of gibbon social behaviour may cause misinterpretation of the overall context and function of the inter- and intra-group behavioural patterns observed. This challenges assumptions associated with nuclear family structure, 'monogamy,' and the underlying explanations for why gibbon groups would enter into conflict (or affiliation) with one another (Bartlett 2007).

How does this situation and change over time reflect my previous discussion of the complexities of fieldwork in measuring meaning and understanding? In turns out that the context and paradigmatic training for decades of fieldworkers provided a set of assumptions that impacted the way in which they 'saw' their data during collection and 'understood' it during analyses. This pattern combined with a heavy usage of a 'species or genus typical pattern' assumption (monogamy and its associated behavioural patterns in this case) led to the propagation of an interpretation pattern of gibbon datasets that was increasingly contradicted by those same datasets. Here we see explanatory mechanisms and social constructs suggesting that 'monogamy' per se was an adaptation exhibited by gibbons and thus gibbons lived in two-adult groups by design. Measures of gibbon behaviour were then based on the assumption of a meaning for a two-adult group: that it equalled social and genetic monogamy. This assumption carried with it specific sub-assumptions about species particular behaviour patterns and thus hypotheses were generated to test these (and not other) assumptions. It turned out that data on gibbon groups and populations are best understood by placing them in the broader context of recent studies on small group, two-adult, and pair bonded primates, a relatively new paradigmatic approach that emerged in the 1990s due to increasingly confounding field datasets on small-grouped primates (Fuentes 1999). While the measuring of gibbon behaviour has changed with the advances in genetic analyses and the increase in long term and additional study sites, the debate on meaning is ongoing. Researchers are currently faced with multiple perspectives regarding explanatory hypotheses of gibbon social structure (Bartlett 2007; Fuentes 2000; Reichard 2003). In the case of the Hylobatids one can see that the patterns and contexts under which research took place coupled with specific apriori paradigmatic assumptions resulted in specific limitations on understanding of the gibbons and their behaviour. This case also highlights the pivotal role of accumulated fieldwork and advances in technologies to move through assumptive barriers and into broader and more accurate attempts as measuring meaning and understanding in primatology.

So what?

In place of separate subjects, each with its own assumptions, methodology, and technical jargon, we must envisage networks of cooperative investigation, with common methods and terminology, all eventually linked up in a comprehensive process of inquiry. This, of course, will mean a radical reorganization of scientific teaching and research.

J. Huxley 1963, in Washburn 1973

Given in 1963, reiterated in 1973, this quote still holds an important call for fieldworkers in primatology and biological anthropology. Our ability to collect, assess, analyze and contextualize high quality datasets is largely reliant on our abilities to follow Huxley's call and see across methodologies, paradigms and contexts in our quest for understanding. In this chapter I suggest that the incorporation or at least recognition of variable methods and an openness to multiple paradigms of analyses lead to better data which in turn facilitates better access to opportunities for understanding. It should be apparent that because of the global anthropogenic impact on our planet, and of the cultural and historical constructs we as researchers hold and encounter that we need to be as biocultural as possible in the field. That is, we need to incorporate and examine interfaces between physiological, cultural, historical and perceptual modalities as parts of dynamic systems not only as distinct and easily separable influences. I suggest that one area that may hold great promise in integrating perspectives and practice from biological anthropology and primatology is the emerging field of ethnoprimatology (Fuentes and Wolfe 2002; Riley 2006).

Because of our increasing realization of the bio-behavioural realities for humans and the need to integrate approaches we can possibly see an engagement with, and respect for, multiple methodologies as a new biological anthropology, a logical extension of Washburn's new physical anthropology. The complexities in fieldwork methodologies, contexts and interpretations fit well with emerging understandings of complexity in evolutionary theory and especially with greater understandings of human niche construction and the integration of organism-environment relations (Fuentes 2004, 2009; Odling-Smee et al. 2003; Potts 2004). Rather than merely responding to environmental challenges organisms can also shape their environment and this in turn alters the selective pressures impacting the system. Evolution is a dynamic process and one in which humans have a significant impact relative to other organisms. Rather than assuming a cultural deconstructionist's cooption of post modernity that favours only hyper relativistic and hyper reflexive narratives we can see a move beyond post-modernity in primatology and biological anthropology wherein a certain amount of reflectivity and reflexivity combined with greater integration across disciplines and fieldwork paradigms produces novel and/or innovative engagements with our datasets and the way we both produce and understand them.

Finally, I conclude this chapter with the following points, as they are central to the future of fieldwork and the data it generates.

- Who owns the truth in the collection of field data? Can it be one or another specific paradigm or one national school over others? No. The concept of multiple truths may not be practical, but there are certainly many ways to create meaning from data and exploring a multiplicity of paths can only be beneficial to our overall abilities to derive meaning from datasets.
- How do we disseminate field data? Where do we publish, in what language do we publish and who are the gate keepers to publishing? These are questions for serious consideration and ones that are worthy of a book on their own. How and where data are presented acts to either solidify current paradigms or challenge them.
- How do we train fieldworkers? Most, if not all, of the contributors to this volume are teachers as well as researchers. We create the next generations of fieldworkers and thus the way we do so shapes the datasets that emerge. Training the practitioners of the future to respect diverse (and possibly divergent) perspectives is one of the strongest tools we have in our quest for the derivation of meaning and the process of understanding data derived from fieldwork in primatology and biological anthropology.

Acknowledgements

I owe a sincere debt of gratitude to Professor Phyllis Dolhinow for instilling in me much of the basal ideas and contexts that underpin this chapter. I wish to thank Professor Jeremy MacClancy for organizing the conference that this book emerged from and Oxford Brookes University for hosting the conference. Funding for the research that this chapter emerged from was provided in part by the University of Notre Dame College of Arts and Letters Office of the Dean, and the Institute for Scholarship in the Liberal Arts.

Bibliography

Barrett, L., R. Dunbar and J. Lycett. 2002. *Human Evolutionary Psychology*. Princeton, Princeton University Press.

Bartlett, T.Q. 2007. 'The Hylobatidae: small apes of Asia' in C.A. Campbell, Fuentes, K.C. MacKinnon, M. Panger and S. Bearder (eds) *Primates in Perspective*. Oxford: Oxford University Press, pp. 274–89.

Brockelman, W.Y., U. Reichard, U. Treesucon and J.J. Raemaekers. 1998. 'Dispersal, pair formation and social structure in gibbons (Hylobates lar)', *Behavioral Ecology and Sociobiology* 42: 329–39.

Brockelman, W.Y. and S. Srikosamatara. 1984. 'Maintenance and evolution of social structure in gibbons' in H. Prueschoft, D.J. Chivers, W.Y. Brockelman, N. Creel (eds) *The Lesser Apes: Evolution, Behaviour, and Biology*. Edinburgh: Edinburgh University Press, pp. 283–323.

Buss, D. and P. Schmitt. 1993. 'Sexual Strategies Theory: an evolutionary perspective on human mating', *Psychology Review* 100: 204–32.

Campbell, C., A. Fuentes, K.C. MacKinnon, M. Panger and S. Bearder. 2006. *Primates in Perspective*. Oxford: Oxford University Press.

Carter, C.S. 2003. 'Developmental Consequences of Oxytocin', *Physiology and Behaviour* 79: 383–97.

Carpenter, R. 1940. 'A field study in Siam of the behaviour and social relations of the gibbon (*Hylobates lar*)', *Comparative Psychology Monographs* 16: 1–212.

Chivers, D.J. 1974. 'The siamang in Malaysia' in *Contributions to Primatology*. Basel: Karger, pp.1–335.

_____ 2005. 'Gibbons: the small apes' in J. Caldecott, and L. Miules (eds) *World Atlas of Great Apes and their Conservation*. Berkeley: University of California Press, pp.205–14.

Dolhinow, P. 1999. 'A mystery: explaining behaviour' in S.C. Strum and D.G. Lindburg (eds) *The New Physical Anthropology: Science, Humanism, and Critical Reflection*. Englewood Cliffs, NJ: Prentice Hall, pp. 119–32.

Di Fiore, A. and P. Gagneux. 2007. 'Molecular Primatology'. In C. Campbell, A. Fuentes, K.C. MacKinnon, M. Panger and S. Bearder (eds), *Primates in Perspective*. Oxford: Oxford University Press, pp. 369–94.

Ellefson, J.O. 1974. *Natural History of White-handed Gibbons in the Malayan Peninsula*. Ph.D. Thesis. Berkeley: University of California.

Fuentes, A. 1999. 'Re-evaluating Primate Monogamy' *American Anthropologist* 100 (4): 890–907.

_____ 2000. 'Hylobatid Communities: changing views on pair bonding and social organization in hominoids' *Yearbook of Physical Anthropology* 43: 33–60.

_____ 2002. 'Patterns and trends in primate pair bonds', *International Journal of Primatology* 23(4): 953–78.

_____ 2004. 'It's Not All Sex and Violence: Integrated Anthropology and the Role of Cooperation and Social Complexity in Human Evolution', *American Anthropologist* 106(4): 710–18.

_____ 2006. 'The humanity of animals and the animality of humans: A view from biological anthropology inspired by J.M. Coetzees' *Elizabeth Costello*' *American Anthropologist* 108(1): 124–32.

_____ 2009. 'Re-situating Anthropological approaches to the evolution of human behavior', *Anthropology Today* 25(3): 12–17.

Fuentes, A. and L.D. Wolfe. 2002. *Primates Face to Face: The Conservation Implications of Human and Nonhuman Primate Interconnections*. Cambridge: Cambridge University Press.

Hrdy, S.B. 1981. *The Woman that Never Evolved.* Cambridge, MA: Harvard University Press.

Imanishi, K. 2002[1941]. *A Japanese View of Nature: The World of Living Things.* P. Asquith, H. Kawakatsu, S. Yagi, and H. Takasaki, trans. New York: Routledge Curzon.

Jolly, A. 1998. 'Pair-bonding, female aggression and the evolution of lemur societies', *Folia Primatol* [Suppl] 64: 1–13.

Kappeler, P.M. and C.P. van Schaik. 2002. 'Evolution of Primate Social Systems', *International Journal of Primatology* 23: 707–40.

Lasley, B.L. and A. Savage. 2007. 'Advances in the understanding of primate reproductive endocrinology' in C. Campbell, A. Fuentes, K.C. MacKinnon, M. Panger and S. Bearder (eds) *Primates in Perspective.* Oxford: Oxford University Press, pp. 356–68.

Leighton, D.R. 1987. 'Gibbons: territoriality and monogamy' in B.B. Smuts, D.L. Cheney, R.M. Seyfarth, R.W. Wrangham, T.T. Struhsaker (eds) *Primate Societies.* Chicago: University of Chicago Press, pp. 135–45.

Lovejoy, C.O. 1981. 'The origins of man', *Science* 211: 341–50.

Malone, N. and A. Fuentes. In press. 'The Ecology and Evolution of Hylobatid Communities: Causal and Contextual Factors Underlying Inter- and Intraspecific Variation' in S. Lappan, D. Whittaker and T. Geissmann (eds) *The Gibbons: New Perspectives on Small Ape Socioecology and Population Biology.* New York: Springer.

Miller, G. 2000. *The Mating Mind: How Sexual Choice Shaped the Evolution of Human Nature.* New York, Doubleday.

Mitani, J.C. 1984. 'The behavioural regulation of monogamy in gibbons', *Behavioral Ecology and Sociobiology* 15: 225–9.

Odling-Smee, F. J., K.N. Laland and M.W. Feldman. 2003. *Niche Construction: The Neglected Process in Evolution.* Princeton: Princeton University Press.

Palombit, R.A. 1999. 'Infanticide and the evolution of pair bonds in nonhuman primates', *Evolutionary Anthropology* 7: 117–29.

Potts, R. 2004. 'Sociality and the Concept of Culture in Human Origins', in R.W. Sussman and A.R. Chapman (eds) *The Origins and Nature of Sociality.* New York: Aldine de Gruyter, pp. 249–69.

Ray, E. 2007. 'Research Questions', in C. Campbell, A. Fuentes, K.C. MacKinnon, M. Panger and S. Bearder (eds) *Primates in Perspective.* Oxford: Oxford University Press, pp. 346–55.

Reichard, U. 1995. 'Extra-pair copulations in a monogamous gibbon (Hylobates lar)', *Ethology* 100: 99–112.

——— 2003. 'Social monogamy in gibbons: the male perspective', in U. Reichard and C. Boesch (eds) *Monogamy: Mating Strategies and Partnerships in Birds, Humans and Other Mammals.* Cambridge: Cambridge University Press, pp. 190–213.

Reichard, U. and V. Sommer. 1997. 'Group encounters in wild gibbons (Hylobates lar): agonism, affiliation, and the concept of infanticide', *Behaviour* 134: 1135–74.

Riley, E. 2006. 'Ethnoprimatology: Toward Reconciliation of Biological and Cultural Anthropology', *Ecological and Environmental Anthropology* 2(2): 75–86.

Sapolsky, R. 2004. 'Social Status and Health in Humans and Other Animals', *Annual Review of Anthropology* 33: 393–418.

Sapolsky, R.M. and L.J. Share. 2004. 'A pacific culture among wild baboons: its emergence and Transmission', *PLoS Biology* 2(4): 106.

Symons, D. 1979. *The Evolution of Human Sexuality.* Oxford: Oxford University Press.

Tilson, R.L. 1980. *Monogamous Mating Systems of Gibbons and Langurs in the Mentawai Islands, Indonesia.* Ph.D. Thesis. Davis: University of California.

van Schaik, C.P. and P.M. Kappeler. 1997. 'Infanticide risk and the evolution of male-female association in primates', *Proceedings of the Royal Society of London* [Biology] 264: 1687–94.

van Schaik, C.P. and R.M. Dunbar. 1990. 'The evolution of monogamy in large primates: a new hypothesis and some crucial tests', *Behaviour* 115: 30–62.

Stamps, J. 2003. 'Behavioural processes affecting development: Tinbergen's fourth question comes of age', *Animal Behaviour* 66: 1–13.

Washburn, S.L. 1951. 'The new physical anthropology', *Transactions of the New York Academy of Science* 13 (2d ser.): 298–304.

——— 1973. 'The promise of primatology', *American Journal of Physical Anthropology* 38: 177–82.

West-Eberhard, M.J. 2003. *Developmental Plasticity and Evolution*. New York: Oxford University Press.

Wittenberger, J.F. and R.L. Tilson. 1980. 'The evolution of monogamy: hypotheses and evidence', *Annual Review of Ecological Systems* 11: 197–232.

Wrangham, R.W, J. Holland Jones, G. Laden, D. Pilbeam and N. Conklin-Brittain. 1999. 'The raw and the stolen. Cooking and the ecology of human origins', *Current Anthropology* 40: 567–94.

9
Fieldwork as Research Process and Community Engagement:
Experiences from the Gambia and Afghanistan

Mark Eggerman and Catherine Panter-Brick

Introduction

This chapter is a reflection on the practice of fieldwork, in which we offer concrete suggestions to encourage an open-ended and iterative attitude to research. This is particularly relevant to situations in which research activities rely on close engagement with local communities for the purposes of scientific data collection and evaluation. We draw upon personal experiences from two contrasting projects. One was action research to address a particular public health problem in the Gambia, namely the prevention of childhood malaria through better usage of mosquito nets. The other was basic research on young people and their families in Afghanistan and refugee camps in Pakistan, to provide baseline data on mental health and to address an important public health issue. Both projects were cross-disciplinary in theoretical outlook and methodology, evaluating biological health outcomes within social and ecological contexts. They posed, however, very different challenges in terms of implementation. We drew on our long-term experience initiating and managing large research teams overseas: directing inter-disciplinary research on health and wellbeing in cross-cultural contexts (Panter-Brick) and international media research in the Middle East and Africa (Eggerman), to devise ways that made research more reflective, relevant and effective on the ground.

Fieldwork is a process, framed by a set of questions

When conducting research, it is useful to keep in mind five basic questions regarding project aims, implementation, and impact: *Why are we doing this? What needs to be done to accomplish it? When and how can we do it? Whom should we involve? What is the significance of the work?* First addressed when conceptualizing a research issue, these questions remain relevant throughout a project's implementation: they may be explicitly asked by local field staff or community participants, or surface when researchers confront particularly difficult logistic or ethical issues. As a set of useful catchphrases (Table 9.1), they also guide our present discussion.

Table 9.1. Fieldwork as research process and community engagement.

1. Fieldwork is guided by questions regarding aims, implementation and impact:
  • why do this?
  • what needs to be done?
  • when and how can this be done?
  • who needs to be involved?
  • so what is the significance of the work?

2. Fieldwork provides opportunities
  • for formulating and refining research ideas
  • for evaluating the research process
  • for collecting data

3. Fieldwork requires
  • interaction between scientific practice and the reality on the ground
  • community engagement, which is often problematic.

Fieldwork provides opportunities for formulating, refining and evaluating research ideas: it is not just the implementation of a ready-made protocol of data collection. By routinely asking oneself 'Why are we doing this in this way?' or 'How can we be doing this better?', one is compelled to evaluate fieldwork activity in terms of intended aims as well as logistic or ethical issues related to implementation. Fieldwork is by necessity an open process: it rests upon ways in which researchers engage with local communities, an engagement which is fundamental to the work but which also can be problematic. Most research projects have to navigate snags and hitches, some of which can be whipped into full-blown storms rising out of an incompatibility between plans for scientific practice and the reality on the ground. Fieldwork is thus a process for exploring issues of both practical and academic importance; furthermore, flexibility is particularly valuable where research is proceeding along interdisciplinary lines.

Action research: designing a successful health intervention

Action research programmes often have built-in answers to the question, 'Why are we doing this?' Research aims are pre-specified to make some form of significant improvement to people's lives. In the field of medical anthropology, for instance, action research may focus on delivering or packaging health services to an area, or simply improving access to existing health care facilities. Our project in the Gambia had such an objective: to improve usage of mosquito nets in order to prevent malaria, the biggest killer of young children in many parts of Africa. Reduction in childhood mortality, achieved by combating unnecessary and preventable infectious diseases, is one of the major Millennium Development Goals (Bryce et al. 2006).

Challenges for anthropology in health research

Health interventions are usually directed at promoting change at the level of communities or individuals (in ways that lessen risk-taking or encourage harm-reducing practices) or promoting change at macro socio-political level (in terms of legislation, resource provision, or media information). It is fair to say that many health interventions directed at modifying individual behaviour have been strikingly unsuccessful (Table 9.2). Both in high and low-resource countries, it has proven extremely difficult to make individuals stop smoking, use condoms for sex, take up physical exercise, eat more nutritious food, or make timely use of existing health care services. Policy needs to be in place to facilitate or compel changes in actual behaviour; examples are mandatory health warnings on cigarette packaging, bans on cigarette advertising, availability of nicotine substitutes, and bans on smoking in public places.

Because the management of health-related behaviours is a central preoccupation in public health, and because social scientists offer valuable 'expertise' on contextualising behaviours within a given society or culture, anthropologists working in health research are often asked what kind of interventions actually work, how they should be designed, and at whom they should be directed.

Table 9.2. The value of fieldwork for action research: designing health interventions.

- Effective behaviour change is notoriously difficult to initiate and sustain, even where communities are well informed about simple means of health-promotion.
- Anthropologists often contribute to the design, implementation, and evaluation of health interventions.
- Strive to be culturally compelling, not merely culturally appropriate, when designing health interventions.
- Fieldwork is the process that helps with community engagement and mobilisation.
- Fieldwork has an important role in research evaluation.

From Panter-Brick et al. (2006).

Culturally-compelling behaviour change

We argue that action research should work towards designing culturally 'compelling' health interventions (Table 9.2), in the sense of providing a package that will entice, seduce or obligate people to change their risk-taking behaviours. Merely designing interventions that are culturally appropriate can be wasted effort (Panter-Brick et al.

2006). This element of compulsion can be engineered at several levels: individual behaviour, community mobilization and social policy.

Take once again the example of what needs to be done to implement a policy on smoking cessation. What makes people stop smoking? Is it the knowledge that 'smoking kills' or is it that 'smoking smells' and is therefore bad for one's love life? Will smokers quit because it is too expensive, because it is actively discouraged by social convention, or because it is made illegal in many public spaces? Recent legislation enforcing a total ban on smoking in public spaces, in parts of North America, Europe and Asia (Fichtenberg and Glantz 2002; Jamrozik 2004), exemplifies one dimension of social coercion brought about to compel behaviour change. Wholesale community mobilisation and censorship, to enforce non-smoking in a small community in Fiji (Groth-Marnat et al. 2001), exemplifies another dimension of culturally-compelling behaviour change. Whether enforced by negative rules impacting personal and social behaviour, or facilitated by policy and resource provision to promote well-being, health interventions owe their success to particular strategies for compelling social action.

In recent years, literature reviews have emphasised two fundamental lessons in public health, namely that interventions must feature both grassroot community mobilization and top-level political and financial commitment (Levine 2004). Some of the models mapping the determinants of behaviour change in the available literature have not been far-reaching or relevant enough. For example, one extensively-used model in public health is based on documenting knowledge, attitudes and practice to uncover what people think and what people do in terms of health. This is empirically useful, but demonstrably limited if promoting the assumption that changes in knowledge and attitudes will bring about changes of practice without due consideration of powerful social, economic and political constraints on human behaviour. In the same vein, models developed within the field of psychology, based on theories of reasoned action or self-efficacy, focus primarily on how psychological factors govern behaviour change, and pay scant attention to socio-political contexts that shape willingness and ability to make effective health-related changes.

The value of fieldwork for community mobilization

Fieldwork is a process which helps one design, implement and evaluate such culturally-compelling interventions. This is a lesson we learnt in the Gambia, working on a project entitled 'A Stitch in Time Saves Lives', the aim of which was to motivate local people to repair tears in their mosquito nets and maintain them in mint condition. The impetus for the project was the observation that Gambian villagers made extensive use of insecticide-treated mosquito nets to prevent falciparum malaria, but that they also allowed them to tear and deteriorate to the point where they afforded no effective protection from biting mosquitoes (Clarke et al. 2001). The project was funded by the Bill and Melinda Gates Foundation as a collaboration between two UK universities (Durham and the London School of Hygiene and Tropical Medicine) and the Medical Research Council in Fajara, the Gambia. Six months of fieldwork were orchestrated by experienced, bilingual local staff, a Masters-level student in Anthropology and senior researchers with cross-disciplinary expertise in epidemiology, entymology, and anthropology (Panter-Brick et al. 2006).

Why didn't local people mend their mosquito nets? It was quickly established that needle and thread were ubiquitous in family compounds, and that professional tailors operated throughout local villages. Interviews and focus groups, however, revealed four major constraints on people's motivation and ability to repair bednets. The first was lack of access to good quality netting material: some nets were old or made with second hand material, including cheap, flimsy netting, or fabric with decorative patchwork and large holes, all of which provided an ineffective barrier to biting mosquitoes. Time and cost were two other significant factors. Thus mosquito populations were largest during the rainy season, the busiest time of the year, due to the concentration of farming activities; however, the window of opportunity for sewing a small tear during daylight hours, or for taking down a net for patching by tailors, was very limited as women were walking six to eight km daily to plant rice in rain-fed fields. Paying for repairs by a tailor or purchasing a net of better quality was financially prohibitive for many families during the financially lean times of the pre-harvest rains, after which the peak malaria risk was past. A final constraint pertained to the nature of social interaction within polygamous households. In those where social relations between a husband and co-wives were strained, it was difficult for a wife to argue priority for repair of her mosquito net (and for the husband to allocate money) if this were seen as favouring one wife over another. By contrast, in cooperating households, nets would be exchanged, repaired or renewed, in line with an agreed household priority to protect newborn babies and the youngest children (Figure 9.1).

Figure 9.1. Women examining mosquito netting in The Gambia.

It was quickly established that a health intervention need not be directed to improve knowledge, attitudes and practice related to usage of mosquito nets: villagers were very familiar with insecticide-treated bednets, knew that mosquitoes carried a killer disease, and showed a great concern with protecting young children against malaria infection. Poverty, however, was an over-arching constraint: lack of money restricted access to good-quality nets, while lack of time due to the pressure of seasonal farm labour limited opportunities for ongoing repairs. In the context of scarce resources, husbands and wives in polygamous households could construe allocation of money as an act of favouritism rather than an act of priority, making it difficult to repair or replace bednets without exacerbating household conflict.

In terms of community-level intervention, how could we facilitate community mobilisation in ways that made bednet repair a priority for today, rather than tomorrow or the day after? The idea that shaped the intervention was generated, quite simply, during fieldwork activities. Cultural immersion provided the main clue regarding how to design an intervention that was culturally compelling, not merely culturally appropriate. Village women, invited to a focus group discussion, unexpectedly broke out in song upon receiving refreshments brought to thank them for participation. One lead singer spontaneously composed short musical phrases about 'enemy mosquitoes', 'tucking children in bed', protecting 'expensive nets', using 'needle and thread', while a chorus clapped, danced, and took up the refrain. Songs were the community's way of formulating meaningful messages across a whole range of contexts: to welcome guests, to motivate labour groups in the rice fields, to communicate important messages about social behaviour. Here, then, was a potentially relevant, authentic and culturally-compelling vehicle for behaviour change. In consultation with villagers, the strategy for the 'intervention' consisted of recording these songs, performed in the village by female singers and male drummers; distributing the tapes to village households; and adopting a 'hands-off' approach as to where and when tapes were played on locally-owned tape recorders. Largely because of this local ownership, the songs provided significant reminders that nets should be repaired sooner rather than later. Bednet repair became a priority endorsed by the community in a very public way.

The value of fieldwork for research evaluation

Fieldwork also proves to be a crucial component of research evaluation, following research design and implementation (Table 9.2). It offers a unique opportunity to evaluate and reflect upon the research process.

In the Gambia, we evaluated the health intervention with both qualitative data (on community perceptions about how effective songs had been in persuading people to sew their nets) and quantitative data (by recording extent of net repairs and counting numbers of malarial mosquitoes captured under bednets, pre- and post-intervention). In terms of behaviour change, community mobilisation was striking: there were rapid and extensive household responses showing a significant increase in bednet repairs. In terms of health impact, however, there was no evidence of a substantial reduction in the number of biting mosquitoes: however much people sewed them, nets continued to tear throughout the rainy season. Too many bednets were in such poor condition, or made with such fragile netting to begin with, that they could not be repaired thoroughly enough.

Significance of the work

What does this example tell us about the value of fieldwork for action research? Asking oneself a bald question – 'So what?' – forces us to think hard about the significance of a particular project. Did the work advance existing knowledge regarding the best strategies for health intervention? Did it advance knowledge about sustainable impact on health and society?

In revisiting the question 'Why do this?', we stress that the project sought to promote a health intervention that was within the reach of the very poor. In answering the question 'Whom to involve?', it sought to provide immediate benefits to poor households with young children, without waiting for the provision of a malaria vaccine or ecological manipulation of mosquito habitat. The provision of insecticide-treated bednets is a major component of malaria prevention, but torn nets, even if treated with insecticide, provide no effective protection (Clarke et al. 2001). Mending nets with needle and thread is hardly newsworthy, but it is a small, practical action that, if taken, can immediately benefit poor households.

Perhaps unusually in the context of a large multidisciplinary team working with a medical research council, fieldwork activities were integral to the formulation of an actual strategy deployed to underpin a health intervention. In addressing the question of how to develop a successful health intervention, project activities were directed to foster engagement with local communities, to be more than just an exercise in data collection. Conceiving fieldwork activities as a process during which we prioritised community engagement helped to develop the specific strategy for intervention, namely to capitalise on the value of creative oral tradition to make both the form and the content of a health message more compelling. While project aims had been elaborated in the UK, cultural immersion and community participation helped the design and implementation of the health intervention.

Fieldwork was also critical for reflective research evaluation. It sharpened our thinking regarding the impact as well as nature of the intervention, in terms of its success and limitations. The fact that the project had effectively promoted behaviour change, but with little impact on health per se, made us reflect on the pervasiveness of constraints on human agency in these Gambian communities. Behaviour change, in matters as simple as repairing mosquito nets, is hampered by local constraints (time, cost, social dynamics) embedded in grinding poverty. It is also structured by macro-level constraints: low access to high-quality netting material, as local markets have been flooded with less-expensive product which has little resistance to wear-and-tear. Research was a process which allowed reflection on the micro- and macro-level factors that will undermine the success of health interventions. One of our recommendations was therefore to focus attention on marketing affordable, tear-resistant netting, not just insecticide-treated bednets, given the fundamental importance of having bednets in mint condition to protect against malaria.

In terms of process, this research project went through three specific stages. The first was a pre-planned examination of community beliefs and practices related to malarial transmission and actual constraints of human agency. The second was concerned with identifying a strategy to promote behaviour change, based on the use of a culturally compelling medium of communication. The third was an evaluation of the success, sustainability, and applicability of the intervention. The value of fieldwork lies not just in 'being there' (Watson 1999), but in making action research more relevant and reflective throughout distinct stages of project design, implementation, and evaluation.

Basic research: addressing scientific and community concerns

Our second example describes basic research into a public health issue of great importance (Horton 2007; Panter-Brick 2010): mental health. Undertaken with Afghan families living in contrasting areas of Afghanistan and among Afghan communities in the North-West Frontier Province (NWFP) of Pakistan, this project aimed to provide sound population-level data pertinent to mental health issues in a population often defined in terms of its past wars and ongoing conflicts, its linguistic and ethnic heterogeneity, the segregation and seclusion of women, and its past and present poverty. The research, funded by the Wellcome Trust over a period of four years (2004–2007), was essentially a population survey to identify the major life stressors, mental health problems, and forms of social resilience among Afghan youth in the aftermath of war and mass population displacement (Panter-Brick et al. 2009; Eggerman and Panter-Brick 2010).

Challenges for anthropology in difficult settings

So why do this research, how best to implement the project, and whom to involve? Anthropologists provide a perspective on mental health which differs from that customarily offered by psychiatrists or epidemiologists, especially when working with communities in conflict zones (Bolton and Betancourt 2004; Boyden and de Berry 2004). The anthropology of suffering is a dimension of the 'painful anthropology of disruption and despair', which focuses attention on hardship, conflict, destabilization and repair; it raises conceptual, logistic and ethical issues quite different from the 'comfortable anthropology of social organization' which focuses on the structures of social order (Davis 1992).

Because the project was intended as a means of enhancing local research capacity, we established collaborations with several local partners: an Afghan clinical psychologist to co-direct research with Pashtuns in rural Afghanistan; a senior academic in social work at the University of Peshawar to head research with Afghan refugees to NWFP Pakistan; and a research agency based in Afghanistan to complete work in Kabul, Bamyan and Balkh provinces. These partners obtained formal research permission to use local schools as research sites, as well as recruited young people and their parents or guardians to participate in the project. They also hired local staff (project supervisors, male and female interviewers, doctors, translators and drivers) to work with us as a field team.

Let us begin by listing some of the commonly cited challenges to research activities in Afghanistan and NWFP Pakistan. Afghan communities have endured three decades of civil war and conflict; the problems of sovereignty, security and rule of law continue. There has been a prolonged and severe drought for much of the past decade, which has decimated livestock and agricultural production. There have been earthquakes and outbreaks of infectious diseases. There have been large displacements of population due to war, ethnic persecution, and economic collapse. Many Afghans and their families have experienced immense suffering, and many continue to suffer. In this context it is often difficult – if not impossible – to justify participation in any activity that does not at least hold out the hope of some real, material benefit.

From a practical standpoint, research in Afghanistan is complicated by a lack of reliable basic data on the population (such as an up-to-date national census, or comprehensive lists of schools or enrolment figures). Communications within the country have improved greatly since the fall of the Taliban in 2001, but at the time of fieldwork the new internet and mobile phone networks do not extend beyond urban centres. There are very real security issues arising from such ongoing political, social and economic problems. Yet another challenge is the sourcing and retention of competent fieldworkers; some of our staff, having benefited from training and project experience, quickly moved onto better-paying jobs with aid organizations. A strict gender divide has to be navigated, as well as inter-generational, ethnic and linguistic differences which affect trust and authority. More importantly, there is little familiarity with academic research as a process; this unfamiliarity, often mixed with the public awareness of the reconstruction effort and the possibility of receiving handouts from various aid programmes, can produce expectations of the research which have no connection with the explanations given by project staff. Many Afghans are non-literate, never having had the opportunity to obtain a formal education: there is often little familiarity with or little understanding of what the aims of a research survey might be (Eggerman 2003, 2005).

For this project, field visits were restricted to key events: training field staff, pre-testing research tools in vernacular languages, participating in the pilot and supervising the start of data collection, translation and evaluation. Our first-hand experiences of research sites and project activities were limited by substantial perceived security risks (sporadic anti-Western riots, kidnappings, and car bombs) and consequent difficulty in securing permission and insurance to participate in fieldwork activities. Our local partners were responsible for most on-the-ground aspects of project management, budget decisions, data collection and community engagement. Mobile phone and face-to-face communication was restricted, but we did hold regular and frequent consultative meetings, both on site and in the UK. After a year of slow progress with one local partner, we moved to a partnership with a Kabul agency that had extensive experience in research leadership and management.

This situation characterises many projects in biological anthropology where large, multi-disciplinary research teams function on the basis of sporadic visits by cultural outsiders and long term ground-work by local collaborators. We contributed critical research experience: for example, what sampling methodology would ensure the representativeness of the data collected. Our *etic* perspective reflected scientific concern to ensure validity, reliability, and cross-cultural comparison. For their part, our local collaborators were much better placed to engage with local communities: to explain the project, to secure community participation, to frame observations more meaningfully within socioeconomic and cultural contexts. They were also versed in deploying the locally relevant vocabulary for talking about psychosocial stress and mental health.

This helped to shift the emphasis of research, with respect to determinants of poor mental health, from an initial focus on past events (related to war and displacement) to local preoccupations (related to current life stressors generated by household socioeconomic circumstances). While competitive funding had been won to appraise links between mental health, violent conflict, and forced displacement, the actual fieldwork activities helped to broaden our focus, to show how suffering was rooted in current circumstances and an unstable, uncertain future. What mattered, in this difficult setting, was good communication between local and external research partners and good communication between the research team and participating communities.

Addressing gaps in understanding

Fieldwork is wrought by the interaction between the demands of scientific practice and those of the reality on the ground. As one seasoned anthropologist has remarked, in a phrase that is usefully terse: 'You don't do fieldwork, fieldwork does you' (Simpson 2006). In Afghanistan, the value of maintaining flexibility in the research process was clear from the outset. Fieldwork helped us evaluate and modify the research process, navigate conflicting and contradictory information, contextualise the information collected, and even to assign value to the unexpected (Table 9.3). Limited opportunity for first-hand fieldwork experiences and devolved project management meant that we had to address important gaps between scientific and local concerns while data collection was underway. In what follows, we describe several gaps of understanding between investigator and participant regarding project aims, the selection of respondents, and expectations related to outcomes. This will illustrate the point that community cooperation and engagement is fundamental to research, but often problematic. We then address issues related to practicing an ethical community engagement; following Bhutta (2002: 116), who argued that if research is regarded as the 'brain' of health systems, then ethics serves as its conscience.

Project aims

Due to unforeseen events, project planning issues, 'What needs to be done? When and how can this be done?', had to be readdressed from the moment fieldwork began in Afghanistan. For example, the unexpected closure of all Kabul schools in advance of the 2004 parliamentary elections required a relocation of work from urban Kabul to one of the rural areas three days before data collection was due to start! Further unexpected changes required us to rearrange the entire fieldwork schedule, given the necessity to avoid the harsh winters in the Afghan mountains (where schools have no heating) and the dusty hot weather in Peshawar refugee camps (where schools have no fans or water coolers). In the end, the work originally planned for Kabul in 2004 did not take place until 2006.

Table 9.3. The value of fieldwork for basic research: bridging research and community concerns.

1. Fieldwork is shaped by: • the demands of scientific practice and reality on-the-ground • communication between researchers and participating communities.
2. First-hand fieldwork experiences help: • address gaps between scientific and local concerns (project aims) • evaluate and modify the research process (refine methodology) • navigate confusing, contradictory information (evaluate data) • contextualise the information collected, give meaning to numbers • give value to the unexpected • confront ethical issues.

From the perspective of local communities, questions about the nature and meaning of the research work were clearly of more central importance: Why do this? So what are the outcomes? These are questions that tend to be forgotten by the field team once the project has been explained, the consent forms are signed, and the data collection has started. Research can be easily misconstrued, even when sustained effort is made to explain the intent of the work to participants. In some schools in Kabul, for example, a rumour circulated that the objective of our project was to select the best students in order to send them on educational scholarships. Despite explanations intended to mitigate unrealistic expectations, respondents held out many hopes – would we be offering medical treatment or financial assistance to the families we were interviewing, or building the much-needed new classrooms the school required, or help provide some form of transport from home to school?

Specific complications came about as a result of our work with Afghan girls. In this conservative, avowedly Islamic country, the public behaviour and reputation of young girls is a central concern to their families, as it has a bearing on their eligibility for marriage and the social standing of the family. A great effort was made to address potential obstacles to participation, including the exclusive use of female interviewers in this context, the assurance of privacy and confidentiality during interviews, and securing the informed consent of school directors, teachers, and parents, as well as of girls themselves. By and large the research proceeded smoothly, and was welcomed, particularly by the parents and relatives who accompanied their daughters, grand-daughters, nieces, or younger sisters to the school as appointed guardians. Nevertheless, there was still a need for vigilance in this sensitive area, as potential disapproval from other relations could pose a problem. At one of the schools for girls, following a day's interviews by female staff, a male relative of one of our participants arrived in an imposing Land Cruiser. He told the school director that the girl would no longer attend her classes, and led her away; the director expressed uncertainty about whether she would be able to return to school at all, even after the completion of our project in the school. Although this was an isolated case which bewildered both the school staff and fieldworkers, it does illustrate the strength of the cultural constraints placed on female behaviour in Afghanistan, and the potential for strong, negative responses to any perceived loosening of these constraints, despite the great care taken to mitigate this.

Selection of participants

Throughout this project, it was clearly important to explain not just what we were doing, but why we were picking just a selection of participants for interviews. Our research plan was to recruit eleven to sixteen year olds, an age group which had been previously studied in several national and community mental health surveys across the world. We planned to access this group through government and NGO-run schools, contacting parents or designated guardians via the intercession of school directors. Our sample would thus be confined to the target age group enrolled in primary or secondary education; due to disruption of education under the Taliban, children of this age range were found even at primary level. Recruitment of a representative sample of adolescent boys and girls outside the schools would have been extremely difficult: parents who were keeping their children – particularly girls – out of formal education (see Oxfam 2006) were not likely to give consent for our staff to conduct face to face, private interviews. An added benefit of this approach was that the research could be conducted within the school gates, a safe location for both staff and participants in the areas we worked in.

To ensure that our data were representative of the population group we were studying, we insisted on multi-stage random sampling, first drawing a random sample of schools, and then a random sample of those students enrolled within selected schools. Given the importance of representative sampling in research within the field of biological anthropology, let us elaborate what was entailed by these sampling procedures.

Our procedure for random sampling was well thought-out, but acquiring the information necessary to implement our strategy was not easy. Obtaining a list of schools in a given area, or a list of students enrolled at a particular school, was at times extremely difficult due to poor on non-existent record-keeping. In Kabul, for example, we compiled a list of all 165 government schools in the municipality, which accounted for some 699,808 students across the sixteen 'educational zones' defined by the authorities. Creation of a master list of schools for Afghanistan's capital involved a special visit to individual zone managers. The Department of Education, while having a list of schools, did not have data which would allow a breakdown of the student population by school, basic information which was needed to properly sample our target group.

Once we had compiled figures for student enrolment by school and educational zone, we randomly selected schools from our master list, using a method which weighted schools by the size of its student population. In this manner, we were effectively using the school system (and the data we had compiled on it) to establish a sampling frame for all eleven to sixteen year old students. Once the schools had been chosen, we drew a random sample of eleven to sixteen year olds within them.

This last step was well explained to school directors and class teachers: because we could not select everyone for participation in the survey, we would select a sample of students by chance.

Random sampling is a notoriously tricky concept to convey. Although we explained and demonstrated the process, many remained unconvinced or simply unclear as to why such a complex method of choosing people was necessary. Why not just pick the most able students, such as the ones who would be more able to provide answers to our questions? Why not interview all the orphans, who have more difficulties than any other students? Why not just interview everyone? This sort of feedback from local participants generated another question regarding the actual practice of fieldwork – what did people think we were really doing (Figure 9.2)? There was clearly scepticism about the need to create a representative sample. One school director commented, 'Really, it is fine to go to boys' schools, but there is no need to go to the girls' schools for this.' There was also genuine incomprehension of the painstaking effort put into compiling class lists for use in the selection process – in Kabul, many secondary schools had over a thousand names to record, with no age-segregated class lists available for our use. One school principal, thinking he could have saved us a lot of trouble by selecting the students himself, exclaimed: 'It's like you are trying to eat with your hands tied behind your back!' Again, despite careful and repeated explanation, random sampling was not a procedure that made much cultural sense to the parents or guardians interviewed. Some parents had explicitly asked that their child be interviewed; when their child was not selected for participation by random sampling procedure, they were likely to say 'Allah did not choose us.'

Expectations of good outcomes

One stage of the research process proved particularly useful to identify problems, clarify meanings, and evaluate the data collected. It was designed as an explicit wave of fieldwork evaluation, to be completed after all data collection had been undertaken in a school. This procedure required a second, smaller wave of face-to-face interviews to be scheduled with the school director and a sub-sample of teachers, pupils and parents, using a structured questionnaire with a randomly-selected sub-sample of respondents. This was difficult to carry out: many fathers did not want to take time off from work, and many mothers could not rearrange an escort by a male relative, to return to the school to be reinterviewed. Nevertheless the evaluation provided some interesting insights as to respondents' attitudes towards the research project and its purpose.

The evaluation was based on fourteen short, direct questions about the project such as: What was this project about? Do you think this project was worthwhile? Do you think the project raised many hopes and expectations? Was the project about things that were important to you? (Table 9.4). Respondents were also asked to give reasons for their replies to some of the evaluative questions. It was clear from the answers collected that even simple, straightforward questions were interpreted and answered on the basis of subtle expectations of 'good outcomes'. The reasons given by some respondents for their answers at times revealed an interesting discrepancy between scientific and local expectations.

Figure 9.2. Fieldwork in Kabul city: the project manager explains to a school director and staff at a school how students will be chosen for participation by random sampling (reproduced with permission).

Table 9.4. A formal questionnaire for fieldwork evaluation (selected items).

Questions asked in face-to-face interviews, recalling participants after data collection:
• What was this project about?
• Was the purpose of the project explained to you before work began?
• Did any of the questions upset you?
• Do you think this project was worthwhile?
• Was it good to run this project in your area?
• Do you think the project raised many hopes and expectations?
• Was the project about things that were important to you?
• Would you participate in a project like this again if you were asked to?

In Kabul, for example, responses regarding our project were overwhelmingly positive, with over 95 per cent of respondents affirming that the project had been clearly explained, that they enjoyed participating in it, that they believed it was worthwhile, and that they would participate again if asked. On the face of it, one would conclude that the work was fully understood by just about everyone involved, and greatly appreciated. But other responses collected on this apparently short, simple questionnaire raised questions about what participants actually thought and demand more careful evaluation.

For example, 90 per cent of respondents thought that the project 'raised many hopes and expectations, for teachers, parents, or children'. This, for Western investigators, is clearly a problematic finding: we are used to conceptualising 'basic research' as a legitimate process of enquiry even though it will not deliver immediate or direct pay-offs to participants. Research applications vetted by research or ethics committees explicitly ask investigators to state whether projects might raise unreasonable expectations in local communities: the implication being that this would be unethical, unless explicitly addressed with project briefs and signed records of informed consent by participants. For Afghan respondents, however, to raise expectations in people is a very good thing. In the words of many of the parents, 'The project raised everyone's expectations', and so 'Everyone is waiting to see what the results will be', results being synonymous with practical assistance in this context. Our research activities only made sense to local people if they led to some form of practical, visible, and above all prompt outcome. Collecting information had to be 'useful' in terms of addressing pressing present needs, and doing so fairly soon; if not, it was considered a waste of time.

On the other hand, many adolescents told us that they liked participating in the project because it was the very first time they had been able to express their feelings, concerns, and aspirations for the future. They viewed their interview experience positively, simply because it was new and different for them; they felt special because they had been chosen, and their ability to complete the interview gave them a boost of confidence. Many teachers also rated the project positively because it was the first time they had been asked to reflect on the mental wellbeing and material circumstances of their pupils, and in some cases, the first time they had had the opportunity to meet with the parents. Mothers rarely, if ever, visit the girls' schools unless specifically requested to do so. They responded very favourably to this project – because of the opportunity to visit the school, to have a free health check, or to talk to our female project staff.

Ethical issues

In certain contexts, fieldwork can be an emotional rollercoaster. In the course of this project, we were confronted with reports of explicit violence, injustice, torture, crime, corruption, ethnic cleansing, domestic abuse, kidnapping and murder. We feel that there is an important responsibility to address issues raised in the personal narratives elicited in face-to-face interviews. To this end, we held a daily debrief of activities. Following each day's interviews, the field team would meet and discuss their work, and any issues or observations arising from it. This allowed the staff to raise and review any difficulties encountered, including important ethical issues.

By way of example, we outline the cases obtained in the course of a single day of fieldwork, in a school which catered for children from very poor families in Kabul. Our interviews featured, among other questionnaires, a traumatic event checklist (adapted from the Harvard Trauma Questionnaire and the checklist used with adolescent refugees in Gaza) as well as an open-ended questionnaire about the most important problems currently faced by the respondent.

The first case was brought to our attention during a lunchtime break by one of the interviewers, who recounted his conversation with an eleven year old boy. The boy said he had witnessed the arrest, torture and murder of a fourteen year old boy by 'the Taliban'. While reports of injustice, violence and execution were frequent, the manner in which the victim had been tortured was uncommon: the murderers had allegedly 'driven nails into his body, all down his arms and legs' prior to executing him. The unusually repulsive nature of this crime caused us to question whether the boy had actually witnessed such a horrific event. Was he exaggerating to attract attention? The ensuing discussion prompted the interviewer to recount his own experience of harassment by the Taliban: he had been stopped on his way to classes, and because his appearance was deemed unacceptable, had had his hair forcibly shaven in the street; he was left with two bands on his skull in the form of a cross, 'north-south like the road from Khost to Kabul, and east-west, like the road of Herat to Kandahar'. The interviewer was convinced that the boy's story was genuine.

Back inside the school, when we were taking measurements of health status, one of the project staff brought over the mother of one of the pupils, whom she had just interviewed. The woman said she was beaten by her husband, who once had hit her with a hot steam iron; she had a deep scar on her upper arm and body. She said her husband was prone to violence because he was addicted to opium; she made it clear there was no one she could turn to for protection or assistance. Her husband would beat 'his mother, his sister, everyone else in the house'. Her inlaws were given to telling her husband that he should beat his wife instead of his blood relatives. Her own family had washed their hands of the matter, because she now 'belonged to her husband's family' and had to accept her fate. Her husband was unemployed, and the family lived off whatever her son could earn by selling plastic bags in the bazaar, after school.

What should be done in a case like this? Though possible, directing this woman to one of the few women's shelters in Kabul could not be recommended: we were told by Afghan staff that a woman who left her marital home in this way, without permission, could face twenty years imprisonment. Moreover, if what transpired in the interview became public knowledge, the husband might feel justified in actually killing his wife. In the end, it was impossible to engineer a way of directly assisting this poor woman: the case was simply beyond our capability. Under these circumstances, is there consolation in the knowledge that research would be raising awareness of the problem of domestic violence, with specific illustration of the suffering it causes?

Other stories of desperation and criminal violence came to light in subsequent interviews. One woman reported that she had just attempted suicide, by taking rat poison, to escape beatings by her husband; she had been discovered and taken promptly to hospital. Another woman, who had no male relatives to support or protect her, flatly stated that she survived on the meagre income her teenage girl obtained from selling sheets of toilet paper in the bazaar; perversely, her biggest worry in life was that her daughter would soon be 'grown up,' ending her current means of survival: once the daughter was recognised as a 'full-grown' woman, she would lose the ability to circulate and sell goods in the market.

The last two interviews of the day were with a female and a male pupil at the school. The girl stated that the most distressing experience she could recall was the kidnapping and murder of her brother, who had been found with his eyes and kidneys missing, thus believed to be the victim of organ traffickers. The boy recounted that his father, having complained to the local baker when his family fell sick after eating some bread, was set upon by the baker's relatives and beaten up so severely he died from his injuries the following day.

The nature of this research, which included eliciting accounts of past and current violence from respondents, meant that we were bound to be confronted with disturbing narratives. It forced us to face some harsh choices. We did not provide material help to participants, many of whom were struggling to make ends meet. Indeed, to have addressed all their hardships would have meant abandoning research altogether, to join instead the ongoing reconstruction of Afghanistan, which is the responsibility of the government and the many non-governmental organizations operating in the country. We confined ourselves to simply thanking participants individually for their time (giving them each a small gift) and providing a substantial, practical gift to each of the schools we worked in (following discussions with school staff, to include, for example, the gift of mats and water coolers, or the provision of cement and cinderblocks for the construction of a much-needed classroom). As it turned out, what mattered most for many of our participants was simply being listened to and treated with respect and empathy. Many children and adults spontaneously thanked our staff for coming to their school to 'hear their story'. One expression of thanks was particularly poignant: upon receiving a cold drink from one of the field staff, one boy stated that it was the first time in his life that anyone had given him anything 'for free'.

Conclusion: linking scientific aims with community concerns

Fieldwork is costly in terms of money, time and effort. As shown in the above examples, it involves risk-taking and can be personally very demanding. Fieldwork is nevertheless the backbone of anthropological research. Our argument is that good fieldwork should do more than simply collect data within a predetermined framework: there is an obligation to reflect on research design and implementation, considerations which will contribute to data interpretation and evaluation.

In the field of biological anthropology, where work is often done in large teams, across several sites, following multiple methodologies, it is essential that we reflect more carefully on issues of process and community engagement. In this chapter, we have looked at two very different field research projects, and set out a number of practical questions to guide the conceptualization and practice of research fieldwork. We have argued that it is important to remain flexible and open-minded when implementing a research project: in some cases even the best-laid plans may go awry; in others they may require substantial modification during the course of the work, as new information comes to light; in yet other cases, community mobilization is actually the engine driving the research process. To regularly ask a set of simple but fundamental questions, why, how, and so what?, should be an iterative exercise that takes place during fieldwork, not just at the planning stage. In this way, the practice of fieldwork becomes a means of linking scientific aims more successfully to local community concerns.

Acknowledgments

Funding was obtained by the Bill and Melinda Gates Foundation for work in the Gambia, and by the Wellcome Trust [grant 073305] for work in Afghanistan and NWFP Pakistan.

References

Bhutta, Z.A. 2002. 'Ethics in international health research: a perspective from the developing world', *Bulletin of the World Health Organization* 80(2): 114–20.

Bolton, P. and T. Betancourt. 2004. 'Mental health in postwar Afghanistan', *Journal of the American Medical Association* 292(5): 626–8.

Boyden, J. and J. de Berry. 2004. *Children and Youth on the Front Line: Ethnography, Armed Conflict and Displacement*. Oxford: Berghahn Books.

Bryce, J., N. Terreri, C.G. Victora, E. Mason, B. Daelmans, Z.A. Bhutta, F. Bustreo, F. Songane, P. Salama, T. Wardlaw. 2006. 'Countdown to 2015: tracking intervention coverage for child survival'. *The Lancet* 368(9541): 1067–76.

Clarke, S., C. Bogh, R. Brown, M. Pinder, G.E.L. Walraven, S.W. Lindsay. 2001. 'Do untreated bed nets protect against malaria?', *Transactions of the Royal Society of Tropical Medicine and Hygiene* 95: 457–62.

Davis, J. 1992. 'The Anthropology of Suffering', *Journal of Refugee Studies* 5(2): 149–61.

Eggerman, M. 2003. 'Afghanistan: A View from the Ground', in O. Zollner (ed.), *Beyond Borders: Research for International Broadcasting*. Bonn: CIBAR, pp. 102–16.

Eggerman, M. (ed.). 2005. 'Questions for Afghanistan: The Impact of Cultural, Social, and Educational Factors on Research', *Targeting International Audiences: Current and Future Approaches to International Broadcasting Research*. Bonn: CIBAR.

Eggerman, M. and C. Panter-Brick. 2010. 'Suffering, hope, and entrapment: Resiliance and cultural values in Afghanistan', *Social Science and Medicine* (online proof 1–13).

Fichtenberg, C. and S. Glantz. 2002. 'Effect of smoke-free workplaces on smoking behaviour: systematic review', *British Medical Journal* 325: 188–94.

Groth-Marnat, G., S. Leslie, M. Renneker, S. Vuniyayawa and M. Molileuu. 2001. 'A Community Approach to Smoking Cessation and Relapse Prevention in a Traditional Fijian Village', in N. Higginbotham, R. Briceno-Leon and N. Johnson *Applying Health Social Science: Best Practice in the Developing World*, London: Seb Books.

Horton, R. 2007. 'Launching a new movement for mental health', *The Lancet* 370: 806.

Jamrozik, K. 2004. 'Population strategies to prevent smoking', *British Medical Journal* 328: 759–62.

Levine, R. 2004. *Millions Saved: Proven Successes in Global Health*. New Jersey: BNT Database Management.

Oxfam. 2006. *Free, Quality Education for Every Afghan Child*, Oxfam Briefing Paper 93.

Panter-Brick, C. 2010. 'Conflict violence and health: Setting a new interdisciplinary agenda' *Social Science and Medicine* 70(1): 1–6.

Panter-Brick, C., S.E. Clarke, H. Lomas, M. Pinder, S.W. Lindsay. 2006. 'Culturally compelling strategies for behaviour change: A social ecology model and case study in malaria prevention', *Social Science and Medicine* 62(11): 2810–25.

Panter-Brick, C., M. Eggerman, V. Gonzalez and S. Safdar. 2009. 'Ongoing violence, social suffering and mental health: A school-based survey in Afghanistan', *The Lancet* 374: 807–16.

Simpson, R. 2006. '"You Don't Do Fieldwork, Fieldwork Does You": Between Subjectivation and Objectivation in Anthropological Fieldwork', in D. Hobbs and R. Wright (eds), *The Sage Handbook of Fieldwork*. London: Sage Publications, pp. 125–38.

Watson, C. (ed.). 1999. *Being There: Fieldwork in Anthropology*. London: Pluto.

10

Framing the Quantitative within the Qualitative:
Why Biological Anthropologists do Fieldwork

Lyliane Rosetta

Introduction

Biological anthropologists have a biological approach to populations and consequently think in terms of physiological and biological adaptation to environment, lifestyle, and cultural habits in the natural context (Baker 1982; Johnston et al. 1990; Beall et al. 1992; Wood 1994; Brush and Harrison 2001; Vitzthum et al. 2004; Pollard et al. 2006; Steegmann 2006). For example, biological anthropologists have compared the level of physical activity and consequent energy requirements in various populations with different lifestyles, like sedentary farmers, nomadic pastoralists or hunter-gatherers; others interested determining the limits of human adaptation have measured adult or children body composition at various ages, and the change in nutritional status with seasonal variation in food availability. A number of biological characteristics were studied among contrasted group of people sharing a common factor of possible inter-individual variation, either living in the same geographical environment or exposed to the same health hazards. Others have studied the adequacy of the diet for women at various physiological status (Leslie et al. 1993; Gray 1994; Benefice et al. 2001; Dufour et al. 2003; Ferrell et al. 2006), or different aspects of human adaptability to their lifestyle like human fertility (Briebiescas 2001; Campbell et al. 2005a, 2005b, 2006; Campbell and Mbizo 2006).

A number of leading scientists around the world (North America, Europe, Asia, Australasia) contributed to the International Biological Program (IBP 1964–1974). Human biologists and biological anthropologists were particularly involved in two out of nine program areas 'Human Adaptability' and 'Environmental Physiology' (see Harrison 1976; Baker 1996). According to the Archives of the National Academies, the IBP was originally promoted in the United States by the International Council of Scientific Unions (ISU) and the International Union of Biological Sciences (IUBS). It was later suggested that 'this research contributed to the ongoing transformation of physical anthropology and related fields from a largely descriptive to an analytical science'. The ten year international programme became the base of several multidisciplinary projects in human biology: 'a subfield of demography within human biology has matured; nutrition, infant and child growth, and health studies have proliferated; and molecular genetics and DNA analysis have superseded the earlier population genetics' (Little and Garruto 2000).

For the last twenty years the main objectives of field research in biological anthropology have been:

- To understand the range in variability in one or many major biological characteristics between populations (Harrison 2001).
- To determine the precise limits of human adaptation to environments and to place each of these characteristics in their functional and evolutionary contexts (Garruto et al. 1999).
- To investigate physiological mechanisms likely to explain inter-variability between populations (Beall et al. 2002).

A few biological anthropologists claim that they can do biological anthropology without doing field research. They are involved in analyzing data collected by others (health workers or medical staff running systematic data collection), acquired by several persons (doctors, nurses or midwives) in various wards or health services, possibly using different methods or instruments of measurement, which can introduce a significant variability between measurements. In France in large hospitals, the public health service has recently created 'clinical research units' in which well-trained statistical technicians analyse the vast amount of data collected daily in medical wards and contribute to improving epidemiological data sets useful to medical or public health planners. Thus biological anthropologists will no longer have any justification for using the same medical data for their research and will have to join their counterparts who base their research on data collected during fieldwork. The salience of research findings can be enhanced by combining different approaches but biological anthropologists will never draw complete insights if they ignore the cultural context and characteristics of the population(s) studied.

Old-fashioned human fertility studies in biological anthropology had a descriptive approach to the main characteristics such as age at menarche, age at menopause and reproductive history: number of live births, miscarriages, abortions, stillbirths, duration of interval between marriage and first birth, interbirth interval, duration of menstrual cycle and the characteristics of menses. In contrast, the aims of current fertility studies are:

- To identify the range of variation in fertility between populations.
- To determine precisely the lower limit and upper limit of the normal female reproductive life and its evolution within a population (menarche or menopause).

- To study the determinants of variability in fecundity or fertility for men or women at the population level (duration of post-partum amenorrhea among lactating women or incidence of menstrual troubles among sportswomen).

This chapter will focus on fertility surveys carried out in biological anthropology during the last twenty years in very different settings and various contexts implying totally different logistics and costs for their achievement. As an example, I will relate the context and different steps of my own participation in field research carried out in developing countries. My main research interest was to try to disentangle the role of different characteristics in the lifestyle of women with suppressed reproductive function in order to assess the role of variables like breastfeeding pattern, nutrition, energy expenditure and body composition in the regulation of fertility in human populations without modern contraception.

A first experience in West Africa

In Africa, the dramatic Sahelian desertification observed between 1968 and 1986 was linked to severe seasonal drought which was highly damaging to both people and the environment. Between 1968 and 1973 successive severe rainfall deficits initiated the whole process. Local people called it the 'Great Drought'. Local authorities in collaboration with Western research institutes and universities decided to set up different research programmes to assess the extent of damage in specific geographic areas and to act to remedy the situation.

As a biological anthropologist, I was involved in a research project in the field of ecology and human biology. The aim of the study was to identify seasonal variation in food availability and food intake in rural agricultural settings and their possible impact on the regulation of human fertility (Rosetta 1986, 1988a, 1988b, 1989; Rosetta and O'Quigley 1990). A survey was conducted between July 1980 and October 1982 among a sample of about 450 people belonging to forty households randomly chosen in the rural community of Ndiaganiao, Senegal, where the national authorities gave me the permission to carry out this research.

Choice of the sample

A preliminary survey had shown the range in family size in this area, according to ethnic groups (Serere people made up a large majority) and the extremely wide range in village size.

The latter required me to stratify in order to allow for a proportional representation of small, medium and large villages. From the official tax records at the regional administration, out of a total of thirty-two villages in the rural community of Ndiaganiao, ten were randomly chosen and four households were then randomly chosen in each village. The randomization was carried out under the supervision of the highest administrator (called a 'sous-prefet'). After the identification of the forty households, the heads of the ten villages were invited to participate in a meeting organized by the administrative authority and the researcher (LR). None of them were missing. The rationale of the research and how their village were chosen was explained to the villagers. We identified the name of the head of each family randomly chosen in each village and the head of the village was asked to inform the four heads of households in his village. We then organized a second meeting to explain the aim of the study and the extent of involvement of each woman who would participate, and answered any question they and heads of households raised. After their approval we started to visit each compound selected in order to meet the women likely to enter in the survey, to explain the duration and the different aspects of the investigation (questionnaires, anthropometric measurements, food survey) and asked for their informed consent before the beginning of data collection. The study included around 450 people, consisting of approximately 200 women, their husbands (90) and their children aged less than five at the beginning of the survey (160). The newborn infants of these women during the two-year survey were then included.

The design of the survey was indexed on the maximum variation in food resources. In Sahelian countries, there is marked seasonality: the rainy season is followed by a long dry season. Peanut was the staple crop grown by many families in this area, and millet was the staple food. Each family depends on the quality and quantity of a single harvest in late September or early October, the end of the rainy season. In each household, the management of food reserves was under the strict responsibility of the head of family. When the total amount of millet is not enough to reach the next harvest, the manager will regularly decrease the daily amount of the staple food to be shared by all members of the family in order to avoid a sudden scarcity. In some families even the number of meals can decrease at the most difficult times. When there is a food shortage it happens during the wet season, the period of the year when people have to work very hard in the field to prepare for the next harvest. In terms of energy balance, a period of lower energy intake coincides for many adults with a period of higher energy expenditure. This is also the peak season for parasitic diseases like malaria or intestinal parasites, and the total health burden is heavy for deprived people. Data collection took place during two consecutive years twice a year, during the middle of the dry season, the period of relative abundance, and at the end of the rainy season, before the harvest starts. The same data were recorded on each occasion.

Ethical issues

A major concern was to keep the number of investigators to a minimum: most of the time the researcher only, accompanied by a local female interpreter belonging to a well-known and esteemed family in the rural community of NDiaganiao, and the driver. When field assistants had to be recruited, trained and supervised for the food survey for example, they were also chosen from the same community among the young people belonging to the same ethnic group. Both reproductive and food issues are delicate issues requiring particular attention. In field studies about female reproduction it is crucial to avoid any male involvement in questioning women on their reproductive health and history. In field studies requiring investigation on food and nutrition, the ethnic affiliation of the field assistant can introduce a bias. In my experience, in rural traditional populations, it is recommended to have field assistants from the same ethnic group to get reliable data. They cannot be cheated as they know the cultural habits in terms of food availability and consumption. But they should be discreet and tactful and maintain the strictest confidentiality about the situation observed in the family surveyed. It is the responsibility of the main researcher to make clear to all assistants that in case of any dereliction of duty of discretion, they will be dismissed.

How to get the confidence of the participants in the survey?

This is a major factor in biological anthropology field surveys. We need a reliable source of information to avoid bias. The population involved in the survey should have every confidence in all the staff who will be in contact with them at every level of responsibility. They also need to understand from the beginning what are for them the advantages or the disadvantages in participation. Food and reproductive issues are private matters which need mutual trust and support between the investigator and the participant in the survey. In developing countries, if we are investigating communities who have recently suffered serious difficulties like natural disaster or major conflict, it seems problematic to ask people to participate fully and honestly if they do not think that their individual participation is beneficial to the community.

The main findings of the study carried out in Senegal were to confirm that there are obvious interactions between nutrition and fertility: long lasting lactational amenorrhea was observed in this population; the composition of the diet was not adequate and resulted in specific nutritional deficiencies likely to impair hormonal metabolism. The long duration of blockade of the reproductive function in this population was explained as a combination of the central suppression of the regulation due to the suckling stimulus, reinforced by the interaction of peripheral factors associated with the composition of the diet. Energy expenditure associated with manual workload was high, particularly during the season of agricultural work and the annual harvest period when the food reserves are at their minimum. Energy balance of these women was found to be low.

The next step of my research was to try to unravel the role of chronic malnutrition (low level of energy intake) from the role of high level of physical activity, and thus to compare the effects of a high level of energy expenditure with the possible function of energy balance in the regulation of fertility. The results of the Senegalese study had also emphasized the nutritional and energetic similarities between amenorrheaic lactating women in developing countries and amenorrheaic female marathon runners in developed countries. I started to carry out parallel investigations on reproductive impairment in Western female endurance runners and to quantify the level of energy balance/ energy expenditure in lactating women living in poor nutritional environments. It was necessary to focus on populations chronically malnourished so that we could compare two groups of women having the same reproductive status. The two categories of women would differ only by one factor supposed to be causal in the regulation of fertility, in this case the level of physical activity.

A survey among chronically malnourished women in Bangladesh

The first challenge was to identify an adequate population of the chronically malnourished, in order to compare two groups of fertile women belonging to the same ethnic group, having the same food habits, and similar resources, but different levels of daily physical activity (Rahman et al. 2002). In Bangladesh in addition to the garment industry in large towns, women are employed as paid workers in the tea industry, a rural activity apparently physically demanding. We choose to focus on female tea workers, as we suspected that women employed as tea pluckers had high levels of daily physical activity and consequently high levels of energy expenditure (Vinoy et al. 2000, 2002). The women who were not employed but lived in the same tea plantation were housewives of male tea workers. From a preliminary survey we had seen that the tea workers in this area in Bangladesh were mainly of Indian origin, had kept over generations their original cultural habits, and were extremely poor.

A longitudinal survey was set up to measure the duration of post-partum amenorrhea in a sample of women recruited in the tea garden, together with the variation of body composition, level of energy intake, energy expenditure, the pattern of breastfeeding and health characteristics (haemoglobin level, detection of parasitic diseases) of the mothers, and the growth and health of their infant.

Data collection started in February 1996 and finished in November 1998, among a sample of women recruited in North East Bangladesh working for the same tea company. We had got permission from one of the major tea companies in Bangladesh to carry out this survey among their employees. We were restricted to investigate only three tea estates in the same geographical area. The socioeconomic situation of the workers was similar in the three plantations. The tea workers and their families lived in villages organized in labour lines inside the tea plantation. They were provided with very simple housing, without electricity or access to schooling and with only rudimentary health care from the tea company. The tea workers were extremely poor and most of them were illiterate. A number of adults and children suffered from chronic malnutrition and parasitic diseases. It was not possible to know a priori if the level of physical activity was quantitatively high (PAL level) among tea pluckers and if their PAL level was significantly different from the group of women living in the same villages but unemployed, i.e., housewives of men working in the tea plantation. Our results showed that the difference was significant, with women employed in the tea plantation having higher levels of physical activity than their unemployed counterparts, although their nutritional status was slightly better since their families probably benefited from a higher income than the families in which only the husband was employed (Rosetta et al. 2005).

To run the protocol, we had the participation of a team composed of researchers, Ph.D. students and research assistants. We recruited a number of local assistants that we had to train and to supervise during the thirty-four months of data collection. Research assistants filled in weekly and monthly questionnaires, recorded anthropometry, and collected biological samples over time. To assess energy intake, energy expenditure and breastfeeding pattern, specialized methods were used, such as heart rate monitoring, doubly-labelled water method, and a minute-by-minute record of activity (Ghosh et al. 2006). The same female assistants attended the same women throughout the survey; also, their number was kept to a minimum.

In this situation, though we had gained informed consent from each participant before the beginning of data collection, we knew that the women had little opportunity to choose whether or not to participate in the survey since the tea manager had approved our project. We made clear to each of them that they had the possibility of withdrawing at any time if they were not able to continue. But none of them left the study before reaching an end-point based on defined criteria of exclusion (new pregnancy, confirmed return of menses, use of hormonal contraception, and others), except for one woman who was seriously ill and unable to participate. It turned out that it was even rewarding for the participants to know that people from outside the tea industry were visiting them regularly and they began to consider that we were looking after them and their infants. The whole team was extremely committed to the survey and supportive of mothers who needed health care for themselves or their children.

Local assistants were recruited from families connected to the tea company; this was partly because of a firm request from the tea manager not to employ assistants from outside the company, and also because these assistants lived near the tea plantation in which the women in the survey stayed, and were locally known as honourable people. We employed female and male assistants with various levels of education. Almost all of them worked in a satisfactory manner; with rare exceptions, they all were extremely respectful to the mothers. Those who did not had to leave the project.

Choice of non-invasive methods of data collection

Biological anthropologists combine interviews (questionnaires) with the collection of biological samples and various measurements like body composition, food intake, daily energy expenditure and other physiological tests (Garnier and Bénéfice 2006). Except for human relationships during the actual survey, the choice of methods of investigation adapted to fieldwork can be crucial for the acceptance by the subjects in the long term and the compliance with frequent and regular sampling. To follow the same group of people during two or three years with data collection every week or even every other day for some variables, is quite a different task from occasional visits and the collection of opportunistic biological samples.

In longitudinal fertility studies, biological anthropologists need to have serial sampling from the same subject in order to establish either hormonal profiles or to detect new pregnancies or early miscarriages. A single sample only is generally useless for this purpose, given that hormonal profiles during a full menstrual cycle inform us about various potential causes of subfertility or infertility. Ovulation is a key indicator. In ovulatory cycles, the respective duration of follicular and luteal phase, and the characteristics of the luteal phase are all reliable sources of information on fertility.

In order to select non-invasive methods of sampling and assay procedures, it is usually preferable to use saliva or urine samples instead of blood sampling, to carry out serial hormonal assays in field studies (O'Connor et al. 2003, 2006). When blood samples are necessary, this is often limited to blood spot sampling (Worthman and Stallings 1997; McDade et al. 2000; Campbell and Mbizo 2006; Campbell et al. 2006). The choice of the fluid to be obtained is also a function of cultural habits and taboos in the population studied. Since the first requirement is total acceptance by the subjects, other needs must be linked to those of the convenience of collection, storage, handling and transport of the whole samples collected from the field to the lab. We generally choose to collect very small volumes, preferably on filter paper, without need of freezing before storage in the lab. Otherwise, preservation of biological samples in field conditions may depend on a reliable electric power supply, access to rapid transport, reasonable cost of storage and transport, which are proportional to volume and weight of the whole amount of samples. Once in the lab biological anthropologists can choose between radio-immunoassays used by clinicians, and enzyme immuno-assays, which are often preferred, to carry out the assays. In urinary or saliva samples one can assay sex steroid hormones glucuronide derivates like Estrone-3–glucuronide (E1–G), Pregnanediol-3a-glucuronide (PdG) during menstrual cycles, or gonadotrophin hormones like luteinizing hormone (LH), human chorionic gonadotropin (hCG), prolactin (PRL) during pregnancy. For example, urinary assays for hCG in field studies were carried out during an eleven month prospective study of fetal loss in rural Bangladesh using a modified pregnancy test for hCG (Holman et al. 1998). Urine samples were collected from 494 women: 330 pregnancies and ninety-three fetal losses were detected with this method. Urinary hormonal assays were also used to study intrauterine mortality in nomadic and settled women in Turkana, Kenya. These assays enabled the detection of pregnancies at an early stage, and early miscarriages. Our results suggest an exceptionally high rate of fetal mortality in the settled Turkana of Morulem but a low rate among the nomadic population. A satisfactory explanation is likely to involve environmental stresses associated with settled life in this semi-arid environment (Leslie et al. 1993; Pike 2005).

Such investigations become very informative and allow one to go deeply into the physiological understanding of human adaptation to environment according to lifestyle. Many large projects have been carried out over years in remote areas (Bailey et al. 1992; Rosetta et al. 2005; Ferrell et al. 2006; Vitzthum et al. 2006). Most of them have combined questionnaires with collection of series of biological samples necessary to run hormonal assays.

How is it possible to introduce biases during fieldwork studies?

In human populations for ethical reasons, studies carried out by biological anthropologists in natural settings are mainly observational, either descriptive or etiological and may have the same bias as epidemiologic surveys. The definition of the sample should comprise criteria for inclusion and exclusion. During fieldwork, loss of follow-up, withdrawal, and censored data are all potential sources of bias. It is then crucial to avoid selection bias during the phase of recruitment by using proper designs. Bias of sampling can be indirect or linked to external factors. They can result from various circumstances: remote place of residence can lead to missing subjects difficult to reach for the investigators. In fertility studies we may have difficulties in recruiting women shortly after delivery, when young women leave their husband's house to stay at their mother's house for a little while: in this case, the short absence of women from home at the time of recruitment can create bias. Medical or psychological factors may also bias recruitment; these factors can also introduce a further bias during follow-up. In addition since young women are more likely to visit their mother's house after delivery than older women, this tradition may introduce a selection bias in age. When we study two groups, the loss in follow-up may be greater in one group compared to the other one and we should suspect a confounding factor which was not clearly understood at the beginning.

Whatever the source of error in the information obtained, a study subject may be misclassified. A selection bias can severely interfere with the conclusions of the study. A variable that potentially affects an outcome variable should be carefully controlled and a pilot survey held to detect potential bias of auto-selection. An example of bias we had to face was as follows: a multinational study of breast-feeding and lactational amenorrhea was carried out in seven different countries by the World Health Organization Task Force on Methods for the Natural Regulation of Fertility (1998a, b). The Bangladeshi study refered to earlier in this chapter (Vinoy et al. 2002; Rosetta et al. 2005; Ghosh et al. 2006) was based on the same protocol with permission of the WHO. Out of the seven centres selected to participate in the multinational study, five were in developing countries (China, Guatemala, India, Nigeria, Chile), and two were in developed countries (Sweden and Australia). Although we applied the same protocol, major differences appear in our results (Table 10.1): in the multinational study, the median duration of lactational amenorrhea ranged between 122 and 282 days (WHO Task force 1998a, 1998b) while in the Bangladeshi survey it was 491 days (Rosetta and Mascie-Taylor 2009). Since another major difference was in the nutritional status of the women included in both studies, we can suspect this factor to have a significant and causal effect on the duration of blockage of ovarian function in women with similar patterns of breastfeeding. Mean Basal Metabolic Index (BMI) ranged between 21.4 to 24.8 in the WHO multinational study, that for the Bangladeshi women was 17.8 ± 1.6 (chronic malnutrition, level III), at three and a half months post-partum. The nutritional status was significantly different between the two studies. If we hypothesize that breastfeeding pattern and duration are not the only determinants of the duration of lactational amenorrhea, nutritional status becomes a key (or confounding) factor.

Table 10.1. Duration of lactational amenorrhea by place and nutritional status of lactating women (WHO multinational study and Bangladeshi study with the same protocol).

	Duration of Lactational Amenorrhea (days)	BMI of the Mother at 6 weeks post-partum (kg/m2)
	Median (95% CI)	Mean ± sd
• CHENGDU	282 (266-304)	21,5 ± 0,08
• GUATEMALA CITY	209 (196-228)	24,8 ± 0,12
• MELBOURNE/SYDNEY	272 (258-285)	24,8 ± 0,14
• NEW DELHI	122 (111-134)	21,4 ± 0,13
• SAGAMU	234 (215-255)	24,5 ± 0,12
• SANTIAGO	171 (156-183)	24,8 ± 0,06
• UPPSALA	230 (221-241)	24,0 ± 0,12
• BANGLADESH STUDY	491 (418-564)	17.8 ± 1,6 (1)

(1) at 15 weeks post-partum

What was the source of bias in this particular example? A single criteria of inclusion was able to modify the composition of the sample population: for practical reasons, WHO choose to include only women able to read and write, so that the women could themselves fill in the forms, whilst in Bangladesh we did not make this requirement but selected women solely by occupation. The tea workers employed in the tea garden were extremely poor, having almost daily, very heavy sessions of work during the plucking season, were illiterate in 99 per cent of cases and unable to fill in forms. We recruited a number of female field assistants to visit the women every week and fill in the questionnaires translated in the language of the tea workers (in this case Hindi). Otherwise all other criteria of inclusion and discontinuation were similar in both studies. The results show that our sample was significantly different from the whole sample of the WHO Multinational Study and highlight the fact that breastfeeding alone cannot explain the variability in duration of post-partum amenorrhea among populations.

Students doing fieldwork: what we teach them about field techniques and what they learn in the field

When we are carrying out fieldwork in countries with different cultures and different socioeconomic levels than in our own, which happens very often, it can be a real experience for students. Since it is for them often their first experience in a developing country, together with their first experience of research in the field, it becomes a new environment added to a personal adventure, which we cannot do in their place, as well as a research experience, and they have to learn. We should pass on our knowledge and help them to avoid difficulties. We also have to train them in field methodology. In biological anthropology we commonly use anthropometry, questionnaires, heart rate monitoring, and many other techniques of record to assess nutritional and energetic variables together with reproductive variables. We often need to set up a pilot survey to test the possible methods of recording and adjust or select the most adapted to the situation.

This preliminary phase is run with voluntary subjects who will never be included in the survey itself and is designed to train research assistants and students to acquire the skills necessary to insure the success of data collection. The process should be closely supervised by researchers since the quality of data (repeatability and precision of the measurements, reliability and accuracy of the measurement) determine the full success of the project. Although the reverse is rare, but may happen, most of the students who embark on field research for an M.Phil or a Ph.D. have an interest in understanding different cultures and how to handle delicate topics with people who are not scientists and who require explanation of what we are doing and how they will contribute.

Another aspect is the relationship between students, research assistants and other collaborators, like computer technicians or other health staff. When students have the role of supervising part of the data collection or part of the project, particularly in developing countries, they must be unpretentious and certainly not arrogant with local staff.

Conclusion

Biological anthropologists do fieldwork to try to disentangle the role of different variables in various aspects of physiological constraints imposed on human beings by their lifestyle. Another aim of fieldwork in biological anthropology is to question the limits of adaptation to the environment in functional and evolutionary contexts. It is then appropriate to test hypotheses among a representative sample of populations, or to examine sub-samples of a population chosen with particular characteristics, in order to control a causal factor and then draw a comparison between other factors. For practical reasons, it is not always possible to select large and representative samples of populations. Subsequent statistical analysis requires careful handling.

Many pilot surveys have led to modification of an original protocol, since one of the permanent challenges during fieldwork is to balance the acceptability to participate for the subjects involved with the number of measurements needed. In addition we have to keep to a minimum the intra- and inter-investigators' variability in measurements. Although fieldwork in difficult settings, in terms of distance, transport facilities, climate, or even accommodation, can be a proper test for the researcher, most biological anthropologists consider that it is also a rewarding and valuable step in their research and they would never change over to analyzing data whose reliability they cannot control.

The greatest chance of bias creeping in is likely to happen when participants are not confident with the investigators, when they are not really willing to participate or when they find the study too demanding. In biological anthropology, during fieldwork, human relationships are crucial to the success of the project, as in other disciplines, but the quality of data collection depends largely on this factor. In field research, all human beings, either voluntary participants, technical collaborators, or local authorities are equally important and should be approached with caring consideration.

References

Bailey, R.C., M.R. Jenike, P.T. Ellison, G.R. Bentley, A.M. Harrigan, and N.R. Peacock. 1992. 'The ecology of birth seasonality among agriculturalists in central Africa', *Journal of Biosocial Science* 24: 393–412.

Baker, P.T. 1996. 'Adventures in human population biology', *Annual Review of Anthropology* 25: 1–18.

Beall, C.M., C.M. Worthman, J. Stallings, K.P. Strohl, G.M. Brittenham, and M. Barragan. 1992. 'Salivary testosterone concentration of Aymara men native to 3600 m', *Annals of Human Biology* 19: 67–78.

Beall, C.M., M.J. Decker, G.M. Brittenham, I. Kushner, A. Gebremedhin, and K.P. Strohl. 2002. 'An Ethiopian pattern of human adaptation to high-altitude hypoxia', *Proceedings of the National Academy of Sciences of the USA,* 99: 17215–8.

Bénéfice, E., D. Garnier, and G. Ndiaye. 2001. 'High levels of habitual physical activity in West African adolescent girls and relationship to maturation, growth, and nutritional status: results from a 3–year prospective study', *American Journal of Human Biology* 13: 808–20.

Bribiescas, R.G. 2001. 'Reproductive ecology and life history of the human male', *American Journal of Physical Anthropology* Suppl 33: 148–76.

Brush, G., and G.A. Harrison. 2001. 'Components of length growth variation in infants from the same population but different environments', *American Journal of Human Biology* 13: 197–203.

Campbell, B., P.B. Gray and P. Leslie. 2005. 'Age-related changes in body composition among Turkana males of Kenya', *American Journal of Human Biology* 17: 601–10.

Campbell, B.C., P.W. Leslie, M.A. Little, and K.L. Campbell. 2005. 'Pubertal timing, hormones, and body composition among adolescent Turkana males', *American Journal of Physical Anthropology* 128: 896–905.

Campbell, B., P. Leslie, and K. Campbell. 2006. 'Age-related changes in testosterone and SHBG among Turkana males', *American Journal of Human Biology* 18: 71–82.

Campbell, B. and M. Mbizo. 2006. 'Reproductive maturation, somatic growth and testosterone among Zimbabwean boys', *Annals of Human Biology* 33: 17–25.

Dufour, D.L., J.C. Reina and G.B. Spurr. 2003. 'Physical activity of poor urban women in Cali, Colombia: a comparison of working and not working women', *American Journal of Human Biology* 15: 490–7.

Ferrell, R.J., K.A. O'Connor, D.J. Holman, E. Brindle, R.C. Miller, G. Rodriguez, J.A. Simon, P.K. Mansfield, J.W. Wood, and M. Weinstein. 2007. 'Monitoring reproductive aging in a 5–year prospective study: aggregate and individual changes in luteinizing hormone and follicle-stimulating hormone with age', *Menopause* 14: 29–37.

Garnier, D. and E. Bénéfice. 2006. 'Reliable method to estimate characteristics of sleep and physical inactivity in free-living conditions using accelerometry', *Annals of Epidemiology* 16: 364–9.

Garruto, R.M., M.A. Little, G.D. James, and D.E. Brown. 1999. 'Natural experimental models: the global search for biomedical paradigms among traditional, modernizing, and modern populations', *Proceedings of the National Academy of Sciences of the USA* 96: 10536–43.

Ghosh, R., C.G.N. Mascie-Taylor and L. Rosetta. 2006. 'Longitudinal study of the frequency and duration of breastfeeding in rural Bangladeshi women', *American Journal of Human Biology* 18: 630–8.

Gray, S.J. 1994. 'Comparison of effects of breast-feeding practices on birth-spacing in three societies: nomadic Turkana, Gainj, and Quechua', *Journal of Biosocial Science* 26: 69–90.

Harrison, G.A. 1976. 'Genetic and anthropological studies in the human adaptability section of the International Biological Programme', *Philosophical Transactions of the Royal Society of Biological Sciences* 274: 437–45.

——— 2001. 'Comparative stress in human societies', *Journal of Physiological Anthropology and Applied Human Science* 20: 49–53.

Holman, D.J., F.N. Rasheed, C.M. Stroud, E. Brindle, K.A. O'Connor and K.L. Campbell. 1998. 'A commercial pregnancy test modified for field studies of fetal loss', *Clinica Chimica Acta* 271: 25–44.

Johnson, P.L., J.W. Wood, and M. Weinstein. 1990. 'Female fecundity in highland Papua New Guinea', *Social Biology* 37: 26–43.

Leslie, P.W., K.L. Campbell and M.A. Little. 1993. 'Pregnancy loss in Nomadic and settled women in Turkana, Kenya: a prospective study', *Human Biology* 65: 237–54.

Little, M.A., and R.M. Garruto. 2000. 'Human adaptability research into the beginning of the third millennium', *Human Biology* 72: 179–99.

McDade, T.W., J.F. Stallings and C.M. Worthman. 2000. 'Culture change and stress in Western Samoan youth: Methodological issues in the cross-cultural study of stress and immune function', *American Journal of Human Biology* 12: 792–802.

O'Connor, K.A., E. Brindle, D.J. Holman, N.A. Klein, M.R. Soules, K.L. Campbell, F. Kohen, C.J. Munro, J.B. Shofer, B.L. Lasley and J.W. Wood. 2003. 'Urinary estrone conjugate and pregnanediol 3–glucuronide enzyme immunoassays for population research', *Clinical Chemistry* 49: 1139–48.

O'Connor, K.A., E. Brindle, R.C. Miller, J.B. Shofer, R.J. Ferrell, N.A. Klein, M.R. Soules, D.J. Holman, P.K. Mansfield and J.W. Wood. 2006. 'Ovulation detection methods for urinary hormones: precision, daily and intermittent sampling and a combined hierarchical method', *Human Reproduction* 21: 1442–52.

Pike, I.L. 2005. 'Maternal stress and fetal responses: evolutionary perspectives on preterm delivery', *American Journal of Human Biology* 17: 55–65.

Pollard, T.M., N.C. Unwin, C.M. Fischbacher and J.K. Chamley. 2006. 'Sex hormone-binding globulin and androgen levels in immigrant and British-born premenopausal British Pakistani women: evidence of early life influences?' *American Journal of Human Biology* 18: 741–7.

Rahman, M., C.G.N. Mascie-Taylor and L. Rosetta. 2002. 'The duration of lactational amenorrhea in urban Bangladeshi women', *Journal of Biosocial Science* 34: 75–89.

Rosetta, L. 1986. 'Sex differences in seasonal variations of the nutritional status of Serere adults in Senegal', *Ecology of Food and Nutrition* 18: 231–44.

——— 1988a. 'Seasonal variations in food consumption by Serere families in Senegal', *Ecology of Food and Nutrition* 20: 275–86.

——— 1988b. 'Seasonal changes and the physical development of young Serere children in Senegal', *Annals of Human Biology* 15: 179–89.

——— 1989. 'Breast feeding and post-partum amenorrhea in Serere women in Senegal', *Annals of Human Biology* 16: 311–20.

Rosetta, L., and J. O'Quigley, 1990. 'Mortality among Serere children in Senegal', *American Journal of Human Biology* 2: 719–26.

Rosetta, L., A. Kurpad, C.G.N. Mascie–Taylor and P.S. Shetty. 2005. 'Total energy expenditure H₂ ¹⁸O, physical activity level and milk output of lactating rural Bangladeshi tea workers and non tea workers', *European Journal of Clinical Nutrition* 59: 623–31.

Rosetta, L. and C.G.N. Mascie-Taylor. 2009. 'Factors in the regulation of fertility in deprived populations', *Annals of Human Biology* 36: 642–52.

Steegmann, A.T. Jr. 2006. 'Physiological Anthropology: Past and Future', *Journal of Physiological Anthropology* 25: 67–73.

Vinoy, S., L. Rosetta and C.G.N. Mascie-Taylor. 2000. 'Repeated measurements of energy intake, energy expenditure and energy balance in lactating Bangladeshi mothers', *European Journal of Clinical Nutrition* 54: 579–85.

Vinoy, S., C.G.N. Mascie-Taylor and L. Rosetta. 2002. 'The relationship between areca nut usage and heart rate in lactating Bangladeshis', *Annals of Human Biology* 29: 488–94.

Vitzthum, V.J., H. Spielvogel and J. Thornburg. 2004. 'Interpopulational differences in progesterone levels during conception and implantation in humans', *Proceedings of the National Academy of Sciences of the USA* 101: 1443–8.

Vitzthum, V.J., H. Spielvogel, J. Thornburg and B. West 2006. 'A prospective study of early pregnancy loss in humans', *Fertility and Sterility* 86: 373–9.

Wood, J.W. 1994. 'Maternal nutrition and reproduction: why demographers and physiologists disagree about a fundamental relationship', *Annals of the New York Academy of Sciences* 709: 101–16.

World Health Organization Task Force on Methods for the Natural Regulation of Fertility. 1998a. 'The World Health Organization Multinational Study of Breast-feeding and Lactational Amenorrhea: I. Description of infant feeding patterns and of the return of menses', *Fertility and Sterility* 70: 448–60.

World Health Organization Task Force on Methods for the Natural Regulation of Fertility. 1998b. 'The World Health Organization Multinational Study of Breast-feeding and Lactational Amenorrhea: II. Factors associated with the length of amenorrhea', *Fertility and Sterility* 70: 461–71.

Worthman, C.M. and J.F. Stallings. 1997. 'Hormone measures in finger-prick blood spot samples: new field methods for reproductive endocrinology', *American Journal of Physical Anthropology* 101: 1–23.

11

Considerations on Field Methods Used to Assess Nonhuman Primate Feeding Behaviour and Human Food Intake in Terms of Nutritional Requirements

Claude Marcel Hladik

Measuring food intake has been a major issue in our multidisciplinary research team, where anthropologists and primatologists worked together aiming at the objective of a better understanding of food preferences and choices in various contexts, especially in environmental settings where indigenous, spontaneous species can cover most of the nutritional requirements. The idea of merging primatological studies with an anthropological approach resulted from the search of methods to differentiate what part of the feeding behaviour is exclusively determined by biological factors and what is shaped by the sociocultural context including symbolic aspects, which can become a major force determining food choices in human groups. This important anthropological basis of human feeding behaviour was the major concern of Igor de Garine, who conducted field studies, mostly in Africa, during the second half of the twentieth century (Garine 1972, 1993). When I met Igor De Garine at the end of the 1970s, and when we decided to construct a research team together, I had conducted fieldwork on several wild primate species, with the aim of understanding the origin and the evolution of feeding behaviour (Hladik 1988). Of course, the differences in our approaches have never been excessively different, since nonhuman primates share with humans several traits that are now considered as 'cultural' (see, for instance, the review by Jolly 1999), whereas some human cultural traits have been understood as biologically adaptive (Pasquet et al. 1993).

Indeed, one of the topics in which our respective primatological and anthropological approaches converged was methodology, for example how to measure accurately feeding behaviour and food intake, in order to compare different ethnic groups, or, among nonhuman primates, different species? Since the time of early field studies our research team has been reshaped and renewed – including young researchers on food perception – under the leadership of Serge Bahuchet, with whom we have conducted surveys of food production in various environments, either 'natural' or partly reshaped by human settlements (Bahuchet et al. 1990). However, the methodology remains a central issue of the field approaches of feeding behaviour (Simmen et al. 2004). In this context some of the new techniques recently introduced in the field will be presented and discussed in relation to the experience of previous fieldwork.

Methods for measuring food intake in nonhuman primates

The field methods used by primatologists to compare feeding behaviour of different primate species, or groups living in various environmental conditions, must be adapted to peculiar aims since no previous approach allows accurate results in both the fields of biology and behaviour, both are necessary to understand the global phenomenon of feeding. The measurement of the actual food intake of wild primates is particularly time consuming and can be done only in a few places where the conditions of visibility are exceptionally good. This is why, in most instances, only the feeding time is recorded, generally with an indirect statistical method (periodical scans of individuals), which allows comparison of behavioural traits, but not necessarily that of the diet.

For instance, during an early primatological survey in Sri Lanka (Hladik 1977), undertaken with a team of the Smithsonian Institution which included students of the University of Peradeniya, we were able to follow a targeted animal, from dawn to dusk, in some study areas. This was possible in the Sacred Area of Polonnaruwa, where Buddhist pilgrims have been in peaceful contact with the monkeys for centuries. In such places, where natural vegetation is partly open, the conditions of visibility allowed the observer to record the exact number of fruits eaten, or the number of mouthfuls when the animal was feeding on large flower bunches or packs of young leaves. It was sometimes necessary to use a tape recorder when the feeding activity was too fast to allow the taking of notes. Calculation of the food ingested during a day necessitates samples to be collected, fruits, flowers and leaves to be weighed and for the mouthfuls including a small number of young leaves and/or flowers, to be reproduced as accurately as possible, after comparing estimates of different observers. Although collecting, weighing and preparing food samples for further biochemical analysis necessitated almost as much time as the daytime observation, the cooperation and relay at midday of the observers allowed them to obtain the series of data presented in Figure 11.1 (each dot along the time axis is a full day of observation), for two species of leaf monkeys, *Semnopithecus entellus* and *S. senex*. The food intake of another species of primate, the toque macaque (*Macaca sinica*) was also recorded in the same area, with the same method, during a period also covering the entire seasonal cycle.

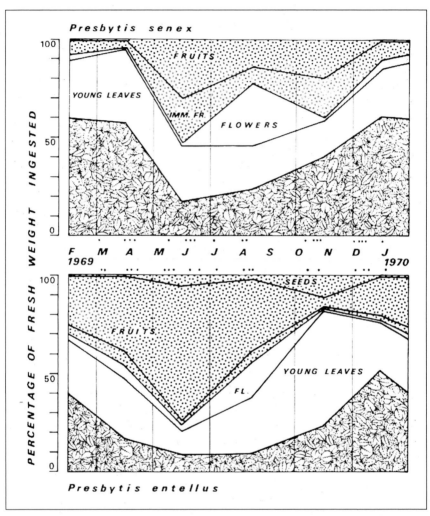

Figure 11.1. Comparison of the seasonal variation of food intake of two species of primates, *Semnopithecus senex*, (upper), and *Semnopithecus entellus*, (lower) in their natural forest habitat. Each dot along the time axis represent a full day of continuous observation focused on one species and followed by a day for collecting and preserving food samples. The field technique used allows one to compare cumulative percentages of actual weights of various foods ingested (along the vertical axis), which vary throughout the seasonal cycle; nevertheless, at any time, *S. senex* is more folivorous than *S. entellus*. Such a specific difference in food choice, also concerned with the type of food plants, corresponds to a difference in energy intake, linked to group size and range size (after Hladik 1977).

The tables 11.1 and 11.2 show examples of the results obtained after full days of observation, during which we have been able, with the help of my colleagues of the Smithsonian Institute (Susan Ripley, Rudy Rudran, Wolfgand Dittus, and their Ceylonese Students) working on territorial and social behaviour of the same primate species, to compare the results obtained with various techniques. It is particularly interesting to consider the feeding time, obtained either by scans (statistically showing the time spent feeding on various food items), or by the actual recording of the time spent feeding by one targeted animal during the whole day. The comparison thus includes the feeding time and our results calculated in terms of the actual weight (in grams) eaten by one individual primate during the same day.

In Table 11.1, concerning the feeding behaviour of *Semnopithecus senex*, the results of various calculations do not much differ, either when considering the feeding time, or the food intake, at least in terms of the percentage of fresh weight of leaves of various tree species that were eaten vs the percentage of feeding time spent on these plant species. This may show the value of using the easy method of scan sampling for recording feeding time, when the speed of feeding is even for plucking, crushing and swallowing leaves, by the whole group of primates.

However, the other example of a full day of records of the feeding behaviour of *Semnopithecus entellus* (Table 11.2), observed after the monsoon rains have stopped, when fruits were available in large amounts, shows such a large difference between the percetage of feeding time and that of the actual food intake (for instance 28 per cent vs 77 per cent for the fruits of *Ficus benghalensis*), that we can consider the comparison of feeding time as totally irrelevant for research on the diet. The discrepancies are even more important for primates (such as macaques) feeding on insect and/or other invertebrates for which the foraging time could be extremely important and the weight of food obtained is low (for instance, in a period of ten minutes, either 50–100 gm of fruit is eaten, or 1–2 gm of small insects are obtained by active foraging) but insects provide fat and protein necessary for a balanced diet.

Accordingly, to compare the annual variation of food intake by two different species as shown in Figure 11.1, it was crucial to utilise the quantitative method based on the fresh weight actually ingested. Furthermore, this type of comparison allows one to investigate the energy balance in relation to the food choices and the relative use of various plant parts and plant species, and the chemical composition of these foods. While there is a parallel trend in the seasonal variation of the diet of both primate species due to seasonal availability of fruits and leaves resulting of the monsoon cycle, the computation shows that the two species obtain the major part of their annual diet from a different set of products. *Semnopithecus senex* is the most folivorous at any time of the year and obtains 70 per cent of its annual food intake from the three most common tree species, especially *Adina cordifolia*, whereas *Semnopithecus entellus* eats more fruit and includes ten tree species (including those used by *S. senex*) to make 70 per cent of its annual intake (Hladik 1981).

In short, one species (*S. senex*) feeds on the most abundant plant parts that provide a low energy return. This is linked to a strategy of low energy expenses, with small groups of four to seven individuals living in small territories (two to seven

Table 11.1. Comparison of the results obtained with various field methods for the measurement of food intake by one *Semnopithecus senex*, observed in Sri Lanka, in April, during one day, from 6:30 to 18:30.

Sample eaten	Time spent feeding (min)	(%)	Amount ingested, fresh weight (g)	(%)	Amount ingested, dry weight (g)	(%)
Fruits of *Ficus benghalensis*	36	28·1	1200	77·3	250·9	71·2
Fruits of *Drypetes sepiaria* (stones not included in weight)	19	14·8	126	8·1	31·5	8·9
Fruits of *Schleichera oleosa*	20	15·6	68	4·4	22·1	6·3
Fruits of *Walsura piscidia* (with seeds eaten)	11	8·6	24	1·5	6·4	1·8
Fruits of *Alseodaphne semecarpifolia*	10	7·8	40	2·6	9·8	2·8
Young leaves of *Streblus asper*	5	3·9	4	0·3	0·7	0·2
Young leaves of *Tamarindus indica*	10	7·8	13	0·8	2·9	0·8
Flowers of *Tamarindus indica*	2	1·6	3	0·2	0·8	0·2
Leaves of *Alangium salviifolium*	6	4·7	60	3·9	23·1	6·6
Leaves of *Mimosa pudica*	9	7·0	14	0·9	4·3	1·2

Time spent feeding annotations:
28·1% of the feeding time spent on [14·8, 15·6, 8·6] 46·8% *Ficus benghalensis*; 7·8 on other fruits.
13·3% on young leaves and flowers [3·9, 7·8, 1·6]; 11·7% on leaves [4·7, 7·0].

Amount ingested, fresh weight annotations:
77·3% of the fresh weight ingested from [8·1, 4·4, 1·5] 16·6% *Ficus benghalensis*; 2·6 from other fruits.
1·3% from young leaves and flowers [0·3, 0·8, 0·2]; 4·8% from leaves [3·9, 0·9].

Amount ingested, dry weight annotations:
71·2% of the dry weight ingested from [8·9, 6·3, 1·8] 19·8% *Ficus benghalensis*; 2·8 from other fruits.
1·2% from young leaves and flowers [0·2, 0·8, 0·2]; 7·8% from leaves [6·6, 1·2].

Table 11.2. Comparison of the results obtained with various field methods for the measurement of food intake by one *Semnopithecus entellus*, observed in Sri Lanka, in June, during one day, from 5:30 to 18:30.

Sample eaten	Time spent feeding (min)	(%)	Amount ingested, fresh weight (g)	(%)	Amount ingested, dry weight (g)	(%)
Mature leaves of *Adina cordifolia*	57	30·0	165	30·0	56·0	29·8
Mature leaves of *Schleichera oleosa*	40	21·1	150	27·3	86·7	46·1
		51·1% of the feeding time spent on leaves		57·3% of the fresh weight ingested from leaves		75·9% of the dry weight ingested from leaves
Young leaves and shoots of *Schleichera oleosa*	52	27·4	115	20·9	22·9	12·2
Young leaves of *Garcinia spicata*	27	14·2	70	12·7	7·1	3·8
Leaf flushes (and some flowers) of *Walsura piscidia*	9	4·7	30	5·5	9·0	4·8
		46·3% on young leaves and shoots		39·1% from young leaves and shoots		20·8% from young leaves and shoots
Green fruits of						

hectares). The other species (*S. entellus*), which lives in larger groups (including twelve to twenty-five individuals) in larger territories (ten to fifteen hectares) obtain a richer diet by spending more energy on moving and finding plant parts providing more energy, especially sweet fruits. The comparison has also been made with the macaque (*Macaca sinica*) living in the same forest with an even higher investment of energy providing a richer diet; however the comparison of the two species of *Semnopithecus* is particularly interesting to consider as a model, because these two species have a similar body weight, and, finally, with an energy investment totally different can reach a similar population density by using a quite different strategy of energy balance.

Considering these published results on the primate diet, that are not easy to produce and not very abundant in the current literature, I was recently extremely surprised by the comments of one of the referees of a paper submitted to an international journal by my colleagues, who obtained reliable and complete results on the actual food intake of a lemur species inhabiting a dry forest in the North West of Madagascar. The referee was asking 'But why has the standard method (scan sampling) not been used?' In this case, the lemur species is mainly frugivorous, implying that a method based on feeding time (scan sampling) is not at all adequate. Because it does not require as much field work as recording the actual food intake, and statistical comparisons are easier, the most used method of sampling is based on feeding time, and most published studies are a result of the use of this field method. Is this a criterion for considering it as a standard?

Methods for measuring energy expenditure

Recent field methods used in primatology could involve more sophisticated techniques. This is the case of studies on energy expenditure carried on in the south of Madagascar. These studies currently follow the work of Rasamimanana et al. (2006) showing that among ringtailed lemurs (*Lemur catta*) the dominance of females is not directly linked to energy expenditure. The energy expenditure of male and female *L. catta* calculated by Rasamimanana has been based on the factorial method, which consists of adding the time spent for various activities affected by a factor representing the level of energy spent (for instance, during walking slowly, or for running) related to body size. Such factors have to be determined for each type of activity (see the review by Pasquet, 2004). Although this requires several tests in the field, the factorial method has been utilised for studies in anthropology allowing comparison of different ethnic groups in Africa (Pasquet and Koppert 1993).

For the studies on the ringtailed lemurs (*Lemur catta*) and on other lemur species of Madagascar, it was not easy to evaluate the accuracy of the factorial method, since it implies adding a series of estimates of energy expenditure, for species whose metabolism slightly differs from that of other primates. Accordingly, the field study that started in 2006, aiming at an accurate measurement of energy expenses, was based on doubly labelled water (water including the stable isotopes deuterium and oxygen 18), a method which is also used for anthropological studies, but which was rarely utilized in the field, and never for wild lemurs. The animals have to be captured (a syringe with ketamine is thrown with a blowpipe) and doubly labelled water is incorporated into the bloodstream. After a few days (four days in this case), the animal has to be re-captured for someone to take another sample of its blood.

The technique consists of measuring the turnover of two isotopes: deuterium (^{2}H) and oxygen 18 (^{18}O) over the period of four days in order to estimate the quantity of carbon dioxide produced and thus the energy expended during this period of time. The energy expenditure is calculated according to the difference in the proportions of deuterium and oxygen 18 found in the blood at the start and at the end of such a field experiment. Of course, the analysis of the blood samples in terms of stable isotopes requires the know-how of a specialized laboratory and the cost of such analysis (including that of doubly labelled water) implies a careful planning for studies on non-human primates as well as for studies in anthropology.

Diet and energy expenditure in human populations

In fieldwork concerning human diet and energy balance, although the backgrounds where human populations are embedded are as much socioculturally as biologically determined, the environmental and biological conditions involve issues that are partly similar to those that we have to face for primatological studies.

The actual measurement of the food ingested could be extremely precise, although the quantitative method requires an important investment in time by a scientific team and should be carefully prepared in terms of contacts and collaboration with the local population that might eventually consider this type of approach as too much invasive. For instance, in the comparative studies conducted in Cameroon on the Yassa, the Mvae, and the Bakola Pygmies (Koppert et al. 1993), the individual portions were actually weighed, as well as the uneaten remains. The information, concerning food intake of forty persons in each village and thirty-three persons in the Pygmy camps, was stored for computation by an iterative process, with a program that was developed by Koppert. This peculiar computation was necessary, because, in several instances, the food was taken from a communal dish (that was weighed), and the expected distribution among the participants has to be calculated. And the results allowed one to compare the seasonal cycle of food intake (Figure 11.2) in these various groups utilizing different parts of the available food resources, in relation to practices, knowledge and beliefs.

Before such field studies, some of the anthropologists of our team, who had previously studied the social structures and ways of life of the ethnic group, had to spend as much time as necessary to prepare the place where the field work on food anthropology could be undertaken. For instance, in the Cameroonian areas where the above described studies have been carried on, meetings were organised under the authority of the chief of the village, to obtain a consensus of the inhabitants, some of whom, in turn, would benefit from temporary paid jobs for participating in the weighing of foods. However, the limit of our inputs in terms of money or other gifts was to avoid interfering with the food system that we were actually measuring. This

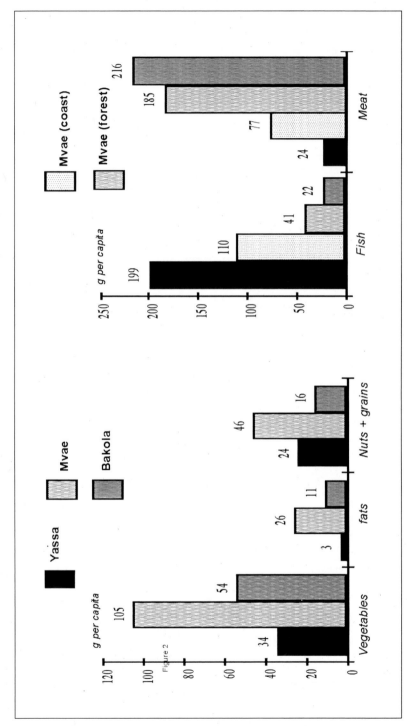

Figure 11.2. Relative importance of different food classes in four populations of southern Cameroon, as percentages of the total intake, respectively for vegetables (left) and meat or fish (after Koppert et al. 1993).

is a classical issue concerning even physicists who know that there is a limit when measuring the trajectory of a particle, since the actual system of measurement might change the trajectory. In our case, we had to be sure that most benefits obtained by the villagers from our study were preferentially invested in the roofing or other improvement of their housing, or for their children's education, etc., rather than for canned food, that was indeed rarely bought and used in the villages where we investigated food anthropology.

The most accurate measurement of individual food consumption in a communal dish might imply wider interference between the system of measurement and what is actually measured. It was carried on during a field study among the Ngbaka of the Central African Republic (Koppert and Hladik 1990). A fast and precise electronic scale, a material which is currently very common in food shops, but was an expensive device for a laboratory at this time, was connected to a micro computer, all these materials being carefully protected against humidity (Figure 11.3). As the participants were picking up the food in the communal dish (either the meat dish, or the dish with yam or cassava), each of the events was recorded after an immediate calculation (by the computer) of the difference in weight of the communal dish before and after taking the food. Thus the field assistant obtained, for each participant, the exact weight actually ingested. The shape and duration of the meal is also recorded by this method. Although requiring a total involvement of the participants in the field research and a period of habituation to forget the unusual setting, the results were fruitful in ethnological terms. The communal dish appears as a way to mask the

Figure 11.3. An accurate measurement of the individual food intake in a communal dish. The dish is placed on a precision scale (one gram for 30,000 gm) protected in a trunk with a thin PVC sheet and dryer. The operator, whose micro-computer is also protected from humidity, records the weight of each helping for each participant.

social status of the participants, since no individual part of the dish is obviously attributed. Whereas the social status generally leads to the adults (especially the adult males) getting a large portion of protein, masking the actual intake of the participants in a communal dish is a way to provide a better share to the children who need a larger portion of protein. Indeed the children actually obtain, in the communal dish, enough protein to cover their nutritional requirements. This social and nutritional function of the communal dish could be verified by such a sophisticated field method. However, this type of exceptional study needs a deep involvement of the participants, who must be sufficiently relaxed to forget the technical context for a while. This was enabled by the network of exchanges and emphatic social links between the team of anthropologists that were established during the years preceding such studies.

The results of the actual food intake can be easily converted in terms of energy, using the FAO tables and/or the results of analysis of food samples collected during the field study. Nevertheless, a study of the energy budget also requires measurements of the energy expenses. The techniques for such measurements are very similar to those described above for nonhuman primates, and again, the factorial method is the one most frequently utilised. In this case the accuracy can be satisfactory, when the energy expense during each type activity is measured. This was performed by recording the production of carbon dioxide during the activities (such as walking, chopping wood with machete, harvesting manioc, etc.) performed by a subject wearing a mask connected to a Douglas bag (Figure 11.4), and analyzing the carbon content of the exhaled gas (Pasquet and Koppert 1993). Again, the technical sophistication of the

Figure 11.4. A Douglas bag receiving the exhaled gas during a specific activity (here preparation of manioc) to determine the energy expenditure for calculation of the energy budget, in a village of southern Cameroon.

methodology, that should be partly forgotten by the habituated observed person, necessitates a previous approach by the team of anthropologists, in order to reach a local consensus, with mutual benefits for carrying out the study.

In southern Cameroon, in the different villages where such measurements have been performed (in parallel with the quantitative study of the diet described above), there was a survey of the time allocation conducted on a total of eighty-seven subjects (twenty-six Yassa men and eighteen Mvae men, twenty-two Yassa women and twenty-one Mvae women). Each subject was followed by a local assistant, to record minute-by-minute activities. The results allowed one to compare activity levels and patterns on work days, as well as the seasonal variation of the activity levels. Those were, as expected, related to the level of energy intake that was calculated according to seasonal variation of food intake, but large differences have been found between fishermen Yassa and among Mvae, with the women showing significantly higher energy expenses during the major dry season, when most time is devoted to agricultural tasks.

The human energy budget has also been studied with the method of the doubly labelled water, which, in this case, is carefully sipped in a glass by a subject in order to estimate the quantity of carbon dioxide produced and thus the energy expended during a standard period of time. This accurate but expensive method was used in northern Cameroon to study the energy balance during a period of traditional intensive overfeeding, the *Guru Walla* (Pasquet et al. 1992). The aim of this study, that was coupled with a social anthropological approach, was to legitimate the induction of some energy-wasting adaptive process (*luxuskonsumption*, or dietary induced thermogenesis) during this extreme case of overfeeding.

Field studies on taste perception and feeding behaviour

Field methodology also shows parallel issues for studies on taste perception among nonhuman primates and human populations. However, whereas verbal communication allows a simplified approach of what is perceived by *Homo sapiens*, for all other primates, studies of taste perception imply a long period of testing to obtain statistically significant results.

Moreover, most studies on nonhuman primates have to be carried out under laboratory conditions, in order to provide access to tasting solutions to an isolated animal. The 'two-bottle test' allows one to determine the difference of consumption between two solutions and after varying the concentrations (a process that can take several months). The taste threshold is the minimum concentration of a solution (for instance of sucrose) which is differentiated from pure water (Simmen et al. 2004).

Field studies on taste perception are thus exceptional in non-human primates. A study on the perception of tannins could be carried out recently on a group of ringtailed lemurs (*Lemur catta*) freely ranging on a large enclosure. In this enclosure, the animals can be followed and the 'two-bottle test' provided in protected boxes giving access to the identified target animal (Simmen et al. 2006). A 'two-bottle test' on free ranging lemurs was also carried on in the south of Madagascar (Simmen

2004) at the edge of the forest, showing the threshold to acid solution of a young lemur, who later is going to feed on the very acidic pulp around the seeds of the tamarind tree (*Tamarindus indica*).

Interestingly, such measurements of the taste responses correspond to the measurements that, in nonhuman primates, could have been carried out on the taste nerve. In the most recent research, the recording of the taste responses to solutions in contact with the tongue have been done on isolated nerve fibres (Hellekant and Danilova 2004) and, in some instances directly on the neurones of the taste areas of the brain of a macaque (Rolls 2004).

Nobody could even think of carrying out such investigations on humans; however, a non-invasive approach to human taste perception, that is easy to carry on in field conditions, led to parallel conclusions about taste sensitivity (Hladik et al. 2003). A total of 412 subjects were tested in Africa, Asia, and Europe. The test solutions of pure compounds (fructose, sucrose, citric acid, sodium chloride, quinine, tannin, etc.) were tested at random, but starting from the most diluted solutions in series prepared with local drinking water. In such blind tests (Figure 11.5), the subject, who has to name, in his/her own language, the quality of the taste, at first perceives the most diluted solution as pure water and can name the taste quality only when the concentration is higher. The lowest concentration correctly named for a given substance is considered as the taste recognition threshold and is among the most important parameters playing a basic role in individual responses to foods.

As for nonhuman primates, the human taste responses to solutions of pure compounds are not measurements of levels of responses to what has been considered as 'basic tastes' (salty, sweet, bitter or acid). Such 'basic tastes' are approximate definitions in various languages, but do not correspond to what is shown by the experiments described above, each taste signal (even for a pure compound) involving simultaneously several types of taste fibres. Testing taste sensitivity with various compounds is just a way to investigate the functioning of the whole taste system, especially when comparing the relationships between the responses to various compounds. Such a comparative approach enabled by interdisciplinary field research was conducted by our team in anthropology and in primatology, led us to consider the former and recent impacts of evolutionary trends on the taste system. It helps to explain the present condition of *Homo sapiens* and the relationships with the cultural parameters that strongly interfere with food preferences and food choices.

A major consequence of natural selection among primates is the dichotomy of the taste system, allowing them to discriminate what is potentially harmful (the bitterness of several alkaloids or the astringency of tannins) from what is beneficial and provide energy, especially the various sugars present in the fruit pulp of the angiosperms that evolved in parallel with primates during the Caenozoic (Hladik et al. 2003). These evolutionary trends also explain the possible utilisation of plant secondary compounds that are harmful and efficient for protecting the plant, but useful as 'preventive medicine' when eaten in small amount by the great apes and can avoid the infestation by parasites (Krief et al. 2005). In such cases, this eventually leads towards cognition and social learning.

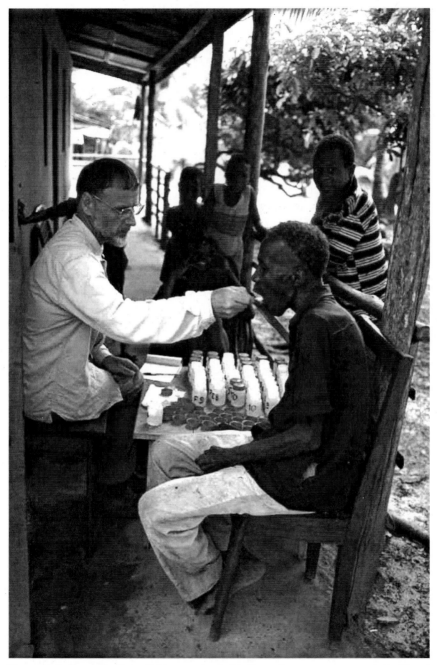

Figure 11.5. Determination of the taste thresholds for various pure compounds in diluted solutions in a village of southern Cameroon.

Finally, the history of humankind has been deeply marked by cooking foods and by the utilization of salt, the most common food additive used to improve the taste of cooked foods. But why has salt and salty taste such an impact in the collective representations of most civilisations, whereas no selective trend has ever induced salt perception in primates? Since the concentration of sodium chloride is below recognition threshold in natural products (except along the seashore, where exceptionally some wild primates live), the functioning of our taste system is based on the gene pool of more remote ancestors than primates, especially fish. And this former ability to perceive salt allowed some of our *Homo* ancestors (not necessarily *H. sapiens*) to make a great discovery in improving food taste (Hladik 2007). The pleasurable utilization of such improved foods, in the context of social contacts, is certainly at the origin of civilization.

References

Bahuchet, S., et al. 1990. 'Agricultural Strategies as Complementary Activities to Hunting and Fishing', in C.M. Hladik, S. Bahuchet and I. de Garine (eds), *Food and Nutrition in the African Rain Forest*. Paris: Unesco, pp. 31–5.

Garine, I. de. 1972. 'The Sociocultural Aspects of Nutrition', *Ecology of Food and Nutrition* 1: 143–64.

――― 1993. 'Food Resources and Preferences in the Cameroonian Forest', in C.M. Hladik, et al. (eds) *Tropical Forests, People and Food: Biocultural Interactions and Applications to Development*. Paris: Unesco-Parthenon, pp. 561–74.

Hellekant, G. and V. Danilova. 2004. 'Coding of Sweet and Bitter Taste: Lessons from the Common Marmoset, *Callithrix jacchus jacchus*', *Primatologie* 6: 47–85.

Hladik, C.M. 1977. 'A comparative study of two sympatric species of Leaf Monkeys: *Presbytis entellus* and *Presbytis senex*', in T.H. Clutton-Brock (ed.) *Primate Ecology: Studies of Feeding and Ranging Behaviour in Lemurs, Monkeys, and Apes*. London: Academic Press, pp. 323–53.

――― 1981. 'Diet and the evolution of feeding strategies among forest primates', in R.S.O. Harding and G. Teleki (eds) *Omnivorous Primates: Gathering and Hunting in Human Evolution*. New York: Columbia University Press, pp. 215–54.

――― 1988. 'Seasonal Variations in Food Supply for Wild Primates' in I. de Garine and G.A. Harrison (eds) *Coping with Uncertainty in Food Supply*. Oxford: Clarendon Press, pp. 1–25.

――― 2007. 'Salt as a non-food: to what extent do gustatory perceptions determine non-food vs food choices?' in H. Macbeth and J. MacClancy (eds) *Consuming the Inedible: Neglected Dimensions of Food Choice*. Oxford: Berghahn Books, pp. 121–30.

Hladik, C.M. et al. 1993. 'Tropical forests, people and food: an overview', in C.M. Hladik et al. (eds) *Tropical Forests, People and Food: Biocultural interactions and Applications to Development*. Paris: Unesco-Parthenon, pp. 3–14.

Hladik, C.M., B. Simmen and P. Pasquet. 2003. 'Primatological and Anthropological Aspects of Taste Perception and the Evolutionary Interpretation of "Basic Tastes"', *Anthropologie* 41: 9–16.

Krief, S., C.M. Hladik and C. Haxaire. 2005. 'Ethnomedicinal and Bioactive Properties of Plants Ingested by Wild Chimpanzees in Uganda', *Journal of Etnopharmacology* 101: 1–15.

Jolly, A. 1999. *Lucy's Legacy: Sex and Intelligence in Human Evolution*. London: Harvard University Press.

Koppert, J.A. et al. 1993. 'Food Consumption in three forest populations of the southern coastal area of Cameroon: Yassa - Mavae – Bakola' in C.M. Hladik, et al. (eds), *Tropical Forests, People and Food: Biocultural Interactions and Applications to Development*. Paris: Unesco-Parthenon, pp. 295–310.

Koppert, J.A. and C.M. Hladik. 1990. 'Measuring Food Consumption', in C.M. Hladik, S. Bahuchet and I. de Garine (eds) *Food and Nutrition in the African Rain Forest*. Paris: Unesco, pp. 58–61.

Pasquet, P. 2004. 'The Concept of Energy Balance and the Quantification of Time Allocation and Energy Expenditure', in H. Macbeth and J. MacClancy (eds) *Researching Food Habits: Methods and Problems*. Oxford: Berghahn Books, pp. 149–60.

Pasquet, P. et al. 1992. 'Massive Overfeeding and Energy Balance in Men: the *Guru Walla* Model', *American Journal of Clinical Nutrition* 56: 483–490.

Pasquet, P., A. Froment and R. Ohtsuka. 1993. 'Adaptive Aspects of Food Consumption and Energy Expenditure — Background', in C.M. Hladik, et al. (eds) *Tropical Forests, People and Food: Biocultural Interactions and Applications to Development*. Paris: Unesco-Parthenon, pp. 249–56.

Pasquet, P. and C.M. Hladik. 2005. 'Theories of Human Evolutionary Trends in Meat Eating and Studies of Primate Intestinal Tracts', in A. Hubert, I. de Garine, and H. Macbeth (eds) *Meat: Environment, Diet and Health*. Mexico: Universidad de Gualararaja. Estudio del Hombre, 19 pp. 21–34.

Pasquet, P. and J.A. Koppert. 1993. 'Activity Patterns and Energy Expenditure in Cameroonian Tropical Forest Populations', in C.M. Hladik, et al. (eds) *Tropical Forests, People and Food: Biocultural Interactions and Applications to Development*. Paris: Unesco-Parthenon, pp. 311–20.

Rasamimanana, H. et al. 2006. 'Male and Female Ringtail Lemurs' Energetic Strategy does not Explain Female Dominance', in A. Jolly et al. (eds) *Ringtail Lemur Biology:* Lemur catta *in Madagascar*. New York: Springer, pp. 271–95.

Rolls, E.T. 2004. 'Taste, Olfactory, Texture and Temperature Multimodal Representations in the Brain, and their Relevance to the Control of Appetite', *Primatologie* 6: 5–32.

Simmen, B. 2004. 'Perception Gustative des Substances de Défense Chimique des Végétaux: Adaptation et Plasticité des Réponses des Primates', *Primatologie* 6: 149–70.

Simmen, B., P. Pasquet and C.M. Hladik. 2004. 'Methods for Assessing Taste Abilities and Hedonic Responses in Human and Non-Human Primates', in H. Macbeth and J. MacClancy (eds) *Researching Food Habits. Methods and Problems*. Oxford: Berghahn Books, pp. 87–99.

Simmen, B., et al. 2006. 'Diet Quality and Taste Perception of Plant Secondary Metabolites by *Lemur catta*' in A. Jolly et al. (eds) *Ringtail Lemur Biology:* Lemur catta *in Madagascar*. New York: Springer, pp. 160–83.

12
Anthropobiological Surveys in the Field:
Reflections on the Bioethics of Human Medical and DNA Surveys

Alain Froment

Anthropobiology is the branch of anthropology that studies humans as a biological species, focusing on evolution and variation, and including areas such as primatology, paleoanthropology, human genetics, and human ecology; some applied fields are bioarchaeology, biometrics and forensic anthropology. It is related to medicine on one side, especially epidemiology and nutrition, and of course to cultural anthropology on the other side, because there is no natural history in humanity without a cultural component: biological evolution shaped hominids towards a bigger and more efficient brain, and the brain became a culture-making organ. That is why bioanthropological practice borrows from both fields (Parkin and Ulijaszek 2007). Here we shall consider only biological research, not medical experiments, which raise completely different issues, such as drug testing. This paper explores some field problems, conceptual as well, met by anthropobiologists, which are common to those faced by cultural anthropologists.

Formerly known as physical anthropology, anthropobiology, the aim of which is to describe and explain human polymorphism, has been suspected in the past century as focussing mainly on racial classifications and as then encouraging or justifying discrimination, inequalities, or even persecutions. Craniology for instance, because of some of the ways it was used in the past, is often mistakenly portrayed as a racist tool, a view shared by some cultural anthropologists, but also popularized by some biologists (Gould 1981). That is why some ethnologists are reluctant to refer to physical anthropology ('You treat people like animals!'), while anthropobiologists have long understood that human evolution is a biocultural process. In genetics for example, the population is the group within which people intermarry preferentially (marriage is here considered as the way to transmit genes to the next generation). It is then defined by marriage circles: most traditional populations are endogamic, i.e., they impose the choice of a spouse within their own culture and vicinity, and sometimes inside the same broad family. It is then clear that biologists rely upon cultural concepts to define their object of study. In human biology, the population is called the *deme*, while an ethnic group is defined not on a genetic basis, but only on cultural traits. These ethnic traits, including food, beliefs and behaviours, are key issues for understanding risk factors in epidemiology, while the deme refers to the genetic substratum (Risch et al. 2002).

Ironically, as genetics made extraordinary progress since Landsteiner's initial discovery of blood groups one century ago, genetic markers are now seen as grossly supporting a reconstruction of races, through a geographical approach (Bamshad et al. 2004). Also, forensic anthropology sometimes uses a racial framework, mainly to comply with administrative requirements. But this approach faces growing difficulties as the proportion of people of mixed ancestry increases (Cox et al. 2006). In fact, because there is never any gap in genetic continuity, frontiers of races are impossible to delineate. A cultural anthropologist trained in biology, Franz Boas, also a leading anti-racist campaigner of the interwar period, was among the first to show, using anthropometry, that any concept of 'race' was merely a social construction. Sociologists and some anthropologists, however, find it interesting and informative to study the popular uses of the race concept.

Field methods

Since Malinowski, cultural anthropologists advocate observation by participation in the local life of the societies they study. The first step is to learn the language and, progressively and painstakingly, to understand the explanation underlying behaviours and beliefs. Such an effort is usually not made by the biologists: first, because they are always in a rush to bring back fragile samples to the lab; second, because they work in various societies and places and could not master all the local languages; and third, because they hope to study biological phenomena at the species level, with large transcultural comparisons. There are vast areas of fieldwork common to social and biological sciences, like collecting genealogies, or data on behaviour. Another, very interesting subject is related to ethnosciences, which deal with the knowledge that indigenous societies have about nature. One aspect, still not very developed, of convergence between human biology and cultural anthropology would be to study how traditional societies invent their own human taxonomy (Cormier 2002), and also, how they see the evolutionary relationship of humans with other animals, especially primates.

The collaboration between biology and social sciences led to enlightening progress in public health, like the discovery of the role of food habits in the occurrence of naso-pharyngeal cancer in South Asia (Hubert et al. 1993), or the involvement of anthropologists in the management of emerging diseases like AIDS, or Ebola (Hewlett et al. 2005). Medical, and especially public health and epidemiology, is thus a growing area of interest common to ethnologists and bioanthropologists (Craig 1986; Gulati 2006; McElroy and Townsend 2003; Trostle and Harwood 2005), generating specific ethical questions (Meskell and Pels 2005).

Anthropometric and epidemiological studies

What may distinguish cultural surveys from biological ones is the qualitative nature of the former, and the quantitative of the latter. For biologists, measuring is the baseline. From initial skull studies by Samuel Morton (1839), until the end of the twentieth century, human variation has been studied through various metric and non-metric methods. Physical anthropology was focusing both on soft parts, to determine growth and nutritional status, and on genetic characters like skin colour, hair structure, and other 'culture-free' traits not evenly distributed among humans, and related to a geographic origin (e.g., eye fold and other anatomic peculiarities). Anthropometry was mostly interested in head or skull size and shape, but also in stature or body proportions. The rationale was that bone measurements (made on the living as well as on skeletons) had a strong genetic component; in the early days when too few blood markers were available, this method proved to be quite reasonable and brought a large amount of data on the history of the human species (Lahr 1996). And obviously, on past populations and fossils where no genetic data are available, only metrics enable taxonomic studies.

Nowadays anthropometric measurements, on adults as well as on children, are mainly used as a tool for assessing nutritional status, for epidemiological surveys. The usual measures are stature, sitting height, weight, arm circumference, and various skin folds. More sophisticated techniques can be used, as the impedance meter, which measures total body fat. Methods to assess energy balance include food consumption surveys (Hladik, this volume), and energy expenditure studies; the latter may involve the use of rather heavy spirometry equipment, and some scoring activities, such as running on a treadmill or riding an ergometric bicycle. Some cultural anthropologists working on food studies understand the important contribution quantitative data can make to their studies (Garine 2006).

Other biological anthropological explorations can be more or less invasive. In the case of taste studies, surveyed people are asked to taste, and spit without swallowing, decreasing dilutions of elements like sugar, salt, or bitter substances, to determine their taste threshold, which relates to a genetic ability. For exploring lactose intolerance, people must drink a fair amount of milk or lactose, and blood sugar (sometimes hydrogen content of expired air) is measured several times; intolerant subjects may suffer transient abdominal pain or diarrhoea, which limits the acceptability of the test, though it is a very interesting way to study the coevolution of man and animal domestication (Beja-Pereira et al. 2003).

Genetic studies

Today, biological anthropologists seeking historical relations between groups carry out direct studies on DNA. Collecting DNA can be more or less invasive: it is easier to collect cheek swabs or saliva than blood. Blood collection is complicated in the field. First, cold conservation is needed, and necessitates a quick return to the lab.

Second, the handling of samples carries the risk of viral disease transmission, like hepatitis and HIV. Third, surveyed people are usually reluctant to be bled. This can be due either to a traditional reason ('blood is sacred', or 'blood cannot regenerate', so that taking even a very small amount is considered an amputation). This aspect requires a highly developed anthropological sensitivity. Interestingly, stools are an alternative source of DNA, which is already proving useful in primatology (Sommer, this volume).

However, collecting blood gives a larger DNA harvest, and allows us to study sera, where the antibodies against infectious diseases are found. Sera can be stored for decades, and can be used as archives for tracing emerging diseases, as in the AIDS example, when sera from the late 1950s were retrieved in freezers and proved the presence of AIDS at this early date. This epidemiological dimension has a great public health interest, and also has potential benefits for the study of evolution, as pathogens coevolved with humans (Wirth et al. 2005). In this manner, many microorganisms can be used as markers of human migrations: e.g., viruses (HTLVs: Black 1997; polyomavirus: Pavesi 2005; HIV: Yusim et al. 2001), bacteria (*Helicobacter pylori*: Suerbaum and Achtman 2004; *Treponema spp*.: Froment 1994; *Streptococcus* agent of dental caries: Caufield et al. 2007), endoparasites (*Plasmodium* of malaria: Kwiatkowski 2005; hookworms: Reinhard et al. 2001, tapeworms: Hoberg et al. 2001) or ectoparasites (lice: Reed et al. 2004; jigger flea: Lucchetti et al. 2006).

In sum, the rationale for conducting anthropological genetics is manifold: to search for human origins; to document human diversity within its ecological context, and to understand the evolutionary forces which shaped it, reconstructing diasporas, past migrations and palaeodemography; to define the evolutionary role of diet and disease, and eventually develop pharmacogenetics, enabling the production of treatments which match people's particular metabolism. To achieve these aims, field studies are mandatory.

Ethical issues and problems
Benefits for surveyed peoples

Essentially, anthropobiological surveys are not harmful to people. Asking them to perform some exercises, or even sampling a tube of blood is of little consequence, from a strictly medical point of view. Often, the visit of a research team is also an occasion for leisure; sometimes, when a time consuming task is requested, it can also be an opportunity for earning some money. Usually there is no payment for blood; the giving of blood is a voluntary act freely participated in: blood cannot be bought. However, because these surveys are conducted in remote areas where no modern medical care is available, the least which can be done for people at the local level is to offer a medical examination, and general acts like systematic deworming, and detection of chronic disease like hypertension (by measuring resting blood pressure), diabetes (by researching sugar in the urine with a lab stick), or sickle-cell anaemia. The first two examinations can be done on the field; the third requires electrophoresis of haemoglobin in the lab, and another field trip to bring back the results to individuals, but it is a highly appreciated practice which allows a follow-up of the survey, and meets the concern of the people: to receive some results about their blood.

One problem is often that non-Westerners living in remote areas imagine that, when their blood is examined, all the diseases they bear can be detected, and eventually cured; researchers must be clear in discouraging such hopes. Also, most of the results obtained from the blood for purposes of research cannot be communicated to donors. For example genetic markers of anthropological interest will be of no use for them; instead, some genetic tests useful in medicine, like detecting sickle-cell anaemia (as seen above), are interesting and can be returned to the participants for their own safety.

Serologies of infectious diseases studied in fundamental research raise delicate issues and it is often questionable whether one should communicate some of the results. First, the presence of antibodies is often the sign that the infection is finished, and cured; second, in the few exceptions when this is not the case (hepatitis B and C), most people are chronic carriers and do not suffer from the infection, so giving a result can be more harmful; third, the treatment is not accessible for economic reasons.

AIDS is a particular case: the incubation is very long, up to ten years, but eventually as far as we know most infected, untreated people will develop the disease; it is very important to monitor patients before they develop signs of the disease; also, drugs are now cheap or free, and even if the disease is not cured, it can be stabilized. But some people are reluctant to give their blood in medical surveys, because they suspect they will be tested for AIDS without their consent. In developing countries, up to 90 per cent of the virus carriers ignore their infection, and they spread the disease without knowing.

However, cheap and quick tests are now available, which can give a good answer in five minutes, so testing can be done on the field for people, in growing number, who ask for it. The key issue here is to preserve the autonomy and freedom of participants in our research.

At the national level, human biology projects, which must be approved by ethics committees, also must bring some benefits to the country. Such initiatives can be, as we did in Cameroon:

- foundation of a gene bank, where samples are deposited for free access to medical research;
- establishment of a sera collection, which acts as a library where all infectious diseases (including those to be discovered) affecting people, can be retrieved;
- academic and practical training of students and colleagues, including going all together into the field, participating in local universities teaching, and training students and colleagues in Europe.

A problematic situation, met by cultural as well as biological anthropologists, occurs when a severe case of disease is met in a village during the field survey. When it is an acute situation like an accident or any surgical emergency, there is usually no major difficulty in evacuating the patient to the nearest hospital. The problem arises when it is a chronic case (from usual chronic hypertension, to severe renal insufficiency, or cancer, or any other life-threatening condition). Local people cannot afford the long, sometimes life-long, and expensive treatments, nor can the research team. Usually, the only solution is an arrangement with local health facilities, but unfortunately treatment of these kinds of cases is often impossible to conduct properly.

In all cases, fundamental research must not lose sight of its ultimate purpose: alleviating the burden of diseases. For example, in 2002, genetics accomplished a triple marvel, sequencing the whole genome of the malaria parasite (*Plasmodium falciparum*), of its vector (*Anopheles gambiae),* and of its victim (*Homo sapiens*). Yet the fact that more than one million victims die of malaria every year, means that this success, if it is to be such, has to be translated into new therapies (see figure 12.1).

Difficulties and constraints
Facing cultural identities

Obviously, when biological surveys are conducted, the basic rights of the surveyed people must be protected. The first medical commandment has always been '*primum non nocere*' (first do no harm). Problems are then not caused by damaging the health of those surveyed but, usually, when local beliefs may be hurt. In the emic/etic dichotomy, cultural anthropologists are more interested studying the emic aspect, i.e., the indigenous point of view, while biologists are more interested in the etic side, i.e., explaining the situation from outside. This general difference of approach can lead to different perceptions of the same reality.

A good example is the broad question of indigenicity. The definition is far from clear (Kuper 2003). At first sight it appears simple; the indigenous peoples are the first settlers and, in a colonial context, in the New World, they represent the survivors of the first nations, who have been invaded, spoiled, and all too often, massacred by outsiders. But things are more complicated, since aborigines and invaders often interbreed, a case also observed during slavery. Indeed in the Ancient World, it is

Figure 12.1. 'Genomic fantastic breakthroughs. Not enough? More than one million people die each year of malaria'. Drawing by Christian Seignobos, IRD©, with author's and editor's permissions.

vain to attempt to define indigenicity. In sub-Saharan Africa for instance, most of the present inhabitants live in areas which their ancestors have occupied since the dawn of mankind. Often herders or hunter-gatherers are presented as indigenes just because they did not adopt agriculture, and therefore because their way of life is endangered by economic development. This leads to apparently ludicrous situations, like in Kenya where Maasai are viewed as indigenous while Kikuyu are not. More generally, each population has its own narrative of origin, and biological theories may be seen to compete with folk explanations regarding human origins. Biblical creationists are not different, in that way, from some Australian, or Native American groups, claiming that God created them locally.

As some Native Americans (here from the Havasupai tribe) put it, they 'were raised to believe that the retreat of waters from a global flood had carved the Grand Canyon, and that the Canyon is the birthplace of the human race' (Rubin 2004). Considering the 'out of Africa' story as insulting their traditions, they deny the results of DNA studies: 'That was like a scientist asking Christians from Nazareth to give blood for a diabetes study, then producing research to suggest that Jesus never existed' (Rubin 2004). Some cultural anthropologists may be sympathetic to this kind of myths, because they express certain values within a community, while many biologists are not at ease with this attitude, because it challenges the biological unity of mankind. One example of this conflict: an organization formed in 1993 to oppose the Human Genome Diversity Project (HGDP), called Indigenous Peoples Council on Biocolonialism (IPCB 2005), accused the worldwide genetic project, nicknamed 'Vampire project', to be racist, because the aim of the HGDP was to target DNA from some indigenous communities.

A similar controversy arose with respect to the study of cannibalism. The debate was started with a book by Arens (1979), later expanded by Barker et al. (1998), claiming that accounts of cannibalism were to a very great extent inventions of travellers or colonialists aiming to despise 'savages'. The debate also involves bioarchaeology, from Neanderthal to recent populations. For example, when apparent evidence of this behaviour-human flesh in a fossil stool-was found in a Precolumbian Anasazi village (Marlar et al. 2000), Native American communities became angry, because it contradicted the stereotype of the Indian-in-harmony-with-Mother-Earth (Dongoske et al. 2000). The subsequent debate, in which the scientific status of the stool analysis was questioned, underlines how very careful and scientifically cautious academics working at the interface of the biological and the social have to be when working with potentially sensitive material and interpretations.

Handling human remains and fluids

In Europe, anthropological museums are full of human remains. Most of these remains are of local origin, but a minority comes from overseas, and is now subject to repatriation demands. Conversely in the US, it is mainly the local, Native American bones, which are the subject of such claims. Biological anthropology is not the only science involved, archaeology is also concerned (Layton 1994; Vitelli 1996). In the Kennewick case (a 9,000 year-old human skeleton claimed for repatriation by local tribes of the Pacific North-West USA), the federal government decided in favour of the tribes, but biological anthropologists appealed, and eventually won their case. Those cultural anthropologists who participated in this debate appear to have been quite divided, some supporting the tribes' point of view, others their biological colleagues. Journalists, who popularize and transmit scientific knowledge to the public, called their readers' attention here to the different kinds of 'truth' that were being debated in this extended controversy (Coleman and Dysart 2005).

Clearly, conservation of human remains (bones, flesh, hair, but also mummies) raises special problems, even when they do not come from oppressed minorities (Turner 2005). Some of these bodies have been collected on battlefields, excavations, or various other ways, including the worst, but there is still a gap in legislation. Archaeological exploration of a burial is, literally, a desecration and still, even in European law, a crime. Also, beyond death, some indigenous peoples refuse that anything from a dead person, bones but also photographs, or names collected for genealogies, can be recalled. Obviously these data are basic tools in field anthropology, and most excellent ethnologists use them despite the reluctance of some tribes. There is then an urgent need of legal texts to allow archaeologists and anthropologists to work, together with the communities, for the benefit of bringing back to light the life of past populations. Guidelines of best-practice for example in the UK (DCMS 2005) are currently developed, acknowledging the fact that some peoples believe the spirits of their people cannot rest in peace until their bones are laid in their native ground (Mihesuah 2000). When the material in question is DNA and, worse, cell lines, or foetuses and still-born babies, the issue is even more sensitive. In all these cases, human remains are kept for research, though some people maintain that medical research cannot lie above their own beliefs.

This fact entails a host of important moral issues: many people waiting for a graft (mainly kidney, heart and liver) die because of a lack of consenting individuals, or families of individuals, who die in such circumstances that an organ donation could be possible. Of course in traditional societies, such a graft was not conceivable, but with modernity a lot of people are ready to accept an evolution of these practices, though most families, in developed countries, are still very reluctant to allow an organ to be taken from the body of a beloved parent. The same is true for blood transfusions: during the First and Second World War, there are stories of German soldiers preferring to die instead of receiving 'racially inferior' blood. Besides this racist view, many religions also forbid transfusion. Forensic anthropology has also difficulties, because it requires the dissection of a human body (Walsh-Haney and Lieberman 2005), for judiciary or medical reasons. Faced with these limitations, biological anthropologists and medical doctors have to defend a higher standard of ethics, where human life is put on the top of all else.

In a deeply controversial book (Tierney 2002) devoted to Amazonia, and namely to the Yanomami group, the anthropologist Napoleon Chagnon was accused of encouraging aggression and homicidal attitudes, while the geneticist James Neel was suspected of spreading measles in order to study natural selection. A specially convened committee of the American Anthropological Association later found that none of these accusations were the case (AAA 2002). But these accusations still fed hate and suspicion against anthropologists dealing with human biology. Today, some indigenes ask for the return of frozen blood from Neel's campaigns, as said Davi Kopenawa, a Yanomami representative, at the Annual Meeting of the Association of American Anthropologists, held in Washington in 2001:

> I would like to speak again about the book and the blood which was taken from my kin and taken from there and today is stored in a refrigerator. I would like to know what they want to do with this blood and why do they keep it. I want them to give the blood back to me so that I can take it back to Brazil and spill it into the river to make the shaman's spirit joyful (CCPY 2001).

This problem clearly illustrates the debate about the fate of any body part, either solid or liquid, removed from a living person, and still in storage after his or her death.

Balancing individual and community rights versus mankind rights

A difficult issue is to obtain written informed consent from surveyed people, especially when they live in remote areas, and are illiterate. How can the biologist be sure that the aims of his/her research is correctly understood? Also, when people give their agreement for one study, and the samples are kept for years, how are we to consider a new development leading to re-use of the material for other studies, which were of course not forecast in the initial survey? Should we destroy the samples after use? Go back to the field and ask for permission anew? Ask the government? Or simply consider that when people agree to give blood for medical research, it encompasses all future developments of biological research (provided that it is conducted with all ethical guarantees)? This is not a theoretical concern. In 2000, Oxford Professor of Biological Anthropology, Ryk Ward promised, after discussion with locals, to give back the blood samples he had collected among the Native American group, the Nuu-Chah-Nulth, because he used them for an anthropological investigation (Ward et al. 1991) which went beyond the initial medical research he had conducted years before (Weiss 2003). In 2004, the Havasupai tribe filed two lawsuits seeking $75 million against Arizona State University, on the basis that blood samples collected in the early 1990s were used for more than the agreed-upon diabetes research (Rubin 2004). For biologists, the ideal situation would be that sampled people give blood to science, and accept any kind of research on their blood, provided that all ethical guarantees are given, but biological anthropologists, like all other fieldworking academics, have to work in league with the peoples they survey.

Problems may arise in field research, when people refuse to allow surveys. For instance, a new virus was recently discovered in a Pygmy of the Cameroonian rainforest by our team (Calattini et al. 2005): HTLV-3 is the third virus of the HTLV (Human-T-Lymphocyte Virus) retroviruses family. It happened that a woman, divorced, with the princeps HTLV-3 case, was married to a man HTLV-2 positive, and had one HTLV-I child among her children. It was then extremely important to get some blood from that lady, who was at the meeting point of the three viruses. We do not know if these viruses can recombine in an individual, but if so, it creates a potentially big health hazard. She refused to be bled, which is her right. It could be argued that ethics, which can protect individual rights, should also consider the issue of rights at a higher level: when mankind is potentially threatened.

In the general context of biopiracy, one of the fears frequently met is that human DNA could be patented for commercial use. There is also an unsound idea that Native genes, more than any others, are treasures which could generate fortunes. Such a conflict rose in 1995, when it was revealed that Carol Jenkins, a skilled biological anthropologist, and her associates at the Papua New Guinea Institute of Medical Research and at the National Institutes of Health (USA), were accused of patenting the genome of a Hagahai tribesman in the highlands of Papua New Guinea. The patent was in fact not on the genome in itself, but on a HTLV-1 virus integrated in this genome; HTLV-1 is a plague, and developing detection tests in blood banks are a great priority. As these tests are commercialized, the felt economic need for patenting rises. Though Jenkins discussed the idea of the patent with the tribe, and was supported by its members, who would earn half the royalties, a small NGO called RAFI (Rural Advancement Foundation International) released a provocative statement on the internet, saying that 'On March 14, 1995, an indigenous man of the Hagahai people ... ceased to own his genetic material.' Eventually the patent was approved but, the next year, withdrawn (Pottage 1998). Even though accounts such as this may be outweighed by the examples where collaboration between biological anthropologists and locals has worked well, to their mutual benefit, the point remains: biological anthropologists working in the field have to be very aware of how their work may be represented by others who may have different interests.

Conclusion

Cultural and biological anthropologists face the same problems on the field, but often choose different perspectives. One of the problems is related to conservation issues: when an indigenous population lives in a park, should it be expelled to ensure peace to wild life, or not? It is a common mistake in anthropology (as in ecology, regarding environment), to consider cultures as immobile.

They are in perpetual evolution, and, due to a vivid dynamics of adaptation, what is true today may not be tomorrow. The strategies used by some activists to defend cultural identity are then more based on a short term agenda than on an immutable cosmogony. A Pygmy can still be a Pygmy, if he be an academic professor or a naked hunter-gatherer. Innumerable societies around the world, adopted Christianity, Islam, or whatever change, without disappearing. One and often two generations after the end of colonialism, the concept of 'ethnocide' (i.e., a cultural killing, while genocide is a physical killing), as formulated by Robert Jaulin (1970, unfortunately never translated into English), should be revisited.

Sensitivity of tribal populations is extremely high, due to the innumerable crimes perpetrated against them during colonization. Listening to their grievances is a way to assume the historical responsibility of Western nations. Because of these crimes, a part of Occidental opinion is ready to be sympathetic to indigenous views; while some cultural anthropologists try to keep a neutral position, others think that the only way to embrace anthropology is to fight alongside with the tribes. Biologists are not involved in such a choice. For example, while Professor Cavalli-Sforza proposed the Human Genome Diversity Project (HGDP) mentioned above as urgent, because of the quick 'disappearance' of indigenous groups, a criticism was that instead of spending money to save DNA it was wiser to act in such a way that these groups do not disappear. This example shows that the two attitudes are not opposed but complementary; most tribal groups do not disappear by physical extinction but by miscegenation.

The fundamental question for anthropologists, both cultural and biological, is then: has Occidental science a universal meaning, or is it just one conception equal to any others? Very important collections (bones, blood) have been saved by biological anthropologists. It can be argued that these collections now belong to mankind's patrimony, destroying them would be an absolute loss and would impoverish not only museums, but also future generations. Also, offering one's blood for epidemiological or genetic studies, not only helps fundamental and applied research, but can be seen as an affirmation of solidarity which connects *ego* to the rest of mankind.

References

AAA (American Anthropological Association). 2002. '*El Dorado Task Force Papers*'. http://www.aaanet.org/edtf/final/vol_one.pdf and vol_two.pdf.

Arens, W. 1979. *The Man-Eating Myth: Anthropology and Anthropophagy*. Oxford: Oxford University Press.

Bamshad, M. et al. 2004. 'Deconstructing the Relationship between Genetics and Race', *Nature Reviews in Genetics* 5: 598–609.

Barker F., P. Hulme and M. Iversen (eds). 1998. *Cannibalism and the Colonial World*. Cambridge: Cambridge University Press.

Beja-Pereira A. et al. 2003. 'Gene-culture Coevolution between Cattle Milk Protein Genes and Human Lactase Genes', *Nature Genetics* 35: 311–13.

Black, F.L. 1997. 'Tracing Prehistoric Migrations by the Viruses they Carry: Human T-Cell Lymphotropic Viruses as Markers of Ethnic Relationships', *Human Biology* 69: 467–82.

Calattini, S., et al. 2005. 'Discovery of a New Human T-Cell Lymphotropic Virus (HTLV-3) in Central Africa', *Retrovirology* 2: 30–8.

Caplan, P. (ed.). 2003. *The Ethics of Anthropology: Debates and Dilemmas*. New York and London: Routledge.

Caufield, P. et al. 2007. 'Population Structure of Plasmid-containing Strains of *Streptococcus mutans*, a Member of the Human Indigenous Biota', *Journal of Bacteriology* 189: 1238–43.

CCPY/Comissão Pró Yanomami. 2001. Associação Americana de Antropologia Discute Coleta de Sangue Yanomami. *Boletim Yanomami*, n° 23, CCPY, Brasilia. Available at: http://www.proyanomami.org.br.

Coleman, C.L. and E.V. Dysart. 2005. 'Framing of Kennewick Man against the Backdrop of a Scientific and Cultural Controversy', *Science Communication* 27: 3–26.

Cormier, L.A. 2002. 'Monkey as Food, Monkey as Child: Guajá Symbolic Cannibalism', in A. Fuentes and L.D. Wolfe (eds) *Primates Face to Face: Conservation Implications of Human and Nonhuman Primate Interconnections*. Cambridge: Cambridge University Press, pp. 63–84.

Cox, K., N.G. Tayles and H.R. Buckley. 2006. 'Forensic Identification of 'Race'. The Issues in New Zealand', *Current Anthropology* 47: 869–74.

Craig, J. (ed.). 1986. *Anthropology and Epidemiology*. Dordrecht: D. Reidel Publ. Co.

DCMS (Department for Culture, Media and Sport, UK). 2005. *Guidance for the Care of Human Remains in Museums*. Available at: http://www.culture.gov.uk/NR/rdonlyres/0017476B-3B86–46F3–BAB3–11E5A5F7F0A1/0/GuidanceHumanRemains11Oct.pdf.

Dongoske, K.E., D.L. Martin and T.J. Ferguson. 2000. 'Critique of the Claim of Cannibalism at Cowboy Wash', *American Antiquity* 65: 179–90.

Froment, A. 1994. 'Les Tréponématoses: une Perspective Historique', in O. Dutour, et al. (eds) *L'origine de la Syphilis en Europe*. Paris: Editions Errance, pp. 260–8.

Garine, I. de. 2006. 'Anthropology of Food and Pluridisciplinarity', in H.Macbeth and J. McClancy (eds) *Researching Food Habits: Methods and Problems*. Oxford: Berghahn Books, pp. 1–28.

Gould, S. J. 1981. *The Mismeasure of Man*. New York: W.W. Norton and Co.

Gulati, M. 2006. 'Epidemiology and Culture (Review)', *Perspectives in Biology and Medicine* 49: 308–11.

Hewlett, B.S. et al. 2005. 'Medical Anthropology and Ebola in Congo: Cultural Models and Humanistic Care', *Bulletin de la Société de Pathologie Exotique* 98: 230–6.

Hoberg, E.P., et al. 2001. 'Out of Africa: Origins of the *Taenia* Tapeworms in Humans', *Proceedings of the Biological Society* 268: 781–7.

Hodgson, J. 2002. 'Introduction: Comparative Perspectives on the Indigenous Rights Movements in Africa and the Americas', *American Anthropologist* 104: 1037–49.

Hubert, A. et al. 1993. 'Anthropology and Epidemiology: a Pluridisciplinary Approach to Nasopharyngeal Carcinoma', in T. Tursz et al. (eds) *Epstein-Barr Virus and Associated Diseases*. Paris: INSERM and John Libbey Eurotext, pp. 775–88.

IPCB. 2005. *IPCB Action Alert to Oppose the Genographic Project*. Available at: http://www.ipcb.org/issues/human_genetics/htmls/action_geno.html.

Jaulin, R. 1970. *La Paix Blanche: Introduction à l'Ethnocide*. Paris: Seuil.

Keele, B.F. et al. 2006. 'Chimpanzee Reservoirs of Pandemic and Nonpandemic HIV-1', *Science* 313: 523–6.

Kuper, A. 2003. 'The return of the Native', *Current Anthropology* 44: 389–402.

Kwiatkowski, D.P. 2005. 'How Malaria has Affected the Human Genome and what Human Genetics can Teach us about Malaria', *American Journal of Human Genetics* 77: 171–92.

Lahr, M.M. 1996. *The Evolution of Modern Human Cranial Diversity: A Study in Cranial Variation*. Cambridge: Cambridge University Press.

Layton, R. (ed.). 1994. *Who Needs the Past?: Indigenous Values and Archaeology*. New York: Routledge.

Lucchetti, A. et al. 2007. 'Genetic Variability of *Tunga penetrans* (Siphonaptera, Tungidae) Sand Fleas across South America and Africa', *Parasitologic Research* 593–8.

Marlar, R.A. et al. 2000. 'Biochemical Evidence of Cannibalism at a Prehistoric Puebloan Site in Southwestern Colorado', *Nature* 407: 74–8.

McElroy, A. and P.K. Townsend. 2003. *Medical Anthropology in Ecological Perspective*. 4th edition. Boulder: Westview Press.

Meel, B.L. 2003. 'The Myth of Child Rape as a Cure for HIV/AIDS in Transkei: a Case Report', *Medical Science and the Law* 43: 85–8.

Meskell, L. and P. Pels (eds). 2005. *Embedding Ethics*. New York and London: Berg.

Mihesuah, D.A. (ed.). 2000. *Repatriation Reader: Who Owns American Indian Remains?* Lincoln: University of Nebraska Press.

Morton, S.G. 1839. *Crania Americana; or, A Comparative View of the Skulls of Various Aboriginal Nations of North and South America: To which is Prefixed An Essay on the Varieties of the Human Species*. Philadelphia: J. Dobson.

Parkin, D. and S. Ulijaszek. 2007. *Holistic Anthropology: Emergence and Convergence*. New York: Berghahn Books.

Pavesi, A. 2005. 'Utility of JC Polyomavirus in Tracing the Pattern of Human Migrations Dating to Prehistoric Times', *Journal of General Virology* 86: 1315–26.

Pottage, A. 1998. 'The Inscription of Life in Law: Genes, Patents, and Bio-politics', *Modern Law Review* 61: 740–65.

Reed, D.L. et al. 2004. 'Genetic Analysis of Lice Supports Direct Contact between Modern and Archaic Humans', *PLoS Biology* Nov. 2(11): e340 (online).

Reinhard, K., et al. 2001. 'American Hookworm Antiquity', *Medical Anthropology* 20: 96–104.

Risch, N. et al. 2002 'Categorization of Humans in Biomedical Research: Genes, Race and Disease', *Genome Biology*. Available at: http://genomebiology.com/content/pdf/gb-2002–3-7–comment2007.pdf.

Rubin, P. 2004. 'Indian Givers. The Havasupai Trusted the White Man to Help with a Diabetes Epidemic. Instead, ASU Tricked them into Bleeding for Academia', *Phoenix New Times*, 27 May 2004.

Stinson, S. et al. (eds). 2000. *Human Biology: An Evolutionary and Biocultural Perspective*. New York: Wiley.

Suerbaum, S. and M. Achtman. 2004. '*Helicobacter pylori*: Recombination, Population Structure and Human Migrations (Review)', *International Journal of Medical Microbiology* 294: 133–9.

Taubes, G. 1995. 'Scientists Attacked for 'Patenting' Pacific Tribe', *Science* 270, news, 17 November 1995.

Tierney, P. 2002. *Darkness in El Dorado: How Scientists and Journalists Devastated the Amazon*. New York: Norton.

Trostle, J.A. and A. Harwood. 2005. *Epidemiology and Culture*. Cambridge Studies in Medical Anthropology N°13, Cambridge Univ Press.

Turner, T. (ed.). 2005. *Biological Anthropology and Ethics: From Repatriation to Genetic Identity*. New York: SUNY Press.

Van Heuverswyn, F. et al. 2006. 'Human Immunodeficiency Viruses: SIV Infection in Wild Gorillas', *Nature* 444: 164.

Vitelli, K.D. (ed.). 1996. *Archaeological Ethics*. Walnut Creek, CA: Altamira Press.

Walsh-Haney, H. and L.S. Lieberman. 2005. 'Ethical Concerns in Forensic Anthropology', in T. Turner (ed.) *Biological Anthropology and Ethics: From Repatriation to Genetic Identity*. New York: SUNY Press, pp: 121–31.

Ward, R.H. et al. 1991. 'Extensive Mitochondrial Diversity within a Single Amerindian Tribe', *Proceedings of the National Academy of Sciences of the USA* 88: 8720–4.

Weasel, L. H. 2004. 'Feminist Intersections in Science: Race, Gender and Sexuality through the Microscope', *Hypatia* 19: 183–93.

Weiss, K.M. 2003. 'Obituary. Richard H. Ward, Ph.D. (1943–2003): Wild Ride of the Valkyries', *American Journal of Human Genetics* 72: 1079–83. See also: http://vancouver.cbc.ca/cgi-bin/templates/view.cgi?/news/2000/09/27/bc_blood000927.

Wirth, T., A. Meyer and M. Achtman. 2005. 'Deciphering Host Migrations and Origins by Means of their Microbes (Review)', *Molecular Ecology* 14: 3289–306.

Yusim, K. et al. 2001. 'Using Human Immunodeficiency Virus Type 1 Sequences to Infer Historical Features of the Acquired Immune Deficiency Syndrome Epidemic and Human Immunodeficiency Virus Evolution', *Philosophical Transactions of the Royal Society of London, ser. B Biological Sciences* 356: 855–66.

Zhu, T., et al. 1998. 'African HIV-1 Sequence from 1959 and Implications for the Origin of the Epidemic', *Nature* 391: 594–7.

13

Field Schools in Central America:

Playing a Pivotal Role in the Formation of Modern Field Primatologists

Katherine C. MacKinnon

Introduction

Recently there has been a renewed debate about the continued existence of various subfields in anthropology, and whether or not biological and cultural anthropology can truly coexist (see Calcagno 2003; Mascia-Lees 2006; Thomas 2006; Riley 2006; Loudon, Howells and Fuentes 2006). For many trained in a traditional North American four-field approach, the very question goes against what attracted them to anthropology in the first place: the holistic exploration of what it means to be human (Peters-Golden 2004). For the aspiring anthropologist at the undergraduate level, one place to experience this holism, and to grasp an understanding of its utmost importance, is a field school where sociocultural and biological anthropology issues are tightly intertwined.

Despite a seemingly scant selection of active primatology field schools (see Appendix 13.A), there are a handful of sites in Central America that have run successful courses on a yearly basis, and which have become the standard for such curricula in undergraduate training for future researchers. Primatology field schools offer students a unique opportunity to learn about nonhuman primates in natural settings while living in a foreign country. Unlike cultural anthropology field schools which may be based in more populated areas, courses on primatology are typically located in forested rural or wilderness areas of the host countries. Thus, they often present more physical challenges to students in terms of exercise, daily hygiene and potential for occasional injury and illness. Additionally, as many field school sites are in areas that do not have continuous twenty-four hour electricity, many comforts of home such as email access and telephone communication may be severely restricted or unavailable.

Throughout this chapter I will underscore what many have noted on the subject of field schools for undergraduate students (e.g., Upham, Trevathan and Wilk 1988; Gmelch and Gmelch 1999; Wallace 1999; Walker and Saitta 2002; Pyburn 2003; Clark, 2008; Lightfoot 2009): above all, their importance in contributing to gaining first-hand experience in anthropology. Moreover, field schools are now becoming a standard component in the training of field primatologists. This trend is reflected in the increasing number of working primatologists who can trace their first field experience to an undergraduate course (Garber, Molina and Molina 2009; P. Garber, personal communication).

My main focus is on field schools in the Central American countries of Costa Rica, Nicaragua and Panamá; I have taught in all three of these countries and have done extensive fieldwork in Costa Rica. I will first give a brief background overview of four successful field school sites in these locations. I will then discuss common themes, highlighting what is taught and also challenges faced in the field. I include comments made by students on what they see as positive and negative aspects of such an experience. Finally, I will argue that field schools serve to impart essential anthropological themes such as cultural relativity and multiple ethical viewpoints, and are a crucial component in the training of future field primatologists.

A selection of field schools in Central America

There are relatively few primate field schools in consistent operation in Central American locations. The following is a selection of four sites in Costa Rica, Nicaragua and Panamá that offer courses every year (Figure 13.1; contact information listed in Appendix 13.B at the time of writing is correct, but check with the individual organisations for the most up-to-date information as field school logistics may change). It should be noted that there are no cultural anthropology field courses currently taught at the sites discussed here; one archaeology course was taught through the organisation listed for Panamá from 2002–2006. [Note: the Organization for Tropical Studies (OTS) and the Office of Study Abroad (OSA) at Duke University, US, have a well-established tradition of offering excellent summer and semester-long field courses in tropical ecology in Costa Rica. As they don't offer specific courses in field primatology *per se*, they are not discussed herein. See their website for more information: http://www.ots.ac.cr].

El Zota Biological Field Station, Costa Rica

El Zota is a relatively new biological field station in Northeastern Costa Rica (10° 33.437′ N, 83° 44.177′ W), and is part of a research area utilized by the Fundación Neotropical, which works on issues of reforestation and sustainable forest use, and DANTA: Association for Conservation in the Tropics. The field station is privately owned by a Costa Rican family, and is located near the Barro del Colorado reserve.

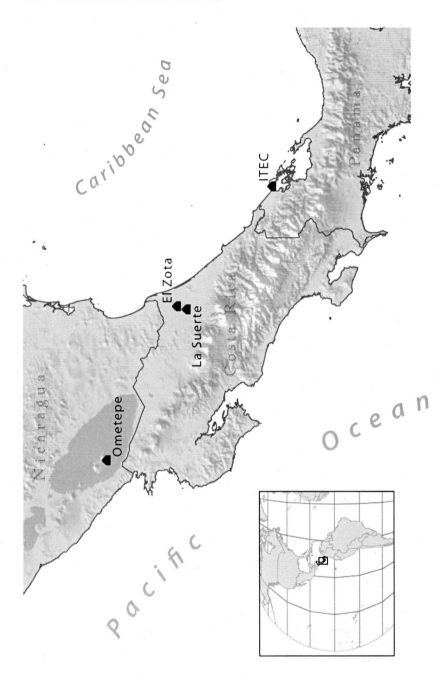

Figure 13.1. Location of the biological field stations discussed in this chapter.
Michelle S. Koo, Museum of Vertebrate Zoology, University of California at Berkeley.

El Zota is predominantly lowland rainforest (~700 hectares), although parts of the station were originally operated as a cattle ranch. Some of the old pasture areas have been converted to planted tree farms for native and exotic species. The stated goals of this field station include helping students learn field techniques that can be used on ecological, behavioural and conservation research questions in the tropics, and also to 'conserve and promote conservation of [this] land and its inhabitants in this portion of Costa Rica' (see website, Appendix 13.B).

La Suerte Biological Field Station, Costa Rica

The Molina family of Nicaragua owns and operates two separate field stations that are both part of the private non-profit Maderas Rainforest Conservancy: La Suerte (Costa Rica) and Ometepe (Nicaragua). La Suerte Biological Field Station (Estación Biología de La Suerte) in Northeastern Costa Rica (10° 26' 30" N, 83° 46'15" W) was established in 1993 (with the first primate course taught in June 1994), and since that time has hosted more than 1,300 students from the United Kingdom, United States, Canada, Latin America, India, Japan, and elsewhere. The site, known as Finca La Suerte ('Lucky Farm') was formerly part of an old cattle ranch, and is now used exclusively for research, education, and conservation. According to their website (Appendix 13.B) the station's goals are: 1) 'to challenge students intellectually and provide them with the problem-solving skills and academic background needed to address key issues in tropical ecology, environmental studies, and conservation'; and 2) 'to foster in students a love of inquiry, exploration, and learning about their natural world...by having the students actively participate in science.'

Ometepe Biological Field Station, Nicaragua

The Ometepe Biological Field Station (Estación Biología de Ometepe) is also part of the private non-profit Maderas Rainforest Conservancy, and started hosting classes in 1997; it is the first of what its founders hope will become a series of research and teaching centres throughout the country. The island of Ometepe lies in Lake Nicaragua (11° 24' 59.73" N, 85° 32' 19.56" W), and at 276 km², is the largest freshwater island in the world (McCrary, Denberghe, and McKaye 2005). Two impressive volcanoes joined by an isthmus dominate the landscape. Volcán Madera (~1,400m) is lushly forested and has been dormant since the thirteenth century, while Volcán Concepción (~1,700m) is more barren in appearance, erupted last in 1957, and had recent seismic activity in 2005 (6.2 on the Richter scale). Ometepe has a population of approximately 30,000 people (most of whom live on the Concepción side of the island), with a local economy based on agriculture (plantains are the dominant crop), livestock and tourism. The majority of island inhabitants are of Chorotegan Indian ancestry, and view themselves as distinct and separate from 'mainlanders'. The goals of the Ometepe Biological Field Station include offering field courses to undergraduate and graduate students; helping to educate and train Nicaraguan students in ecology, conservation, and field biology; and initiating long term research to obtain scientific information for management and conservation decisions (see website for complete list of stated goals).

Institute for Tropical Ecology and Conservation (ITEC), Panamá

The Institute for Tropical Ecology and Conservation (ITEC) is a non-profit education, research and conservation corporation, and operates the Bocas del Toro Biological Station in Panamá (9° 24' 51.60" N, 82° 19' 52.81" W). Located on the north end of Isla Colón, a large island in the Bocas del Toro Archipelago, the station offers field courses to undergraduate and graduate students, and also helps the local community with educational programs and workshops on conservation, reforestation, and pollution control. ITEC also tries to provide additional employment opportunities that have minimal environmental impact in the region. They have instigated a long term sea turtle conservation program which aims to relieve poaching pressure through education outreach programs and the establishment of alternative economic activities (e.g., ecotourism and promotion of indigenous and local folk art). The goal is to restore turtle nesting populations back to historic levels (see website for complete description of ITEC's programs and goals).

All sites offer four-week primatology courses, although some have shorter sessions of two to three weeks over the winter or spring academic breaks (see Appendix 13.C for a sample of course titles). Class size is usually limited to about twenty people, with one professor and up to three teaching assistants. All facilities try to ensure a small student-to-faculty ratio, so the assistants are a necessity for courses with higher enrolments. Students must be a minimum of eighteen years of age to enrol.

Housing varies somewhat, but generally four to six same-sex students are assigned to cabins or dormitory rooms with bunk beds. Faculty may share rooms or have their own, and they are typically placed in buildings separate from the students. At all field school sites discussed here flush toilets and showers are available, and a generator provides electricity for several hours each evening. Clothing is typically washed by hand in cold water and air-dried outside. Meals based on the local cuisine (vegetarian and non-vegetarian options) are eaten in a large communal dining area, and there are kitchen rotations each night (students and faculty) to help the local workers with clean-up and some food preparation.

Generally speaking there are very few serious health concerns for students travelling in Central American countries. Basic precautions should be taken regarding drinking water (i.e., know the source or drink bottled water), certain vaccinations should be current, and malarial prophylaxes should be taken if current local conditions require it.

Course curricula

The four-week primatology field schools generally include two components: field exercises and lectures during the first half, and independent research projects during the second half (see below and Appendix 13.B). The goal of any primate field course is to teach students the process of observation, data collection, hypothesis testing, and writing of a final paper in a scientific journal format, based on original data. If an undergraduate plans on graduate work in anthropology, biology, or a related discipline, gaining early field experience is worthwhile preparation for what is to come in their academic careers. The ambitious student may even publish their work:

a participant in my 2004 Nicaragua course used data she collected during the four-week session, as well as data collected over an additional two-week period after the course had ended, to publish a useful description of age differences in prehensile tail-use in mantled howler monkeys (Russak 2005). Other students have presented their findings in paper or poster format at their home universities or at regional and national professional meetings. Such experiences are invaluable for future primatologists, as the opportunity to participate in scientific meetings at an early stage in their academic careers gives them a distinct advantage in the following ways: presenting original work instils confidence, listening to other papers can stimulate original ideas, undergraduates can interact with graduate students and professors they might not otherwise have immediate access to, and the meeting environment exposes them to current scientific work and engages them more fully in anthropological discourse.

Sample course curriculum Part I: Field exercises & lectures

The first half of the course involves supervised participation in data collecting techniques and field methods. There are daily lectures and activities in the forest (Figure 13.2). Usually primate courses provide instruction and experience in the following field techniques: 1) methods of habitat description in tropical rainforests, 2) methods of collecting information on temporal changes in resource availability in the rainforest (phenology and productivity), 3) primate census and identification, 4) ethogram construction, and 5) methods of collecting standardized data on the social behaviour and ecology of free-ranging nonhuman primates (e.g., scan sampling, focal animal sampling, identifying plant species and part eaten, estimating quantity consumed).

Sample course curriculum Part II: Independent research projects

The independent research project component of the second half of the class allows students to design and implement an original scientific study (Figure 13.3). Students are graded on organization, interpretation and evaluation of field data, and the preparation of a written report based on those original data. The following components are usually required: 1) writing a research proposal, 2) collecting data, 3) analyzing data and writing a final report, and 4) an oral presentation of research results.

The combination of these two components provides students with valuable, practical skills which include research design and hypothesis testing, how to take behaviour al observations, and the use of various methods of data analyses (see Appendix A for sample course syllabi and variations on this theme). All are invaluable for students going on to graduate school in any social or natural science discipline. It should be noted that in 1994, Dr. Paul Garber (University of Illinois, Urbana-Champaign), the Director of Research and Education at La Suerte and Ometepe, designed the course structure and lesson plans that are largely followed today by most instructors at various sites (and see Garber, Molina and Molina 2009).

Many field schools also offer opportunities for travel in addition to the regular academic curricula or after a course has ended. For example, the biological field station at La Suerte, Costa Rica offers a ten-day trip called 'Eco Challenge', which includes activities in neighboring Nicaragua such as hiking extinct volcanoes, visiting sites with pre-Columbian artifacts, mountain biking, kayaking, shopping at local markets and exploring colonial cities. Until recently, ITEC offered students a special two-week course called 'Tropical Ecosystems and Indigenous Cultures of Panamá', which included travel to different areas where students were hosted by Kuna Indians in the San Blas archipelago and the Emberá Indians of the Darien region (refer to the websites listed in Appendix 13.B for updated information on these and other courses mentioned throughout; depending on personnel and funding availability, some courses may not be taught every year, new courses may be added, or some may be discontinued).

During the field school experience students are also exposed to content in concurrent courses; for example, a student taking a primate ecology course may also interact with archaeology and herpetology (the study of reptiles and amphibians) students during mealtimes and group lectures. Due to space limitations at most sites, students from a variety of courses are housed together and have many opportunities to discuss their assignments and independent research projects. These experiences augment the learning environment and students gain additional understanding and respect for a variety of disciplines they might otherwise not be exposed to. They are able to see linkages among the plants, insects, other animals, and human inhabitants of an area, and begin to grasp how various biological components fit into the tropical forest ecosystem. This type of informational cross-pollination also serves as an excellent example of how multi-discipline research teams are of great value to field studies.

Figure 13.2. Students taking behavioural data on a social group of mantled howler monkeys (*Alouatta palliata*), in the tropical dry forest of Ometepe, Nicaragua.

Figure 13.3. Students observing an adult female mantled howler monkey (*Alouatta palliata*) with her infant, Ometepe, Nicaragua.

Challenges

Field school settings pose a particular set of challenges to the instructor and the students. Challenges for the instructor can include: being available and accessible virtually around the clock, dealing with student conflicts, health problems, long intense days, unpredictable logistical issues (e.g., consistently locating the primate study groups, and handling field site difficulties such as missing equipment, lack of supplies, and so on), and time away from one's own research. Challenges for students might include: dealing with culture shock (e.g., various ethical issues, language differences, new foods, seeing poverty up-close, transportation delays) (and see Ward 1999), managing homesickness, interpersonal conflicts (often exacerbated by tight living quarters), demanding academic expectations and challenging physical conditions. Competent teaching assistants can make life easier for both instructors and students. They perform many tasks the instructor might not have time for; they help with grading assignments, and can also serve as sounding boards and mediators for student problems (particularly if some students feel reluctant in talking to the professor about such matters).

I have had many students tell me they signed up for a course because they wanted to see if they were 'cut out for' fieldwork. Some immediately fall into a daily rhythm, grabbing hold of each new challenge with a positive and humorous attitude, while others are dismayed to find the work is much more challenging than they had originally thought. Some may find reality falls short of their romanticized pre-course ideals, and feel downtrodden by the workload, while others are enchanted with each new experience and become energized from the work. Even in the most positive student, a psychological 'roller coaster ride' is to be expected, and thus, I include a discussion of this phenomenon in my course introduction. Letting students know that mood swings are a natural part of the experience can lessen anxiety; a strong support system from site coordinators, instructors, teaching assistants, and peers is crucial for a student's positive experience. Instructors can lead by example, recounting humorous stories from past fieldwork seasons (see Bearder et al., 2003), and focusing on the positives in trying situations. Running into a wasp nest while following a primate group can ruin one's day, but it can also be turned into a painfully (literally) funny tale to tell back at camp that evening. The small day-to-day irritations such as mosquito bites, rain, mud, dirty clothes, and cold showers take on greater significance than they might hold back home. A last-pair-of-clean-socks that did not dry overnight can result in a very grumpy fieldworker. It is worth reminding students that these minor annoyances will quickly fade with time, and that rather, the majority of their memories will be filled with the enjoyable times they spent in the forest, at the field site, and with each other.

Phobias: snakes, spiders, and very large insects

Field school students may arrive with many phobias, the most common being aversions to crawling and slithering creatures. Central American orb weaver spiders reach lengths of over three inches and females construct their webs from about three to six feet off the ground to higher up in the canopy (many webs are placed at face-height, which can be annoying for some on early morning walks). Tarantulas are large and dramatic looking, scorpions make unwanted appearances in living quarters and shower stalls, and brown recluse spiders (one of the most poisonous, yet least conspicuous of the Central American arachnids) are virtually everywhere. Students at the beginning of their trip are generally amazed at the sheer abundance of invertebrate and vertebrate life. Some can merely cope with it, some have a very difficult time, and still others are fascinated by the diversity of forms. I have had students in every field school say to me, 'I do not know how I am going to deal with the bugs!' and I am always surprised at the ability of most to become desensitised to what initially scares them most. Instructors must be sensitive to students' phobias. Usually being with others in the forest helps tremendously, as does learning about the natural history of the organisms. Rendering them as 'familiar,' 'interesting,' and a crucial part of the forest ecosystem serves to take off the scary edge; I try to gently introduce some of the fellow inhabitants of a field site to students who are interested. Many want to overcome their fears, and simply need a safe arena in which to do so. Also, in many of these locations, courses on herpetology are taught at the same time as primate courses, and students have access to experts who can demystify this group of animals. Herpetology instructors can also give helpful pointers to the whole camp for identifying non-venomous versus venomous snakes. This is basic information everyone should have, and students should not be allowed to pick up any snake unless under the close supervision of a herpetologist or extremely knowledgeable and experienced instructor.

Overall, links to the 'big picture' are important to highlight: invertebrates as indicators of forest health, insects as valuable additions to diet in some cultures (e.g., beetle grubs, crickets, termites); mythology and symbolism constructed around snakes and other wildlife. Finding large insects in your hair, seeing them crawling on the walls, or having them occasionally fly into your plate of food, is a reality in rural tropical settings. Most students adapt very well, even if they are initially disturbed. All of these encounters serve to normalize the forest experience and prepare students for longer stretches should they continue on in fieldwork-based anthropology.

Processing reality: emotional stages

There appears to be a general progression through four emotional stages for most students during a field course: a) initial excitement, b) acceptance of the situation and settling into a routine of hard work, c) a slight depression or lull in overall outlook, and d) a mixture of contrasting feelings as the course comes to a close. In the first stage, the student is often infectiously giddy with excitement just to be in an 'exotic' locale. They have often planned for this trip for months (or years), sometimes working an extra job during the academic year to save up needed funds. The first journey to a tropical country in Latin America by nonresidents is quite exhilarating: the warm, humid air that envelops like a soft blanket, the new sights, smells, and sounds at every turn, a foreign language in the air (for native English speakers), the explosion of insect life, and the buzz of human activity one experiences in urban areas upon arrival (which can include the stark reality of being faced with extreme poverty). Above all, students generally feel liberated: physically and psychologically, distanced from their familiar environment back home, and plunged headfirst into a new social group that will (for better or worse) become their extended family for a few weeks. Bonding with others happens immediately, and sets the stage for social connections that may continue throughout the course and beyond.

The second stage involves the true rigors of fieldwork. A routine is quickly set in place, and students are submerged in a demanding schedule of lectures, field exercises, required reading, independent project development, and sunrise-to-sunset activities. Social connections are further strengthened or frayed during this phase, as individual differences are highlighted, cliques are formed, and seemingly small issues can be magnified. The third stage of a slight depression in outlook might seem a peculiar one to those familiar with much longer periods in the field. I have found that it really does not matter if one is away four weeks, four months, or a year: we have the ability to divide the experience into 'manageable units'. Invariably this entails a period of homesickness, exhaustion, and being tired of whatever situation one is in and the group of people one is with – this phenomenon is readily apparent in field school students. It is during this third stage that a distracting intervention by the instructors is useful. Some professors pack away special treats like chocolate or other candy for mood lifters (especially appreciated after a mid-course exam). Celebrating any birthdays that occur during the class is also helpful, in addition to scheduling a mid-course 'break' of a day or two (which might include travel to a nearby beach, or a trip into town). By this point, the entire group has spent a great deal of energy, and all are thankful for a bit of rest.

Finally, as the course nears its end, a mixture of emotions emerge from the students. Many are surprised to find that despite experiencing some degree of homesickness, the end has come too quickly and they are not ready to leave. Some become more introspective and begin to truly savour their last days in the forest, and all collect contact information from those classmates who have become trusted friends and close companions. The extremely early mornings, long tiring days in the hot buggy forest, wet and smelly field clothes, and any personal conflicts that may have occurred in previous weeks, all fade to the background as the sense of the experience 'being over too soon' settles into everyone's mind. During the final days instructors may hear students describe their time in the course as 'life-changing,' 'magical,' 'spiritual,' 'awesome,' and 'amazing'.

All of the above contributes to the training of future primatologists in that they become familiar with extended periods of isolation, homesickness, boredom, and the hard work that will be required if they pursue graduate training. Becoming acquainted with the emotional (and psychological) aspects of fieldwork is just as crucial for success as learning the methodology of field-based science.

The ethnoprimatological context

Primate field schools teach more than primatology. Students are actively engaged with course material while living in a culture different from their own. While doing so, many students come face to face with perceptions of primates that differ radically from what they might be used to. For North American and European students, primates embody the exotic experience of the tropical forest. Many feel strong emotions upon seeing their first primate in the wild, and I have had several students tell me it is one of the most amazing experiences they have ever had. All students have seen primates in zoo settings, and most have grown up watching nature documentaries that depict the lives of wild animals. However, encountering a social group of primates several metres away in a natural forest setting is a visceral experience for many – an event which brings a hush of awed silence, widened eyes, and then excited whispers as they process the experience with their own primate cohort. Finding out that local people might occasionally shoot primates as crop pests, hunt them for food, or keep them as pets, can be quite disturbing for many students not accustomed to such practices. Placing such realities in a broader cultural context is necessary so that students (and instructors) can more accurately examine their own values and the values of local people (see Sponsel 1997; Cormier 2002, 2006; Fuentes 2002, 2006; Lizarralde 2002; Sprague 2002; Jones-Engle, Schillaci, and Engle 2003; Riley 2005, 2006, 2007; Loudon, Howells and Fuentes 2006; and Sprague and Iwasaki 2006 for examinations of these topics).

Nearly all instructors make mention of nurturing some degree of cross-cultural sensitivity and awareness in their students. For the vast majority of students this is a significant experience, especially while travelling and living in a developing country where the local people earn far less than the poor in their home countries (see Eudey 2002). Respecting local customs is a necessity for faculty and students alike.

Finally, with regard to gender issues, it is important to note that we typically see a preponderance of female students in late twentieth and early twenty-first century primatology field courses. In 2004 I had a total of sixteen students, fourteen of who were female (Figure 13.4); apparently about a one-third/two-thirds split between men and women students is characteristic of all US study abroad programmes (Wallace 1999). This gender 'imbalance' can make for lighthearted fun during a course. (Heterosexual) male students playfully joke they will boast to their friends back home that they were in a beautiful tropical setting with far more women than men, and women have fun 'one-upping' the men in forest field exercises. Gender equality quickly becomes the rule of the day: everyone undergoes the same physical discomforts and challenges, and all are required to do the same academic exercises. For the instructor, highlighting field school demographics can be an excellent opportunity to discuss gender in science (e.g., see Fedigan 1994 and Haraway 2000 for examinations of this topic), assumed normative roles of male and female behaviour (e.g., I have found it is often the male students who are more fearful of spiders and snakes in this setting), and what characterizes 'masculine' and 'feminine' at home and in other cultures.

Discussion

Teaching Ethics: The broader role of primatology field schools

One of the characteristics that distinguish anthropology from other disciplines is a reliance on fieldwork and ethnography as research methodologies (e.g., see Malinowski 1922; Mead 1928; Evans-Pritchard 1940; Geertz 1983; Bourgois 2003; Boellstorff 2008). For anthropologically-trained field primatologists (I would argue for all field biologists as well), engaging in the cultural landscape of a research site should be as crucial as learning the diets, home ranges, social interactions, and individual identities of our nonhuman primate study subjects (see Wheatley 1999; Fuentes and Wolfe 2002; Jones-Engle, Schillaci, and Engle 2003; Fuentes 2006; Loudon, Howells and Fuentes 2006; Riley 2005, 2006, 2007; Garber, Molina and Molina, 2009). Yet, comparatively little emphasis is placed on the importance of such issues in the training of most primatologists. Field schools stand out as an excellent setting in which to encourage values of cultural relativity and sensitivity.

In particular, to address the questions of professional ethics in primatology (and see Hill 2002; Carlsson et al. 2004; Wolfe and Nash 2005), we must ask – and urge our students to ask – three main questions. First, what information do we already have that can inform the debate on how we treat other animals or influence their lives? Second, what information should we seek to better resolve conflicting views of conservation and management? Third, how are intersections between primate researchers in host countries and local people best traversed? Students either already understand, or quickly observe, that fieldwork of any sort is not carried out in a vacuum. They should be encouraged to think about the negative and positive impacts scientific data could have on both the local people and the primates being studied (see Fuentes 2002, 2006; Loudon, Howells and Fuentes 2006; Riley 2005, 2006,

Figure 13.4. Students and teaching assistants in the author's 2004 Primate Behaviour and Ecology class, Ometepe, Nicaragua.

2007; Garber, Molina and Molina, 2009). In a field school setting students may be confronted with real life problems for which there are no easy solutions; these experiences can result in rich conversations and may encourage students to explore such topics further. In that setting, they can better see the reality of economic and sociopolitical complexities involved in many of these issues – issues that might have been viewed in more black and white frameworks back home. I provide the following questions as examples for field-based discussions:

- What are primatologists' roles as conservation/management ambassadors and educators when faced with long term embedded local traditions of human-primate interactions (e.g., primates as pets, as food, as crop pests, as tourist attractions)?
- How far should our involvement extend in terms of providing educational opportunities in host countries (e.g., training and providing support for field assistants and local high school or college students, developing information for younger children in educational programmes)?
- What does one actually do when confronted with hunting ban violations in a national park, or local animal exporters who supply the demand for biomedical research to countries that do not have a ban on importing wild-caught monkeys?
- Is it our responsibility to address land-use practices that might present short-term gain in an impoverished area, but which pose dangerous long-term effects to both local human communities and the natural habitat?

The landscape upon which all of these questions play out involves multiple ethical standards and norms. Field school students are introduced to a reality many primatologists and anthropologists face: that is, working within two (or more) sets of ethical standards (i.e., in our home countries and fieldwork locales). Students in the field, far more than in the classroom, can begin to see the potential difficulties of managing a plurality of understood ethical values, some of which originate in vastly different constructs of religious, economic and colonial histories.

One of the responsibilities we have as field primatologists is to better educate our students along these lines. Field schools, relevant coursework, and/or a required seminar before students go on to engage in any type of independent field research (either at the advanced undergraduate or graduate level) should be essential. Specific topics might include information on a particular country's history, the ethnic groups and identities currently present, the socioeconomic status of people in cities versus more rural areas, and cultural taboos.

A twitch and a wink: cultural awareness and sensitivity

Clifford Geertz (1973) once described the goal of an anthropologist as being able to tell the difference between a twitch and a wink. He notes that a twitch and a wink are physically the same action, but they carry deeply different meanings. Being able to operate within a local culture – to understanding the meanings that people attribute to words and actions, at least in certain contexts – is often crucial for success in field primatology. Obviously, learning the particularities of a culture takes time, and picking up information through conversation and observation can be a very slow process. Yet any attempt to get to know the local customs better pays off in the end for the field primatologist. We cannot forget that our very presence as researchers affects the communities in which we live (see Fuentes 2002). We are usually, after all, outsiders. As many have pointed out (e.g., Wolfe and Nash 2005), primatologists that do fieldwork have a responsibility to act in a manner so that future researchers will be able to conduct their work. Thinking about and processing these issues at the undergraduate level begins to prepare future fieldworkers for their role in the broader cultural context.

Unfortunately, the view that a local human population is something one just 'needs to deal with' in the process of getting primate-focused data, exists amongst at least some primatologists. Hopefully this attitude is uncommon, however it is remarkable to come across graduate students who, while in the extremely fortunate position of living in another country for a year or more during their dissertation fieldwork, remain isolated from the local people. There are precious few minutes left in the day after data collection, data entry, food preparation and laundry, but the field experience should be anthropological, which of course includes interacting with local people. Field schools offer a unique way of introducing undergraduates to this reality, so that they might be more open to cultural experiences as graduate students and beyond.

What the students say

I recently asked some of my 2004 field school students about their overall experiences in the primatology class. All respondents were between the ages of twenty and twenty-two when they took the course, and most had prior travel experience in Europe. None of the respondents had travelled previously in Central America. When asked if they could better appreciate multi-cultural viewpoints, and better apply cultural relativism since that experience, some responses were:

Sure. I think any experience outside of your own 'bubble' helps to alleviate preconceived ideas of others. Being in a foreign environment and being an outsider helps you see that there are many ways to live, and even though we are most accustomed to our way of life, it's not the only way.

Sure, anytime you spend a significant time in another culture you gain at least a little more understanding of those culturally different from you.

Probably. I think that before going to Nicaragua as well as after my return, I was in touch with cultural relativism. This may be because I had already studied abroad. Either way, I think that traveling is immensely important to shaping how people see their own culture, other cultures, and the intersection of the two.

When asked if they thought the primate field course was a valuable cultural experience, one student responded with several colourful examples:

Yes. Though we were in the jungle most of the day, all other times were spent in the culture surrounding us. The food, the roads and trucks they used for transportation as well as the ferry, the day in the city, watching women wash cloths on rocks, the football games, rum and cokes out of plastic cups in a woman's backyard, class outside in a hut with lizards covering the walls and farm animals eating next to you … I'd say that's culture.

Another student added:

I think any experience that introduces new people and new ideas will help to expand a person's ability to see things from different perspectives.

One student also pointed out the potential predilection for anthropology-oriented primate students to gain more (culturally) from a field course experience:

I think that the field school added to my understanding of cultural differences, but I also think that for the most part, people who are studying primates (thus studying anthropology), are more likely to try to maintain this state of mind anyway, which I found to be true of the people I met through the program.

However, some students felt that the safety and secluded nature of this particular site hampered interaction with local people:

I definitely think that interacting with local people was one part of the field experience that I did not really get to enjoy. I think this was primarily due to the set-up of the field school (a.k.a. living at the field station and spending the day out in the forest away from the rest of society). Most importantly, I did not speak Spanish. So when I saw people on the street, I wasn't able to speak to them. Thus, my only interactions with passers-by were when I got whistled at by men on the street. I went to church one day to try to see that aspect of the culture and ended up having a very long, difficult 'conversation' with some of the parishioners. [However] I think that my experience at the church and the night when the children came to dance [traditional folk dances] were my best experiences of [the] culture.

The issue of language came up again when another student stated:

I was frustrated at times because I wanted to talk with [the local people] or be able to understand what they asked me…I went into the trip knowing no Spanish, thus, I was at a bit of a disadvantage.

While the field sites discussed in this chapter offer their courses in English (save for one ITEC course on neotropical birds), all mention that some knowledge of Spanish would enrich the students' experiences.

I also asked the students if, in their view, they thought that field primatologists should work in isolation or minimal contact with the local people, or if they should be more active participants in that local community. One response in particular struck me as convergent with an issue sociocultural anthropologists have to struggle with in terms of local gossip:

> Oh definitely more active in the community. When foreigners go into a quiet community and remain quiet, they leave themselves … open to rumours, which might evolve into hate/dislike. If people are open and smile and offer [to] help, then they are welcomed into the community and respected. [The local people] know that [the researchers] are not there spying, stealing or destroying their land.

This student continued, expressing the following concern:

> However, [working in a community] can get out of hand and cause a dramatic shift in the culture. If a particular village is often used by primatologists, then the area might become 'touristy' and thus, they [primatologists] might introduce commercial [economic] hardships into the area.

As I did not follow up on this question, I can only assume this student meant that perhaps the local inhabitants might get left behind economically if there is a resulting surge in eco-tourism due to the presence of (habituated) primates. Other students' responses point to the necessity of involving local communities in successful conservation efforts. For example:

> I think part of the focus of primatology [should be] to include the local community in the excitement of studying primates. A huge part of conservation is understanding, and if local people don't understand why an animal is endangered and why it is important to do work to save it, then fieldwork is essentially pointless. If the primates are not there, then there is nothing to study. So educating the local people and gaining their support will ultimately be necessary in order to do fieldwork. Working in isolation may be the best technique when actually collecting data, but in general I think contact should be maintained with the people in the area.

And:

> I think that primatologists must work in cooperation with the local people. It is important for safety and for creating a hospitable environment around a study sight. It is wrong for an outsider to come into an area and not take the local people into consideration. Additionally, I think that the involvement of local people is essential for conservation efforts. This may not apply to all primatology studies, but I think that all studies should

consider conservation to some extent. It is hard to study a species if the local community is decimating it because of local or foreign demand.

Finally, when asked if they would rate their 2004 Nicaragua experience as positive, neutral or negative, the responses included:

Very Positive! Friendly, beautiful, safe environment to get exposure to field methods and monkey tracking.

Positive!! When else do you get to enjoy meeting others with similar interests and truly getting to know them ... getting up before dawn to hike to a familiar spot ... the experience of having your body rumble due to the howlers [monkeys] waking up and greeting the day ... walking down peaceful dirt roads with only the chirping bugs and animals around you ... and who would not call getting pooped on by a monkey a positive experience?!

Positive. I had a good time, I learned a lot, I went somewhere I'd never been before, I saw monkeys, I got to practice Spanish, I ate a lot of beans and rice (and bugs), I got to ride a donkey ... I got to sleep on a bag of rice in the ferry, I got to uses crutches meant for a 6-foot man, I got to see an amazing waterfall, I got to take awesome pictures, I got to read a lot of books, and most importantly I met interesting people.

As the above comments illustrate, the field school experience gets students thinking about some of these issues in a more visceral and informed way than perhaps is possible in the traditional classroom. Witnessing the day-to-day realities of life in a rural tropical environment allows insight into the complexities of doing fieldwork, and thus, is excellent preparation for students intending to pursue anthropological studies. The field school serves to demonstrate to students that they are seeking the right personal academic path, or not ('it's what I've always wanted to do' versus 'this is definitely not for me'). For most, it solidifies their academic and professional interests. As of this writing, at least thirteen of sixteen students in my last field course are currently in graduate programs in anthropology or the biological sciences. During a recent meeting of the American Society of Primatologists, an invited session was held, titled: *Field Primatology of Today: Navigating the Ethical Landscape* (see Baden et al., 2009 for review). In that symposium, Garber, Molina and Molina (2009) presented the paper, "Putting the Community Back in Community Ecology and Education", which summarized 15 years of education, research, and conservation at La Suerte and Ometepe Biological Research Stations. Strikingly, they note that over 120 of field school students thus far have received doctoral degrees or are currently in graduate programmes. Additionally, four doctoral dissertations, several MA theses, and approximately 20 scientific articles have been published based on research conducted at these sites (Garber, Molina and Molina, 2009; P. Garber and M. Bezanson, personal communication; and see Bezanson 2006). This is a highly successful model, showing how undergraduates and graduate students can not only learn to conduct original scientific research in a field school setting, but can also positively impact an area, learn about conservation issues first-hand, and experience local cultures

The future

Maintaining and building upon successful programmes takes continued interest from universities and colleges abroad. Tuition from North America and European students in particular brings much needed revenue for day-to-day operations, payment of faculty salaries, site maintenance, purchased supplies, local transportation costs and payment of local employees. Enough revenue also allows these organisations to offer reduced fees for students from host countries. There is an obvious inequity in these programmes, and addressing the under-representation of students from host countries is crucial for their long term success. For the sites mentioned here, offering more courses in Spanish would greatly increase the participation of advanced high school and college students from the host countries. Training 'ecological and cultural ambassadors' might afford local students greater success in finding alternative employment and educational opportunities, such as establishing contacts for graduate study, being field guides and naturalists, and working as valued assistants for national and international researchers.

Incorporating ethnographic perspectives into primatology field schools in Latin America is a useful exercise, and would strengthen sociocultural content in some research projects. Specifically, certain students (perhaps those who have a tough time adapting to the forest, and/or those who speak some Spanish) could design projects that include participant observation techniques as well as semi-structured interviews with local people about their views on nonhuman primates and the field station. Local participants could be a valued resource for those students interested in 'big picture' questions surrounding human-nonhuman primate dynamics. Furthermore, an incorporation of local people into the students' field projects might better secure a lasting positive attitude towards the presence of foreign researchers in the area. Finally, although relatively short in length, the four-week field sessions discussed here can produce useful information on primate population densities as well as accurate censuses of local study groups (and see Appendix 13.D for independent project titles from a recent course). Accumulated year after year, these data can provide a baseline for in-depth demographic studies and might also illuminate certain pressures that primates face at various times of the year (see Estrada 2006, 2009; Estrada and Garber 2009). The applications for conservation and management of wild primate populations via primatology field schools should not be overlooked (see Winkler et al. 2005).

Summary

A field school can spark in some a strong resolution to travel more, and an intense desire to experience different cultures. For others, it is an experience that will serve to demonstrate how they are not a good match for this type of life and work. Either outcome is beneficial for students figuring out which paths to take in their educational and professional lives, and either way, students learn what Wallace (1999) calls the 'intangibles': they learn about the culture they visit, they become more mature and better understand themselves and others, they become more sensitive to rural life in developing countries – including race and class issues in these localities – and they might also return home with a renewed appreciation for their own advantages and educational opportunities.

As first and foremost a social construct, primatology has never occurred in isolation from the culture in which it is practiced, embedded, and where training occurs. There is an interface among scientific endeavors, the scientists themselves, and the societies in which they work. An outcome of this confluence is the need for responsibility to the study subjects (the primates), the local cultures, societies at large, and the global environment in which we all live. Providing students an opportunity to do original research at the undergraduate level further strengthens in them a passion for cultural and biological investigation that may already be in place. It also informs them of the complex realities of conservation and management *vis a vis* idealistic notions of the way situations should be and the histories of human-primate interactions in a given area. Such training provides a solid footing for future anthropologists and prepares them well for the challenges and epiphanies only fieldwork can produce.

References

Baden, A.L., A. Lu and S. R. Tecot. 2009. 'Review of the 2009 Annual American Society of Primatologists Meeting', *Evolutionary Anthropology* 18: 164–165.

Bearder, S.K., K.A.I. Nekaris, D.J. Curtis, J.L. Dew, J.N. Lloyd and J.M. Setchell, 2003. 'Tips from the Bush: An A-Z of Suggestions for Successful Fieldwork', in J.M. Setchell and D.J. Curtis (eds) *Field and Laboratory Methods in Primatology*. Cambridge: Cambridge University Press, pp. 309–323.

Bezanson, M. 2006. *Ontogenetic patterns of positional behavior in Cebus capucinus and Alouatta palliata*. PhD. Thesis, University of Arizona.

Boellstorff, T. 2008. *Coming of Age in Second Life: An Anthropologist Explores the Virtually Human*. Princeton NJ: Princeton University Press.

Bourgois, P. 2003. *In Search of Respect: Selling Crack in El Barrio* (2nd edition). New York: Cambridge University Press.

Calcagno, J.M. 2003. 'Keeping Biological Anthropology in Anthropology, and Anthropology in Biology', *American Anthropologist* 105(1): 6–15.

Carlsson, H-E., S.J. Schapiro, I. Farah and J. Hau. 2004. 'Use of Primates in Research: A Global Overview', *American Journal of Primatology* 63: 225–37.

Clark, B.J. 2008. 'Artifact versus Relic: Ethics and the Archaeology of the Recent Past', *Anthropology News* 49(7): 23.

Cormier, L.A. 2002. 'Monkey as Food, Monkey as Child: Guaja Symbolic Cannibalism', in A. Fuentes and L. Wolfe (eds) *Primates Face to Face: Conservation Implications of Human-Nonhuman Primate Interconnections*. New York: Cambridge University Press, pp. 63–84.

——— 2006. 'A Preliminary Review of Neotropical Primates in the Subsistence and Symbolism of Indigenous Lowland South American Peoples', *Ecological and Environmental Anthropology* 2(1): 14–32.

Estrada, A. 2006. 'Human and Nonhuman Primate Coexistence in the Neotropics: A Preliminary View of Some Agricultural Practices as a Complement for Primate Conservation', *Ecological and Environmental Anthropology* 2(2): 17–29.

_____ 2009. 'Primate Conservation in South America: The Human and Ecological Dimensions of the Problem', in P.A. Garber, A. Estrada, J.C. Bicca-Marques, E.W. Heymann and K.B. Strier (eds) *South American Primates: Comparative Perspectives in The Study of Behaviour , Ecology, And Conservation*. New York: Springer Press, pp. 463–505.

Estrada, A. and P.A. Garber. 2009. 'Comparative Perspectives in the Study of South American Primates: Research Priorities and Conservation Imperatives', in P.A. Garber, A. Estrada, J.C. Bicca-Marques, E.W. Heymann and K.B. Strier (eds) *South American Primates: Comparative Perspectives in the Study of Behaviour, Ecology, and Conservation*. New York: Springer Press, pp. 509–31.

Evans-Pritchard, E.E. 1940. *The Nuer: A Description of the Modes of Livelihood and Political Institutions of a Nilotic People*. Oxford: Oxford University Press.

Eudey, A.A. 2002. 'The Primatologist as Minority Advocate', in A. Fuentes and L. Wolfe (eds) *Primates Face to Face: Conservation Implications of Human-Nonhuman Primate Interconnections*. New York: Cambridge University Press, pp. 277–87.

Fedigan, L.M. 1994. 'Science and the Successful Female: Why There Are So Many Women Primatologists', *American Anthropologist* 96(3): 529–40.

Fuentes, A. 2002. 'Monkeys, Humans and Politics in the Mentawai Islands: No Simple Solutions in a Complex World', in A. Fuentes and L. Wolfe (eds) *Primates Face to Face: Conservation Implications of Human-Nonhuman Primate Interconnections*. New York: Cambridge University Press, pp. 187–207.

_____ 2006. 'Human-Nonhuman Primate Interconnections and their Relevance to Anthropology', *Ecological and Environmental Anthropology* 2(2): 1–11.

Fuentes, A. and L.D. Wolfe (eds). 2002. *Primates Face to Face: The Conservation Implications of Human and Nonhuman Primate Interconnections*. New York: Cambridge University Press.

Garber, P. A., A. Molina and R. Molina 2009. Putting the Community Back in Community Ecology and Education. *American Journal of Primatology*. 71 (suppl. 1): 31.

Geertz, C. 1973. *Interpretation of Cultures: Selected Essays*. New York: Basic Books.

_____ 1983. *Local Knowledge: Further Essays in Interpretive Anthropology*. New York: Basic Books.

Gmelch, G. and S.B. Gmelch. 1999. 'An Ethnographic Field School: What Students Do and Learn', *Anthropology & Education Quarterly* 30(2): 220–7.

Haraway, D. 2000. 'Morphing in the Order: Flexible Strategies, Feminist Science Studies, and Primate Revisions', in S.C. Strum and L.M. Fedigan (eds) *Primate Encounters: Models of Science, Gender, and Society*. Chicago: University of Chicago Press, pp. 398–420.

Hill, C.M. 2002. 'Primate Conservation and Local Communities: Ethical Issues and Debates', *American Anthropologist* 104(4): 1184–94.

Jones-Engle, L., M. A., Schillaci, and G. A Engle. 2003. 'Human-nonhuman primate interactions: An ethnoprimatological approach', in J.M. Setchell and D.J. Curtis (eds.), *Field and Laboratory Methods in Primatology*. Cambridge: Cambridge University Press, pp. 15–24.

Lightfoot, K. G. 2008. 'Collaborative Research Programs: Implications for the Practice of North American Archaeology', in S.W. Silliman (ed.) *Collaborating at the Trowel's Edge: Teaching and Learning in Indigenous Archaeology*. Tucson: University of Arizona Press, pp. 211–27.

Lightfoot, K.G. 2009. 'Anthropology Field Schools for the 21st Century', *General Anthropology: Bulletin of the General Anthropology Division of the AAA* 16(1): 1–4.

Lizarralde, M. 2002. 'Ethnoecology of Monkeys Among the Barí of Venezuela: Perception, Use and Conservation', in A. Fuentes and L. Wolfe (eds) *Primates Face To Face: Conservation Implications Of Human-Nonhuman Primate Interconnections*. New York: Cambridge University Press, pp. 85–100.

Loudon, J.E., M.E. Howells and A. Fuentes. 2006. 'The importance of integrative anthropology: a preliminary investigation employing primatological and cultural anthropological data collection methods in assessing human-monkey co-existence in Bali, Indonesia', *Ecological and Environmental Anthropology* 2(1): 2–13.

Malinowski, B. 1922. *Argonauts of the Western Pacific: An Account of Native Enterprise and Adventure in the Archipelagoes of Melanesian New Guinea*. London: George Routledge & Sons, Ltd.

Mascia-Lees, F. 2006. 'Can biological and cultural anthropology coexist?', *Anthropology News* 47(1): 9–13.

McCrary, J.K., E.P. van Denberghe and K.R. McKaye. 2005. 'A breeding population of *theraps underwoodi* (Teleostei: Cichlidae) on Ometepe Island, Nicaragua, and implications for its dispersal mechanisms', *Caribbean Journal of Science*, 41(4): 874–76.

Mead, M. 1928. *Coming of Age in Samoa*. New York: William Morrow.

Mills, B.J. 2005. 'Curricular Matters: The Impact of Archaeological Field Schools on Southwest Archaeology', in L.S. Cordell and D.D. Fowler (eds) *Southwest Archaeology in the Twentieth Century*. Salt Lake City: University of Utah Press, pp. 60–80.

Peters-Golden, H. 2004. 'Thinking Holistically', in P.C. Salzman and P.C. Rice (eds) *Thinking Anthropologically: A Practical Guide for Students*. Upper Saddle River, New Jersey: Pearson Prentice Hall, pp. 17–27.

Pyburn, A.K. 2003. 'What Are We Really Teaching in Archaeological Field Schools?', in M.J. Lynott and A. Wylie (eds) *Ethics and American Archaeology: Challenges for the 1990s*. Washington DC: Society for American Archaeology, pp. 71–6.

Riley, E.P. 2005. *Ethnoprimatology of Macaca tonkeana: The Interface of Primate Ecology, Human Ecology, and Conservation in Lore Lindu National Park, Sulawesi, Indonesia*. Ph.D. Thesis, University of Georgia.

Riley, E.P. 2006. 'Ethnoprimatology: towards reconciliation of biological and cultural anthropology', *Ecological and Environmental Anthropology* 2(2): 75–86.

——— 2007. 'The human-macaque interface: conservation implications of current and future overlap and conflict in Lore Lindu National Park, Sulawesi, Indonesia.', *American Anthropology* 109(3): 473–84.

Russak, S.M. 2005. 'Getting the hang of it: age differences in tail-use by mantled howling monkeys (*Alouatta palliata*)', *Neotropical Primates* 13(1): 5–7.

Sponsel, L.E. 1997. 'The Human Niche in Amazonia: Explorations in Ethnoprimatology', in W. G. Kinzey (ed.) *New World Primates*. New York: Aldine De Gruyter, pp. 143–65.

Sprague, D.S. 2002. 'Monkeys in the Backyard: Encroaching Wildlife and Rural Communities in Japan', in A. Fuentes and L. Wolfe (eds) *Primates Face to Face: Conservation Implications of Human-Nonhuman Interconnections*. Cambridge: Cambridge University Press, pp. 254–72.

Sprague, D.S. and N. Iwasaki. 2006. 'Coexistence and exclusion between humans and monkeys in Japan: is either really possible?', *Ecological and Environmental Anthropology* 2(2): 30–43.

Thomas, R.B. 2006. 'Anthropology for the next generation', *Anthropology News* 47(1): 9–11.

Upham, S., W.R. Trevathan and R.R. Wilk. 1988. 'Teaching anthropology: research, students, and the marketplace', *Anthropology & Education Quarterly* 19(3): 203–17.

Walker, M. and D.J. Saitta. 2002. 'Teaching the craft of archaeology: theory, practice, and the field school', *International. Journal of Historical Archaeology.* 6(3): 199–207.

Wallace, J.M.T. 1999. 'Mentoring apprentice ethnographers through field schools', *Anthropology and Education Quarterly* 30(2): 210–19.

Ward, M.C. 1999. 'Managing student culture and culture shock: a case from european Tirol'. *Anthropology & Education Quarterly* 30(2): 228–37.

Wheatley, B.P. 1999. *The Sacred Monkeys of Bali.* Prospect Heights, IL: Waveland Press.

Winkler, L.A., X.C. Zhang, R. Ferrell, R. Wagner, J. Dahl, G. Peter and R. Sohn. 2004. 'Geographic Microsatellite Variability in Central American Howling Monkeys', *International Journal of Primatology* 25(1): 197–210.

Wolfe, L. and L.T. Nash. 2005. 'Ethical issues in primatology', *Anthropology News* Feb, 2005: 6.

Appendices

Appendix 13.A: Listings of field schools on professional websites.

The vast majority of anthropology-related field schools around the world are in archaeology, and a quick glance at the Archaeological Institute of America's webpage (http://www.archaeological.org/webinfo.php?page=10016) reveals many potential opportunities for students. A recent viewing (February 2010) of the American Anthropological Association's (AAA) website revealed that of the 29 field school programmes currently listed (http://www.aaanet.org/profdev/coop.cfm, click on 'search announcements' and then select 'field school' in the 'type' box), 11 are in sociocultural anthropology/ethnography and 18 are in archaeology/bioarchaeology/paleoanthropology (note: the listings on the AAA site change on a continual basis, as sessions begin and end). Primatology field schools are more rare. The Biological Anthropology Section (BAS) of the AAA has a listing of eight primate field schools (as of February 2010), however six of the eight links are broken or out of date (http://www.as.ua.edu/bas/FieldSchools.htm). On the Primate Info Net site, operated by the National Primate Research Centre at the University of Wisconsin, Madison, WI, US, there are four primatology field schools listed (as of February 2010), however the vast majority of listings are for volunteer field assistant positions, not structured courses (http://pin.primate.wisc.edu/jobs/list/avail). The Canadian Association for Physical Anthropology currently lists two primatology field schools that are also listed on the BAS site (http://www.utsc.utoronto.ca/~chan/capa/resources/field_schools.html). The American Association of Physical Anthropologists (AAPA) website currently lists no primatology field schools, nor does the Royal Anthropological Institute of Great Britain and Ireland (RAI).

Appendix 13.B: Websites and sample syllabi for primate field courses mentioned.

Organisation Fieldsites

El Zota Biological Field Station, Costa Rica
http://www.danta.info/ezb.php

La Suerte Biological Field Station, Costa Ric
http://www.maderasrfc.org/Maderas_Rainforest_Conservancy/La_Suerte_B.F.S..html
Ometepe Biological Field Station, Nicaragua
http://www.maderasrfc.org/Maderas_Rainforest_Conservancy/Ometepe_B.F.S..html

Institute for Tropical Ecology and Conservation (ITEC), Panamá
http://www.itec-edu.org/index.html

Sample primate field course syllabi online:

El Zota Biological Field Station, Costa Rica
http://www.esu.edu/~tcladuke/el_zota/Primates/primate_syl.htm

La Suerte Biological Field Station, Costa Rica
http://www.lasuerte.org/syllabus/coursedesadv_Garber.html

Ometepe Biological Field Station, Nicaragua
http://www.lasuerte.org/syllabus/halloran_syllabus_ome_08.pdf

Institute for Tropical Ecology and Conservation (ITEC), Panamá
http://www.itec-edu.org/primatology01.html

Appendix 13.C: Sampling of courses offered during 2010-2011 (listed alphabetically). Check websites for the latest information.

La Suerte Biological Field Station, Costa Rica

Advanced Primate Behaviour and Ecology
Comparative Skeletal Anatomy and Function
Dance Workshop in the Forest
Eco Challenge
Global Ecology
Mixed Media in the Rain Forest
Neotropical Ethnobotany
Photography Workshop in the Neotropics
Primate Behaviour and Ecology
Rain Forest Ecology: Birds
Rain Forest Ecology: Entomology
Tropical Cooking
Tropical Ecology: Rainforest Ecology and Conservation
Tropical Herpetology

Ometepe Biological Field Station, Nicaragua

Advanced Primate Behaviour and Ecology
Cloud Forest Ecology
Eco Challenge

Neotropical Ethnobotany
Primate Behaviour and Ecology
Primate Communication
Primate Survey and Assessment: BIOBLITZ
Tropical Herpetology
Veterinary Field Medicine

Institute for Tropical Ecology and Conservation (ITEC), Panamá

Adventure Photography
Canopy Access Techniques
Central American and Carbonate Geology
Coral Reef Ecology
Ecología y Conservación de Aves Tropicales (Spanish language course on Tropical Bird Ecology and Conservation)
Neotropical Herpetology
Neotropical Ornithology
Photography in the Environment
Primate Ecology
Tropical Animal Behaviour
Tropical Conservation Ecology
Tropical Ethnobotany
Tropical Rainforest and Canopy Ecology
Tropical Rainforest Mycology
El Zota Biological Field Station, Costa Rica
Primate Behaviour and Conservation
Tropical Biology and Conservation
Tropical Ornithology

Appendix 13.D: Examples of independent research project titles from students in the author's 2004 primate behaviour and ecology field course (Ometepe, Nicaragua)

'Getting the hang of it: Age-related patterns in tail use by mantled howler monkeys (*Alouatta palliata*).' (see Russak 2005).

'Association patterns among female howlers (*Alouatta palliata*) in the volcano forest, Isla de Ometepe, Nicaragua.'

'Sources of dietary variation in mantled howler monkeys (*Alouatta palliata*).'

'Travel patterns and associated travel cues of mantled howlers, *Alouatta palliata*, on Ometepe Island, Nicaragua.'

'Adult male and immature interactions in howler monkeys (*Alouatta palliata*).'

'Intersexual social relationships in mantled howler monkeys (*Alouatta palliata*).

'General activity budgets of adult male and female mantled howlers (*Alouatta palliata*).'

'Female positional changes associated with approaches by males in mantled howler monkeys (*Alouatta palliata*).'

14

The Narrator's Stance:
Story-telling and Science at Berenty Reserve

Alison Jolly

Introduction

Donna Haraway's *Primate Visions* (1989) delighted academics in the humanities and annoyed many primatologists when she analysed personal influences on the professional study of primatology. In the crucible of field work the primatologist meets and begins to comprehend an alien species, while simultaneously dealing with unfamiliar cultures of people, undergoing a personal transformation in the process. The primatologist's own story involves the struggle to narrate what she sees. That story is often worth telling. But there is a further question: to what extent does individual narrative substitute, or compensate for, the attempt to be objective about a statistically valid sample of the lemurs or people one is seeing?

In *Lords and Lemurs* (2004), I used first-person narrative to describe members of four societies who interact at Berenty Reserve, Madagascar: ringtailed lemurs, the scientists who cross the world to watch the lemurs, French ex-colonial capitalists, and Tandroy tribespeople. I focused on the drama of individual lives. I also hoped to illuminate something more general about each society, even though the more you know about an individual the less he or she seems typical of any wider group.

I believe I knew enough background to give a fair picture of the both scientists and lemurs, although I deliberately chose an extreme lemur individual as heroine. An anonymous reviewer saved me from gross misrepresentation of the colonialists. I had initially recounted only the tumultuous history of the de Heaulme family who own Berenty, who are in some ways benevolent capitalists, or rather, feudal lords for good and bad. Until the reviewer savaged my first draft I had mistakenly assumed readers would fill in the background of colonial oppression for themselves. For the most challenging case, the Tandroy, I have had no feedback. There are few Tandroy anthropologists and my interlocutors first didn't speak English, second were mostly not literate, and third were old and some now dead. Still, their own society of people, who descend from nobles, commoners or slaves, fits them well to understand the feudal de Heaulmes. I can only hope I did them justice.

I found that it is easier for the duration of fieldwork to relate to lemurs than to people, and it is certainly easier to write about them. The narrator's stance comes naturally when you know you are not a lemur. Taking that stance toward other people works best when they also accept you as an alien whom they themselves privilege as narrator. I conclude that individual life histories, whether of people or lemurs or even myself, is storytelling, not science. Personal narrative, however rich the interpretation, is not enough by itself. Broader conclusions should rest on broader evidence.

Primate Visions and the struggle for objectivity

The field worker who intends to write of what she sees plays a treacherous role. She is perpetually both a sentient subject and an observer storing notes for later public use. This is even more acute if she intends to tell individual stories, not just a broad statistical sample with individuality concealed. There is yet another layer: if she is recounting the individual story in part to illuminate the context of a society, how to be sure that the individual is representative enough, or illuminating enough to be worth telling? Even if it is her own life story, the fact that she felt or saw something in her own limited context may not make it true in any wider sense.

The scientist tries to sort out some more lasting generalization in this welter of interconnections. The novelist plunges into the connectedness as deep as his courage will take him. The journalist skims the surface, plucking some good quotes here and there. But the anthropologist – the anthropologist is lost between all possibilities at once.

When Jeremy MacClancy surveyed literary images of anthropology and anthropologists, he unearthed a panoply of bizarre human characters. Anthropologists in fiction appear as:

> heroic, or (much more common) pathetic. Fieldwork marks them out as distinctive, and makes ordinary anthropologists odd and the already odd ones even odder ... In sum, fieldwork is emotionally intense, psychologically enriching, potentially traumatic, possibly dangerous ... in these dramatic settings ... extremes are exposed and may even collide (MacClancy 2005: 549, 558).

In sober academic publications, as in fiction, we find constant tension between the anthropologists' love for the people and their culture which engulf him or her for the duration of the field work, and the effort to maintain an outsider's view. Even in the field the evening's notes may struggle to recapture the dispassionate tone the anthropologist must eventually adopt in thesis or monograph. This is also true if the anthropologist loathes and fears the people around. The worst sin of all, MacClancy points out, would be to find the people boring. Boredom is saved for the academic write-up.

In her book *Primate Visions*, Haraway showed that for field primatologists the personal and the professional are also inextricably linked (Haraway 1989). Some may not remember primatologists' first reactions to that book. We hated it. We felt betrayed. Haraway talked about the context of what we tried to do without addressing what we ourselves thought we were trying to do. Of course the personal context, our gender, social class, colour and nationality had bolstered or hindered our work. We reacted to, or ignored, the people at our field site in ways dictated by local colonial history. However we saw primatology itself as a pure flame of observation that burned through all the dross. We were reaching out to animals so different from ourselves that we could only watch their lives, never imagine or even influence anything so new, exciting and real.

Of all the reviews I read of *Primate Visions*, and there were many, I remember only one good one by a scientist (Patty Gowaty), and no bad ones by people in the arts. My literary daughter and I wrote a joint review with me outraged, her admiring. I said, '[Haraway] analyses field primatology as though it were science fiction. Fragmented views of lemur or baboon need never rejoin, any more than you would try to reconcile Warhol with Canaletto. Haraway does not accept the effort of science to discover, not merely create.' My daughter Margaretta answered, 'When you oppose the scientist to the artist, the attempt to discover against the desire to create, you misunderstand the essence of Haraway's project. Far from proposing that all scientific findings are entirely relative or individual, she shows instead the wider social consensus that shapes the scientific and the scientist.' Meanwhile physical anthropologist Matt Cartmill fumed, 'This is a book which clatters around in a closet of irrelevancies for 450 pages before it bumps accidentally into its own index and stops; but that is not a criticism ... because its author finds it gratifying and refreshing to bang unrelated ideas together as a rebuke to stuffy minds' (Jolly and Jolly 1990; Cartmill 1991; Gowaty 1991; Jolly 1999).

The humanities indeed found it gratifying and refreshing. They welcomed Haraway as a prophet of postmodernism. I have just reread her account of me. I confess that I now feel flattered by every word. As always, the original text is far more detailed and nuanced than simplified memories of the passage. However, Donna was quoting not from my scientific writings about lemurs, but from *A World like our Own*, a first person account of travels with Malagasy scientists, written to campaign for conservation in Madagascar (Jolly 1980).

Lords and Lemurs

Recently I have again written a first-person book, *Lords and Lemurs*, an account of the history of Berenty Reserve (Jolly 2004). It presents a multispecies, multicultural society in far from academic terms. Major characters include a ringtailed lemur called Frightful Fan, scientists Alison Jolly and Hanta Rasamimanana, Tandroy tribesmen Tsiaketraky (He-who-Cannot-be-Thrown-to-Earth) and Jaona Tsiminono (He-who-Never-Suckled), whose lives have been spent on Berenty Estate, and above all, the de Heaulme family, the 'Lords of the Helm'.

I stumbled onto Berenty Reserve as a field site beyond compare for the study of lemur social behaviour in 1963. I did not decide to write about the people of Berenty until 1999. The impetus was literary: the biography of Jean de Heaulme, owner of Berenty, is an irresistible tale to tell. The highs and lows of de Heaulme family fortunes from grandeur to imprisonment and back again have an actual turning point: the night in prison when Jean learned that his own workers were coming over the mountains to confront the government inquisitors and demand his release. In that white night he made his decision to tell his workers not to shed blood, their own or others', on his behalf. However, he would remain in Madagascar, not flee to France. He would stay true to his own father's vision and to the thousands of people who worked for him in the face of all that a xenophobic central government could do to him. His biography embraces the political changes of twentieth-century Madagascar, and how his family transformed the lives of the Tandroy people of the spiny forest, a tribe of warriors and pastoralists who still carry spears on all ceremonial occasions.

The de Heaulme family's claim to wider fame is not their wealth and power, but the fact that on their 6,000 hectare sisal plantation, 1,000 hectares are protected natural forest. Berenty Reserve proper, the largest parcel, is the site of my own field research and that of many others scientists: Malagasy, North American, European, Japanese. It is the high point of many tourists' visit to Madagascar. In the October birth season of 2005 we had five different TV teams overlapping at Berenty; in 2006 cinematographers shot a ten-part lemur 'soap opera' for Channel 5 and Animal Planet. Madagascar itself is a mini-continent a thousand miles long, with evergreen rainforest, alpine heath, majestic baobabs, and surreal spiny desert, not to mention the richness of various human cultures from intertwined Afro-Asian origins. If you have a mental picture of the Great Red Island, though, it is probably starts with promenading ringtailed lemurs or dancing white sifaka, filmed in the front five hectares of Berenty.

How to tell this multiple story? Did my experience of lemur field work qualify me for constructing the book which became *Lords and Lemurs?* (Jolly 2004). I am an anthropologist of lemurs but only a journalist of people. I actually had to go and do a new kind of field work among the people: cross-cultural interviews about their lives within the history of Berenty Estate. I had managed to put off that particular exposure of my own ignorance for almost forty years.

The observer and narrator

Aged nine: The Unitarian Sunday School of Ithaca, New York.

Little hope to be chosen Mary in the Christmas pageant, but perhaps the white-winged Angel, or a resplendent King?

'Oh, no, no, Alison,' said the teacher. 'You will wear a black robe and read the story from a lectern at the side. You will be Narrator. You were always meant to be Narrator.'

Aged fourteen: Athens, Greece.

Madagascar was not, for me, the first experience of an alien culture. That was the American High School of Athens, Greece. (It still exists, having celebrated its fifty-year reunion.) My father held a Fulbright professorship in Athens for the academic year of 1951–1952. When I arrived as a very young sophomore, the sole goal of any 1950s high school culture I had known was to scale the ladder of peer-pressure up to the heights of being popular. The resident American teenagers demanded that I sing the current Radio Hit Parade of the USA, in order from the top. They really wanted to learn the songs. Most were army offspring stationed in Athens after the years of civil war with the Communists. They were homesick. I was cowed. I didn't know any songs on the Hit Parade.

Social structure of the ninety-student school revolved around 'going steady' because the kids believed that was compulsory in America. It usually meant fairly modest kissing in the movies (we didn't have cars). In the top three classes everyone paired off except myself, my two best girlfriends, and a boy who eventually had a nervous breakdown. Midway through the year the alpha male and female broke up, which necessitated rearrangements all down the line since they obviously could not remain unattached.

Meanwhile in the Athenian upper classes a girl was not supposed to be alone with a boy, let alone kiss him, until they were engaged. If you met a stranger you liked at a friend's house there was no way to see him again unless you asked your friend's parents to introduce his parents to your parents, by which time all concerned assumed that you were pregnant. One father told me of his horror at an American movie where the boy drove up in his hot rod, honked, and the girl ran out of her house to join him while her parents continued calmly eating dinner. Athenians assumed that the teenagers were eloping and the parents dead to decency, not that boy and girl were off to share an ice cream soda in the local drugstore.

No way to conform to both sets of rules: maybe standing outside was an option even for a teenager?

Further trips to Europe made it seem that I could gradually learn to cope as a foreigner in many countries, especially in the multilingual 'civilized' layers of society where people are proud of their own culture but fully aware that other cultures exist, and so did not expect me to conform. I assumed that dealing with people in independent Madagascar would be more of the same.

Oddly, it was.

Aged twenty-five: Fort Dauphin, Madagascar.

With American ignorance of colonialism, I was surprised to find that whenever I wanted something official or unofficial in the Madagascar of 1962–1964, a door opened to reveal a Frenchman. I arrived two years after Madagascar's independence:

an 'independence' where France stabilized the franc and the budget, officially handled foreign affairs, the military, and education, and unofficially continued to run almost all profitable enterprise.

During the first two months of my stay I travelled throughout the island-continent looking for a field site. Everywhere Frenchmen and their wives made me welcome. At last, stumbling on the private nature reserve of Berenty, I met the de Heaulme family. They were an extreme of the courtesy I'd found elsewhere: indeed, they seemed to be aristocrats who had never quite noticed the French Revolution. They welcomed me as a naturalist to their private reserve as they might have accepted a librarian for their library, or as they later did, encouraged an anthropologist to design their museum of local culture. I felt that I had driven my Landrover straight into the eighteenth century, where I could park under a tamarind tree and start watching lemurs (Jolly 2004).

On my odd weekends off in the nearby town of Fort Dauphin it seemed that the dual world of the Athens adolescents had somehow returned. Fort Dauphin held two varieties of Caucasians who managed to totally avoid each other. Perhaps 150 French and around forty Americans (not counting children) lived in separate spheres within a very small town.

They did it mostly through timing, like an elaborate minuet. At almost any hour of the day either the Catholic French or the Lutheran Norwegian-Americans would be at home eating, but not at the same times. During the few remaining hours they bought groceries and dry goods in identical wooden shops that sold everything from sugar to sardines to wrap skirt cloths, but different identical shops. Their children went to different schools. On Sundays of course they went to different churches. The greeting rituals of each faction completely excluded the other. In that sweltering climate as you come into any house the host or hostess must offer drink. Among the missionaries it was lemonade or pineapple juice, proud home-made concentrates diluted with water, and like as not a home-baked chocolate-chip cookie to go with it. The French tipped a few drops of Johnny Walker whiskey into water: a concoction paler gold than missionary lemonade. Tee-total Lutherans and alcohol-oriented French never crossed each others' thresholds.

These were not newcomers ignorantly continuing the habits of other continents. Some of the French were third-generation residents; some of the missionaries fifth-generation. Up to that time missionaries had home leave only every fifth year. They travelled by boat to spend their year in the snows of Minnesota. Like the teenagers at the Athens High School they created a parody of home, with prohibitions on almost all small pleasures of life except food: chocolate-chip cookies, pumpkin pie made of local squash, and hoarded packets of Jell-O carried all the way from the USA. Their real home, of course, was Madagascar. They married each other through the generations and sent their children to the family-like mission school they had attended themselves. They firmly believed in the Malagasy devils whom they could exorcise by name from the possessed penitents in their flock.

Fort Dauphin held not only Americans and French, but Indians, Chinese, Tanosy people whose ancestors had always lived there on the coast, Tandroy people from the dry country inland around Berenty Reserve, Merina civil servants from the capitol on Madagascar's central plateau. All maintained their own identities. Each group had its own sub-groups. One Gujurati asked me to dinner to meet his family. In the course of the evening he explained that he would have to import a wife from India, because it was unthinkable that he might marry a girl from any other caste and clan but his own and there were none in all Madagascar. The forty or fifty Indians of Fort Dauphin had almost as many impenetrable barriers as there were families. Dessert was rose-perfumed agar-agar made from local seaweed, a quivering echo of the missionaries' precious Jell-O.

I somehow swam between all factions. I was non-Catholic American, which suited one lot. I drank and danced and spoke French, which suited another. Everyone in Fort Dauphin shared an exquisitely anthropological sense of cultural relativity. They were quite able to cope with a temporary newcomer who arrived as a culture of one. I was finally perfectly free to be myself.

What I did not do, though, was to reach out to ordinary Malagasy. Colonial education meant that in almost every village someone spoke enough French to help a passing stranger. The elite whom I did meet and know were bilingual. I had work enough to do trying to understand the lemurs. It was easiest to stick to the languages I already spoke and people whom I could just about comprehend.

First wild lemurs

I am not going to write much about what it feels like to be in a tropical woodland among creatures of utter physical beauty and alien minds, particularly in contrast to the muddles of humanity. Much better to read Thoreau or Aldo Leopold or Darwin's first glimpse of Brazil. I am convinced that E.O. Wilson is right to argue that 'biophilia' is an instinct that runs deep in human nature, though shaped in our own culture to a particular romantic vein (Wilson 1984).

Let me simply quote a letter I wrote to my parents on 28 February 1963. Perhaps it conveys a little of the forest that was possessing me. Even though this was early on, before I deciphered much of what I saw, by the last paragraph I am among the lemurs: hidden observers of an alien human being:

> I drive through the gate ... Immediately I am in a warm green gloom full of bird calls. Tufty grass springs up between the two wheel marks of the car. Something causes a great stir in the grass—three guinea-fowl with red and blue heads, accompanied by 14 scuttling brown chicks ...

> And the lemurs. Lemurs are everywhere. They leap about at 60 feet in the kily tops, with a great swishing of foliage, and they swagger about on the ground with their tails in the air ... The Lemur go in gangs of 20, black masks and noses into everything, tufted white ears forward with interest or back with suspicion, black-and-white ringed tails semaphoring. When upset slightly they growl, when lonesome they meow, when mobbing me they come and yap all together very loud like very obstreperous terriers. All these

noises are catching. Sometimes at dusk one will throw back its head and howl, but I don't know why ...

And then there are *Propithecus,* the sifaka. I am afraid I think of them as huge white teddy bears, just like Avalanche [the stuffed polar bear I loved dearly from the age of 3]. They live in families of 4 to 8, and they hop. When active they hop 20 feet, when not so active they hop 1 foot. When they feel like it, they come down and hop on the ground. They have black faces and a brown or blond skull cap. The white crescent of fur, between, goes down in the middle and up to their tufty ears, which always gives them a worried expression. How can one help loving anything with a perfectly round head and a heart-shaped face? ... I am seeing new things every day—things thousands of Malgache hunters may have seen, but no one ever has looked at.

And it is a thrill just to be in these woods, wandering happily about outdoors all day, writing down earnest descriptions of birds I can't identify and plants I can't identify and something at first couldn't even classify to phylum but finally decided was a six inch long flatworm (Oh for Borradaile and Potts on the Invertebrates) and getting rained on and eating bread and oranges and sitting on lianas which are not as comfortable as they look in the movies and watching lemurs ... .

One morning I was sitting watching *L. catta,* way into the woods, when I heard a liquid whistling far in the distance. The *catta* sat where they were, too, ears forward, tails hanging down. I sat still, too, which makes one practically invisible to people. The whistling changed to singing—a repeated minor cadence, not particularly African, maybe like a herdsman in the near east. The man had a beautiful high baritone voice. He sang loud, without forcing, so that his singing seemed to fill all the spaces between the trees. He would start on the same high note and hold it, swelling, while he decided how to descend with grace notes and quavers and bits of fast talking rhythm—perhaps he was telling some long story—to the low note he always ended on. I could just catch just a glimpse of his herd through the leaves: white humped zebu, looking suddenly huge after the lemurs. Then they passed, the singing gradually faded in the distance but went on for a long, long time with an obligato of bird calls.

The lemurs shook themselves and stretched in heraldic poses and began to talk again (Jolly 2004: 160–62).

Telling ringtailed lemurs

Forty years later I finally sat down to describe Berenty for public readers. The backbone of the story was the biography of Jean de Heaulme, but to tell it, I must also tell of the Reserve's lemurs and Berenty's Tandroy people. Describing the lemurs was relatively easy. Describing the de Heaulmes turned out to be almost disastrous. And the Tandroy? I don't know how that came out at all.

There is no basic problem writing about lemurs in a popular vein. I recycle phrases from my very first book and popular article: how males wave their perfumed tails at each other 'like outraged feather dusters' in the course of their 'stink-fights', how subordinate animals make 'spat calls' at each other, how white sifaka when alarmed 'spring apart like popcorn', or carry out their own territorial confrontations 'like arboreal chess games' (Jolly 1966; 1970).

By now, though, in the birth season you find at least a dozen scientists and students earnestly following their troops, and at least one television team. For an introduction to link the different worlds, I picked a French TV crew come to publicise the release of the French version of Disney's movie 'Dinosaur'. Jean de Heaulme gave them a dinner party, and told of his own arrival in the south of Madagascar as a six month old baby in the sidecar of his father's Harley-Davidson. They had only three days to film, so instead of doing their own homework they grabbed available talent to explain animals to the camera. It happened we had three beautiful female students that year: Japanese Takayo Soma, English-Argentinean Erica Moret, and Malagasy Dina Felantsoa. That suited the French film crew of course, but also suited me to indicate the mix of studies and nationalities typical of Berenty research.

A more fundamental choice was how to present ringtailed lemurs themselves, not only to bring out the similarities and differences in their society and ours, but to show that lemurs are also people. I wanted to emphasise the role of territoriality among lemur troops in part to foreshadow the conflict between colonials and tribespeople over rights to Malagasy land, and also, of course, to explain ringtails' female-dominant society, where troop status is a female concern.

I focussed on the rise and fall of Frightful Fan, by all odds the nastiest lemur I have known. Her troop, the A-Team, split in two in 1992. Fan's group, A1, were dominants who targeted the subordinate females and drove them away amid intense aggression and the death of A2 infants. A1 miscalculated. A2 became one of only two cases among twenty-three seen by Berenty researchers which successfully fought back to claim the better part of the core range of their former dominants. Fan, who became A1's alpha female, spent an extraordinary amount of effort both fighting to keep what remained of the A1 territory, and spitefully harassing subordinates within her own troop. Eventually she reduced her own troop size by targeting and exiling a cousin along with the cousin's four young kin. One by one those exiles disappeared or died. Fan's aggressiveness toward her neighbours and her kin clearly saved her troop (Hood 1993; Hood and Jolly 1995; Dubovick 1998; Ichino and Koyama 2006; Jolly et al. 2006).

Simplified life stories, soap operas, fit well with lemur personal relations. But why pick Fan? Robert Sussman remarks that I have a penchant for telling samurai stories. Very true. He calculates the social behaviour of ringtailed lemurs in different sites and seasons takes up only 2.6 to 8.5 per cent of their day. Some 75 per cent to 90 per cent of that time is affiliative, while aggression is a mere 10 per cent to 20 per cent of the social time. Why focus on that? (Sussman et al. 2005.)

Well, aggression is important. Lemurs do cuddle and groom far more than they fight, but a troop fission, or targeting and exile, will determine where you live and who you live with, perhaps whether you live at all. The relative importance of affiliation and aggression is a bit like comparing foraging and predation. Foraging takes up much of every day while predation is very, very rare: but a single episode of being eaten is a life-changing experience.

So I plead guilty to hyping up lemur life for narrative purposes, not beyond what actually happened to the animal in question, and with components which are all shown by other lemurs, but I did choose a candidate for 'Desperate Housewives' as my focus rather than a more humdrum mum. To let people see the crucial long term importance of lemur status and territory, I felt I couldn't choose a more revealing heroine than Frightful Fan.

Telling of feudal lords

It was Jean de Heaulme's life story that I could not resist as a writer of stories. His life and his family's lives are a drama with shape and a turning point, like this:

No matter how good the tale, though, the ups and downs of one rich family was not worth three years of research and writing. (Maybe for Danielle Steele, but she'd do it in six months.) The wider significance was that they founded and preserved what has become one of the best research sites in Madagascar. And that they were and are feudal lords in a multicultural society.

The de Heaulme family are friends, although they are friends on fairly formal terms: we each have our own sphere. Jean de Heaulme, a fundamentally social man, has always been affable to visiting scientists. As Jean and I grow older he has become more and more confiding about his life. I am one of the few people now who

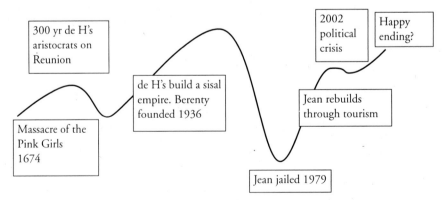

Figure 14.1. The de Heaulme family history is a drama of highs and lows with a turning point that might tempt any author to tell the story.

remember his redoubtable father Henry de Heaulme, founder of the plantation, and his sister Chantal whose life work was nursing Berenty personnel and delivering their babies. Of course I made choices in writing about a living person and his family, but they were predictable choices. If I had felt that honesty would cost me his friendship I would not have started the book.

The problem which nearly destroyed the book was political stance. The de Heaulmes arrived in Madagascar as colonial settlers in the 1920s, after 300 years as slave-holding plantation owners on Réunion. Berenty Estate is still run on feudal lines today, with the 'Patron' as patriarch. I point out repeatedly that this is why it has survived the post-independence changes in Madagascar. It is nonetheless hard to balance the fact that by western standards, their workers are underpaid, under-housed, dispossessed of the land that was theirs, against the opposing fact that the workers are better off than almost anyone in Tandroy villages outside the estate, where indeed hundreds of families depend on wages remitted by people at Berenty. Fifty years ago one might see Tandroy poverty as either the simple nobility of a 'primitive' culture or a result of colonial repression. By now it is far more due to overpopulation of a fragile environment. That arguably results in part from health benefits of the modern world which has denied the Tandroy the economic benefits of that world. Work on sisal estates is one of the few benefits they get.

When I wrote the first draft of *Lords and Lemurs* it was criticized by an anonymous reviewer, a social anthropologist, for being far too kind to the colonialists. The criticism was harsh, but justified. When I got over being furious I realized I had made a fundamental mistake. I have known for four decades that colonialism involves violations of human rights and destruction of the culture of the colonized. I thought everyone started from the same assumptions. My first draft emphasised that some colonists actually brought some benefits, because for me that was the new and interesting point. The de Heaulme family had negotiated with villagers, offering salaries as a buffer against recurrent devastating famines. They became blood-brothers to local chiefs. Jean de Heaulme's father was a noted Tandroy orator, fascinated by Tandroy customs, and so loved the landscape that he preserved parts of it as the reserves where the primatologists study, again in collaboration with local clans.

When I read the anthropologist's criticism I realized I had to rethink my book draft. Few people have much sense of history (it comes with being old). Fewer still in the West have any real knowledge of colonialism in the third world. I started over to explain the national background, not just what I had personally seen of the de Heaulmes. I underlined the role of head tax, forced labour and land appropriation. In particular, I told of the great 'rebellion' of 1947–1949, Madagascar's War of Independence. It was suppressed by the French with torture, imprisonment, mass execution. And no news allowed to the outside world. Its atrocities were no worse, but no better, than the wars in French Indochina and Algeria which finally led to the dissolution of the French Empire.

In short, writing only my personal experiences of the de Heaulmes and Berenty was so biased as to have been flat wrong. I was fascinated when Arlette Petter-Rousseaux said the same thing. She and her husband made the first great studies of wild lemur behaviour in 1956–1957 (Petter 1962; Petter-Rousseaux 1962). They spent a year touring all over Madagascar, just seven years after the 'rebellion' ended. It was not until she read *Lords and Lemurs* that she had any idea how the French had treated the Malagasy during the 1947–1949 War of Independence.

To compare with the section on lemurs, I felt safe telling Fan's story because I do have enough wider experience of ringtailed lemurs to know where she was typical, where extreme. Oddly, I was on much less secure ground telling my own story and that of close human friends. To set them in context needed much more explanation than the lemurs did. I could not count on readers to start from my own assumptions.

Telling of Tandroy

This brings me to the really challenging dilemma, the one I worried about from the start: how to describe the Tandroy workers on Berenty Estate. For background I read every scrap of the meagre anthropological writing on the tribe (DeCary 1930, 1933; Frère 1958; Guérin 1977; Heurtebize 1986, 1992, 1997; Fee 1996, 2000; Tsimamandro 1998; Middleton 2000), as well as the extraordinary account by Robert Drury, a cockney midshipman who became a Tandroy slave after his shipwreck in 1703 (Drury 1729; Parker-Pearson 1996; Parker-Pearson and Godden 2002).

Tandroy were and are a pastoral people. Their wealth is measured in humped, long-horned zebu cattle, with goats and sheep as small change. A man cannot marry until he gives at least one zebu to his father-in-law. A family's whole prestige depends on the scale of its funerals and tombs, accompanied by sacrifice of zebu at every stage of the proceedings. A hundred years ago Tandroy were famous warriors. They had local kings, derived from lighter-skinned people who, by tradition, came from across the sea and had a taboo on eating pork. Their descendents are still known as the noble caste. In spite of kingly relationship, clan warred against clan, killing the men and taking women and children as slaves.

Tandroy are proud of their strength to live in the 'Spiny Forest', where cactus-like plants stretch thorn-studded fingers into the sky and baobabs loom above thickets of bloated sausage-trees or whip-stemmed scratchy *roy* bushes. About once a decade drought leads to terrible famine. In some droughts half the children under five may die. In the old days, though, children born and raised between famines could grow to six feet tall on a diet rich in zebu yogurt, with plenty of beef to share at funerals. Tandroy have wholly patriarchal inheritance, but there is a paradox: women laugh loud, stride free, and take remarkable initiative in choosing lovers. A Tandroy proverb announces, 'Better to have a child's umbilical cord cut by a strong woman than a weak man.'

Their heritage leads to a second paradox. Tandroy are simultaneously among the most conservative and the most enterprising people of Madagascar. The tradition of young men travelling with the herds has turned into sending away young men to earn money, often temporarily, to raise cash for brideprice or an elder's funeral. Forced migration during famine leads whole families to work in distant regions. Nowadays many Tandroy still live in their thorn-encircled villages, but others are plantation field hands, mechanics, charcoal burners, rickshaw pullers throughout the length of

Madagascar's island-continent. When the paler, Indonesian-derived people of the central plateau want a security guard they hire a tall, dark, fearsome Tandroy.

But for *Lords and Lemurs* I was not writing about a distillation of traditional Tandroy social norms. I was trying to describe Berenty's sisal plantation. I hardly knew where to start. Over forty years, I had had minimal contact with the actual people of the region. Scandalous? Of course. The lemurs were plenty to occupy me. Furthermore, it was not my place to mess with the running of Berenty Estate.

Therefore to write my book I had to go out and do interviews. Guided by Lahivano, chauffeur, Andreas Miha and Benoit Damy, tourist guides, Hanta Rasamimanana, my lemur-watching colleague, and Georges Heurtebize and Philibert Tsimamandro, actual anthropologists. I interviewed a total of eleven men and four women, most of them on several occasions. Only five made it into the book as characters.

The five people that I quoted covered a spectrum of the earliest plantation workers, foremen and commanders, and one noble who had opted out because it was much more important to take care of his cattle. They at least gave me some history of the peculiar place I work in. They would spread a clean palm-straw mat outside the hut, where I sat with my colleague-interpreter. Everyone in the family or village crowded round to hear: if the children pack tight enough, eighty people can surround a village mat. All my interlocutors were pleased to talk and immensely courteous hosts. Even though most had very little idea what it meant to be in a book, I had no qualms about taping and writing: the stories were clearly the public versions which everyone was supposed to hear. It helped, too, that by now I was old: that leant mutual respect to my seeking them out and asking their opinions.

Rehomaha (The Abandoned) fulsomely declared that he would let his head be cut off if it would help the de Heaulmes. When he was a fatherless ten year old, M. de Heaulme senior had given him a boy's job to keep himself and his mother alive. For him, the plantation was his family. Another man was frank enough to sum up the early de Heaulme negotiations with the villagers: 'They took our land, and all they gave us was some zebu for a party.' The grandest of them, Tsiaketraky (He-Who-Cannot-Be-Thrown-to-Earth), had been a field commander of a thousand men and women in the plantation's heyday. He told me how he rose from his origins as a young army deserter to his present eminence. He concluded, 'The old customs are being forgotten ... even I am now Christian ... I am old and must think about my funeral. If I am Christian, my sons do not have to kill all my three hundred cattle, perhaps only twenty-five of them. So I converted ... which ensures an inheritance for my sons'(Jolly 2004: 42). Over and over, people spoke of the continuity of the plantation. Under the feudal rule of the de Heaulmes their workers expect jobs for the future. In spite of the low wages (also a recurrent theme) there was no industrial unrest at Berenty, because, 'Here the sons inherit.'

To place the people I met into their own wider culture, I described a grand funeral, the high point of Tandroy rites of passage. Valiotaky (Troubled-by-Others'-Talk) celebrated the interment of his older brother, head of his clan. A great zebu was killed at the moment of death so that its breath would carry the dying man's breath into the next world. The corpse lay in a sealed coffin of corrugated iron roofing sheets for the three months it took to prepare the funeral. A thousand guests attended. Spear-waving runners stampeded herds of cattle through the village amid gunfire and oratory and dancing and sacrifices and sex. Women danced, spines in an S-curve and bottoms thrust back, with a straw hat held forward to requisition gifts of cash from any man they danced to. Scores of goats were killed and roasted to feed the assemblage. After two weeks, at the grand climax, the dead man's sons sacrificed twenty-three fat steers to become their father's new herd. The sons dispatched each zebu with a single spear-thrust to the heart. A fitting send-off for the Ancestor!

Valiotaky's family fortunes were based on his wages as a sisal commander on Berenty estate, cannily multiplied by the herd of interest-bearing cattle. His elderly wife was from a distant clan: he had met her while working in the sisal sheds. Far from being generic 'primitive tradition', during that funeral I watched tradition operating in the same plantation world that was sheltering me, the scientists, the lemurs, tourists and TV crews.

I would hardly dare to write about lemurs citing five individuals from a total sample of fifteen. The Tandroy chapters were clearly journalism, not science. I hope that I placed my chosen five in the appropriate background, better than I had managed with the de Heaulmes, their feudal masters. But maybe I did not, and I have no way of knowing. Social anthropologists are deep in discussion about the value of personal testimony by observers and observed: what is called 'autoethnography' (Watson 2001). I figured if I read one single book of this self-reflective criticism, I was lost. I think in the end I did a respectable job of explaining about the Tandroy, but the last thing I want is some Donna Haraway doing a meta-analysis of how it should have been better!

Berenty scientists and the narrator's stance

How does this consideration of the personal and professional, or of individual experiences and the validity of generalization, bear on scientists at Berenty and their experience of studying lemurs? Do they 'go bush' or 'go primate'?

I think of one scientist who almost totally identified with her lemur troop. She was at the intersection of female heartbreak, Japanese personification of individual animals, twelve to fifteen hour continuous focal sampling, and the general madness that affects people too long in the field and students too long in graduate school. I think of another who had the kind of narrowly focussed Western-style observational intensity which I had at the beginning, except that even I never would have set up a focal sample regime with ten second recording intervals. One way or another, it is possible at Berenty to shut out much of the world beyond the lemurs you are watching. If you don't speak either French or Malagasy, in a place with no TV, phone, or email, you soon forget there is an outside world. Even if you maintain an almost rational view that lemurs are just small mammals, the puzzles you set yourself take over your own mind.

There is always an edge of drama. It may be as simple as will you find the troop this morning? Who are the mysterious strangers you glimpsed yesterday? Will you see a birth during siesta? Will the infant survive? Who wins this territorial skirmish? Even, will that blasted animal turn its face to the light so you can take its photograph? Somehow all that becomes far more important and exciting than battles and elections and scandals in far-away lands.

So yes, in a sense we all become obsessed with the lemurs, to the point where dinner table gossip is only the daily soap opera of the troops. On the other hand, we do not imagine that we actually are lemurs.

Conclusion

The narrator's stance, the trajectory allotted to me aged nine in the Unitarian Sunday School, applies easily to the lemurs. It is far more awkward towards other people, as anthropologists know. In fact, I suspect that it requires their complicity. Habituated ringtails who have neither been fed nor hunted treat scientists as an irrelevant primate species, much like the white sifaka who also share their woods. One moves freely among them, neither threat nor benefactor. Humans who deal with an inquisitive foreigner also have to decide how much to accept him or her. The narrator's stance only works when your hosts agree to accommodate a stranger who can never truly integrate into their tribe.

The heartbreak comes when you try to be initiated and fail: you can't sing the songs on the Hit Parade. The liberation comes when people accept your difference: you are American, not French or Tandroy. And even as an American, you may never hope to become a Midwestern Norwegian Lutheran who knows the names of Tandroy devils.

There is a final question, though. Is the narrator's stance enough?

There, the answer, to me, is 'No'. It is not enough to tell your own impressions of the few people or lemurs you come to know well.

The personal, whether my life or Frightful Fan's life, or Jean de Heaulme's life, or Valiotaky's grand funeral for his brother, or a student's tears over the death of a lemur baby, are notes for a private or public diary. The public diary is a literary construction. Like all literature, it hopes to stir feelings, to seek depths of understanding with a nimbus of connotations which spread into surrounding worlds of the reader's mind. It may have an ulterior goal: to press for a cause like conservation, or to convey the richness of another culture. It may even be an attempt to show the limitations of a supposedly scientific account of a culture, and how few people, with what mixed motives, are actually involved. But if it is not set in a wider context than its own story, it is literary propaganda, for good or for bad.

In my first draft of writing about the de Heaulme family, personal knowledge was clearly not to be trusted when it got the context wrong. In my writing about the Tandroy, one needs more systematic analysis of modern plantation life to even find out if my version has some validity. Only in writing about the lemurs do I think I knew enough scientific background to be sure I targeted Frightful Fan's story accurately. The depth of my personal identification with all of these societies has led me to write with passion, but has little to do with the accuracy of my accounts.

The scientists' attempt to gather a wider data set may seem earnest and dull. Our defined intellectual boundaries are self-limiting: I did my best to analyze this, I did not try to know that. But the discipline of looking broadly enough to actually see what may be statistically valid, what may be typical rather than just individual, what may be verified by other observers, even by a whole community of scientists rather than just one's individual self: that is the search for what can stand, at least for a while, as truth.

References

Cartmill, M. 1991. 'Book review: *Primate Visions: Gender, Race, and Nature in the World of Modern Science*, by Donna Haraway', *International Journal of Primatology* 12: 67–75.

DeCary, R. 1930, 1933. *L'Androy*. Paris: Société d'Editions Géographiques, Maritimes, et Coloniales.

Drury, R. 1729. *Madagascar, or Robert Drury's Journal during Fifteen Years' Captivity on that Island*. London: W. Meadow.

Dubovick, T.H. 1998. 'A historical, social and ecological analysis of three tourist ranging troops of *Lemur catta*, Berenty Reserve, Madagascar', *Department of Ecology and Evolutionary Biology*. Princeton NJ: Princeton.

Fee, S. 1996. *Bibliographie Thematique de Tandroy*: 1–16.

____ 2000. 'Note introductive sur le genre à Madagascar', *Taloha, Revue du Musée d'Art et d'Archéologie de Madagascar,* Repenser 'la femme malgache': numéro spéciale: 13–39.

Frère, S. 1958. *Panorama de l'Androy*. Paris: Ed. Aframpe.

Gowaty, P.A. 1991. 'Review of *Primate Visions: Gender, Race, and Nature in the World of Modern Science*, by Donna Haraway', *Animal Behaviour* 42: 166–8.

Guérin, M. 1977. *Le Defi: L'Androy et l'appel à la vie*. Fianarantsoa, Madagascar: Librairie Ambozontany.

Haraway, D. 1989. *Primate Visions: Gender, Race and Nature in the World of Modern Science*. New York: Routledge.

Heurtebize, G. 1986. *Histoire des Afomarolahy (Extrême-sud de Madagascar)*. Paris: CNRS.

____ 1992. *L'Habitat Traditionelle Tandroy*. Antananarivo: Centre d'Information et de Documentation Technique.

____ 1997. *Marriage et Deuil dans l'Extrême-Sud de Madagascar*. Paris: L'Harmattan.

Hood, L.C. 1993. 'The saga of A-Troop: infanticide and female competition among ringtailed lemurs (*Lemur catta*) at Berenty Reserve, Madagascar', *American Journal of Primatology*. 16(6): 997–1015.

Hood, L.C. and A. Jolly. 1995. 'Troop fission in female *Lemur catta* at Berenty Reserve, Madagascar', *International Journal of Primatology* 16: 997–1016.

Ichino, S. and N. Koyama. 2006. 'Social changes in a wild population of ring-tailed lemurs (*Lemur catta*) at Berenty, Madagascar', in A. Jolly, R.W. Sussman, N. Koyama and H.R. Rasamimanana *Ringtailed Lemur Biology: Lemur catta in Madagascar*. New York: Springer, pp. 233–44.

Jolly, A. 1966. *Lemur Behavior*. Chicago: University of Chicago Press.

____ 1970. 'Malagasy lemurs–clues to our past', *Animal Kingdom* 70: 66–75.

____ 1980. *A World like our Own: Man and Nature in Madagascar*. New Haven: Yale University Press.

_____ 1999. *Lucy's Legacy: Sex and Intelligence in Human Evolution.* Cambridge, MA: Harvard University Press.

_____ 2004. *Lords and Lemurs: Mad Scientists, Kings with Spears, and the Survival of Diversity in Madagascar.* Boston: Houghton Mifflin.

Jolly, A. and M. Jolly. 1990. 'A view from the other end of the telescope (Review of Haraway, *Primate Visions*)'. *New Scientist* (April 21): 58.

Jolly, A., H. Rasamimanana, et al. 2006. 'Territory as bet-hedging: *Lemur catta* in a rich forest and an erratic climate', in A. Jolly, R.W. Sussman, N. Koyama and H. Rasamimanana, *Ringtailed Lemur Biology: Lemur catta in Madagascar.* New York: Springer, pp. 187–207.

MacClancy, J. 2005. 'The literary image of anthropologist', *Journal of the Royal Anthropological Institute* (N.S.) 11: 549–75.

Middleton, K. 2000. 'The rights and wrongs of loin-washing', *Taloha, Revue du Musée d'Art et d'Archéologie de Madagascar,* Repenser 'la femme malgache': numéro spéciale, pp. 63–99.

Parker-Pearson, M. 1996. 'Reassessing *Robert Drury's Journal* as a historical source for southern Madagscar', *History in Africa* 23: 1–23.

Parker-Pearson, M. and K. Godden 2002. *The Red Slave.* Thrupp, Stroud: Sutton Publishing.

Petter, J-J. 1962. 'Ecological and behavioral studies of Madagascar lemurs in the field', *Annals of the New York Academy of Science* 102: 267–81.

Petter-Rousseaux, A. 1962. 'Recherches sur la Biologie de la Réproduction des Primates Inférieurs', *Mammalia* A: 3794: 1–87.

Sussman, R.W., P.A. Garber, et al. 2005. 'The importance of cooperation and affiliation in the evolution of primate sociality' *American Journal of Physical Anthropology* 128: 84–97.

Tsimamandro, P. 1998. 'Le Kokolampo: essai d'interpretation d'un phénomène de possession dans la région Est de l'Androy', *Anthropology Department.* Tuléar, Madagascar: Université de Tuléar.

Watson, J. 2001. 'Autoethnography', in M. Jolly (ed.) *Encyclopedia of Life Writing.* London: Fitzroy Dearborn. I, pp. 83–5.

Wilson, E.O. 1984. *Biophilia.* Cambridge, MA: Harvard University Press.

15
Natural Homes:
Primate Fieldwork and the Anthropological Method

Pamela J. Asquith

Introduction

'It can be no secret', wrote social anthropologist Graham Watson, 'that for many North American cultural anthropologists, British social anthropologists constitute a negative reference group, and that the British reciprocate the antagonism in full measure' (Watson 1984: 351). The author, a British trained anthropologist teaching in a Canadian university, pointed out what he saw as the hopeless circle of argument and counter-argument about what the disciplines 'really' are; hopeless because views of the disciplines do not refer to any particular reality but rather are 'texts of embedded interpretive practices' by means of which anthropologists construe them as disciplines in the first place (ibid. 352). Written in the early days of sociology of science and postmodern critique, Watson suggested that until we reveal what these embedded interpretive practices are, controversy about the disciplinary status of the various fields of anthropology will remain unfruitful.

As the editors of this volume point out, methodology, or the content and process of fieldwork itself, became a legitimate object of analysis from the mid 1980s in social anthropology. Indeed, the prior (and rather few) ethnographic memoirs that had given some insights into field methodologies, were largely replaced by 'narrative ethnographies', in which the ethnographic process, rather than the ethnographer, was the focus of study. There has not been a similar sustained reflection about field methodology on the part of biological anthropologists although there have been many theoretical developments over the same period that have influenced methodology in all of its subfields. The task posed by the conference organizers for biological anthropologists and primatologists to reflect on their fieldwork practices produced some surprises. What at first had seemed to be a rather forced exercise (for those who 'just get on with the fieldwork'), instead provided a powerful tool for finding disciplinary boundaries in anthropology in the widest sense. For the field of primatology, which is examined here, a much deeper and more dynamic connection between anthropology and primatology became apparent. That is, in addition to the familiar argument from evolutionary kinship as the rationale for primatology being aligned with anthropology, significant parallels in the fieldwork process itself bind ethnography and primatology.

There have been eleven narrative accounts of fieldwork written by primatologists between 1964 and the present. These (a kind of 'narrative primatology') go to the heart of the fieldwork experience for primatologists studying animals in their natural habitats. Almost all introductions to scientific monographs include something about the primatologists' relationship with the animals they studied. The narrative accounts, however, are exceptional in that they provide sustained reports on the fieldwork experience and hence very much richer examples about methodology, about the nature of the relationship between the observers and animals, and that among the animals themselves. These books are not confined to describing the 'ethnographic process' in fieldwork: they are part personal memoir, part research report, and part enriched descriptive accounts of whole animal lives. These reports provide a picture of a community of actors playing out their lives in their 'village of birth' rather than being confined to addressing a particular question for a scientific publication, although in so doing they contribute important scientific data to the discipline.

My intent is to point out that anthropology is an appropriate home for primatology, based as much on some common fundamentals of methodology as for reasons of evolutionary kinship with humans.[1] In recognizing those commonalities we can at the same time feel more secure about accommodating significant differences that have been at the heart of anthropologists' doubts about disciplinary connections with primatology. The root of those doubts can be traced in part to Claud Lévi-Strauss' proposal of reciprocal exogamy as a universal structural feature of human society that was uniquely human and that marked the transition from nature to culture in his 'Les Structures Elémentaires de la Parenté' ('The Elementary Sructures of Kinship', published in 1949) (Chapais 2008: 10). More recently, another source of aggravation for social anthropologists is 'the question of culture' (and of rationality) in humans and animals. However, the twin dilemmas of, for social anthropologists, the (mis)appropriation of the term 'culture' by primatologists, and for primatologists, the insistence on inventing definitions of culture to enable use of the term to refer to behavioural plasticity in nonhuman primates, are, I will argue, simply unnecessary.

Disciplinary settings

In departments of anthropology in England (where I was trained) and North America (where I have taught), there has been a more or less pronounced division or wall of incomprehension on the part of social anthropologists toward primatology. This has been displayed in terms of competition for limited resources for library acquisitions, hiring of faculty, and facilities for graduate students, as well as the apparent absence of common goals in training new anthropologists across the subspecialties of the discipline. While primatologists may be viewed as contributors to speculations about past hominid behaviour, social anthropologists take a dim view of the appropriation of terms such as 'culture', 'kinship' and a host of what is perceived as anthropomorphic terminology by their colleagues to describe primate society. Given the taxonomic Order under consideration, the response that departments of anthropology should more correctly be named departments of primatology is treated as a poor joke or with derision.

Such tensions within the anthropological fold were played out publicly in 1998 and 1999 at Stanford University. There, the former Department of Anthropology was divided into two new departments, each with separate administrative units and degree programs. Although the source of the rift at Stanford was ostensibly between 'scientific' people and postmodernists, the resulting departments reflected a clear division of training for students in anthropology of human culture versus holistic anthropology even while retaining some of the same subfields (linguistic and medical anthropology). The Stanford website states that the newly-named Department of Anthropological Sciences takes as its subject matter the nature and evolution of our species, and that faculty 'have a common interest in the interrelations of biology, culture, environment and language.'[2] The descriptor of the second Department, 'Cultural and Social Anthropology', notes that that department offers a wide range of approaches to various subfields and topics within anthropology as well as training in ethnographic research. Biological anthropology and primatology are not included among the subfields of this department and 'students interested in biological and evolutionary approaches to anthropology are urged to consult the Department of Anthropological Sciences'.[3]

Primatology faces further challenges finding a disciplinary home in the sciences. It is considered to be 'not quite science' by zoologists, although often a zoologist (and a statistician) will be included on supervisory and examining committees for graduate students in primatology. For more than two decades one of the most pressing concerns for primatologists has been the conservation of primate species and their habitats. It is surprising, therefore, that their presence has not increased in departments of ecology or general zoology. Zoologists find the long term field studies of primates difficult to justify when one could obtain demographic and behavioural data through cross-sectional studies of animal populations and perhaps some clever manipulation of environmental or social conditions. There are a few field primatologists who work in departments of ecology but they are very much in the minority. Those primatologists who work in departments of psychology or medicine are usually never engaged in fieldwork[4] and perhaps would not be called primatologists, but rather people who use nonhuman primates in their laboratories.

While primatology has often sat uneasily within anthropology, anthropology has usually been regarded as its natural home, especially in North America, since the original focus of research was to contribute to our understanding of human behaviour and its evolution.[5] In England the history of primatology has had greater disciplinary diversity, giving but three recent examples, affiliation with an animal behaviour unit (Madingley, Cambridge), a former Biological Anthropology unit (Oxford),[6] and an anthropology department (Oxford Brookes University). In these days when more and more primatologists are studying endangered species simply for knowledge about them, rather than about people, the wide publicity in both media and science circles attending any findings that can be applied to 'human nature' is striking. Indeed, the argument for preservation of primate species often devolves to their evolutionary closeness to humans. The connections to anthropology tend to be resurrected through these findings of 'basic natures' (e.g., 'rape', 'monogamy', 'cheating', 'murder', 'infanticide', 'warfare', etc.) reported in both scientific and popular form. There are likewise glimmerings of the obverse argument whereby knowledge of human behaviour is called upon to try to understand primate behaviour. Bradshaw and Sapolsky (2006: 488) call this 'inferential symmetry', whereby human-to-animal and animal-to-human inferences have become legitimately symmetric, based on a deeper understanding of brain biology.

'Narrative' primatology

The question posed by the conference organizers provides an entirely different avenue by which to explore disciplinary links with primatology. That is, through examining the process of fieldwork, not only in terms of logistics, hypothesis testing, etc., but through what the researchers report about coping with, being changed by, and forming a view of their objects of study, we gain insight into similarities of experiences for primatologists and social anthropologists. Primatologists will be familiar with many of the books of this narrative genre in their discipline, but a brief overview will provide the context for those who have not read them. Six of the books describe longterm fieldwork experiences and the lives of the great apes (gorillas, chimpanzees and orangutans [none has yet been written on bonobos, or pygmy chimpanzees]). Four of the books are based on fieldwork with baboon species, and one is about a New World monkey, the muriqui or woolly spider monkey, of Brazil. These books also can profitably be mined for insights into fieldwork methodologies that appear counter to strictly 'scientific method', for insights into the meaning of humanness, or for the political consequences of 'public productions of primate personality' (see Rees 2007).[7]

The mountain gorilla (*Gorilla gorilla beringei*) is featured in George Schaller's (1963) *Year of the Gorilla*, Dian Fossey's (1983) *Gorillas in the Mist* and Bill Weber and Amy Vedder's (2002) *In the Kingdom of the Gorillas*. Schaller's research was based at Kabara, in what was then the Albert National Park, Congo, now Zaire. Other researchers and travellers had watched gorillas there before, but with his wife, Schaller was the first to habituate and to study the social life of the gorillas. The book is based on research that began in 1959 and lasted approximately a year. His work at Kabara ended in September 1960, although supplementary observations of gorillas and other primates were made before fieldwork terminated in January 1961.

Dian Fossey began her study of the mountain gorillas in 1967 at the same site where Schaller had worked in the Congo. Abandoning the site as a result of political instability she eventually founded the Karisoke research station in the Parc National des Volcans in Rwanda. Her book is based on her experiences there from 1968 until

1980, when she returned to the United States to teach. She returned to Karisoke in 1983, and was murdered there in 1985. Her life has been the subject of several biographies and a Hollywood movie. A foundation in her name continues to raise funds for the protection of the remaining mountain gorillas.

Weber and Vedder (2002) began their work in 1978 at Fossey's site at Karisoke, and expanded to other sites in the area to encourage conservation by habituating gorillas for tourist groups. Work was disrupted by the genocide experienced in Rwanda in the 1990s, but work on the gorillas continues to the present. Besides describing the gorillas, their book is another (though this one very critical) portrait of Dian Fossey and her work, as well as a report of the very considerable challenges of local poverty, politics and sheer physical and emotional difficulties faced by the researchers.

Study of the second great ape species, the orangutan (*Pongo pygmaeus*), was undertaken by Birute Galdikas (1995) from 1971 in Tanjung Putin Reserve, in Borneo. Much of her work was also concerned with returning captive orangutans to the wild and continues to the present.

Jane Goodall (1990) began work on the third species, chimpanzees (*Pan troglodytes*), at Gombe in Tanzania in 1960.[8] The Gombe Stream Research Centre was founded in 1967. Work at the site was disrupted in 1975, when Zairian rebels kidnapped four foreign students from the site. Tanzanian research assistants continued data collection until foreign students and researchers were allowed to return to the site in 1989, and work there has continued ever since. Goodall for many years has split her time between research at Gombe and fundraising trips worldwide for the protection of chimpanzees both in the wild and in captivity.

The sixth study, also on chimpanzees, by Vernon Reynolds (1965) was in Budongo, in northwestern Uganda. The work described in this book began in 1962 and lasted approximately a year. Again political unrest interrupted research there for years, which recommenced in 1990, when Reynolds and colleagues set up the Budongo Forest Project. Research on the chimpanzees continues to the present day, along with conservation efforts essential to all the great ape study sites.

Of the four books of this genre on baboon species, Hans Kummer (1995) began research on hamadryas baboons (*Papio cynocephalus hamadryas*) in Ethiopia with his colleague and assistant Fred Kurt in 1960. The initial year long study was followed by a series of later projects from 1967 to 1977 (not continuous) when research stopped as a result of the war with Somalia. Robert Sapolsky's (2001) account of his research with the olive baboons (*Papio cynocephalus anubis*) in the Serengeti, Tanzania began in 1979. The research has not been continuous, but takes place during three months of the year, to the present. The third researcher, Barbara Smuts (1985), began studying olive baboons (*Papio c. anubis*) at Kekopey, near Gilgil in Kenya, in 1976. A second edition of Smuts' book was published in 1999. The fourth researcher, Shirley Strum (1987), who was co-director of the Gilgil Baboon Project when Smuts arrived, also worked on the olive baboons of Kekopey, and was responsible for their translocation to Chololo in 1984. Research on the baboon troops continues to the present. A second edition of Strum's book was published in 2001.

Karen Strier's (1992) work on the muriqui or woolly spider monkey (*Brachyteles arachnoides*), the largest South American primate, began at Fazenda Montes Claros in Minas Gerais, Brazil in 1982, and has continued to the present day. With the exception of Schaller's and Reynolds' reports, these records were published ten to thirty years after the initial fieldwork. It is therefore unsurprising to find 'thick description' of primate lives and their impacts on the observers. These are powerful and charming texts that draw the reader into the lives of primates and primatologist observers. They are enjoyed equally by other primatologists and by the public for whom they were written.

Methodologies

To most primatologists, 'field methods' could be summed up by Jeanne Altmann's paper 'Observational study of behaviour: sampling methods' published in the journal *Behaviour* in 1974. This paper is arguably the most influential methodological survey in primatology. It is cited in practically any paper or monograph in primatology you pull off the shelf. Altmann, who was a mathematician before turning to primatology, demanded that more attention be paid to the choice of a systematic sampling method (such as focal animal sampling, *ad libitum* sampling, etc.) in order to ensure that the data collected would not be biased, that it would be capable of statistical testing, and that data collected from different field sites could actually be compared. It seems that no one has felt any need in the intervening 33 years to improve on the guidelines that she provided.

What Altmann did not address was the 'heart' of fieldwork. This is what the primate studies memoirs provide. In fact, the twin necessities of habituating the animals to the observer's presence so that they do not panic or hide themselves, and of distinguishing one animal from the other (individual identification) were implicit in Altmann's sampling methods, though most early primatologists wrote in more general terms of males, females, juveniles, and identified high-ranking animals where they could easily be discerned.[9] By contrast, the primate fieldwork memoirs bring us to the reality of just what is involved in habituating wild animals and identifying fast moving individuals. Strier (1992: 37) records that this entailed staying put while branches and faeces rained down around and upon her from frightened muriquis, while Goodall (1990) famously waited nearly two years to be accepted by the chimpanzees. Galdikas (1995) reports enduring months of trials in the rainforest before getting her first glimpses of the elusive orangutans who then on occasion would attempt to push dead branchless trees, called snags, onto her in a bid to run her off, or kill her, she thought.

For purposes of comparing similarities and differences with anthropological fieldwork experiences, a few features common to all the reports will be highlighted. These fall into the following categories: the relationship of observer with the subjects of study, the kind of data gathered, and the experiences of researchers in terms of the mental and physical process of fieldwork, and of being changed by the foreign social environment.

Karen Strier (1992: xv–xvii), who began her study in 1982, described a brief incident that occurred early in her fieldwork that marked a turning point when the research became more than a dispassionate study motivated solely by scientific questions. She had been studying one group of muriquis. A muriqui male of another group was trying to join the group. This is a very tense time in primate social life. The male solicited the support of four females of the group he wished to join. The females instead chased off the male and returned to Strier to offer a gesture of reassurance to her. The gesture took the form of hanging upsidedown and proferring outstretched hands to her, as they do when they reassure other muriquis. At this point Strier noted:

> It took all of my scientific training and willpower to resist the temptation - and the clear invitation- to reach back. I had never touched the muriquis before, and I knew that I could not touch them now and still hope to remain the passive observer that was so essential to my ability to record their behavior for the remainder of the study … . The entire interaction, from the moment the Jaó male approached until the females had returned to their sleeping sites, took less than 10 minutes. But it shaped all subsequent years of the research. (Ibid: xvi–xvii)

Shirley Strum (1987) relates the turning point for her research some time after she had decided to leave the safety of having her vehicle in proximity and simply go where the baboons went. This again was an instance of a baboon who solicited Strum's help in his bid to become part of the troop. This he ('Ray') did by slapping the ground with his hand, looking first at Strum, and then staring at the two troop males who were threatening him. Strum noted: 'This handsome, powerful male struggling to become part of the troop spoke strongly to something in me. I badly wanted to help him, but I couldn't. I signaled this by turning away completely … Ray won his struggle alone, but I shall never forget how honored I felt by the compliment he paid me.' Strum continued, 'There was nothing different about the day; I was different. My mind was full of new questions and my heart of new emotions' (Ibid., 37, italics as in original). Smuts' (1985) *Sex and Friendship in Baboons* reads more like a straight research monograph than the other books. However, she notes that within a strict evolutionary perspective as the context for interpreting results during data analysis:

> The research itself … often took on a very different character due to the powerful influence of my subjects – the baboons. … What captured my interest and motivated me to return to observe my subjects again and again was the daily drama of baboon life (Ibid., 8).

Galdikas' (1995) story of the orphaned female orangutan, Akmad, whom she met soon after her arrival in Borneo, unfolds with the same emotional power. Akmad had been rescued from her captors and, as she matured, would disappear into the forest for as long as a year at a time. One day Akmad returned with her newborn infant. Galdikas (1995: 16) relates:

> In a moment of absolute clarity I realized the intensity of the bond that I had forged with Akmad. ... It had taken me more than a decade of living with orangutans in their great forest home, to understand finally that orangutans are not just simpler versions of ourselves. All those years that orangutans had walked by me, seemingly oblivious, I had despaired of ever reaching them. For a split second, Akmad had allowed me a clear glimpse of her universe. And yet, without knowing it, I already had been allowed into that world years before. What I had taken as indifference and rejection was the orangutan expression of acceptance ... In that moment everything I had been through – the heat, the mud, the humidity, the torrential rains, the fire ants, the leeches, the cobras, pythons, and pit vipers, the fevers, the deaths, the frustrations – became insignificant. I knew that my journey ... into the uncharted depths of the rain forest and the orangutan mind ... had truly begun.

These turning points in their relationship with the animals mark in each case the beginning of pursuing new research questions, of seeing with different eyes the nature of the social lives they had come to document, an experience that will be familiar to ethnographers. Smuts commented that all of her larger questions about baboon life composed with evolutionary outcomes in mind quickly became translated into a series of much more immediate, often compelling questions about phenomena of immediate concern to the baboons themselves (Smuts 1985: 8).

In addition to coming to recognize the subtleties of another species' behaviour, the 'stories about the monkeys' are important for other reasons. Strier (1992: xvii–xviii) remarks:

> Quantitative data are essential for valid comparisons with other studies. ... Behavior is recorded according to a carefully developed protocol. But these data alone do not convey what the day-to-day experience of accompanying muriquis has been like, and many special events and interactions elude neat, numerically coded categories. This book includes these anecdotes because it is the stories about the monkeys and the progress of the research that provide an essential context for the scientific findings.

Yet another reason is provided by George Schaller, who remarks in his foreword to Strum's *Almost Human*, that she ' ... captures both the science of the animal and its being. The baboons are individuals, not mere statistical entities. Scientific papers cannot express the fundamental charm, the fleeting social entanglements, the perishable moments of a baboon's life' (Strum 1987: xii). Schaller continues, 'Books such as hers create an awareness that animals too have unique and complex societies as worth of study and preservation as our own' (Ibid., xiii).

The foreword to Barbara Smuts' book by Irven deVore (an anthropologist) notes, like Schaller (who is a zoologist), that:

While adhering to the most scrupulous methodological strictures, the author maintains an open research strategy- respecting her subjects by approaching them with the open mind of an ethnographer immersing herself in the complexities of baboon social life before formulating her research design … She was able to shift the baboons well along the continuum from 'subject' to 'informant' through her proximity with them (Smuts 1985: xii).

Smuts confirms this when she relates that she began ' … by trying to adopt the attitude of an ethnographer confronted with a previously undescribed society. … I tried to let the baboons themselves "tell" me what was important' (Ibid.: 30).

A final example of a book on primates that is not of the memoir genre is typical of how researchers relate their feelings about doing field work. Boesch and Boesch-Achermann (2002) studied chimpanzees over a period of sixteen years in the Taï Forest of the Côte d'Ivoire in western Africa. In their preface they state two goals that have informed the conception of their book. One was to present new and original conclusions about chimpanzees. The second was to document what is emerging as the main characteristic of the chimpanzee: its wide and generalized behavioural diversity. 'It becomes difficult', they write, 'to state that the chimpanzee behaves in such and such a way: rather we need to say that Gombe chimpanzees behave like this, whereas Mahale chimpanzees do that and Taï chimpanzees behave in yet another way. An ethnological approach to the chimpanzee seems required' (Ibid.: vi). The authors further state:

> … [S]cience is not just about collecting data systematically; it is just as much about not missing the unexpected and the unknown. For this a certain intimacy with the animals is the best tool available. During the weeks and the months … we learned to know them individually. Some of them have impressed themselves upon us more than others, and the trust and admiration that we developed for them has helped us to make some of our most important observations (Ibid., vi).

The nature of the relationship from the observer's point of view is to get to 'know,' as far as is humanly possible, the primates' perspective on what is happening. Although they do not wish to influence the animals' behaviour, and hence do not join in and try not to interfere with their lives, they recognize individuality in the primates and respond emotionally at least to that. Sapolsky (2001: 233) remarked of a particular baboon to whom he devoted a chapter of his book, 'I didn't much like Nick, and neither did the rest of the troop, in that he had one of the most unappealing personalities I'd encountered in a long time.' Indeed, as Smuts (1985) noted, many primate field workers compare their jobs to watching soap operas, except that the characters are real and they do not speak. Similarly, Strier (1992: 82–3) relates that '[f]ollowing the muriquis' life histories is like following a soap opera, because just as in humans, each individual's life history is unique.' Strum (1987: 296) gives a vivid description of watching the baboons while 'the early morning soap opera plays on.'

Additionally for Strum (1987: 55) simply 'being with [the baboons] satisfied most of my social needs' and Strier (1992: 40) remarked that 'the lack of human company never seemed so oppressive when I was with the muriquis.' Carrying out research in the field is hard, lonely and strenuous, though no more so than for fieldworkers studying less ebullient characters, such as bats or voles. The soap opera quality of the daily displays of primate social life comes more perhaps from their more readily recognizable physiognomy for human observers. Schaller (1965: 135) remarked that he felt that the 'gorillas talked to [him] at times with their expressive eyes.'

Having come to know individual animals with unique life histories and characters, primatologists see their role as that of their amanuensis who will record these biographies and histories in order to come to understand their way of life. Further, rather than use the 'hiding in blinds' methods adopted with some success by previous ethologists, particularly ornithologists, Kummer (1995) approached his baboons openly, to gain the confidence of the animals through displaying predictable behaviour. This approach appealed to Kummer as it was ' ... based on politeness and respect. An ethnologist trying to study a human tribal community from hiding places, using night vision apparatus and concealed microphones, would seem boorish. ...' (1995: 85). He felt that the hamadryas baboons have 'found their biographer' in him, that in order to study the animals, he must learn 'hamadryish', and that like the ancient Egyptians, '[b]oth the ancient and I wrote down what the hamadryas told us' (1995: 22, 23, 27). So too, Jane Goodall feels that she 'has been privileged ... to compile the history of a group of beings who have no written language of their own' (Goodall 1990: 198).

A final example of what the researcher has to say when individual identification and habituation have not occurred serves to highlight the fundamentally different quality of data gathered between the 'ethnographic-type' method and that done without. Vernon Reynolds (1965: 45) with his wife Frankie studied chimpanzees for a year in Uganda before writing his book. He wrote that they failed to habituate the chimpanzees probably due to three factors: they were three people (including a tracker) instead of just one, the chimpanzees could not see them distinctly in the dense forest, and were rarely seeing the same chimpanzees on every occasion, so they remained strangers. In fact they tried to hide from the chimpanzees so as not to alarm them when they came across them, having been frightened by an episode with the chimpanzees that Reynolds described as displaying a kind of mob anger, tinged with curiosity (Reynolds 1965: 38). As a result of not knowing individuals, though they had developed certain theories about the nature of chimpanzee society, they did not yet know which chimpanzees went where (Ibid. 193), and while they gathered a lot of information about their feeding habits, daily routines and (they felt) social life, they remained puzzled about chimpanzee social organization (Ibid. 172). Perhaps the most telling difference to the experiences related by the other primatologists is that for Reynolds (1965: 135) '... the most striking thing about chimpanzee life was the utter tedium of it.' This has changed radically for Reynolds in the ensuing years and, with the reopening of the field site in 1990, he and many students and colleagues remain as fascinated by chimpanzee lives as any of the other researchers.

But obviously, the twin methodologies of individual identification and habituation profoundly affect data collection and the field experience of the researchers.

Certainly, it is not enough to say that because the primatologists felt they were approaching their study groups in some respects as ethnographers that their methodology was ethnography. Important differences between ethnography and primate fieldwork are readily apparent. The ethnographer attempts to become a participant observer, to gain an 'emic' (insider's) view as does the primatologist, but the means differ. The ethnographer participates in the lives of the society s/he studies; the primatologist does his best not to participate so as not to influence the animals' 'natural' lives. As Strier (1992: 82–83) notes,

> … [I]t is the unpredictable individual differences that make nonhuman primates such intriguing subjects, but sorting out these nuances from more general patterns of behaviour takes many years. Unlike cultural anthropologists, who can interview their human subjects about their personal histories, primatologists must rely on observations, which accumulate only as fast as the animals develop. And muriquis … are very slow to grow up.

This of course is also the answer to zoologists who wonder why primatologists devote so many years to gain insights into animal behaviour that could be won more easily, they feel, with behavioural sampling or interventionist observation.

The culture question

In suggesting that there are affinities between primatology and anthropology we are referring to the practices of the researchers, not to the lives of the research subjects. However, it reasonable that social anthropologists would assume that, given the kinds of experiences described by primatologists, they are also making inferences regarding the mental lives of the animals. In this they are correct, just as inferences have to be made with regard to mental processes in other human beings, as Gilbert Ryle (1949) pointed out so many years ago. Given too, as Rees (2007) notes, that the lives of primates have been cited frequently in attempts to 'normalise' or rather, 'naturalise' different aspects of human life, attempts to understand and to come to terms with the relationship between categories such as 'human', 'non-human', 'nature' or 'culture' have been at the heart of primatological theoretical and methodological debates. For anthropologists and primatologists there arose two related questions: one is, 'Can the observed social behaviour of other primates be assumed to be anything like the human behaviour of which it reminds us?' The question of anthropomorphism has been amply discussed in this regard. The other question is, 'Can we attribute a nonanthropomorphic rationality to these animals?' These issues in turn underlie the refusal to give primate 'culture' a place in anthropological literature.

To address the last point first, I think that primatology has done itself a disservice in trying to equate simple habits, such as 'hand clasping', methods of cracking nuts, 'stone play', etc. and the diffusion of those habits, with culture (e.g., McGrew 1992).[10] Variety in habits among different groups of a single species and the passing down of learned habits through generations is not equivalent to what anthropologists mean by human culture in terms of such things as beliefs and rituals attending death, fertility, hierarchy, sexuality, gender, and so on. However, it is not necessary to ascribe culture to animals in order to take them seriously. They can and should be taken seriously in their own right, as sentient creatures, expressing rational behaviour within their own kinds of lives.

Moral philosopher Mary Midgley (2005) resolved the apparent human/ nonhuman/nature/culture conundrum long ago. Reflecting back on what she wrote in 1978 in *Beast and Man,* Midgley maintains, '… [R]eason can't mean just deductive logic but must cover what makes sense for beings who have a certain sort of emotional nature' (Midgley 2005: 191). Counter to human exceptionalism, ideas of rationality should be expressible in forms suited to the emotional lives of other species. Primatologists who have gotten to know their animal subjects over many years have, I submit, done this with great success, to the extent that they can predict behaviour in some situations, as much as anyone can predict another's behaviour, and can respond appropriately in 'baboon' or 'gorilla' terms to incidents in which the animals have involved them.[11] Other primate species' abilities to learn, invent, have a social memory and strategize should not need to be defended just because humans also do them. At the same time, in providing us with such a full picture of their lives, we have enough of a context to understand the concepts in 'baboon terms', if you like, without fear of naïve anthropomorphism. The complex and interesting lives that long term field studies have revealed about primates do far more to defend the animals' intrinsic worth, kinship with humans and support the ethnographical methodology of primatology than does invoking the notion of 'culture' in terms of gestures and foraging strategies. One might also add, as Midgley (2005: 192) noted, human nature is complex and our tendency to form cultures is one part of it.

Recently, a challenge that goes to the heart of social anthropologists' self-defined exemption from evolutionary continuity with human social systems has been made by Bernard Chapais (2008). In *Primeval Kinship* Chapais notes that while the study of kinship has been central to many studies by social anthropologists writing about the dawn of human society, our current knowledge of kinship and society in nonhuman primates in fact supports and informs ideas first put forward by Claude Lévi-Strauss. Although Lévi-Strauss felt that kinship systems are fundamentally a cultural construct unique to humans, Chapais (2008: 306) argues the opposite: that its basis is composed of three basic bonds that have deep evolutionary roots – a kinship bond, a sexual bond and a parental bond – and that this basic kinship structure is an integral part of *human nature* (italics in original). Here, the study of kinship and social organization can provide a link between social and biological anthropology.

Conclusion

The juxtaposition of ethnological and evolutionary perspectives is what makes primatology so special, and yet has made for a sense of disciplinary ambiguity. However, as molecular studies increasingly replace 'whole animal biology' in modern zoology, departments of anthropology will become even more important as a home for studies of primate societies. Revelations of field diaries aside, the often-touted holistic nature of anthropology can surely encompass ecological and psychological studies of primates within the rubrics of evolutionary continuity, conservation and simply intrinsic interest of knowledge about their lives.

Acknowledgements

I am grateful to Jeremy MacClancy, Kate Hill, Anna Nekaris and Chris McDonaugh for their kind invitation and for prompting this evaluation of fieldwork experience. I also thank Amanda Rees and the editor of *Social Studies of Science* for permission to quote from forthcoming material.

Notes

1. My remarks are probably more relevant to the North American than to the European context since the majority of primatologists are in departments of anthropology in Canada and the United States. However, such debates about proper placement of primatologists are not unknown in, for instance, the UK as will be mentioned later.
2. http://www.stanford.edu/dept/anthsci/. Retrieved 10 February 2006.
3. http://www.stanford.edu/dept/anthroCASA/about.html/. Retrieved 10 February 2006. In Japan this dichotomy is hardly present. It is not unusual for field primatologists to study people as well. Anthropologists and primatologists participate and report on their fieldwork in the same student seminars. As Juichi Yamagiwa's contribution (this volume) shows, ecological anthropologists and primatologists derive much from each other and some individuals work in both fields.
4. There are exceptions to this of course, one of the most notable being Robert Sapolsky (2001), a neuroscientist, who has written one of the field memoirs cited here. However, I am making a general and legitimate point about trends which can be substantiated by examining which departments advertise for primatologists. By far the majority are departments of anthropology.
5. Strictly speaking, field studies of primates in North America began on the suggestion of comparative psychologist, Robert Mearns Yerkes, in the 1930s as a supplement to laboratory studies. However, primatology as a field of study really got underway in the 1950s under the aegis of anthropology there.
6. The situation there remains fluid, however, as shown by debates about whether a recent new appointment in primatology at Oxford should be placed in Anthropology or Zoology. In the meantime, The Institute of Biological Anthropology was subsumed under Social and Cultural Anthropology a few years ago, the latter itself having been renamed from the Institute of Social Anthropology, with Ethnology formerly a separate unit.
7. Rees (2007) provides a cogent discussion from the perspective of a sociologist of science of why these primatologists do not attempt to avoid anthropomorphism and how, in attributing social agency to the animals, they raise a flag of caution about the political consequences of science speaking for the voiceless.
8. Jane Goodall's first book, *In the Shadow of Man*, was published in 1965.

9. This is in marked contrast to Japanese researchers who, from the first, saw the importance of identifying individual members of a group. C.R. Carpenter had also seen this necessity in the 1930s, though many western researchers did not follow his lead in the first decades of their research.

10. A great many similar reports on primate culture have followed on McGrew's book and his definition of culture.

11. Rees (2007: 895) neatly observes that 'rather than habituating primates to human observation, the process of habituation may well be the process of learning from the primates how to live a primate life.'

References

Altmann, J. 1974. 'Observational Studies of Behaviour: Sampling Methods', *Behaviour* 49: 227–65.

Boesch, C. and H. Boesch-Achermann. 2000. *The Chimpanzees of the Ta Forest: Behavioural Ecology and Evolution*. Oxford: Oxford University Press.

Bradshaw, G.A. and R.M. Sapolsky. 2006. 'Mirror, Mirror', *American Scientist* 94(6): 487–9.

Chapais, B. 2008. *Primeval Kinship: How Pair-Bonding Gave Birth to Human Society*. Cambridge, MA. and London: Harvard University Press.

Fossey, D. 1983. *Gorillas in the Mist*. London: Hodder and Stoughton.

Galdikas, B. 1995. *Reflections of Eden: My Life with the Orangutans of Borneo*. London: Gollancz.

Goodall, J. 1990. *Through a Window: Thirty Years with the Chimpanzees of Gombe*. London: Weidenfeld and Nicholson.

Kummer, H. 1995. *In Quest of the Sacred Baboon: A Scientist's Journey*. Princeton NJ: Princeton University Press (trans. M. Ann Biederman-Thorson).

McGrew, W.C. 1992. *Chimpanzee Material Culture: Implications for Human Evolution*. Cambridge: Cambridge University Press.

Midgley, M. 2005. *The Owl of Minerva: A Memoir*. London and New York: Routledge.

Rees, A. 2007. 'Reflections on the Field – Primatology, Popular Science and the Politics of Personhood', *Social Studies of Science* 37(6): 881–907.

Reynolds, V. 1965. *Budongo: A Forest and its Chimpanzee*. London: Methuen and Co.

Ryle, G. 1949. *The Concept of Mind*. Chicago: University of Chicago Press.

Sapolsky, R. 2001. *A Primate's Memoir: Love, Death and Baboons in East Africa*. London: Random House.

Schaller, G. 1965. *The Year of the Gorilla*. London: Penguin.

Smuts, B. 1985. *Sex and Friendship in Baboons*. Cambridge MA Harvard University Press, (2nd edition, 1999).

Strier, K. 1992. *Faces in the Forest: The Endangered Muriqui Monkeys of Brazil*. New York: Oxford University Press.

Strum, S. 1987. *Almost Human: A Journey into the World of Baboons*. London: Elm Tree Books (2nd edition, 2001).

Watson, G. 1984. 'The social construction of boundaries between social and cultural anthropology in Britain and North America', *Journal of Anthropological Research* 40(3): 351–66.

Weber, B. and A. Vedder. 2002. *In the Kingdom of Gorillas: The Quest to Save Rwanda's Mountain Gorilla*. London: Aurum Press.

16
Popularizing Fieldwork:
Examples from Primatology
and Biological Anthropology

Jeremy MacClancy

Fieldwork is the self-vaunted method of social anthropology. It is the major mode of generating ethnographic information, a badge of initiation, the grounds for a disputable claim to disciplinary distinctiveness, and a central symbol of a romantic, quasi-mystical conception of our subject. It feeds our myths and in turn feeds on them. At this rate, without fieldwork, what are we? Armchair academics? God help us, no!

Fieldwork owes its privileged place within social anthropology thanks above all to the propagandizing efforts of Bronislaw Malinowski, himself one of the greatest myth-makers of the discipline. According to this vision, as propagated by him and his illustrious students, fieldwork was an essentially individualistic, heroic process practised by young gentlemen (and a few gentlewomen) who dared pursue hitherto-unobtained knowledge gleaned from very different peoples in exotic, faraway settings. It was a testing task for an aspiring intellectual with the personal resources to risk 'going bush'. No effete hanging-out in dusty libraries for this courageous bunch.

Fieldwork was a rite de passage, a solitary transformative ordeal which made men into accredited anthropologists, if they could pass the test. One was meant to 'sink or swim' while seeking 'total immersion' in a deeply foreign culture and language. It was not taught, it was learned on the spot: that was part of the ordeal. Indeed, it was commonly believed it could not be taught. As one put it, emphasizing the roles of ignorance and serendipity, 'How can one program the unpredictable?' (Freilich 1970: 15). Following this logic, the capacity to fieldwork well was thought 'an ability or knack which came naturally or not at all' (Berreman 1968: 340).

But these high standards come with their own price. Jackson, interviewing fieldworkers about their experiences, found:

> A general pattern for most interviewees is to couch their answers in terms
> of how much their fieldwork—and hence note-taking—differs from the
> stereotype. In part, this signals a defensiveness about one's fieldwork not
> living up to an imagined standard ... A substantial number of interviewees
> expressed pride in the uniqueness of their field sites, in their own iconoclasm,
> and in being autodidacts at fieldnote-taking (Jackson 1990: 19).

Wellin and Fine use this to underline the fact that many anthropologists celebrate
their reaction to supposed disciplinary routines. This self-congratulatory strategy
runs the obvious risk of lauding ethnography as the enigmatic product of theoretical
orientation, unprompted insight, and physical presence (Wellin and Fine 2001: 326).
In the process the frequent necessity of going it alone is transformed into a virtue, if
not an imperative. These themes come together in the image of anthropologists as
outsiders, discontents in their own culture who find a common home as interpreters
between cultures. When I entered anthropology as a graduate student in 1976 at
Oxford these self-flattering attitudes were still current, especially the feeling that
fieldwork was better practised than studied. As the professor stated in his introductory
lecture to us fledglings, 'And just how fieldwork is done remains a mystery'.

New voices were heard from the late 1960s on. Bob Scholte, writing in the seminal
Reinventing Anthropology (1972), argued that fieldwork should not be represented as
the meeting of a subject and an object, or even as that between two subjects. Rather,
it was an encounter of intersubjectivities, that of the anthropologist and of the local
he/she was working with. This meant anthropologists did not study a culture as
such, but worked at the dynamic interface between different intersubjectivities. Thus
anthropologists could not claim they were coasting in an 'ethnographic present', that
once-enabling fiction which allowed them to ignore history. Another consequence of
this approach was that the data fieldworkers generated were not absolute but relational.
A further consequence was the need for reflexivity, i.e., using the ethnographic analysis
to reflect back on our own way of life. Jim Clifford argued similarly a decade later
with his portrayal of fieldwork as an intersubjective process of co-informants leading
to the complicit manufacture of intercultural texts (Clifford 1982). In his terms,
we no longer produce falsifiable generalizations, but 'partial truths', and our literary
products, to avoid closure, should be open to multiple voices and the possibility of
reinterpretations. The adaptation of these ideas, and of feminist critiques, has led to
a swathe of experimental ethnographies, some of which eschew the elucidation of an
overly systematized culture for the sake of discerning 'partial connections' (Strathern
1991), where our understanding of the contexts in play cannot be prescribed but
continues to evolve. Others have given up the idea of stationary fieldwork, instead
producing multi-sited ethnographies, based on following the studied people or
cultural object wherever they go. In the process traditional ethnographies became
ever rarer and their stylization ever more patent.

Popular accounts by anthropologists of their fieldwork colour and refract
these interpretations, usually emphasizing the sustained contingency and deeply
interpersonal nature of their time learning from others. They may characterize their

fieldwork selves as gumshoe (Descola 1996), pilgrim (Bohannan 1954; MacClancy 1996), 'jester in shorts' (Barley 1983), whore (MacClancy 1988), and even terrorist (Zulaika 1995), among other guises. But a rigorous study of popular anthropology cannot be confined to texts authored by academics. The popularization of a discipline must not be seen in simplistic diffusionist terms, as though the only mode of making it broadly known was dissemination from authoritative sources. There is no space here for altitudinal metaphors of information coming from 'on high'. Rather, as Strum suggests, we should talk of 'circulation' and 'transformation' (Strum 2000: 489). In other words, it is necessary to look at the public reception and understanding of these texts as well. One way to recognize the diversity of anthropologies in this sense is to examine fictional accounts of fieldwork. What an analysis of these shows is that fieldwork is popularly perceived as emotionally intense, psychologically enriching, potentially traumatic, and possibly dangerous (MacClancy 2005). In the process one might learn something about other peoples, though many authors of fiction tend not to dwell on that.

I wish here to extend that analysis, in an interdisciplinary vein, by looking at popular accounts of fieldwork penned by primatologists and biological anthropologists. I choose these disciplines because their popular accounts of fieldwork have never been subjected to the same level of academic scrutiny as has occurred in social anthropology (e.g., MacClancy and McDonaugh 1996; Robben and Sluka 2007). This is particularly surprising in the case of primatology since several personal books on fieldwork have sold very well indeed. The only important exception to this generalization about scholarly focus was the work of Haraway in the 1980s (Haraway 1989).[1]

In this chapter, my aim is explicitly comparative: I wish to discern what is common and what distinctive about the ways fieldwork is portrayed by practitioners of these three related disciplines. For primatology, I have to consider, among other works, famed texts by Jane Goodall and Dian Fossey. Mention of these works may make primatologists grimace and their noses wrinkle, but these books, much re-issued and never out of print, are still the key texts by which the nonprimatological public come to learn of the discipline. Just because these field accounts are very popular is no reason for dismissing them. In fact, it is the very reason for taking them seriously.

The touch, the look

One thing almost every pop primatologist emphasizes is 'the touch', the manual meeting, interpreted as friendship, between a researcher and a studied primate. Whether placed at the very beginning or the very end of the book, this brief moment of physical contact is presented as a transcendental experience, releasing the most charged emotion the fieldworker has ever felt. This hand-on-hand encounter is given as an oceanic, boundary-melting experience where considerations of race, gender, class and nationality are all set miraculously aside. Human being meets fellow primate, and on that basis. It is an experience made all the more indescribable because it is (still) so rare. There are no former models, no pre-existing set of phrases in which to couch the event. Some authors turn to metaphor, some revert to biological figures of speech, others simply admit they are left beggars for description. I am not exaggerating. The first account, by Jane Goodall, who uses it to close her book, has remained an exemplar for all her successors:

> One day, as I sat near him at the bank of a tiny trickle of crystal-clear water, I saw a ripe red palm nut lying on the ground. I picked it up and held it out to him on my open palm. He turned his head away. When I moved my hand closer he looked at it, and then at me, and then he took the fruit, and at the same time held my hand firmly and gently with his own. As I sat motionless, he released his hand, looked down at the nut, and dropped it to the ground.

> At that moment there was no need of any scientific knowledge to understand his communication of reassurance. The soft pressure of his fingers spoke to me not through my intellect but through a more primitive channel: the barrier of untold centuries which has grown up through the separate evolution of man and chimpanzee was, for those few seconds, broken down.

> It was a reward far beyond my greatest hopes. (Goodall 1971: 240–1)

Thirty years later a pair of gorilla-watchers are still just as stumped for words:

> On this first encounter, Kweli gingerly touched the hem of Amy's jeans, then twirled slowly away in a comic series of spins that brought him back to his mother's side. We looked at each other with wide eyes and full smiles. Inside, our hearts were pounding as our minds raced to place the experience in some kind of context. But there was no precedent for the wonder of such direct contact across species lines. (Weber and Vedder 2001: 30; see also p.49, and Strum 1987: 57–8; Hayes 1991: 245; Powzyk 1998: n. 23)

My third example comes from George Schaller, the first academic to study gorillas intensively, in the late 1950s, and famed as the greatest American naturalist of the late twentieth century, with a particularly extensive and long experience of fieldwork. Even he could still be deeply moved by physical contact when revisiting his study site in the mid-1990s. While standing on a narrow path, he is taken by surprise:

> Something touches my lower leg, a gentle tap as if with the back of the hand. A female gorilla called Gurukunda, with an infant on her back, is beside me, trying to get by. "Oops, sorry," I say and step aside. She squeezes by. This is the most wonderful wildlife experience I have had. Or rather, it is more than that. It was an honor and a compliment to be treated just like another gorilla. Gurukunda touched me. (Schaller 2007: 81)

Primatologist colleagues, who run the Masters in Primate Conservation at Oxford Brookes University, said to me they were initially sceptical when so many candidates for their course confessed the reason for their commitment was due to an initial, manual contact with a primate, usually in a zoo. For these wannabe primatologists, the touch was an unforgettable, life-changing moment, and they wanted to build from it. (S. Bearder, A. Nekaris, personal communication.)[2]

Of course the unasked question here is what, on making physical contact, does the primate think he/she is doing? What, for instance, was going through David Greybeard's mind as he stretched his hand toward Goodall's? It is all too tempting here to puncture her earnestness and imagine his thought: 'Reluctantly, after so much pressure, I give this bountiful giver of bananas what she obviously desires: a touch.' My comment might be facetious in tone but the point, I like to think, is still apposite. For how could anyone know what David's touch was meant to convey, if anything?[3]

'The look', though not mentioned quite so much, is valued almost as greatly as 'the touch'. It is interpreted in similarly profound terms, and for much the same reasons forces the primatologist to grapple with language. Perhaps the significant difference here is that this mutual gaze, or even wide-eyed stare, tends to stimulate reflection more than emotion, and that reflection can be more literal than figurative. George Schaller, caught in a session of mutual staring, wonders if his gorilla observer 'recognized the kinship that bound us' (Schaller 1964: 48). He develops the point forty years later:

> No one who looks into a gorilla's eyes—intelligent, gentle, vulnerable—can remain unchanged, for the gap between ape and human vanishes: we know that the gorilla still lives within us. Do gorillas also recognize this ancient connexion? (Schaller 2007: 84)

Weber and Vedder, also speaking of mountain gorillas, mention 'the eyes, the deep brown reflecting pools in which we sometimes see ourselves' (Weber and Vedder 2001: 60). Biruté Galdikas, the pioneer primatologist of orangutans, states:

> I have looked into the eyes of a wild orangutan and seen that orangutan looking back at me. The experience is almost indescribable. (Galdikas 1995: 389)

In fact, thirty pages earlier, she had already tackled that task well:

> Looking into the eyes of an adult male orang-utan is like looking into pools of deep, dark water, ... and seeing oneself reflected back—not one's actual self, but the individual one might aspire to be, the tranquil, serene, strong, independent individual who, with no allies but the resources of his mind, body, and soul, pits himself against all others, one on one, until he can endure no more. That is why we find the adult male orang-utan so compelling. In his eyes we see a precarious balance of ruthless strength and

brutality on the one hand, and gentleness and serenity on the other. The eyes of the male orang-utan remind us of the awkward combination of angel and beast that characterizes the human soul. (Galdikas 1995: 356. See also Fossey 1983: 201, Hayes 1991: 14; Goodall 1999: 80)

It is noticeable that all bar one of those cited above, who experience and laud both 'the touch' and 'the look', are women. The only exception is Schaller. Perhaps this apparent gender-bias should cause no surprise, as the great majority of primatologists are female. Some might argue that it is unsurprising above all because female primatologists appear more predisposed to value the touch, and perhaps elicit it, and then in turn to praise the event in print. What, however, does seem to be common to all pop primatologists, whether men or women, is how deeply they value almost any form of inter-species communication, whether coping with a male baboon's sham-attack (Kummer 1995: 130), playing peekaboo or exchanging head-shakes with juvenile gorillas (Schaller 1964: 133, 137), facing down a silverback's bluff-charge (Hayes 1991; 150), or face-pulling with a baboon as 'an almost daily interspecies ritual' (Sapolsky 2001: 236). Strier, six months into her research among muriquis, was threatened by a visiting male and, to her surprise, was defended by four females who had come to accept her: 'The entire interaction took less than ten minutes... but it shaped all subsequent years of the research' (Strier 1992: xxix). Jahme, author of a study on female primatologists, claims these kinds of communication are grounded on *complicité,* an elusive form of intimate understanding, where language is superfluous, between the very best of friends or a mother and her child. For her, female primatologists, because of their biology, are far better than men at achieving this (Jahme 2000: 14, 357). Smuts, who studied baboons, noted that women researchers evoked less fear than male primatologists (Smuts 1985: 28). Either way, the idea that primatological research is inherently gender-biased remains deeply controversial, and is judged worthy of further research (see e.g., Fedigan 2000).

These non-physical forms of inter-species communication are now all the more valued, given the shift in primatological thinking away from bodily contact, even if the invitation to touch is apparently prompted by the primates themselves and not initiated by the human (e.g., Strier 1992: xxix; Weber and Vedder 2001: 57). Strum, petitioned for help by a threatened male baboon, 'shall never forget how honoured I felt by the compliment he paid me' (Strum 1987: 36–7). Sapolsky adds to this boundary-dissolving exercise by claiming common reactions, across species, to the ten-foot fall of a juvenile baboon: he and five females 'gasped as one'; realizing the child is unhurt, 'as a chorus, we all started clucking to each other in unison' (Sapolsky 2001: 240. See also Galdikas 1995: 241). The less positive side of this communication is only occasionally displayed in these books, whether that be pummelling by a gorilla or rape by an orangutan (Galdikas 1995: 293–4). But whatever the precise form of communication, whether physical, ocular or social, primatologists can still pride themselves that, in contrast to their privileged experiences, an entomologist, to take one example, 'will never have the pleasure of being regarded as a conspecific by his animals' (Kummer 1995: 82).

Over time some field-worn primatologists, perhaps secure in their acquaintance with the primates they have studied, lay less stress on close encounters and come instead to value a gentle, unspoken companionship (e.g., Strum 1987: 55; Goodall 1999: 171). Sapolsky, for instance, ends his book with a vignette of him sharing digestive biscuits with an aged baboon, while sitting in the sun, watching the giraffes and clouds (Sapolsky 2001: 304). Some have gone further, and come to see the animals they study in frankly familial terms. Galdikas, who has nurtured several infant orphaned orangutans, lauds the companionship offered by the now adult members of her 'forest family' (Galdikas 1995: 6, 16–18, 374). Fossey, famously, treated the gorillas she habituated as friends, and believed they reciprocated the love she had for them (Hayes 1991: 316, 318). To Fossey, it was 'an extraordinary feeling to be able to sit in the middle of a resting group of gorillas and contribute to a contented chorus of belch vocalizers' (Fossey 1983: 54. See also p. 205). Keith Lloyd, keeper of the gorillas at London Zoo, admitted much the same. When interviewed in 2006 about the removal of the gorillas to another zoo and his departure from the job, he stated:

> I'll miss the gorillas big time when they go away. They have been an incredibly large part of my life for a very long period of time. But they are going to good places, so that's one consolation. I'll be leaving the Zoological Society of London to pursue a career with orangutans in Borneo. I'll miss the gorillas but at least I'll still be with large hairy apes and that's what makes me me. If I ain't with them, I ain't me. (Kugler 2005)

Neither Goodall nor Fossey could have put it better.

Pop primatologists are, on the whole, keen to portray the tribulations and ordeals they have had to endure in order to win the confidence of their chosen primates. It is as though these sustained privations legitimated the weight of their words and the acuity of their insights. Thanks to their laudably self-denying dedication, these fieldworkers finally manage to accustom the observed to the observer. Little, however, is ever said about the other side of the equation. Thus the legitimate question to ask becomes, who exactly is fitting in with whom? As there are suggestions in this literature that the primates are training their observer in the rules of encounter as much as vice versa:

> Members of Group 5 immediately accepted Amy's presence in their midst, but resisted the idea of being closely trailed... On two occasions, the dominant silverback grabbed her forearm,... as he gently, but forcefully, squeezed. Amy took the warnings to heart and worked at making herself less intrusive. (Weber and Vedder 2001: 48)

> Clearly, TP had become habituated, but so, I realized, had I. The process was reciprocal. Gradually, TP and I worked out an unspoken agreement. If he didn't want me to advance, he would angrily slap or shake the vegetation

near him until I stopped moving. I learned that if I didn't make eye contact with TP, I could come within ten feet. (Galdikas 1995: 184)

Our visits *(with small groups of tourists)* lasted no more than an hour and were designed to approximate the gorillas' typical mid-morning rest period. In fact, Group 11 seemed to choreograph *its* schedule to fit our visits. Soon after we arrived each morning, Stilgar and the adult females would find an appropriate area with good visibility. They they would settle down to rest while the younger generation played around them. Forty-five minutes to an hour later, they would begin to move off, signaling the end of our visit. This pattern held with remarkable consistency, whether we arrived at 9:00 am or noon. (Weber and Vedder 2002: 193, inserted italics)

At times it seems as though the primatologist and the primates they studied form a mutually beneficial social group. The researcher gains her data and the studied take whatever advantage they can. Kummer describes how the baboons his team habituated learnt to keep quiet and at a distance whenever the Westerners negotiated with local nomads for access to watering-holes. They also learnt, when confronted by a hostile troop of fellow baboons, to close ranks around 'their' observer (Kummer 1995: 87–8).

Field primatologists, by spending so long with one collection of animals, come to know them as individual personalities and as a group, with their own histories of copulation, companionship, and fights. Several refer to the daily unfolding of these interactions as akin to a 'soap opera', and with all the connotations of TV addiction that come with that phrase (e.g., Strier 1992: 83; Galdikas 1995: 249; Jolly this volume).[4] Perhaps Galdikas is more exact, but also more patronizing, when she terms what she has observed 'commedia dell'arte', with its associations of improvised high farce grounded on a repertory of conventional behaviours: jealousy, greed, old age, love (Galdikas 1995: 150). In this context, de Waal appears disconcertingly precise when he compares the continuing story of the chimp colony at Arnhem Zoo, the Netherlands, to *Big Brother* (de Waal 2001: 308), with all its associations of pressurized sociability within a restricted space open to observation by others. Perhaps the corresponding term to 'soap-opera' for social anthropologists, who can after all talk one-on-one with the locals they are studying, would be a less oculocentric word more open to the diversity of native interpretation: multiple narratives.

The fieldworker

It is a premise of fieldwork among social anthropologists that one has to participate as much as observe. In a parallel fashion, some primatologists have tried to act like the animals they are studying. It is called 'going chimp'. Janis Carter, who effectively lived alone for seven years with ten apes on an island in the River Gambia, states that each time her visiting boyfriend saw her, 'I was more chimp-like in my behaviour'. On return from a break, it only took a day for her to 'be a chimp again. I travelled with them as they moved around, I slept with them, I *was* one of them.' Her body responded accordingly, moving onto a thirty-five day menstrual cycle, the same as a chimp's (Jahme 2000: 165–9, original italics). When I contacted Stella Marsden (neé Brewer), who worked with Carter for many years, about 'going chimp', she stressed that the term is not necessarily derogatory:

> If you are dealing with a group of individuals where the depth of your knowledge or understanding of them determines how well you are able to carry out set objectives, then in my position 'going chimp' can only be a good thing, as it gives me the best chance of successfully rehabilitating or relating to the chimps in my care. (S. Marsden, personal communication 23 iv 2006)

Fossey appears to be the limit case here. She even referred to the process as 'going bushy'. According to a friend, she approached habituation 'as though she were another gorilla' (Hayes 1991: 25, 213). And very successful she was at it, to our benefit.

As every social anthropologist knows, fieldwork is an intense, very stressful process, by turns frustrating then rewarding; routine then surprising. Primatologists are no different. They can be just as obsessive about details (e.g., Strier 1992: 72), just as territorial about their fieldsite (de Waal 2001: 268), and just as self-centred in their exploitation of fieldwork for their own ends. Sapolsky confesses to a vengeful field-agenda:

> I have always liked Old Testament names,... Plus, clearly, I was still irritated by the years I spent toting my Time-Life books on evolution to show my Hebrew school teachers, having them blanch at such sacrilege...; it felt like a pleasing revenge to hand out the names of the patriarchs to a bunch of baboons on the African plains. And, with some sort of perversity that I suspect powers a lot of what primatologists do, I couldn't wait for the inevitable day that I could record in my field notebook that Nebuchanezzar and Naomi were off screwing in the bushes (Sapolsky 2001: 14).

To some, fieldwork is a salve, a form of therapy, an especial opportunity to strive again for harmony. For Kummer, wandering with baboons is a chance to re-enact a Palaeolithic, gathering lifestyle (Kummer 1995; 237). Galdikas, claiming her husband could not fill all her emotional needs, 'developed relationships, single-sided ones but relationships nonetheless, with the wild adult female orangutans' (Galdikas 1995: 250). Sapolsky found his fieldtrips to Kenya a good way to escape the lab, with all its attendant ills: killing and cutting up animals. (Sapolsky 2001: 220)

Some primatologists, when asked whether Fossey was very odd, answer, 'Does a normal person go live in the rainforest and spend day after day watching primates? They do not.' Indeed some recognize and a few take pride in their ability to reject human company. Goodall did not begrudge solitude after her mother left Gombe:

'Always I have enjoyed aloneness' (Goodall 1999: 71). Kummer admits he and his professor are 'a bit shy with people'. He realized he 'needed to experience the world as it would be almost without people ... That I really did have this profound Adam experience has been one of the deepest joys of my life'. (Kummer 1995: 57, 61)

The stress of fieldwork does not end on quitting the site. Re-entry brings a new set of problems, usually grouped under the umbrella term 'cultural dissonance'. Strum, who was 'only truly happy when I was with the monkeys', argues that social anthropologists have it relatively easy; at least they have always been among humans, no matter how seemingly different their society. Primatologists have no such strut: 'returning to the human realm is difficult; for some it becomes impossible' (Strum 1987: 159). Goodall, on her first trip home, realized how much she had changed and how the man-made world was horribly ugly, spiritually impoverished, and 'terribly, terribly wasteful' (Goodall 1999: 84–5). Kummer found he had become easily angered: when a man pushed in front at a market stall, he immediately grabbed the queue-barger by the collar (*Kummer 1995: 166*).

For some the effect of fieldwork is profound and long-lasting, altering forever the way they view both life and themselves. Goodall, from her watching of chimps, learnt how to be a better mother (Goodall 1999: 87, 90). Galdikas says the same (1995: 316). She also states that observing primates day after day taught her to be more patient, more tolerant, more accepting, and to live more in the present. Contemplating orangutans forced her to come to turns with the 'weakness of being human' (Galdikas 1995: 335, 398). Kummer, from his adolescent years on, had a dreadful sense of the loneliness of man. Experiencing a primate's way of life at close hand, made that picture of extreme solitude recede: we are all part of a larger circle of life, he realized (Kummer 1995: 320). Strum learnt one could have strong emotions, such as the special attachment she felt for a particular baboon, and still do good science. 'Best of all, feeling strongly about the baboons made the science more rewarding' (Strum 1987: 203). Sarah Hrdy confessed:

> I really do feel some of the issues I set out to understand about my own nature, such as parental investment strategies, sibling rivalry and female sexuality. I now understand. I'm much more open-minded and have a general level of understanding that I would never have achieved otherwise. So I would certainly say I now feel closer to understanding myself. (quoted in Jahme 2000: 327)

It was Galdikas who summed up this life-changing process in the most general, most personal terms:

> Fieldwork forces you not only to confront situations you could never have anticipated, but also to confront elements of your own character you might never have known. Every trip into the field is also a trip into yourself. (Galdikas 1995: 337)

Most are affected by the primates in particular. A few are also moved by the primate environment in general. Enchanted by the rainforest, they unleash their imaginations. Identification with the primates is extended to the whole milieu (e.g. Schaller 1964: 144, 154, 194; Fossey 1983: 22, 24, 203; see also Reynolds 1965: 64–5). And from there it is just a short step to a full-blown, ecologically-centred spirituality. Goodall, who went into the field a dedicated Christian, emerged from it a New Age leader:

> Those months at Gombe helped to shape the person I am today … All the time I was getting closer to the animals and nature, and as a result, closer to myself and more and more in tune with the spiritual power I felt all around. For those who have experienced the joy of being alone with nature there is really little need for me to say much more; for those who have not, no words of mine can ever describe the powerful, almost mystical knowledge of beauty and eternity that come, suddenly, and all unexpected. The beauty was all there, but moments of true awareness were rare. They would come, unannounced. (Goodall 1999: 72)

On the death of her second husband, she returned to the ancient forest, unchanged 'since the time of Jesus', to achieve serenity, regain inner peace and so heal herself, successfully (Goodall 1999: 78–9, 169–81). In a similar vein, Galdikas claims 'The tropical rain forest is the most complex thing an ordinary human being can experience on the plant. A walk in the rain forest is a walk into the mind of God.' (Galdikas 1995: 91)

But not everything in this rainforest Eden is idyllic. The sun-dappled green dream can take on sombre tones, as the fieldwork takes over the life, leading to deadly end or misguided failure. Hayes named his biography *The Dark Romance of Dian Fossey*, and Spalding her exposé of Galdikas *A Dark Place in the Jungle* (Hayes 1991; Spalding 1998). The use of shady metaphor here serves to remind that the enlightened view of rainforest harmony is just a modern alternative to the much longer-established idea of the jungle as a corrupting heart of darkness.

If, to some, this seems all too much, fieldworkers can at least console themselves with the knowledge that they are experiencing things very few others have the chance to. And the pioneer primatologists can take pride that they were the first to have experienced what they underwent. They are unabashedly explicit about their distinction. As her fieldwork progressed, Goodall 'was able to penetrate farther and farther into a magic world that no human had explored before' (Goodall 1999: 71. See also p. 172). Galdikas claims she 'was probably the first human being in history who was truly an orangutan infant's grandmother' (Galdikas 1995: 16). Schaller, recounting one of his first meetings with gorillas, admits, 'It was a wonderful feeling to sit near these animals and to record their actions as no one had ever done before' (Schaller 1964: 50; see also Schaller 2007: 83). For Kummer, 'the hamadryas baboons are like a tribe of people whose customs no one since the ancient Egyptians has perhaps understood as well as my collaborators and I' (Kummer 1995: xvi).

Scrutinizing these accounts of pop primatology for gender differences revealed surprisingly little. According to Strum, the media stereotype of a female primatologist is of one who escapes from Culture to commune with Nature and revel in the primates she studies. Goodall, Fossey and Galdikas are the notorious exemplars here. Despite her original intentions Strum finds that she too falls into the typecast role, and enjoys herself in the process (Strum 1987: 61). But the male primatologists can do much the same, pleasuring in the primate environment and savouring their privileged parenthesis from Western living (e.g., Kummer 1995 passim). And some of them can display their emotions just as easily as their female counterparts: Sapolsky writes of his tears as a plague of TB felled the group he had followed for so long, and then lists the dead in a moving Old Testament pastiche (Sapolsky 2001: ch. 29). Moreover, not all women write emotionally charged books (e.g. Strier 1992), for some can be as dry as the most dessicated accounts produced by their male colleagues. It has been argued that men primatologists originally focused on dominant males and behaviours such as aggression, leaving it to woman primatologists to realize the importance of female associations. Maybe so, but by the time some of these men have come to write their popular accounts this sexual division of academic labour had to a great extent disappeared. The only gender difference that I can spot is the deliberately jokey style of Sapolsky, who delights in exposing his rounded personality, even the less attractive aspects (e.g., Sapolsky 2001: ch.3). So far, to my knowledge, no female primatologist has adopted this literary pose.

The locals

As a social anthropologist, what surprises me about so much of this literature is the primatologists' common lack of concern for the locals, as though the primates lived on their own, and any interaction they had with indigenes was either negative, and thus to be damned, or simply ignored, and thus not discussed. Strum, once habituated to her field site, felt more at ease there than in the nearby town: 'People, not wild animals, seemed dangerous' (Strum 1987: 60). It was not until eight years after establishing her fieldsite that she began to talk to local farmers, only to find that the first day she did it 'changed my life and my mind' (Strum 1987: 189). Fossey, once again, is the extreme case here, making no attempt to interact with the locals, or to see their problems (Hayes 1991: 296. See also pp. 165, 192). When discussing this general point with primatologist colleagues, my strong impression has been that, while there are honourable exceptions, the majority of fieldworkers are grateful for their trackers and field assistants but regard most locals as potential liabilities if not also obstacles to the aims of their research. Perhaps the disciplinary difference here is that an astute social anthropologist with broad interests can turn problems with the locals into case material; most primatologists cannot.[5]

Not surprising, then, that in these circumstances locals may see primatologists as strange, even at times as alien beings (e.g., Goodall 1971: 59; Kummer 1995: 77). Fossey, notoriously, deliberately created a persona of herself as someone with magical powers, in order to scare away poachers (Hayes 1991: 320). To the locals in

Galdikas' field-area, the work of she and Rod her husband was incomprehensible, so they were considered unpredictable and therefore assumed to be powerful. Rumours circulated she was a ghost; people acted as though she and Rod were apparitions. When she tried to control an angry large male organutan, talk circulated she was a *pawong*, a person with the mystical power to call wild animals and command them. These stories, plus the couple's righteous belief in their cause, gave them, she claims, the undisputed power to evict unwanted others from their reserve (Galdikas 1995: 223, 233, 262–5, 293).

Perhaps we should extend the concept of 'locals', to include fieldsite visitors, and so acknowledge how the observers themselves may be observed and perceived as part of the area, for this, in our increasingly tourist-centred world, is more and more the context within which primatologists will have to operate. Jolly comes close to making this point when she remarks in *Lords and Lemurs* that, at the Malagasy reserve where she works:

> Tourists and restaurant waiters looked on amazed at apparent track meets between gaggles of ring-tailed lemurs and a blond student sprinting down the road clutching a clipboard and check-sheets. (Jolly 2004: 24)

Biological anthropologists

In comparison with the plethora of pop primatology, biological anthropologists appear a mute lot. There is disappointingly little published by them in a popular vein about fieldwork. I found the meagre total of three examples. One biological anthropologist whom I contacted tried to explain reasons for this dearth: 'Since bio-anthro is so methodologically diverse, and bio-anthros are not known for their cultural sensitivity, I think they tend to bury their fieldwork rather than seeing it as "the blood of the martyrs", or whatever Seligman called fieldwork way back when'. Moreover, since some genetic anthropologists have been branded 'vampires' for collecting blood samples, 'they are tending to be a bit more tight-lipped about fieldwork these days' (Anon, personal communication. For the Seligman quote, see Knight 1995: 21). An example:

> On one occasion when Cavalli-Sforza was taking blood from schoolchildren in a rural region of the Central African Republic, he was confronted by an angry farmer brandishing an ax. Recalls the scientist, 'I remember him saying, "If you take the blood of the children, I'll take yours"' (Subramanian 1995: 54, quoted in Marks 2003: 3).[6]

The first impression from my unrepresentative sample is that when biological anthropologists engage in fieldwork, they feel or are made to feel that they are not doing the 'real' thing. The distinguished Gabriel Lasker, in his memoirs, speaks of others, not himself, as doing 'real' anthropology or 'real' fieldwork (Lasker 1999: 57, 133). Survey methods just don't cut the mustard. Dettwyler, in her revealing account of work in Mali, is pained to state that, once back in the USA, her 'fellow graduate students treated us with some disdain because we did not "live like the natives" but inhabited the nearby expatriate community' (Dettwyler 1994: 19).

Otherwise, a succession of stories in her account will ring bells in any social anthropologist's memory. There are the familiar tales of cross-cultural confusion, with all the attendant frustrations and anger as almost daily occurrence (see also Bribiescas 2006: 4–7). But there are also tales of minor successes and of fun, as she deploys her use of the local language to entertain the locals, and so try to reciprocate in small measure what they were giving her. She narrates moments of self-revelation stimulated by cross-cultural reflection and recognizes the continuing obsessiveness of her work: she is unable, even once back home, to stop looking at people without automatically cataloguing their physical condition. The only significant difference I have spotted is the reassurance quantitative methods give her:

> In just a few weeks, we measured hundreds of children. Hard data! Row upon row of numbers, marching across the page. No slippery interpretations to be made here, no guesses, no language barriers. (Dettwyler 1994: 132)

It is very hard to imagine a social anthropologist writing a passage like that.

The continuing story

It is easy to identify features of fieldwork common to all fieldworkers, whether they study humans, primates, elephants or ants: obsessiveness, privations, a break from university routine, a chance to gawp at nature. But the possibility of communication with fellow humans, usually from a very different background, or fellow primates seems to mark out the broad anthropological enterprise. What distinguishes primatology from either social or biological anthropology is the nature of that communication and the relationships forged with nonhuman locals. Monkeys might be nonverbal but they can't talk back; it is impossible to enter a hermeneutic circle of understanding with them. In contrast, social and biological anthropologists cannot shun the locals; they're the reason for their visit. What unites biological anthropologists and most primatologists, marking them out from their socially minded colleagues, is their apparent satisfaction with numerical data. As one biological anthropologist rather smugly put it:

> Ethnography has an important place in anthropology. However, many questions cannot be answered by ethnographic inquiry; instead, they need to be formulated in a fashion that produces testable hypotheses. Explanations and answers that are based solely on subjective interpretations or are otherwise untestable are often counterproductive and do not serve to support anthropology as a science. (Bribiescas 2006: 7)

What appears to unite many primatologists and social anthropologists is territorial possessiveness: jealously keeping others out of their fieldsite. Some social anthropologists call this strategy 'ethnographic imperialism'. Biological anthropologists, who tend not to remain in one site for a prolonged period, seem not to suffer this fieldworkers' ailment.

But these are just provisional generalizations. They are only the story so far. For we can appropriately end by asking, What will future forms of pop primatology focus on? What aspects of fieldwork will narrative biological anthropologists choose to single out? I look forward to the answers.

Acknowledgements

I thank Agustín Fuentes for suggestive comments, and Jon Marks for directing me to further references in biological anthropology.

Notes

1. I did not become aware of the excellent work of Amanda Rees (2006, 2007) until revising the final draft of this chapter.
2. Even a travelwriter may describe his encounter with gorillas in similarly enchanted terms (Unwin 2008).
3. For a further example of close monkey-human interaction where the humans are clearly imposing their own meanings on the nature of the encounter, see Knight 2005.
4. It appears gorillas do enjoy watching soap-operas on television. Clearly we do not know how much they understand, but if a TV is placed by their cage, they watch soap-operas. In contrast bonobos like watching televised wrestling matches. In one zoo, when the televison broke down, the bonobos were said to become 'depressed'. When a TV repairman returned the fixed machine and placed it outside their cage, they lined up to watch. The technician is reported to have stated, 'They're not going to believe me back at work when I tell them this' (A. Jolly and P. Asquith, personal communication).
5. A hopeful exception to this tendency is Fuentes and Wolfe 2002.
6. On parallel difficulties of collecting biological samples from various human populations, see Crawford 2007.

References

Barley, N. 1983. *The Innocent Anthropologist: Notes from a Mud Hut.* London: British Museum.
Berreman, G. 1968. 'Ethnography: method and product', in J. Clifton (ed.) *Introduction to Cultural Anthropology.* New York: Houghton Mifflin.
Bohannan, L. (using pseudonym E. Bowen Smith). 1954. *Return to Laughter An Anthropological Novel.* New York: Harper and Bros.
Bribiescas, R. 2006. *Man: Evolutionary and Life History.* Cambridge, MA: Harvard University Press.
Clifford, J. 1982. *Person and Myth: Maurice Leenhardt in the Melanesian World.* Berkeley: University of California Press.

Crawford, M.H. 2007. 'The importance of field research in anthropological genetics: methods, experiences and results', in M.H. Crawford (ed.) *Anthropological Genetics: Theory, Methods and Applications*. Cambridge: Cambridge University Press.

De Waal, F. 2001. *The Ape and the Sushi Master. Cultural Reflections by a Primatologist*. Harmondsworth, Middlesex: Penguin Books.

Descola, P. 1996. 'A *bricoleur's* workshop: writing *Les lances du crepuscule*', in J. MacClancy and C. McDonaugh (eds) *Popularizing Anthropology*, pp. 208–24.

Dettwyler, K.A. 1994. *Dancing skeletons: Life and death in West Africa*. Prospect Heights, ILL: Waveland.

Eriksen, T. H. 2006. *Engaging Anthropology: The Case for a Public Presence*. Oxford: Berg.

Fedigan, L.M. 2000. 'Gender encounters', in S.C.Strum and Linda Marie Fedigan (eds) *Primate Encounters: Models of Science, gender and Society*. Chicago: University of Chicago Press, pp. 498–520.

Freilich, M. (ed.). 1970. *Marginal Natives: Anthropologists at Work*. New York: Harper and Row.

Fossey, D. 1983. *Gorillas in the Mist*. London: Hodder and Stoughton.

Fuentes, A. and Wolfe, L.D. (eds). 2002. *Primates Face to Face: The Conservation Implications of Human-Nonhuman Primate Interconnections*. Cambridge Studies in Biological and Evolutionary Anthropology, No. 29. Cambridge: Cambridge University Press.

Galdikas, B. 1995. *Reflections of Eden: My Years with the Orangutans of Borneo*. Boston: Little, Brown.

Goodall, J. 1971. *In the Shadow of Man*. London: Collins.

———— 1999. *Reason for Hope: A Spiritual Journey*. New York: Warner

Haraway, D. 1989. *Primate Visions Gender, Race and Nature in the World of Modern Science*. London: Routledge.

Hayes, H. 1991. *The Dark Romance of Dian Fossey*. London: Chatto and Windus.

Jackson, J. 1990. '"I am a fieldnote": fieldnotes as a symbol of professional identity', in R. Sanjek (ed.) *Fieldnotes*. Ithaca, NY: Cornell University Press.

Jahme, C. 2000. *Beauty and the Beasts: Woman, Ape and Evolution*. London: Virago.

Jolly, A. 2004. *Lords and Lemurs: Mad Scientists, Kings with Spears, and the Survival of Diversity in Madagascar*. Boston: Houghton Mifflin.

Knight, J. 1995. 'LSE's double century', *Anthropology Today* 11(5), October: 21–2

———— 2005 'Feeding Mr. Monkey: cross-species food "exchange" in Japanese monkey parks', in J.Knight (ed.) *Animals in Person: Cultural Perspectives on Human-Animal Intimacies*. Oxford: Berg.

Kugler, O. 2005. 'Kugler's People', *The Guardian*, London, 16 December.

Kummer, H. 1995. *In Quest of the Sacred Baboon: A Scientist's Journey*. Princeton, NJ: Princeton University Press.

Lasker, G. 1999. *Happenings and Hearsay: Experiences of a Biological Anthropologist*. Detroit: Savoyard.

MacClancy, J. 1996. 'Fieldwork styles: Bohannan, Barley, and Gardner', in J. MacClancy and C. McDonaugh (eds) *Popularizing Anthropology*, pp. 225–44.

———— 1988. 'Going nowhere: From Melanesia to the Mediterranean' *JASO XIX* (3) Michelmas: 233–40.

———— 2005. 'The literary image of anthropologists', *Journal of the Royal Anthropological Institute* 11(3), September 2005: 549–75.

MacClancy, J., and C. McDonaugh, (eds). 1996. *Popularizing Anthropology*. London: Routledge.

Marks, J. 2003. 'Human genome diversity project: impact on indigenous communities', in *Encyclopedia of the Human Genome*. London: Macmillan.

Powzyk, J.A. 1998. *In Search of Lemurs: My Days and Nights in a Madagascar Rain Forest*. Washington, DC: National Geographic Society.

Rees, A. 2006. 'A place that answers questions: primatological field sites and the making of authentic observations', *Studies in History and Philosophy of Biological and Biomedical Sciences* 37: 311–33.

—— 2007. 'Reflections on the field: primatology, popular sciences and the politics of personhood', *Social Studies of Science* 37: 1–27.

Reynolds, V. 1965. *Budongo: a Forest and its Chimpanzees*. London: Methuen.

Robben, A.C.G.M. and Jeffery Sluka (eds). 2007. *Ethnographic Fieldwork: An Anthropological Reader*. Oxford: Blackwell.

Sapolsky, R.M. 2001. *A Primate's Memoir: Love, Death and Baboons in East Africa*. London: Jonathan Cape.

Schaller, G.B. 1964. *The year of the gorilla*. London: Collins.

—— 2007. *A Naturalist and Other Beasts: Tales from a Life in the Field*. Berkeley: University of California Press.

Spalding, L. 1998. *A Dark Place in the Jungle: Following Leakey's Last Angel into Borneo*. New York: Seal.

Scholte, B. 1972. 'Toward a critical and reflexive anthropology', in D. Hymes (ed.) *Reinventing Anthropology*. New York: Pantheon, pp. 430–57.

Smuts, B. 1985. *Sex and Friendship in Baboons*. Cambridge, MA: Harvard University Press.

Strathern, M. 1991. *Partial Connections*. Savage, Md: Rowan & Littefield.

Strier, K.B. 1992 *Faces in the Forest: The Endangered Muriqui Monkeys of Brazil*. Cambridge, MA: Harvard University Press.

Strum, S.C. 1987. *Almost human. A journey into the world of baboons*. London: Elm Tree Books.

—— 2000. 'Science encounters', in S.C. Strum and L.M. Fedigan (eds) *Primate Encounters: Models of Science, Gender and Society*. Chicago: University of Chicago Press, pp. 475–95.

Subramanian, S. 1995. 'The story in our genes', *Time*, January 16, pp. 54–5.

Unwin, M. 2008. 'Hope in the hills', *The Independent*, Traveller supplement, 5 July, pp. 4–7.

Weber, B. and A. Vedder. 2001. *In the Kingdom of Gorillas: Fragile Species in a Dangerous Land*. New York: Simon and Schuster.

Wellin, C. and Gary A. Fine. 2001. 'Ethnography as work: career socialization, settings and problems', in P. Atkinson, A. Coffey, S. Delamont, J. Lofland and L. Lofland (eds) *Handbook of Ethnography*. London: Sage, pp. 323–38.

Zulaika, J. 1995. 'The anthropologist as terrorist', in Carolyn Nordstrom (ed.) *Fieldwork Under Fire: Contemporary Studies of Violence and Survival*. Berkeley: University of California Press, pp. 203–222.

Notes on Contributors

Pamela J. Asquith, DPhil (Oxon) is Professor of Anthropology, affiliated with the University of Alberta, Canada, and the School of Environmental Studies, University of Victoria, BC. Her fields of study are: the anthropology of science, Japanese primatology, modern Japanese society, Japanese views of nature. Her recent projects include: the digital archiving of the scientific notes and diaries of Kinji Imanishi; and the public perception and response in Japan to the scientific, agricultural and government policy around TSE ('mad cow') incidents in Hokkaido and Honshu.

Mark Eggerman is a Research Fellow at Yale University and an independent fieldwork management consultant, specialising in the Middle East and Islamic societies. His work has included studies of public opinion, media use, and education for clients such as the BBC World Service, the Intermedia Survey Research Institute, and the Afghanistan Research and Evaluation Unit. He recently carried out a 3-year Wellcome Trust-funded study of adolescent mental health in Afghanistan and Pakistan.

Alain Froment is a medical doctor and biological anthropologist, Research Director at the French Institut de Recherche pour le Développement, and adjunct professor of anthropology at the University of Maryland at College Park (USA). He is in charge of the collections of biological anthropology at the Musée de l'Homme, Paris. His field work conducted in Senegal, Burkina Faso and Cameroon relates to genetics and the epidemiology of nutrition and emerging diseases.

Agustín Fuentes is Professor of Anthropology at the University of Notre Dame. He completed a B.A. in Zoology and Anthropology, and an M.A. and Ph.D. in Anthropology at the University of California, Berkeley. Fuentes' recent published work includes *Evolution of Human Behavior* (Oxford University Press, 2008), *Health, Risk, and Adversity* (co-edited, Berghahn Books, 2008), *Core Concepts in Biological Anthropology* (McGraw-Hill, 2006) and *Primates in Perspective* (co-edited, Oxford University Press, 2006).

Geoffrey A. Harrison is Emeritus Professor of Biological Anthropology at Oxford, Honorary Professor of Anthropology, Durham and an Emeritus Fellow of Linacre College, Oxford. He was educated at Trinity College, Cambridge and Christ Church, Oxford. He has undertaken field work in Namibia, Ethiopia, Brazil, India, Papua, New Guinea, Australia and the U.K. He has published some 250 scientific papers and books, mainly on various aspects of human adaptation.

Claude Marcel Hladik is an emeritus research director at the Museum of Natural History of Paris. He has, for about 30 years, been conducting field studies on the diet of wild primates (lemurs, monkeys and apes), analysing the composition of available foods in their natural settings. He has also conducted field studies on human food choices and food perceptions in the context of a research team that he co-directed with Igor de Garine, to bring together anthropologists and primatologists in an interdisciplinary approach to the socio-cultural and environmental factors surrounding food perception.

Alison Jolly is a senior visiting fellow in the School of Biology and Environmental Science at Sussex University. She has studied ring-tailed lemurs in Madagascar since 1963. Among her books are *Lucy's Legacy* (Harvard University Press, 1999), *Lords and Lemurs* (Harvard University Press, 2004), and *The Evolution of Primate Behavior* (Harvard University Press, 1972), as well as two recent children's stories, *Ako the Aye-Aye* (Lemur Conservation Foundation, 2005) and *Bitika the Mouse Lemur* (Durrell Wildlife Conservation Trust, 2007).

Nobuyuki Kutsukake is Assistant Professor at Hayama Center for Advanced Studies and Department of Evolutionary Studies of Biosystems, The Graduate University for Advanced Studies, Japan. He is also the PRESTO researcher at Japan Science and Technology (JST). He is interested in evolutionary and behavioural ecology in animals and has been studying social behaviour in primates, carnivores and rodents.

Phyllis Lee is an ethologist and conservation biologist, and Professor of Psychology at the University of Stirling. She researches elephants, primates and human perceptions of animals in the context of human-animal interaction from Africa to India and Indonesia. She has published widely in journals and has edited several volumes, the most recent being *Comparative Primate Socioecology* (Cambridge University Press, 1999).

Jeremy MacClancy is Professor of Social Anthropology, Oxford Brookes University, and Director of its Anthropological Centre for Conservation, the Environment and Development (ACCEND). He has carried out major fieldwork in Vanuatu and the Basque Country. He has published widely on Melanesia and Europe, as well as on the anthropologies of art, sport, food, popular anthropology and the history of anthropology. His latest book is 'Expressing Identities in the Basque arena' (James Currey, 2007)

Katherine C. MacKinnon is Associate Professor of Anthropology, and Faculty Fellow of the Center for International Studies, at Saint Louis University. She holds a B.A. and Ph.D. in Anthropology from the University of California, Berkeley, and a M.A. in Anthropology from the University of Alberta, Canada. She has published on primate behavior and ecology, and recently co-edited the volume *Primates in Perspective* (Oxford University Press, 2006). MacKinnon has done fieldwork in Costa

Rica, Nicaragua, Panama, and Suriname, and her research interests include infant and juvenile social development, complexity in behavior, and conservation issues in Central and South America.

Catherine Panter-Brick is Professor of Anthropology, Health and Global Affairs at Yale University. Her research focuses on critical risks to health and wellbeing across key stages of human development, giving special attention to the impact of poverty, disease, malnutrition, armed conflict and social marginalization. She has edited several books to bridge research findings into teaching practice, including *Health, Risk and Adversity* (Berghahn Books, 2009); *Hunter Gatherers* (Cambridge University Press, 2001); *Abandoned Children* (Cambridge University Press, 2000); *Hormones, Health and Behaviour* (Cambridge University Press, 1999); and *Biosocial Perspectives on Children* (Cambridge University Press, 1998). She has directed large inter-disciplinary research projects in Afghanistan, Ethiopia, the Gambia, Nepal, Niger, Pakistan, Saudi Arabia, Tanzania and the United Kingdom. She is Senior Editor (Medical Anthropology section) for *Social Science & Medicine*.

Lyliane Rosetta, a human biologist, was until April 2009 a Senior Researcher in Biological Anthropology at Centre National de la Recherche Scientifique (CNRS), in Paris, France. Her major research interest is in energetics, stress and reproduction. She carried out fieldwork mainly in France, Britain, Senegal, and Bangladesh. She has published widely on the regulation of reproductive function in humans and non-human primates, and has contributed chapters to eleven monographs and co-edited two of them with C.G.N. Mascie-Taylor, *Variability in Human Fertility* (CUP 1996) and *Reproduction and Adaptation* (CUP, (in preparation)).

Volker Sommer is Professor of Evolutionary Anthropology in the University of London and Pro-Provost for the International Strategy (Africa) of University College London. He conducts long-term field research into the socioecology and conservation of primates, in particular langur monkeys in India (since 1981), gibbons in Thailand (since 1989), and chimpanzees in Nigeria (since 2000). His publications include *Homosexual Behaviour in Animals* (co-edited, Cambridge University Press, 2006), *Darwinisch denken* (Hirzel, 2007), *Primates of Gashaka* (co-edited, Springer, 2011).

Robert W. Sussman is Professor of Anthropology and Environmental Science, Washington University, St. Louis. He is currently Editor of the *Yearbook of Physical Anthropology* and Editor Emeritus of American Anthropologist. His recent books include *Primate Ecology and Social Structure, vols 1 & 2* (Pearson Custom Publishing, 2003), *The Origins and Nature of Sociality* (co-edited, Adline Transaction, 2004), *Ringtailed Lemur Biology* (co-edited, Springer, 2006), and *Man the Hunted: Primates, Predators, and Human Evolution* (co-authored with Donna Hart, Basic Books, 2005). He has conducted research in Madagascar, Mauritius, Costa Rica, and Guyana and is co-founder of the Beza Mahafaly Special Reserve in Madagascar.

Juichi Yamagiwa is Professor of Anthropology at Kyoto University, Japan, and currently serving as the president of the International Primatological Society (IPS). He has carried out fieldwork of social ecology on Japanese macaques at Yakushima Island (Japan), on mountain gorillas (Rwanda), and on sympatric populations of gorillas and chimpanzees (DRC and Gabon). He has published on various topics of social and ecological flexibility of non-human primates in relation to human evolution. He has edited three special issues of *Primates* on social ecology of Japanese macaques, cercopithecines and the great apes, and is now editing two books on comparative social ecology of cetaceans and primates (Chicago University Press and Springer, forthcoming). Since 1992, he has served as an advisory member of the Pole Pole Foundation, a local NGO in DRC, that aims for the coexistence of people and wildlife in and around the Kahuzi-Biega National Park.

Index